Antonin Scalia's Jurisprudence

Antonin Scalia's Jurisprudence

Text and Tradition

Ralph A. Rossum

UNIVERSITY PRESS OF KANSAS

Published by the University Press of Kansas (Lawrence, Kansas 66045), which was organized by the Kansas Board of Regents and is operated and funded by Emporia State University, Fort Hays State University, Kansas State University, Pittsburg State University, the University of Kansas, and Wichita State University

Library of Congress Cataloging-in-Publication Data

Rossum, Ralph A., 1946-
  Antonin Scalia's jurisprudence : text and tradition / Ralph A. Rossum.
      p. cm.
  Includes bibliographical references and index.
  ISBN 0-7006-1447-8 (cloth : alk. paper)
  1. Scalia, Antonin.   2. United States. Supreme Court—Biography.   3.
Constitutional history—United States.   4. Constitutional law—United States—
Interpretation and construction.   I. Title.
  KF8745.S33R67 2005
  347.73'2634—dc22   2005026959

British Library Cataloguing-in-Publication Data is available.

Printed in the United States of America

10 9 8 7 6 5 4 3 2 1

To D. Alan Heslop
Friend, mentor, colleague

CONTENTS

PREFACE

This book represents an attempt to articulate the contours of Justice Antonin Scalia's understanding of constitutional and statutory interpretation and the role of the Court. I rely heavily on Scalia's majority opinions, concurring opinions, and dissents written during his nineteen years of service on the Supreme Court. Numbering over 600, Scalia's opinions are carefully wrought, passionately argued, highly principled, and filled with well-turned phrases. They reveal him to be an eloquent defender of a text-and-tradition approach — an "original-meaning" jurisprudence that accords primacy to the text of the Constitution or the statute being interpreted and that declares it to be the duty of the judge to apply that text when it is clear or the specific legal tradition flowing from that text (i.e., what it meant to the society that adopted it) when it is not.

My intention in this book is to understand Scalia as he understands himself. My focus is on his arguments and words. By a careful analysis primarily of his Supreme Court opinions (but also of his Court of Appeal opinions for the D.C. Circuit, his major law review articles as a law professor and judge, and his provocative essay entitled "Common-Law Courts in a Civil Law System: The Role of United States Federal Courts in Interpreting the Constitution and Laws" in A *Matter of Interpretation*[1]), I attempt to state affirmatively his understanding of such key structural arrangements as separation of powers and federalism and such key constitutional provisions as the Commerce Clause of Article I, § 8; the Suspension Clause of Article I, § 9; the Take Care Clause of Article II, § 3; the judicial power as spelled out in Article III, § 2; the Due Process Clauses of the Fifth and Fourteenth Amendments; the Free Speech and Free Press Clauses and the Religion Clauses of the First Amendment; the criminal procedural provisions of Amendments Four through Eight; the protection of state sovereign immunity in the Eleventh Amendment; the Equal Protection Clause of § 1 of the Fourteenth Amendment; and Congress's enforcement powers as granted in § 5 of the Fourteenth Amendment.

I concentrate primarily on the opinions that Scalia himself has written. Although he insists that, to his knowledge, he has never joined an opinion in which he has not agreed with both the holding and the reasoning of that opinion,[2] a book that addresses all the opinions he has joined would no longer be a book on Scalia but on the overall work of the Rehnquist Court. For the same reason, I do not focus particularly on the extensive legal literature that Scalia's tenure on the Court has generated; for the most part, that literature explores Scalia's views on particular trees rather than his understanding of the forest as a whole.

It would be fair to say that this book is a generally sympathetic account of Scalia's original-meaning jurisprudence. Since his appointment to the Supreme Court, he has been remarkably consistent in his approach to questions of constitutional and statutory interpretation, and his opinions have provided considerable instruction on what it means to be a principled and intelligent textualist. Scalia has occasionally drifted from his text-and-tradition moorings on such important matters as state sovereign immunity, Congress's power under § 5 of the Fourteenth Amendment, the incorporation doctrine, and retroactive application of criminal procedural guarantees; when he has done so, I am quick to point this out. In fact, I find that his defense of both constitutional structure and constitutional liberties is invariably most ardent when most textually based. These occasional departures, however, serve only to highlight his overall consistency of approach and to remind the reader of the jurisprudential commitments of one of the Court's most intellectually able justices.

I wish to acknowledge my gratitude to Judge Susan A. Ehrlich of the Arizona Court of Appeals and Professor R. Shep Melnick of Boston College for their careful reading of the entire manuscript and for their valuable substantive and stylistic recommendations, which have made it a much better book; to the Earhart Foundation for its financial support; to Claremont McKenna College for a faculty research grant and time off to complete the manuscript; to my wife, Professor Constance Rossum of the University of LaVerne, for her encouragement and thoughtful editorial suggestions; and to Joan Sherman, copyeditor; Susan McRory, senior production editor; Susan Schott, assistant director and marketing manager; and Fred Woodward, director, who have made my association with the University Press of Kansas so pleasant and rewarding.

Ralph A. Rossum
Claremont, California
July 25, 2005

Notes

1. Antonin Scalia, *A Matter of Interpretation: Federal Courts and the Law* (Princeton, N.J.: Princeton University Press, 1997).
2. Personal interview with Justice Antonin Scalia, Washington, D.C., June 11, 2003.

Chapter One

Introduction

On June 17, 1986, Antonin Scalia—at the time a judge on the U.S. Court of Appeals for the District of Columbia Circuit—was nominated by President Ronald Reagan to serve as an associate justice of the U.S. Supreme Court. On September 17 (Constitution Day), he was confirmed by the Senate by a vote of ninety-eight to zero, and he took his seat nine days later. During his subsequent years on the high bench, the gregarious, poker-playing, opera-loving former University of Chicago law professor has emerged as the Court's most outspoken, intellectually interesting, high-profile, and colorful member.

"On a bench lined with solemn gray figures" who often sit "as silently as pigeons on a railing," Scalia has been described as standing out "like a talking parrot."[1] He relishes the cut and thrust of debate and has institutionalized the practice of hiring, and then carefully listening to, a "counter-clerk" with liberal views at odds with his own and those of his other three clerks as a means of sharpening his thinking.[2] With a distinctly aggressive style of questioning that is by turns testy, confrontational, provocative, and witty, he frequently asks questions during oral argument that are at once intellectually demanding and laced with impish humor. On one occasion, he told a flustered attorney who was frantically searching his brief for information that Scalia had requested, "Just shout 'Bingo' when you find it." On another occasion, he told an attorney who was all too eager to reserve the remainder of his time for reply, "You've got to be kidding."

He is an equally colorful and incisive writer of opinions that are carefully wrought, powerfully argued, highly principled, and filled with well-turned phrases. He has penned many memorable lines; what follows are only four examples, each of which provides insight into his textualist approach and understanding of the role of the Supreme Court:

> The Court transforms the meaning of § 2, not because the ordinary meaning is irrational, or inconsistent with other parts of the statute, but because it does not fit the Court's conception of what Congress must have had in mind. When we adopt a method that psychoanalyzes Congress rather than reads its laws, when we employ a tinkerer's toolbox, we do great harm. Not only do we reach the wrong result with respect to the statute at hand, but

1

we poison the well of future legislation, depriving legislators of the assurance that ordinary terms, used in an ordinary context, will be given a predictable meaning.[3]

Let there be no mistake about our belief that burning a cross in someone's front yard is reprehensible. But St. Paul has sufficient means at its disposal to prevent such behavior without adding the First Amendment to the fire.[4]

[N]o government official is "tempted" to place restraints upon his own freedom of action, which is why Lord Acton did not say "Power tends to purify." The Court's temptation is in the quite opposite and more natural direction—towards systematically eliminating checks upon its own power; and it succumbs.[5]

Consulting States that bar the death penalty concerning the necessity of making an exception to the penalty for offenders under 18 is rather like including old-order Amishmen in a consumer-preference poll on the electric car. Of course they don't like it, but that sheds no light whatever on the point at issue.[6]

Scalia is an eloquent defender of textualism—an "original-meaning" interpretive approach that accords primacy to the text and tradition of the document being interpreted and that declares that the duty of the judge is to apply the textual language of the Constitution or statute when it is clear and to apply the specific legal tradition flowing from that text (i.e., what it meant to the society that adopted it) when it is not.[7] He is an equally fierce critic of judicial activism and what he terms the "Living Constitution"—an interpretative approach asserting that the meaning of a law "grows and changes from age to age, in order to meet the needs of a changing society" and that it is appropriate for the judge to "determine those needs and 'find' that changing law."[8] Scalia's majority, concurring, and dissenting opinions—now numbering over 600[9]—are uniformly reflective of his textualist jurisprudence concerning how the Constitution, statutory law, and administrative regulations are to be interpreted. They have also had a profound impact on the overall work product of the Supreme Court. Ronald Dworkin, professor of law at New York University and professor of jurisprudence at Oxford University and a critic of Scalia, admits that, as a result of Scalia's persuasive and persistent arguments, "we are all originalists now." Mark Tushnet of the Georgetown University Law Center concurs: "Before Scalia, until the late '80s, the justices would issue a ruling and say, 'Here is why our opinion makes sense,' and then support it with some law and history. But now everyone is much more conscious about looking at what the text says—and quite often less conscious about how that might fit into a social or practical context."[10]

Scalia's Pre-Judicial Life

Antonin ("Nino" to his family and friends) Scalia was born on March 11, 1936, in Trenton, New Jersey, the only child of S. Eugene Scalia and Catherine Panaro Scalia. His father, who was born in Sicily and emigrated to the United States as a young man, was a professor of Romance languages. His mother, born to Italian immigrant parents, was a schoolteacher. The appointment of Antonin Scalia, the first justice of Italian heritage, was proclaimed by many as an example of the fulfillment of the American dream.

When Scalia was five years old, his father joined the faculty of Brooklyn College, and his family moved to Elmhurst, a section of Queens, New York. He initially attended public schools in Queens and later St. Francis Xavier, a military prep school in Manhattan, from which he graduated as valedictorian. It is a reflection of how much things have changed in American society over the past half century that he was able, without complaint or alarm, to carry his military rifle with him daily on a crowded subway as he traveled back and forth between his home in Queens and his school in Manhattan.[11]

Scalia's academic success continued at Georgetown University, from which he received his AB summa cum laude in history and graduated as valedictorian in 1957. Scalia went on to Harvard Law School, where he served as notes editor of the *Harvard Law Review* and from which he received his LLB magna cum laude in 1960. After graduation, he traveled in Europe for a year as a Sheldon Fellow of Harvard.

While at Harvard, Scalia had met and become engaged to Maureen McCarthy, an English major at Radcliffe College and the daughter of a Massachusetts physician. They were married on September 10, 1960, and have nine children: Ann Forrest, Eugene, John Francis, Catherine Elisabeth, Mary Clare, Paul David, Matthew, Christopher James, and Margaret Jane. Their marriage has been strengthened by their deep faith in Roman Catholicism.[12]

Scalia began his legal career in 1961 as an associate of the law firm of Jones, Day, Cockley & Reavis in Cleveland, Ohio. A highly unusual scene during his interview for the position provides a window into his personality. James T. Lynn, a former partner at the firm, told the *New York Times* at the time of Scalia's nomination to the Supreme Court that, at a party held for potential recruits at Lynn's home, Scalia immediately made an impression upon eight or so senior partners by engaging them in an all-night debate on Sunday blue laws, which Scalia passionately defended and they all opposed. Lynn said: "He enjoyed taking a position with respect to an issue that was complicated to defend. It didn't bother him at all that here he was with these top partners in the firm."[13]

He was admitted to the Ohio Bar in 1962 and worked at Jones, Day in a number of different areas of law, including real estate, corporate finance, labor, and antitrust. Five years later, he left to become a professor of law at the University of Virginia. In 1971, he began a distinguished career in government service when he took leave from his academic post to serve as general counsel for the Office of Telecommunications Policy in the administration of President Richard Nixon. There, he successfully negotiated a major agreement among industry groups that provided the framework for the growth of cable television in the United States. From 1972 to 1974, he served as chairman of the Administrative Conference of the United States, an independent agency charged with the task of improving the effectiveness and efficiency of administrative processes in the federal government. In 1974, he was nominated by President Nixon to be assistant attorney general for the Office of Legal Counsel. Although the Watergate scandal forced Nixon to resign, Scalia was nonetheless confirmed by the Senate and remained in this position, as legal adviser to the president and the attorney general, under President Gerald Ford, who assigned him the task of determining the legal ownership of Nixon's tapes and documents. Scalia decided in favor of Nixon, concluding that Nixon had a property right in his presidential papers; however, the Supreme Court soon ruled against this conclusion. It was in this position that Scalia began to think more deeply about and articulate his understanding of the constitutional dimensions of the presidency in a scheme of separated powers—an understanding later reflected in his opinions in *Morrison v. Olson*,[14] *Lujan v. Defenders of Wildlife*,[15] and *Printz v. United States*.[16]

With Jimmy Carter's election as president, Scalia left government service to work as a resident scholar at the American Enterprise Institute. He also taught briefly at the Georgetown University Law Center before joining the faculty of the University of Chicago Law School. He stayed at Chicago from 1977 to 1982, leaving only to spend a year as a visiting professor of law at Stanford University. While teaching at Chicago, he also served as chairman of the American Bar Association (ABA) Section of Administrative Law from 1981 to 1982; he was also named chairman of the ABA Conference of Section Chairmen, a recognition by his peers of his leadership abilities. While at Chicago, he cofounded, with Murray Weidenbaum, *Regulation* magazine and served as its founding coeditor from 1977 to 1982. What is particularly noteworthy about Scalia's background prior to his service on the bench is his extensive experience in the practice of law, the teaching of law, "inside the Beltway" Washington politics, and ABA politics. When he became a judge, he knew how law is practiced, taught, and used for corporate, political, and constitutional objectives.

In 1982, Scalia received another chance to return to public service. In July, President Reagan appointed him to the U.S. Court of Appeals for the District of Columbia Circuit, widely considered second in importance only to the Supreme Court. He was confirmed uneventfully in early August. At the time, he was described by the *New York Times* as a "politically conservative academic with impeccable scholarly credentials" and "a reputation for exceptional intellectual ability"[17] and by the *Washington Post* as having "been a co-editor of *Regulation,* a publication that keeps a critical eye on government rulemaking for the American Enterprise Institute, a conservative think tank. Scalia's area of expertise is administrative law, which deals with interpretation of federal regulations, and constitutional law."[18]

Scalia's Appellate Jurisprudence

Once on the bench, Scalia developed the reputation of being a well-prepared, amiable colleague who worked hard and thoroughly enjoyed using oral argument as a vehicle for debating questions of law. During his four years on the D.C. Circuit, he wrote 121 signed opinions: 91 majority opinions, 5 concurring opinions, 18 dissents, and 7 opinions concurring in part and dissenting in part. Since the bulk of that court's caseload involves review of complex federal regulations made by government agencies whose meanings are vigorously contested by affected parties, it is not surprising that in 103 of these opinions, he addressed various aspects of administrative law; 7, however, touched on freedom of speech and the press, 6 on criminal procedure, and 5 on questions of racial discrimination and equal protection.

His appellate opinions plainly revealed his view of the role of the federal judiciary and displayed his consistent adherence to the principles of judicial restraint. They sketched the outlines of the textualist jurisprudence that he would fully elaborate once he was on the Supreme Court.

Scalia on Standing

The "cases and controversies" language of Article III of the U.S. Constitution prevents federal courts from becoming "forums for the ventilation of public grievances" by requiring that legal questions be presented to the courts only "in a concrete factual context."[19] For a party to be able to invoke judicial authority, i.e., to have "standing," it must show, at a minimum, that it personally suffered some actual or threatened injury from the defendant's conduct. In one of his first cases after his appointment, *Community Nutrition Institute v. Block,*[20] Scalia showed his keen interest in keeping the constitutional standards for standing high; he dissented from that part of the majority opinion that conferred standing on three individual consumers of milk who were concerned about the price of fluid milk and who were seeking to challenge the manner in which reconstituted milk was regulated under milk-market orders adopted pursuant to the Agricultural Marketing Agreement Act (AMAA). He declared that he did not believe that a "class as generalized as the one here (viz., all consumers of fluid milk products—which cannot exclude many of the nation's households) can be found" to have standing;[21] they had only a "generalized grievance" about how the Department of Agriculture, through its implementation of the AMAA, was shifting costs from milk producers to milk handlers and therefore ultimately to milk consumers. For Scalia, it was inappropriate for the Court to address this kind of generalized harm grievance; as he declared, "Governmental mischief whose effects are widely distributed is more readily remedied through the political process, and does not call into play the distinctive function of the courts as guardians against oppression of the few by the many." Then introducing an argument upon which he would elaborate at length once he was on the Supreme Court,[22] he continued, "Thus, for such matters it is less likely that Congress intended the creation of private attorneys general to supplement, through the courts, the President's primary responsibility to 'take care that the laws be faithfully executed.'"[23]

Scalia's ability to connect the question of standing to the principle of separation of powers was evident in *Moore v. U.S. House of Representatives*,[24] in which eighteen members of the House of Representatives for the Ninety-seventh Congress sued the House and Senate in the District Court for the District of Columbia seeking a declaratory judgment that the Tax Equity and Fiscal Responsibility Act of 1982 was unconstitutional because it originated in the Senate in contravention of the Origination Clause of the U.S. Constitution.[25] The district court dismissed the complaint on the ground that the legislators lacked standing. They appealed to the D.C. Circuit, which held that, although the appellants did in fact have standing to sue, they would nevertheless be denied declaratory relief for their claim under the doctrine of remedial discretion, a doctrine that "permits the court to exercise judicial self-restraint in particular matters intruding upon a coordinate branch of government."[26] Scalia concurred only in the judgment because, as he said, "while agreeing that we should abstain from deciding this dispute, I view that abstention to be the result not of our discretion but of constitutional command. As the District Court correctly found, these plaintiffs have no standing to press their grievance before this Branch."[27]

Scalia formulated what he regarded as "the only test of congressional standing that is both consistent with our constitutional traditions and susceptible of principled application (*i.e.*, an application undistorted by the *ad-hoc* ery of 'remedial discretion')." That test has "as its point of departure the principle that we sit here neither to supervise the internal workings of the executive and legislative branches nor to umpire disputes between those branches regarding their respective powers. Unless and until those internal workings, or the resolution of those inter-branch disputes through the system of checks and balances brings forth a result that harms private rights, it is no part of our constitutional province, which is 'solely, to decide on the rights of individuals.'" That principle, he continued, "is reduced to meaninglessness, and the system of checks and balances replaced by a system of judicial refereeship, if the officers of the political branches are deemed to have a personal, 'private' interest in the powers that have been conferred upon them (whether specifically or vaguely) by Constitution or statute." For Scalia, standing required something more: "Unless those powers have been denied in such fashion as to produce a *governmental result* that harms some entity or individual who brings the matter before us, we have no constitutional power to interfere."[28]

In *United Presbyterian Church v. Reagan*,[29] Scalia wrote a unanimous opinion affirming a district court's dismissal of a suit for lack of standing brought by various political and religious organizations challenging the legality of a number of features of President Reagan's Executive Order No. 12333, entitled "United States Intelligence Activities." The organizations asserted that the order violated the principle of separation of powers because it was promulgated without congressional authorization and that various of its provisions on their face violated their First Amendment rights of freedom of speech, political belief, association, and free exercise of religion, despite the fact that the order prescribed that nothing contained in it "shall be construed to authorize any activity in violation of the Constitution or statutes of the United States." The plaintiffs claimed they had standing to challenge this order because it caused them to suffer the "harm of a chilling effect,"[30] in that they were likely to refrain from engaging in various constitutionally protected activities out of fear that such activities would cause them to be targeted for surveillance under the order.

Scalia agreed with the district court that the plaintiffs' "alleged grievances [were] insufficient to satisfy the injury-in-fact standing requirement imposed by Article III of the Constitution."[31] He noted that the problem with their attempt to rely upon the harm of a "chilling effect" to establish standing was that "they have not adequately averred that any specific action is threatened or even contemplated against them." Harm cannot be merely speculative. As he wrote, "It must be borne in mind that this order does not *direct* intelligence-gathering activities against all persons who could conceivably come within its scope, but merely *authorizes* them." He drove the point home with an analogy: "To give these plaintiffs standing on the basis of threatened injury would be to acknowledge, for example, that all churches would have standing to challenge a statute which provides that search warrants may be sought for church property if there is reason to believe that felons have taken refuge there. That is not the law."[32]

Scalia's last major circuit court discussion of standing was in his dissent in *Center for Auto Safety v. National Highway Traffic Safety Administration* [NHTSA].[33]

The Center for Auto Safety and three other nonprofit consumer organizations working to promote energy conservation challenged the 1985 and 1986 model years' mandatory fuel economy standards for light trucks set by the NHTSA pursuant to the Energy Policy and Conservation Act of 1975. They alleged that the NHTSA had violated the act's requirement that the agency designate standards at "the maximum feasible average fuel economy level" and that it had instead given impermissible weight to shifts in consumer demand toward larger, less fuel-efficient trucks. The threshold question was, of course, standing. What specific harm had they suffered by the NHTSA's standards? The majority of the panel had no difficulty whatsoever providing an answer: "[T]he petitioners plainly have standing to bring this action in a representative capacity for members of their organizations. Their members have suffered injury-in-fact because the vehicles available for purchase will likely be less fuel efficient than if the fuel economy standards were more demanding. This injury can be traced to NHTSA's rulemaking and is likely to be redressed by a favorable decision. Thus, all of Article III's requirements for standing are met."[34]

Scalia began his dissent by declaring that "[i]f the injuries hypothesized by the interest groups suing in the present cases are sufficient, it is difficult to imagine a contemplated public benefit under any law which cannot—simply by believing in it ardently enough—be made the basis for judicial intrusion into the business of the political branches." He described the majority's decision not as "judicial vindication of private rights" but rather "judicial infringement upon the people's prerogative to have their elected representatives determine how laws that do not bear upon private rights shall be applied."[35] He rejected as insufficient for Article III purposes the "petitioners' bald assertion, unsupported by concrete factual allegations, that unidentified members of their organizations may be unable to purchase unidentified types of fuel-efficient light trucks or light-truck model options"; the complainants were not alleging facts establishing that they would suffer "a concrete, palpable, and distinct injury."[36] He also addressed another element of standing that he would later emphasize once on the Supreme Court: redressability.[37] He observed that a court order to the NHTSA requiring the agency to raise the mandatory fuel economy standard for light trucks would not necessarily redress the plaintiffs' "alleged inability to purchase unidentified types of light trucks or light-truck model options" because the light truck manufacturers might prefer to "pay noncompliance fines (and perhaps to pass them through to customers) rather than take drastic measures to comply with the standard."[38]

Judicial Deference to Administrative Discretion

The fact that a party may have standing to obtain judicial review of agency action does not assure that the courts will provide review. Under the Administrative Procedure Act (APA), although final agency action is generally subject to judicial review, it is not when "(1) statutes preclude judicial review; or (2) agency action is committed to agency discretion by law."[39] Scalia's appellate decisions displayed his emerging textualism and his refusal to read statutes as providing judicial review when they did not. These opinions showed his aversion to judicial policymaking; his understanding that it was the constitutional duty of the executive branch, and not the courts, to enforce the law; and his conviction that, absent clear textual language to the contrary, the courts should defer to agency action.

Gott v. Walters involved the first of the APA's two exceptions to judicial review.[40] This case involved certain methodologies used by the Veterans Administration (VA) to help resolve claims of injury from exposure to radiation during military service. The complaint was that the methodologies were promulgated and adopted without complying with the rule-making procedures and publication requirements of the APA. Scalia wrote the majority opinion that instructed the district court to dismiss the case for lack of jurisdiction, finding that the APA's general language on judicial review did not apply because the veterans' benefits statute clearly stated: "[T]he decisions of the Administrator on any question of law or fact under any law administered by the Veterans' Administration providing benefits for veterans and their dependents or survivors shall be final and conclusive and no other official or any court of the United States shall have power or jurisdiction to review any such decision by an action in the nature of mandamus or otherwise."[41] In light of that language, he held that the courts were barred from considering the appellee's complaint.[42]

Judge Patricia Wald dissented; she could not "believe that [the statute] was intended to allow the VA to defy with impunity the traditional, government-wide constraints on agency action."[43] Scalia responded that what was "truly incomprehensible to the dissent" was not "the nonreviewability of rules" but rather "the whole concept of a system of administrative justice, even in a field of government benefits, without general judicial supervision." However, he said, that concept was "precisely what the veterans' benefit laws enacted, plainly rejecting the judicialization, and even the lawyerization, of this field." His conclusion revealed both this commitment to a textualist reading of statutes and his sense of the proper role of the judiciary: "[O]ur function in cases such as this is not to devise plausible ways of depriving statutory language of its apparent meaning, but rather to give honest effect to the 'fairly discernible' intent of Congress to preclude judicial review."[44]

Chaney v. Heckler involved the APA's second exception to judicial review of agency action,[45] namely, action "committed to agency discretion by law." The case dealt with what Scalia termed "the implausible result" that the Food and Drug Administration (FDA) was required to exercise its enforcement power to ensure that states only used drugs that are "safe and effective" for human execution.[46]

The plaintiffs were eight prison inmates under sentence of death in Texas and Oklahoma who filed suit in U.S. District Court for the District of Columbia, claiming that the FDA had arbitrarily and capriciously refused to prevent the use of drugs not proven safe and effective as a means of human execution. Their petition to the FDA asserted that use of barbiturates and paralytics as capital punishment devices, without prior FDA approval, violated the "new drug" and "misbranding" provisions of the Food, Drug, and Cosmetics Act.[47] In response, the FDA asserted that its jurisdiction did not extend to the regulation of state-sanctioned use of lethal injections and that, even if it did, the FDA would, as a matter of its inherent enforcement discretion, undertake no investigatory or regulatory activity. The district court granted summary judgment against the plaintiffs' challenge to the FDA's refusal to act. On appeal, the D.C. Circuit reversed, finding that "the FDA arbitrarily and capriciously refused to exercise its regulatory jurisdiction."[48]

Scalia dissented, declaring that "[g]enerally speaking, enforcement priorities are not the business of this Branch, but of the Executive—to whom, and not to the courts, the Constitution confides the responsibility to 'take Care that the Laws be faithfully executed.'" For him, "[p]reserving that sound allocation of responsibility was one of the purposes, and has been perhaps the primary application, of that provision of the Administrative Procedure Act which excludes from judicial review 'agency action . . . committed to agency discretion by law.'"[49] He complained that his colleagues' determination that there existed a "general presumption of reviewability" of the FDA's enforcement decisions "distort[ed] the law and usurp[ed] the authority of the Executive Branch." They distorted the law by rendering "quite literally meaningless" the APA's express exclusion of judicial review in those cases in which "agency action is committed to agency discretion by law" by having that language turn on "such pragmatic considerations as whether judicial supervision is necessary to safeguard plaintiffs' interests, whether judicial review will unnecessarily impede the agency in effectively carrying out its congressionally assigned role, and whether the issues are appropriate for judicial review." These pragmatic considerations, he continued, could be summarized as follows: "[W]e intervene when we think it a good idea."[50] And they "usurped the authority of the Executive Branch" by assuming that judges are "the only public officials endowed with intelligence and worthy of trust" and by ignoring that "our system of laws has committed the relative evaluation of public health concerns to others."[51] He concluded by criticizing his colleagues for inappropriately interjecting themselves into the debate over capital punishment. The Court majority attributed the FDA's refusal to exercise enforcement discretion to its wish not to become "embroiled in an issue so morally and constitutionally troubling as the death penalty."[52] Scalia suggested a different reason: "[T]he agency was properly refusing to permit its powers and the laws it is charged with enforcing from being wrongfully enlisted in a cause that has less to do with assuring safe and effective drugs than with preventing the states' constitutionally permissible imposition of capital punishment." He declared that the court "should have done the same. It is our embroilment, rather than the FDA's abstention, that is remarkable."[53]

Scalia's Opposition to the Use of Legislative History

Scalia's appellate opinions also revealed another aspect of his emerging textualist jurisprudence: his opposition to the use of legislative history to ascertain legislative intent. For example, in his concurring opinion in *Hirschey v. Federal Energy Regulatory Commission* [FERC],[54] he seized on a footnote in the majority opinion that referred to a statement in a House committee report that the 1985 amendments to the Equal Access to Justice Act (EAJA) "ratified" an earlier D.C. Circuit decision concerning the granting of attorney's fees under EAJA, and he launched into an attack on the use of such evidence, according it "the weight of an equivalently unreasoned law review article." He would have accorded it "authoritative" weight only if he had found it "reasonable" to assume that the views expressed in the report were "reflected in the law which *Congress* adopted." But, he continued, "I frankly doubt that it is ever reasonable to assume that the details, as opposed to the broad outlines of purpose, set forth in a committee report come to the attention of, much less are approved by, the house which enacts the committee's bill."[55] He stressed to his colleagues that the time had come for them "to become concerned about the fact that routine deference to the detail of committee reports, and the predictable expansion in that detail which routine deference has produced, are converting a system of judicial construction into a system of committee-staff prescription." Scalia was doubly concerned that, in the instant case, the committee report dealt not with the meaning of statutory language drafted by the committee itself but rather with language drafted by an earlier Congress that was simply "reenacted, *unamended*" in the 1985 law. For him, the question before the court should have been resolved "not on the basis of what the committee report said, but on the basis of what we judge to be the most rational reconciliation of the relevant provisions of law Congress had adopted." Even then, the court might not have reconciled them as he would, but he would at least have "had the comfort . . . of thinking that the court was wrong for the right reason."[56]

For Scalia, the use of legislative history can "mask the underlying choices made by the judge in construing a statute" and can confer "a false impression that elected representatives actually considered and intended the result reached by the judge."[57] It can also upset delicate legislative compromises that "are best found" in the actual language of the statute."[58] Scalia underscored the importance of this last point in his dissent in *Illinois Commerce Commission v. Interstate Commerce Commission* [ICC], in which the majority held that the Staggers Rail Act of 1980 authorized the ICC to preempt the regulation of intrastate railroad rates. The court did so in large part because of a statement in the conference report that declared that "the Act preempts state authority over rail rates, classifications, rules and practices."[59] But as Scalia pointed out, the Staggers Act was filled with language indicating that "pro- and anti-preemption legislators" had reached a "compromise between . . . total federal preemption and . . . continued deferral to traditional state regulation of intrastate carriage."[60] By relying on legislative history and giving the conference report more weight than the actual language of the statute, Scalia declared that the majority had engaged in a "betrayal of that compromise."[61] And for him, betrayals of this kind threaten the very integrity of the legislative process. As he well understood, given his extensive knowledge of Washington politics, compromise is essential to the legislative process, and yet, "[l]egislative compromise (which is to say most intelligent legislation) becomes impossible when there is no assurance that the statutory words in which it is contained will be honored."[62]

In the Veterans Administration case, *Gott v. Walters*, Scalia also addressed the use of what he considered to be a still more problematic form of legislative history: a form that "has become known (with a disappointing lack of sense for the paradoxical) as 'subsequent legislative history'—i.e., legislative 'history' that postdates the statute in question."[63] In her dissent, Judge Wald argued for judicial review in part because of statements made by a senator during debate over a subsequent veterans' benefit law, indicating that, in the senator's estimation, the statute at issue in *Gott* had already granted judicial review.[64] Scalia responded that reliance on such after-the-fact remarks would allow advocates of judicial review "to achieve the result they were unable to obtain through the legislative process."[65]

Scalia's Narrow Reading of Freedom of Speech and Press

Scalia's circuit appellate opinions concerning freedom of speech and press revealed a judge who was guided only by the text and "historical practices" permitted by the First Amendment,[66] opposed to the "constitutional evolution" of its provisions, and convinced that the solutions to the "modern problems it poses" were "better sought through democratic change than through judicial pronouncement."[67] One of his very first appellate opinions was his dissent in *Community for Creative Non-Violence* [*CCNV*] *v. Watt*,[68] in which the D.C. Circuit held, in a six-to-five en banc decision, that a general ban on camping in the memorial core area parks of the District of Columbia could not be invoked to prevent camping that constituted an integral and expressive part of a demonstration otherwise protected by the First Amendment. CCNV sought a permit to conduct a round-the-clock demonstration, commencing on the first day of winter, on the Mall and in Lafayette Park in Washington, D.C., in order to impress upon the Reagan administration, the Congress, and the public the plight of the poor and the homeless. The National Park Service granted CCNV permits to set up symbolic campsites and to maintain a twenty-four-hour presence there but denied the participants a permit to sleep at the campsites, based on its anticamping regulations. CCNV sued; it claimed, and a majority on the D.C. Circuit agreed, that this prohibition struck at the core message the demonstrators wished to convey—that homeless people had no permanent place to sleep—and represented an unconstitutional restriction on their freedom of expression. Scalia filed a spirited dissent, denying "that sleeping is or can ever be speech for First Amendment purposes."[69] He found the majority decision to "endanger the great right of free speech by making it ridiculous and obnoxious, more than the Park Service regulation in question menaces free speech by proscribing sleep."[70]

Scalia started from the textualist premise that "speech" means "speech" and not all forms of expression. Otherwise, as he noted, it would have been unnecessary for those who drafted the First Amendment "to address 'freedom of the press' separately." For him, to confer free speech protections on all acts "conducted for the purpose of 'making a point' is to stretch the Constitution not only beyond its meaning but beyond reason, and beyond the capacity of any legal system to accommodate."[71]

He readily acknowledged that there are occasions when "expressive conduct" must be protected: a law "directed at the communicative nature of conduct must, like a law directed at speech itself, be justified by the substantial showing of need that the First Amendment requires." But, he insisted, the Park Service's refusal to grant a permit for camping and sleeping in D.C.'s memorial parks was not such an occasion because the Park Service's anticamping and antisleeping regulations were not directed at the communicative nature of that conduct. They proscribed camping and sleeping for a reason having nothing to do with those activities' communicative character. For Scalia, that was "the end of the matter so far as First Amendment guarantees are concerned."[72] He remarked that it was "a commentary upon how far judicial and scholarly discussion of this basic constitutional guarantee has strayed from common and common-sense understanding" that his statement was viewed as a "bold assertion."[73]

His next major First Amendment opinion was a dissent in the libel case of *Ollman v. Evans and Novak*.[74] Bertell Ollman, a Marxist political science professor at New York University, brought a defamation action against Rowland Evans and Robert Novak for their newspaper column criticizing him for using his faculty position to indoctrinate his students with Marxist revolutionary philosophy. The columnists quoted an unnamed political scientist who said that Ollman had "no status" within his profession and that he was "a pure and simple activist."[75] These statements led the administration at the University of Maryland to deny Ollman's appointment as chairman of its Political Science Department. The D.C. Circuit, sitting en banc, rejected his defamation suit and voted six to five that these statements were not facts but rather protected expression of opinion under the First Amendment. Four of the six judges who voted against Ollman declined to join the court opinion by Judge Kenneth Starr and instead signed Judge Robert Bork's concurrence. In his dissent, Scalia focused his attention on that opinion.

Bork expressed concern that there had been in the preceding few years a "remarkable upsurge in libel actions, accompanied by a startling inflation of damage awards" that was threatening "to impose a self-censorship on the press which can as effectively inhibit debate and criticism as would overt governmental regulation that the First Amendment most certainly would not permit." He argued that the test for proving libel was becoming too easy to meet, and so he proposed an "evolution in doctrine" that would replace the old test with a new one[76]—one based on the "totality of circumstances" that would consider "the context in which the statement occurs" in order to "determine both its meaning and the extent to which making it actionable would burden freedom of speech or press." He acknowledged that the test he was proposing admitted "into the law an element of judicial subjectivity." But, he insisted, a totality-of-circumstances test for protecting free speech and press, with all of its attendant judicial subjectivity, was "better than no protection at all."[77] Moreover, he lashed out, any "judge who refuse[d] to see [these] new threats to an established constitutional value" and who refused to accept this "evolution in [constitutional] doctrine" was "fail[ing] in his judicial duty."[78]

Unsurprising for one opposed to the "Living Constitution" because of "its incompatibility with the whole antievolutionary purpose of a constitution,"[79] Scalia organized his dissent around Bork's call for a "continuing evolution of doctrine."[80] He argued, first of all, that there was no need for evolution in libel law; the existing test to prove libel,[81] he insisted, provided "ample protection against the entire list of horribles supposedly confronting the defenseless modern publicist."[82]

Next he argued that his colleagues should reject "the risk of judicial subjectivity present in an approach which embraces 'a continuing evolution of doctrine'" based on nothing more than "judicially perceived 'modern problems.'"[83] Scalia insisted that the identification of "modern problems" that need to be remedied is "quintessentially legislative rather than judicial business" because it is "such a subjective judgment" and depends on "personal assessments" of so many "sociological factors." The remedies should be legislative; they should "be sought through democratic change rather than through judicial pronouncement that the Constitution now prohibits what it did not prohibit before."[84]

And he argued, finally, that when modern problems necessitate evolution of doctrine concerning libel law, those changes should come from the legislature rather than the courts. He used press shield laws as an example.

The omnipresence of the modern press, the popularity of "investigative reportage," and the eagerness of many dissident groups actively to seek out press coverage, have with increasing frequency caused members of the press to be in possession of information regarding unlawful activity, necessary for the detection or prevention of crime. The [Supreme] Court was asked, as the concurrence asks us here, not to take a "wooden" or "mechanical" view of the First Amendment, and to proclaim that in modern circumstances it prevents the subpoena of such information. Of course the Court declined. And of course the problem has not gone unaddressed. Many states have enacted "press shield" laws . . . which approach the issue in a much more calibrated fashion than judicial prohibition could achieve.[85]

Another major free speech and press opinion written by Scalia was *In Re the Reporters Committee for Freedom of the Press*,[86] in which he denied that there is a First Amendment right of public access to court records pertaining to private civil actions prior to judgment. In this case, the Reporters Committee for Freedom of the Press appealed two district court orders delaying, until after trial and entry of judgment, the public's access to court records consisting of documents produced and depositions furnished by the officers of Mobil Oil; these documents and depositions were provided in the course of third-party discovery in a libel suit brought by the president of Mobil Oil against the *Washington Post* and used in connection with summary judgment and trial proceedings. This was an issue of first impression; as Scalia noted, "No Supreme Court decision deals with the precise issue of the public's First Amendment rights to court records in civil cases." The text of the First Amendment clearly did not resolve the issue, so Scalia turned for guidance to historical practice. He justified doing so because, if courts were governed by "neither the constraint of text nor the constraint of historical practice, nothing would separate the judicial task of constitutional interpretation from the political task of enacting laws currently deemed essential."[87]

After an exhaustive review of historical practice, Scalia found in the available authorities only "weak support" for a general rule prohibiting access to prejudgment records in private civil cases. But that was sufficient: "[W]hen laid beside our inability to find *any* historical authority, holding or dictum, to the contrary, they are more than enough to rule out a general tradition of *access* to such records." He could not "discern an historic practice of such clarity, generality and duration as to justify the pronouncement of a *constitutional rule* preventing federal courts and the states from treating the records of private civil actions as private matters until trial or judgment," and for Scalia, that ended the matter.[88] Under the Constitution's scheme of separated powers, the question whether there should be such a rule was for the political branches to decide, not the courts.

One final First Amendment case needs to be mentioned. Scalia wrote the unanimous opinion for the D.C. Circuit in *Block v. Meese*,[89] in which the U.S. distributor and prospective exhibitors of three Canadian documentary films critical of Washington's nuclear-deterrence strategy and of its policy on acid rain challenged on First Amendment grounds the Justice Department's classification of these films as "political propaganda" under the Foreign Agents Registration Act. The plaintiffs argued that classifying these films as political propaganda expressed governmental disapproval of the ideas in question. Scalia rejected that claim. He did so because, he insisted, the term *political propaganda* did not express disapproval; not only had the term been applied to "material disseminated by our closest friends and allies (such as Canada)" but also "many specific items so classified have fostered policy positions consistently supported by the United States—for example, a film distributed on behalf of the Consulate General of Israel entitled *Plight of the Soviet Jewry: Let My People Go.*" He also rejected the claim because even if the plaintiffs were correct in their assertion that the classification of their films as political propaganda constituted an expression of official government disapproval of the ideas in question, "neither precedent nor reason would justify us in finding such an expression *in itself* unlawful."[90] A rule that would exclude official criticism of ideas would lead, he noted, "to the strange conclusion that it is permissible for the government to prohibit racial discrimination, but not to criticize racial bias; to criminalize polygamy, but not to praise the monogamous family; to make war on Hitler's Germany, but not to denounce Nazism." He flatly rejected the premise that "the only subjects off-limits to the government are those as to which there is less than substantial unanimity among the people—thus permitting official positions on war heroism and motherhood, but excluding nuclear disarmament and acid rain." That distinction, he wryly observed, would raise "the intolerable prospect" that it is the proper role of the courts to decide "what ideas are sufficiently popular to be granted government support—the object being, presumably, to assure that only the ideas of insular minorities will suffer official disparagement."[91] He concluded by observing that the control of government expression "is no more practicable, and no more appealing, than control of political expression by anyone else."[92]

Scalia on Separation of Powers

In a per curiam opinion in *Synar v. United States*,[93] a three-judge district court panel presided over by Scalia held that the automatic deficit-reduction process established by the Gramm-Rudman-Hollings budget-balancing statute (officially known as the Balanced Budget and Emergency Deficit Control Act of 1985), under which the president was required to issue a sequestration order implementing the budget-reduction specifications of a report prepared by the comptroller general, was unconstitutional on the ground that it vested executive power in the comptroller general, an officer removable only by Congress. Scalia was widely rumored to be the author of the per curiam opinion[94] — and for good reason: he was the only court of appeals judge on the panel; the opinion's lengthy treatment of the nondelegation doctrine, reliance on the Take Care Clause, and emphasis on the "technical provisions" of separation of powers have his fingerprints all over it;[95] and the biographical portrait of Scalia prepared by the Supreme Court Historical Society (which he has not requested that it correct) calls it a "Scalia opinion."[96]

The major argument for the plaintiffs was that when the Congress gave the comptroller general the power to make the economic calculations that determined the estimated federal deficit and hence the size of the required budget cuts, it engaged in an unconstitutional delegation of legislative power. The panel rejected that argument; it found that "through specification of maximum deficit amounts, establishment of a detailed administrative mechanism, and determination of the standards governing administrative decisionmaking, Congress has made the policy decisions which constitute the essence of the legislative function."[97] What the panel found decisive instead was the fact that by assigning tasks that "cannot be regarded as anything but executive powers in the constitutional sense" to the comptroller general, a legislative branch official subject to removal only by Congress, the act violated Article II, § 3 of the Constitution, which charges the president alone with the obligation to "take care that the laws be faithfully executed."[98] The panel held that the Constitution flatly denies Congress the power to remove "an officer who actually participates in the execution of the laws," for "once an officer is appointed, it is only the authority that can remove him, and not the authority that appointed him, that he must fear and, in the performance of his functions, obey."[99] The court noted that it "may seem odd" that "an important and hard-fought legislative program" such as the balanced budget act should be invalidated because of "the relative technicality of authority over the Comptroller General's removal," but in language that foreshadowed Scalia's discussion in *Plaut v. Spendthrift Farm*,[100] it declared that "the balance of separated powers established by the Constitution consists precisely of a series of technical provisions that are more important to liberty than superficially appears, and whose observance cannot be approved or rejected by the courts as the times seem to require."[101]

The court interestingly concluded by observing that although it had rejected the plaintiffs' argument based upon the doctrine of unconstitutional delegation, "the more technical separation-of-powers requirements we have relied upon may serve to further the policy of that doctrine more effectively than the doctrine itself." Since in two centuries the federal courts had only twice invoked unconstitutional delegation to invalidate legislation, the possibility of such invalidation, at least in modern times, was "not a credible deterrent against the human propensity to leave difficult questions to somebody else."[102] The technical requirements of separation of powers were far more effective in that respect. Clearly anticipating Scalia's argument in his dissents in *Morrison v. Olson*[103] and *Mistretta v. United States*,[104] the per curiam opinion closed by suggesting that there have been "innumerable" instances in which Congress has been disinclined to delegate its legislative powers to others and has "chosen to decide a difficult issue itself because of its reluctance to leave the decision—as our holding today reaffirms it must—to an officer within the control of the executive branch."[105]

Scalia's Nomination and Confirmation as Associate Justice of the Supreme Court

During his first term in office, President Reagan was able to make only one appointment to the Supreme Court: in 1982, he named Sandra Day O'Connor to fill the vacancy created by the retirement of Justice Potter Stewart. As the 1984 election approached, speculation on what other justices might retire over the next four years and whom Reagan might appoint as their replacements if he were reelected began in earnest. Scalia was always mentioned, along with Robert Bork and Richard Posner.[106] With Reagan's landslide reelection, the speculation intensified,[107] and Scalia's role in *Synar v. United States* was seen as boosting his prospects for an appointment.[108] Then, on June 17, 1986, at a surprise news conference at the White House, President Reagan announced the retirement of Chief Justice Warren Burger,[109] the nomination of Associate Justice William Rehnquist to be chief justice, and the nomination of Scalia as associate justice to succeed Rehnquist.[110]

Initial press coverage of Scalia's nomination was uniformly positive; he was variously described as "intellectually brilliant," "highly qualified," "charming," "delightful," "an intellectually formidable advocate of conservative views and judicial restraint," and "energetic and very gregarious."[111] In-depth profiles followed, and they were equally laudatory. In one, he was called "one of the smartest, wittiest and most cogent stylists on the Federal courts, using a combination of rigorous logic, caustic irony and elegant rhetoric to skewer his opponents."[112] In another, his conservatism was characterized as consisting "of not allowing judges to place their stamp upon public policy."[113] By contrast, Rehnquist's nomination as chief justice was met with controversy and contention.

Rehnquist was a lightning rod for criticism and invective for several reasons: the fact that his confirmation in 1971 as associate justice had been controversial (at the time, he received as many negative votes, twenty-six, as any confirmed justice in U.S. history); the fact that he had served as an associate justice for sixteen years and had written hundreds of opinions, many in lone dissent, challenging the liberal activism that characterized much of the Burger Court's work; and the fact that his engaging personality and powerful intellect were feared by many as likely to provide the leadership necessary to take the Supreme Court in a more conservative direction. His confirmation hearing was especially acrimonious; occurring the week before Scalia's, it was scheduled to last two days but in fact took four. The vote of the Judiciary Committee recommending Rehnquist's confirmation to the full Senate was 13 to 5. Debate in the full Senate was intense; it took five days and ended only after the Senate voted 68 to 31 in favor of a petition by the leadership to cut off further debate and bring the nomination to a vote. He was finally confirmed on a vote of 65 to 33, which, until then, was the highest number of negative votes received by a confirmed justice.[114]

The heavy guns fired on Rehnquist were never even trained on Scalia, even though he was widely considered to be as conservative as Rehnquist. Three factors account for that.

First, it helped a great deal that he was the first Italian American nominated to serve on the Supreme Court; even Robert Byrd of West Virginia, Senate minority leader at the time, saw that it was in his interest to invite Scalia, by then unanimously recommended for confirmation by the Senate Judiciary Committee, to join him at a state Italian heritage festival that year. By so doing, Byrd was named the event's "Honorary Italian of the Year," and Scalia was able to proclaim: "If and when I get there [to the Supreme Court], it should not just be an honor to all Italian-Americans, but to stand for just what kind of a country the United States is. My father came to this country when he was just 15, so I was the son of an immigrant and look where I am today."[115]

Second, unlike Rehnquist—who had already served on the Supreme Court and had voted on such controversial issues as abortion, affirmative action, and criminal procedure—Scalia refused to answer any questions about his views of these and other matters by saying that otherwise he could later be accused of not being impartial. This repeated refrain (although consistent with the approach taken by past nominees, including Justice O'Connor) frustrated the senators but effectively denied them an opening to attack his views.

And third, Scalia's critics knew that if they were successful in killing Rehnquist's nomination, they would succeed in killing Scalia's as well; if Rehnquist were rejected as chief justice, he would retain his seat as associate justice and there would be no position for Scalia to assume. His critics could attack Rehnquist and yet appear friendly to Scalia, thereby quelling the criticism that they were simply opposed to anyone Reagan would nominate while potentially killing the nomination of both.

Scalia's confirmation hearing was held on August 5 and 6, 1986. Scalia testified before the Senate Judiciary Committee on the afternoon and into the evening of August 5. Senator Joseph Biden, ranking Democrat on the committee, told

Scalia that compared with the fireworks at the Rehnquist hearing the week before, the proceedings were "pretty boring."[116] Seven recurrent themes emerged from Scalia's colloquy with the senators.

The first theme involved Scalia's refusal to answer all questions about his views on any constitutional question that might come before the Court. He refused even to answer whether he agreed with Chief Justice John Marshall's 1803 decision in *Marbury v. Madison*,[117] in which the Court asserted its power of judicial review— i.e., the power to declare unconstitutional acts of the other branches of the federal government.[118] The most dramatic refusal was his response to Senator Edward Kennedy, whose very first query was: "Judge Scalia, if you were confirmed, do you expect to overrule the *Roe v. Wade*?" Scalia calmly replied that it would be improper for him to answer that question. He explained why:

> Let us assume that I have people arguing before me to do it or not to do it. I think it is quite a thing to be arguing to somebody who you know has made a representation in the course of his confirmation hearings, and that is, by way of condition to his being confirmed, that he will do this or do that. I think I would be in a very bad position to adjudicate the case without being accused of having a less than impartial view of the matter.[119]

Scalia's repeated refusal to express an opinion on whether any of the existing law of the Supreme Court was right or wrong exasperated the senators.[120] Senator Arlen Specter expressed this frustration to him: "The question I have for you is how does a Senator make a judgment on what a Supreme Court nominee is going to do if we do not get really categorical answers to fundamental questions?" Scalia responded that the question was "very hard" only for "someone who does not have a track record," who has not written "opinions in the past dealing with the important features of the Constitution and of statutes," and who has not demonstrated "veneration for the important principles that you are concerned about." But, he continued, it was not hard at all in his case, given his four years on the court of appeals, his "extensive writings on administrative law and constitutional law" as a professor, and his "testimony and statements" when he was in the executive branch.[121] He continued by declaring that he had thought about "this issue a long time" as he was preparing to appear before the committee and that he had come to the following conclusion: if his answer to a question from Senator Specter or any other member of the committee "is obvious, then you do not need an answer, because your judgment of my record and my reasonableness and my moderation will lead you to conclude . . . [that] anybody that we think is not a nutty-nutty would have to come out that way." By contrast, if his answer to one of their questions "is not obvious, then I am really prejudicing future litigants." On balance, he concluded, "the only safe position that I can take in conscience is to simply not say that there is any particular case regarding which I would absolutely vote against a litigant who urges a position that is contrary to it."[122]

A second recurrent theme was Scalia's rhetorical sophistication in parrying certain lines of inquiry. In response to Senator Charles Mathias's veiled suggestion that, since Scalia had "a very deeply held personal position" on the abortion question and had expressed his views in print on that matter, he "should recuse himself" from hearing any challenges to *Roe v. Wade*, Scalia stated, "It is not at all unusual for Justices to have to confront" cases about which they feel strongly concerning "the morality of the issue." He cleverly mentioned *United States v. Reynolds*,[123] in which the Supreme Court held that Congress did not violate the Free Exercise Clause of the First Amendment when it prohibited polygamy in the federal territories: "Now that was certainly a moral issue. The issue of monogamy for the Justices sitting on that case. They obviously—at least many of them—must have had religious views about the matter and they did not feel it necessary, those who had those views, to disqualify themselves."[124]

Another example of Scalia's deft employment of rhetoric was found in one of his explanations as to why he would not indicate his views about various Supreme Court cases (such as *Roe v. Wade*) that certain members of the committee wanted to consider settled. He pointed out that even *Plessy v. Ferguson*,[125] upholding as constitutional racial segregation, was "considered a settled question at one time, but a litigant should have been able to come in and say, 'It is wrong,' and get a judge who has not committed himself to a committee as a condition of his confirmation to adhering to it."[126] He put those who would protect *Roe* on the defensive by placing them in the same category as those who had protected *Plessy*.

A final example came when Scalia was criticized by Senator Paul Simon for being weak on the First Amendment because of his dissenting opinion in *Ollman v. Evans and Novak*. Scalia responded that he was being put in "a sort of damned-if-you-do-damned-if-you-don't situation. I could have been criticized as being against Marxists had I come out the other way. It was a suit by a Marxist against conservative columnists."[127]

A third recurrent theme during Scalia's testimony was his commitment to an original-meaning approach to constitutional interpretation and his rejection of the "Living Constitution." In response to several senators, Scalia made clear that "in any case, I start from the original meaning," that is, "the text of the document and what it meant to the society that adopted it." He declared that his textualist, original-meaning approach was part of his "whole philosophy, which is essentially a democratic philosophy that even the Constitution is, at bottom, a democratic document." He contrasted the words *original meaning* with *original intent* and said that if "somebody should discover that the secret intent of the framers was

quite different from what the words seem to connote, it would not make any difference" for him.[128] He confessed that he did not have "a fully framed omnibus
view of the Constitution,"[129] and some of his comments made that clear. Despite
his criticisms of Judge Bork's call for a "continuing evolution of doctrine" in *Ollman,* he volunteered that "there are some provisions of the Constitution," including the Cruel and Unusual Punishments Clause of the Eighth Amendment, "that
may have a certain amount of evolutionary content within them," and he acknowledged that he had "always had trouble with [the constitutionality of] lashing."[130]

Although Scalia may not have developed "a full constitutional matrix" by the
time of his nomination, he had clearly thought through many of the most difficult problems of treating the Constitution as so "evolvable" that "in effect a court
of nine judges can treat it as though it is a bring-along-with-me statute and fill it
up with whatever context the current times seem to require."[131] The "Living Constitution" approach to constitutional interpretation, he warned, allows the Court
to employ especially the Due Process Clauses of the Fifth and Fourteenth Amendments to find contrary to "the most fundamental beliefs of our society" a practice
"that was in existence when the Constitutional provision in question was adopted
and is still in existence" today.[132] Yet judges have no guidance, other than their
"own intuition, to say what are the deepest and most profound beliefs of our society." Speaking personally, he worried "that I am left with nothing to tell me what
are our most profound beliefs except my own little voice inside. I do not want to
govern this society on the basis of that."[133]

A fourth recurrent theme was Scalia's opposition to the use by courts of legislative history. He told a fairly incredulous Senator Charles Grassley that "Congress does not act in committee reports. I will say that flat out. Congress acts by
passing a law." What the whole Congress intended, he insisted, was best found in
the words it used rather than in statements "on the floor by a single Senator" or
in committee reports. And thus, he explained to Senator Grassley, he avoided the
use of legislative history in order to make "sure that we are not disenfranchising
the Congress and getting you, as a member of the Senate, committed to a position which in fact you knew nothing about and would disagree with."[134] He went
so far as to tell Senator Simon that if he "could create the world anew," he "would
call all legislative history into question,"[135] and he was so bold as to say that his
views on the matter were "the wave of the future."[136]

A fifth recurrent theme was Scalia's understanding of the problem of overbroad
delegation of power by Congress. Scalia presented it not so much as a constitutional problem but as a democratic one. As he told Senator Kennedy, "The more
specific Congress can be, the more democratic the judgment is, because if Congress is not specific, the judgment is made by the courts, and the courts are not
democratic institutions."[137] Senator Grassley endeavored to enlist him as a defender

of the legislative veto by suggesting that Congress "cannot anticipate crises, and I hope you accept that it is unreasonable to expect Congress to do otherwise" and by speculating that, were the "Founding Fathers" alive "today," they would find the legislative veto "a fair and practical way to deal with bureaucracy." Scalia deftly sidestepped Grassley's entreaty by admitting that it was "conceivable that had they envisioned the kind of system that would develop, they would have made provision in the Constitution for a legislative veto." But, he noted, "they did not."[138]

A sixth theme was introduced when Senator Howell Heflin questioned Scalia about his "general philosophy of the role of the judiciary relative to federalism." Scalia's answers to most of the questions the committee posed to him were predictable and based on his appellate opinions; his answer to this question, however, was more illuminating, for he had written no previous opinions on federalism — not surprising given that he served on D.C. Circuit. He made it clear that he thought "the primary institution to strike the right balance" between the federal government and the states "is the Congress."[139] He described federalism in terms of line drawing and declared that it is "very hard" to find a clear line "between those matters that are appropriate for the States and those that are appropriate for the Federal Government." Difficult as that task may be, however, he insisted that "finding that line is much easier for a legislature than for a court," and he hinted that "the history of this century" had shown that the Supreme Court, after years of struggle, had appropriately come to that conclusion.[140] His steadfast refusal to answer questions about his views on any constitutional question that might come before the Court contrasted strikingly with his willingness to answer the question about whether he thought the courts should defer to Congress's decision of where to draw the line between federal and state power.[141]

Finally, a seventh recurrent theme was Scalia's understanding of freedom of speech and the press. Scalia's circuit opinions in *Ollman* and *CCNV v. Watt* had prompted William Safire of the *New York Times* to brand him "the worst enemy of free speech in America today,"[142] and the committee members were interested in exploring at length Scalia's view on this matter. Scalia immediately began by establishing his bona fides. He told Senator Strom Thurmond within minutes of the opening of his hearing that "I am the first academic to be nominated to the Court since [Justice Felix] Frankfurter. I have spent my life in the field that the first amendment is most designed to protect." He also pointed out, "I think I am one of the few Supreme Court nominees that has been the editor of a magazine." He suggested that if he were to have "a skewed view of the first amendment, it would be in just the opposite direction."[143]

Senator Biden was especially interested in Scalia's dissent in the *Watt* case, causing Scalia to lead Biden through a series of careful distinctions. He began by defining "speech as any communicative activity," and he acknowledged that sleeping could

be a form of communication. But, he continued, whether the government could prohibit that communication without running afoul of the First Amendment would
depend on whether it had "passed a law that allows all other sleeping but only prohibits sleeping where it is intended to communicate." He pointed out that a law that
applies to "an activity which in itself is normally not communicative, such as sleeping
[or] spitting," is not subject "to the heightened standards of the First Amendment." By
contrast, a law that does apply to "communicative activity, naturally communicative
activity—writing, speech, and so forth—any law, even if it is general, across the board,
has to meet those higher standards." Biden wondered how Scalia's understanding
would apply to those civil rights demonstrators of the 1960s who had engaged in sit-
ins in segregated restaurants to protest Jim Crow legislation. Scalia responded forth-
rightly, insisting that those protests were outside the ambit of First Amendment
protection: "If you want to protest, as a means of civil disobedience, and take the
penalty, that is fine. But if the law is not itself directed against demonstrations or
against communication, I do not think it is the kind of law that in and of itself requires
heightened scrutiny."[144] After their colloquy, Biden remarked that his apprehensions
were allayed and his mind put "at ease a great deal."[145] He observed, however, that
without the additional explanation Scalia had just given, someone could well have
concluded that Scalia was the enemy of free speech Safire accused him of being, to
which, in typical fashion, Scalia quipped, "I will have to write longer opinions."[146]

Scalia's confirmation hearing continued the next day (August 6), with the committee receiving testimony from twenty-one different individuals who represented
a wide range of opinion, including: Robert B. Fiske, chairman of the Standing
Committee on the Federal Judiciary of the American Bar Association, who
announced that his fourteen-member committee had unanimously voted Scalia
"well qualified," the highest of three possible ratings for Supreme Court nominees; Gerhard Casper, dean of the University of Chicago Law School, who praised
Scalia's legal brilliance and powerful intellect; Eleanor Smeal, president of the
National Organization for Women, who predicted that Scalia's confirmation
would have "disastrous" consequences for women; and Joseph Rauh, appearing
on behalf of Americans for Democratic Action and the Leadership Conference
on Civil Rights, who decried Scalia's "right-wing" views and denounced his nomination as "a tragedy for our county."[147]

On August 14, the Senate Judiciary Committee gave unanimous approval to
Scalia's nomination, and on the evening of September 17, after a five-day debate
on the confirmation of Rehnquist as chief justice, the full Senate spent fewer than
five minutes before it confirmed Scalia's nomination by a vote of ninety-eight to
zero.[148] Scalia was sworn in as the 103rd member of the Supreme Court on Friday, September 26, and he took his seat at the beginning of the 1986–1987 term
of the Court on October 6. On November 4, he issued his first opinion in *O'Con-*

nor v. United States,[149] writing for a unanimous court that U.S. citizens working in Panama for the Panama Canal Commission were not exempt from paying federal income taxes on their salaries. It is a long-standing Court tradition to give a new justice an easy, unanimous opinion for the first assignment.[150] Not surprisingly, though, Scalia used this occasion to stake out immediately his ground as a textualist. In a nine-page opinion, he parsed the language of the Panama Canal Treaty of 1977 and concluded that, "in our view of the text," neither the United States nor Panama intended to create such a tax exemption.[151]

Conclusions

When he appeared before the Senate Judiciary Committee, Scalia insisted that he did not have a "fully-framed" view of the Constitution. However, no one familiar with his pre-judicial career (especially his service in the Office of Legal Counsel in the Justice Department and his firsthand involvement in Washington politics), his opinions while on the D.C. Circuit, or his lively interactions with members of the Senate during his confirmation hearing would have been in the least bit surprised by the jurisprudential approach he would take once on the Supreme Court. His advice to President Ford as assistant attorney general revealed the importance he placed on the Constitution's separation of powers and his textualist approach to the Take Care Clause of Article II; so, too, did his appellate opinions on standing and his per curiam opinion in *Synar.* His editorial stances in *Regulation* and his appellate opinions refusing to read the APA as authorizing judicial review of agency actions when its text did not provide for it supplied evidence of his emerging textualist approach to questions of constitutional and statutory interpretation; the same can also be said for his principled refusal to employ legislative history while on the D.C. Circuit and for his bold prediction to the members of the Senate Judiciary Committee that his rejection of legislative history represented "the wave of the future." His appellate opinions insisting that the constitutional standards for standing should be kept high and his conviction as expressed before the Senate that questions concerning where to draw the line between the powers of the federal government and those of the states are best addressed by Congress (and not by the judiciary) clearly presaged his repeatedly affirmed commitment to judicial restraint once on the Supreme Court. Finally, his declaration in *Ollman* that the meaning of the First Amendment does not evolve over time and his message to the Senate Judiciary Committee that the Constitution is not a "bring-along-with-me statute" that nine justices are free to fill with "whatever context the current times seem to require" announced his unequivocal rejection of the "Living Constitution" approach to constitutional interpretation.

Chapter Two systematically presents Scalia's affirmative approach to the interpretive enterprise. It is a textualist approach that he could do little more than outline in his D.C. Circuit opinions and in his testimony before the Senate but that he has been able subsequently to articulate fully and refine at length in his many Supreme Court opinions, concurrences, and dissents and in his extensive extrajudicial writings.

Chapter Two

"Text and Tradition":
Scalia's Understanding of the Interpretive Enterprise

Since his elevation to the Supreme Court, Justice Scalia has assiduously and consistently pursued a textualist jurisprudence. He argues that primacy must be accorded to the text, structure, and history of the document being interpreted and that the job of the judge is to apply either the clear textual language[1] of the Constitution or statute[2] or the critical structural principle necessarily implicit in the text.[3] If the text is ambiguous, yielding several conflicting interpretations, Scalia turns to the specific legal tradition flowing from that text[4]—to "what it meant to the society that adopted it."[5] *Text and tradition* is a phrase that fills Justice Scalia's opinions.[6] Judges are to be governed only by the "text and tradition of the Constitution," not by their "intellectual, moral, and personal perceptions."[7] As he remarked in his concurring opinion in *Schad v. Arizona*, "[W]hen judges test their individual notions of 'fairness' against an American tradition that is deep and broad and continuing, it is not the tradition that is on trial, but the judges."[8]

"Text and Tradition" Explained

For Scalia, reliance on text and tradition is a means of constraining judicial discretion.[9] He believes that "the main danger in judicial interpretation of the Constitution"—or, for that matter, in judicial interpretation of any law[10]—"is that the judges will mistake their own predilections for the law."[11] Faithful adherence to the text of a constitutional or statutory provision or, if that is ambiguous, to the traditional understanding of those who originally adopted it reduces the danger that judges will substitute their beliefs for society's.[12] As Scalia observed in response to a question by Senator Howard Metzenbaum during his Senate confirmation hearings:

> [A] constitution has to have ultimately majoritarian underpinnings. To be sure a constitution is a document that protects against future democratic excesses. But when it is adopted, it is adopted by democratic process. That is what legitimates it. . . . [I]f the majority that adopted it did not believe this unspecified right, which is not reflected clearly in the language, if their laws at the time do not reflect that that right existed, nor do the laws at the

27

present date reflect that the society believes that right exists, I worry about my deciding that it exists. I worry that I am not reflecting the most fundamental, deeply felt beliefs of our society, which is what a constitution means, but rather, I am reflecting the most deeply felt beliefs of Scalia, which is not what I want to impose on the society.[13]

For Scalia, the Court's opinions in the companion cases of *Board of County Commissioners, Wabaunsee County, Kansas v. Umbehr*[14] and *O'Hare Truck Service v. Northlake*[15] fully demonstrate the justices' willingness to substitute their beliefs for the traditional beliefs of society. In his combined dissent in these cases, he ridiculed the "Court's Constitution-making process" that prompted his colleagues to declare that the Freedom of Speech Clause of the First Amendment protects private contractors from government retaliation for their exercise of political speech.[16] In the former case, a trash hauler alleged that he had lost a county contract after he criticized the board in a letter to the editor of a local newspaper; in the latter case, a towing firm alleged that it was barred from getting towing referrals after the owner refused to contribute to the mayor's reelection. Scalia noted that "rewarding one's allies" while "refusing to reward one's opponents" is "an American political tradition as old as the Republic." Zeroing in on this tradition, he asked: "If that long and unbroken tradition of our people does not decide these cases, then what does? The constitutional text is assuredly as susceptible of one meaning as of the other; in that circumstance, what constitutes a 'law abridging the freedom of speech' is either a matter of history or else it is a matter of opinion. Why are not libel laws such an 'abridgment'? The only satisfactory answer is that they never were." Scalia's anger was palpable: "What secret knowledge, one must wonder, is breathed into lawyers when they become Justices of this Court, that enables them to discern that a practice which the text of the Constitution does not clearly proscribe, and which our people have regarded as constitutional for 200 years, is in fact unconstitutional?"[17]

Scalia fully understands that the Constitution creates two conflicting systems of rights: One is democratic—the right of the majority to rule individuals; the other is antidemocratic—the right of individuals to have certain liberties protected from majority rule. He relies on the Constitution's text to define the respective spheres of majority and minority freedom, and when that fails to provide definitive guidance, Scalia turns to tradition. He argues that tradition, and not the personal values of the justices, is to tell the Court when the majoritarian process is to be overruled in favor of individual rights.[18] He believes that by identifying those areas of life traditionally protected from majority rule, the Court can objectively determine which individual freedoms the Constitution protects.[19] As he argued in his combined dissent in *Umbehr* and *O'Hare Truck Service*, "I would separate the permissible from the impermissible on the basis of our Nation's traditions, which is what I believe sound constitutional adjudication requires."[20]

Scalia therefore would overrule the majority only when it has infringed upon an individual right explicitly protected by the text of the Constitution or by specific legal traditions flowing from that text.[21] In his dissent in *United States v. Virginia*,[22] in which the Court proclaimed that the exclusively male admission policy of the Virginia Military Institute violated the Equal Protection Clause of the Fourteenth Amendment, he declared that the function of the Court is to "preserve our society's values, not to revise them; to prevent backsliding from the degree of restriction the Constitution imposed upon democratic government, not to prescribe, on our own authority, progressively higher degrees." The Court is not to "supersede" but rather is to "reflect" those "constant and unbroken national traditions that embody the people's understanding of ambiguous constitutional texts."[23] As he powerfully argued in his dissent in *Rutan v. Republican Party of Illinois*, in which the Court held that political patronage violates the free speech rights of public employees:

> The provisions of the Bill of Rights were designed to restrain transient majorities from impairing long-recognized personal liberties. They did not create by implication novel individual rights overturning accepted political norms. Thus, when a practice not expressly prohibited by the text of the Bill of Rights bears the endorsement of a long tradition of open, widespread, and unchallenged use that dates back to the beginning of the Republic, we have no proper basis for striking it down. Such a venerable and accepted tradition is not to be laid on the examining table and scrutinized for its conformity to some abstract principle of First Amendment adjudication devised by this Court. . . . When it appears that the latest "rule," or "three-part test," or "balancing test" devised by the Court has placed us on a collision course with such a landmark practice, it is the former that must be recalculated by us, and not the latter that must be abandoned by our citizens.[24]

Scalia's Employment of "Text and Tradition"

In *Harmelin v. Michigan*,[25] Scalia's text-and-tradition approach was on full display. In it, he held that the Cruel and Unusual Punishments Clause of the Eighth Amendment does not prohibit the imposition of a mandatory term of life in prison without possibility of parole for possessing more than 650 grams of cocaine. Announcing the judgment of the Court, he rejected Ronald Harmelin's contention that his sentence was unconstitutional because it was "significantly disproportionate" to the crime he had committed. Scalia noted that "this claim has no support in the text and history of the Eighth Amendment."[26] Concerning the text, he observed that "to use the phrase 'cruel and unusual punishment' to describe a requirement of proportionality would have been an exceedingly vague and oblique way of saying what Americans were well accustomed to saying more directly."[27] Concerning history, he surveyed English constitutional history since the promulgation of the English Declaration of Rights as well as eighteenth- and nineteenth-century American constitutional and legal history to show that the Cruel and Unusual Punishments Clause was understood only "to outlaw particular modes of punishment" (e.g., drawing and quartering, breaking on the wheel, and flaying alive), not to require that "all punishments be proportioned to the offense."[28] He was led, therefore, to argue that *Solem v. Helms*,[29] in which the Court had held that the Eighth Amendment does contain a proportionality guarantee, was "wrong" and should be overturned.[30]

Although his textualist approach led Scalia to reject a criminal defendant's claim in *Harmelin*, it does not do so invariably. Thus, in *Coy v. Iowa*,[31] it led him to uphold the right of a defendant literally to "be confronted with the witnesses against him" and to overturn his conviction because Iowa law allowed the two thirteen-year-old girls he was charged with sexually assaulting to testify behind a large screen that shielded them from the defendant. For Scalia, the text was unequivocal and governing:

> Simply as a matter of English, it confers at least "a right to meet face to face all those who appear and give evidence at trial." Simply as a matter of Latin as well, since the word "confront" ultimately derives from the prefix "con-" (from "contra" meaning "against" or "opposed") and the noun "frons" (forehead). Shakespeare was thus describing the root meaning of confrontation when he had Richard the Second say: "Then call them to our presence—face to face, and frowning brow to brow, ourselves will hear the accuser and the accused freely speak."[32]

Likewise, in *Rogers v. Tennessee*,[33] Scalia's text-and-tradition approach led him to conclude in his dissent that the Tennessee Supreme Court's retroactive abolition of the common-law "year-and-a-day" rule concerning murder convictions (i.e., no defendant could be convicted of murder unless the victim died by the defendant's act within a year and a day of the act) violated the Due Process Clause of the Fourteenth Amendment insofar as that clause contains the principle applied against state legislatures by the Ex Post Facto Clause of Article I, § 10: "Such retroactive revision of a concededly valid legal rule . . . was unheard-of at the time the original due process clause was adopted."[34]

Scalia does not restrict his text-and-tradition approach to criminal procedural matters; he applies it across the constitutional board. He applied it, for example, in *Pacific Mutual Life Insurance Co. v. Haslip* when he declared that the Due Process Clause does not place limits on the size of punitive-damage awards. He cited Sir Edward Coke, William Blackstone, James Kent, and Joseph Story, all of whom had argued that due process meant simply the "law of the land," and he concluded that a defendant receives due process of law if the trial is conducted according to the settled course of judicial proceedings.[35] "[I]f the government chooses to follow a historically approved procedure, it necessarily provides due process," he stated.[36] And in *Vieth v. Jubelirer*, he applied his text-and-tradition approach when he held that political gerrymandering was a nonjusticiable political question "entrusted to one of the political branches":

> [T]he Framers provided a remedy for such practices in the Constitution. Article 1, § 4, while leaving in state legislatures the initial power to draw districts for federal elections, permitted Congress to "make or alter" those districts if it wished. Many objected to the congressional oversight established by this provision. In the course of the debates in the Constitutional Convention, Charles Pinkney and John Rutledge moved to strike the relevant language. James Madison responded in defense of the provision that Congress must be given the power to check partisan manipulation of the election process by the States.[37]

Scalia has also applied his text-and-tradition approach to the Religion Clauses. It led him to conclude in his dissent in *Lee v. Weisman* that the Establishment Clause "was adopted to prohibit such an establishment of religion at the federal level [as in England was represented by the Church of England] and to protect state establishments of religion from federal interference" and that it therefore did not bar nonsectarian prayers at public school graduation ceremonies.[38] Likewise, it led him to complain in *Board of Education of Kiryas Joel v. Grumet* that

> [t]he Founding Fathers would be astonished to find that the Establishment Clause—which they designed "to ensure that no one powerful sect or combination of sects would use political or governmental power to punish dissenters"—has been employed to prohibit characteristically and admirably American accommodation of the religious practices (or more precisely, cultural peculiarities) of a tiny minority sect. I, however, am not surprised. Once this Court has abandoned text and history as guides, nothing prevents it from calling religious tolerance the establishment of religion.[39]

And concerning the Free Exercise Clause, Scalia's text-and-tradition approach led him to conclude in his controversial majority opinion in *Employment Division, Department of Human Resources of Oregon v. Smith* that, "as a textual matter," there is no need to provide a religious exemption to a generally applicable statute because "to make an individual's obligation to obey such a law contingent upon the law's coincidence with his religious beliefs, except where the State's interest is 'compelling'—permitting him, by virtue of his beliefs, 'to become a law unto himself,'—contradicts both constitutional tradition and common sense."[40]

Scalia believes deeply in following his text-and-tradition approach. His duty, as he described it in his dissent in *Planned Parenthood v. Casey*, is to "read the text and discern our society's traditional understanding of that text."[41] Discerning the original meaning is, he told the Senate Judiciary Committee during his confirmation hearings, "the starting point and the beginning of wisdom."[42] And when that meaning is discerned, the justices are expected to follow it without agonizing over the lost opportunities to engage in activist reform that their professionally required adherence to the text obliges them to forgo. As Scalia lectured an equivocating Justice Anthony Kennedy in *Vieth v. Jubelirer* (who, while he recognized with Scalia that political gerrymandering was a nonjusticiable political question, insisted nevertheless on retaining judicial oversight): "When it has come to determining what areas fall beyond our Article III authority to adjudicate, this Court's practice, from the earliest days of the Republic to the present, has been more reminiscent of Hannibal than of Hamlet."[43]

Nevertheless, Scalia appears occasionally to drift from his text-and-tradition moorings. *Texas v. Johnson*,[44] the Texas flag-burning case in which he joined in Justice William Brennan's majority opinion[45] striking down Texas' ban on burning the American flag, is a case in point. During his Senate confirmation hearings, Scalia defined speech as "any communicative activity,"[46] and by that definition, flag burning is communicative activity and thereby speech and therefore protected by the First Amendment. What appears problematic, however, is not that Scalia's conclusion does not follow logically from his premise but rather the premise itself. There is absolutely no textual or historical evidence to support the contention that the society that adopted the First Amendment understood it to cover such communicative activity as flag burning.[47] Scalia's understanding that the Free Speech Clause covers all intentionally communicative activity is discussed at length in Chapter Five.

Another example, examined in Chapter Six, is Scalia's unquestioned acceptance of the incorporation doctrine. In response to questioning by Senator Arlen Specter during his Senate confirmation hearing, Scalia declared that the Court's incorporation through the Fourteenth Amendment of various Bill of Rights provisions to apply to the states—an interpretation inconsistent with both the text of the Fourteenth Amendment and the understanding of those who drafted and rat-ified it—"is a very accepted and settled part of our current system" and that "it would be quite a jolt to the existing system to suddenly discover that those series of protections against state actions do not exist."[48] At the time, his answer may have been no more than a prudent way of parrying Specter's questions, but Scalia's opinions once on the Supreme Court show a continued reluctance to launch a textualist challenge against the incorporation doctrine. As he observed in *Albright v. Oliver,* "[O]ur decisions have included within the Fourteenth Amendment cer-tain explicit substantive protections of the Bill of Rights—*an extension I accept because it is both long established and narrowly limited.*"[49]

A third example, extensively discussed in Chapter Four, is Scalia's consistent embrace of the Court's "state sovereign immunity" jurisprudence. In his 1991 opinion for the Court in *Blatchford v. Native Village of Noatak,* he expressed the decidedly nontextualist view that the Eleventh Amendment bars all suits against a state in federal court, even though its text is much narrower and bars only suits "commenced or prosecuted against one of the United States by citizens of another State, or by the Citizens or Subjects of any Foreign State." By its terms, the Eleventh Amendment precludes individuals from bringing suit against states in the federal courts only when the basis of jurisdiction is state-citizen diversity; it says nothing about precluding suits against the states in federal court that are based on the existence of a federal question. Nonetheless, Scalia insisted that the amend-ment stood "not so much for what it says, but for the presupposition . . . which it confirms"—that presupposition being the doctrine that a state cannot be sued in federal court without its consent.[50] And in seven cases since 1996,[51] he has invari-ably joined majority opinions that openly dismiss textualism and repeat the words of Chief Justice Rehnquist, first uttered in *Seminole Tribe of Florida v. Florida,* that "a blind reliance upon the text of the Eleventh Amendment" would be "overly exacting."[52]

Scalia believes that "the rule of law is the law of rules"—which reflects the title of his Oliver Wendell Holmes Jr. Lecture delivered at Harvard Law School in 1989.[53] He argues that, when the text embodies a rule, judges are simply to apply that rule as the law.[54] When text and tradition fail to supply a rule, there is no rule, no law for judges to apply to contradict the actions of the popular branches, and therefore no warrant for judicial intervention. This was his argu-ment in *Troxel v. Granville,*[55] in which he dissented from the Supreme Court's invalidation of a Washington State statute providing visitation rights for nonpar-ents of a child if a judge found it would be in the best interests of the child, on the grounds that the statute unconstitutionally infringed on the fundamental right of parents to rear their children. Scalia found the law offensive, declaring that "[i]n my view, a right of parents to direct the upbringing of their children is among the 'unalienable Rights' with which the Declaration of Independence proclaims 'all Men . . . are endowed by their Creator.' "[56] But, he continued, offensive laws are not unconstitutional in the absence of clear text making them so.

> Judicial vindication of "parental rights" under a Constitution that does not even mention them requires not only a judicially crafted definition of parents, but also — unless, as no one believes, the parental rights are to be absolute — judicially approved assessments of "harm to the child" and judicially defined gradations of other persons (grandparents, extended family, adoptive family in an adoption later found to be invalid, long-term guardians, etc.) who may have some claim against the wishes of the parents. If we embrace this unenumerated right, I think it obvious . . . that we will be ushering in a new regime of judicially prescribed, and federally prescribed, family law. I have no reason to believe that federal judges will be better at this than state legislatures; and state legislatures have the great advantages of doing harm in a more circumscribed area, of being able to correct their mistakes in a flash, and of being removable by the people.[57]

This was also his argument in *Romer v. Evans,* in which he unleashed a powerful attack on the Court for "tak[ing] sides in the culture war" and invalidating Colorado's Amendment 2 denying preferential treatment to homosexuals.[58] "Since the Constitution of the United States says nothing about this subject," he commented, "it is left to be resolved by normal democratic means, including the democratic adoption of provisions in state constitutions. This Court has no business imposing upon all Americans the resolution favored by the elite class from which the Members of this institution are selected, pronouncing that 'animosity' toward homosexuality is evil."[59] And this was his argument in his concurring opinion in *Cruzan v. Director, Missouri Department of Health,* in which the Court rejected the contention that Nancy Cruzan had a "right to die." Scalia wrote:

> While I agree with the Court's analysis today, and therefore join in its opinion, I would have preferred that we announce, clearly and promptly, that the federal courts have no business in this field; that American law has always accorded the State the power to prevent, by force if necessary, suicide — including suicide by refusing to take appropriate measures necessary to preserve one's life; that the point at which life becomes "worthless," and the point at which the means necessary to preserve it become "extraordinary" or "inappropriate," are neither set forth in the Constitution nor known to the nine Justices of this Court any better than they are known to nine people picked at random from the Kansas City telephone

directory; and hence, that even when it is demonstrated by clear and convincing evidence that a patient no longer wishes certain measures to be taken to preserve her life, it is up to the citizens of Missouri to decide, through their elected representatives, whether that wish will be honored. It is quite impossible that those citizens will decide upon a line less lawful than the one we would choose; and it is unlikely (because we know no more about "life-and-death" than they do) that they will decide upon a line less reasonable.[60]

In *A Matter of Interpretation*, Justice Scalia succinctly spelled out both the origins of judicial policymaking and his reasons for rejecting it. Judicial policymaking arose, he noted, in the old common-law system in England, in which judges, unconstrained by statutes or a written constitution, exercised the "exhilarating" function of making law. From there, it eventually spread to American law schools, where impressionable "law students, having drunk at this intoxicating well," come away thinking that the highest function of the judge is "devising, out of the brilliance of one's own mind, those laws that ought to govern mankind. How exciting!"[61] He noted a key problem with this approach: it is a "trend in government that has developed in recent centuries, called democracy."[62] As Scalia insisted, "It is simply not compatible with democratic theory that laws mean whatever they ought to mean, and that unelected judges decide what that is."[63]

In several powerful dissents, Scalia has castigated his colleagues (and, thereby, the judges of the lower courts) for their contemptuous disregard for the democratic principle. Thus, in his dissent in the companion cases of *Umbehr* and *O'Hare Truck Service*, he accused the Court majority of "living in another world. Day by day, case by case, it is busy designing a Constitution for a country I do not recognize." He warned the public that "[w]hile the present Court sits, a major, undemocratic restructuring of our national institutions and mores is constantly in progress."[64] Likewise, in his dissent in *United States v. Virginia*, he acerbically noted that much of the Court's opinion concerning Virginia Military Institute and its all-male student body was "devoted to deprecating the closed-mindedness of our forebears with regard to women's education." He therefore felt obliged to "counterbalance" the Court's criticism of our ancestors and to say a word in their praise: "They left us free to change." The virtue of the democratic system expressing itself in the Constitution with its First Amendment "that we inherited from our forebears" is that "it readily enables the people, over time, to be persuaded that what they took for granted is not so, and to change their laws accordingly." That system, he continued, "is destroyed if the smug assurances of each age are removed from the democratic process and written into the Constitution." But, Scalia charged, that is exactly what "this most illiberal Court" has been doing; it

has "embarked on a course of inscribing one after another of the current preferences of the society (and in some cases only the counter-majoritarian preferences
of the society's law-trained elite) into our Basic Law."[65]

Scalia's Understanding of the "Whole Theory of Democracy"

Scalia is criticized for having a "vulgar majoritarian" understanding of democracy.[66] This criticism is based in large part on a lecture he gave in May 1996 at the
Gregorian University in Rome (where his son was a student). During the ques-
tion-and-answer period that followed, Scalia declared that "it just seems to me
incompatible with democratic theory that it's good and right for the state to do
something that the majority of the people do not want done. Once you adopt
democratic theory, it seems to me, you accept that proposition. If the people, for
example, want abortion the state should permit abortion. If the people do not want
it, the state should be able to prohibit it." He went on to declare that "the whole
theory of democracy . . . is that the majority rules; that is the whole theory of it.
You protect minorities only because the majority determines that there are certain minority positions that deserve protection."[67]

The criticism that Scalia has a vulgar majoritarian understanding of democracy is also based on statements he made in A *Matter of Interpretation*. This book
begins with Scalia's essay "Common-Law Courts in a Civil Law System: The Role
of United States Federal Courts in Interpreting the Constitution and Laws," based
on his 1995 Tanner Lectures on Human Values delivered at Princeton University; it is followed by commentaries on his essay by four prominent scholars (Gor-
don S. Wood, Laurence H. Tribe, Mary Ann Glendon, and Ronald Dworkin) and
by Scalia's replies to these commentators. In his commentary, Tribe rejected
Scalia's textualism in favor of what he called an "aspirational" theory of constitutional interpretation. In his reply, Scalia dismissed Tribe's emphasis on aspirations:
"If you want aspirations, you can read the Declaration of Independence, with its
pronouncements that 'all men are created equal' with 'unalienable Rights' that
include 'Life, Liberty, and the Pursuit of Happiness.' Or you can read the French
Declaration of the Rights of Man." But, he continued, "[t]here is no such philos-
ophizing in our Constitution, which, unlike the Declaration of Independence
and the Declaration of the Rights of Man, is a practical and pragmatic charter of
government."[68]

Scalia's critics point out that his theory of democracy bears no relation to the
nation's traditional understanding of the limits of the principle of majority rule,
so perfectly captured by Thomas Jefferson in his first inaugural address: "All, too,
will bear in mind this sacred principle, that though the will of the majority is in
all cases to prevail, that will to be rightful must be reasonable; that the minority

possess their equal rights, which equal laws must protect, and to violate would be oppression."[69] According to Jefferson and the traditional American understanding, "the minority possess their equal rights" independently of the majority; their equal rights are antecedent to majority rule, and majority rule is circumscribed by them. As Harry V. Jaffa has written, the traditional American understanding was that "the foundation of all our free institutions is the doctrine that, under the laws of nature and nature's God, all human beings are endowed with certain unalienable rights, and that it is for the sake of these rights that governments are instituted. As these rights belong *a priori* to every person, they are of necessity the rights of every minority."[70] Scalia's critics also wonder how someone who argues, as he does, that "[i]n textual interpretation, context is everything"[71] could fail to consider the Declaration of Independence and its theory of democracy in constitutional context.

Scalia is vulnerable to the first criticism. He simply has not developed a well-thought-out understanding of the principles of democracy and, perhaps as a consequence, appears to assume that democracy everywhere operates as it does in the United States at the beginning of the new millennium—in a place where the Constitution, as amended, protects the rights of minorities; where both the Constitution and its subsequent amendments were ratified by extraordinary majorities; and where the principal threat to democracy is not majority rule trampling on the rights of minorities but the Court itself threatening the right of the majority to rule itself. However, concerning the second criticism—that he has rejected an aspirational theory of constitutional interpretation—Scalia is on firmer ground. He has defended himself by observing that, at least with respect to the Bill of Rights,

> [t]he context suggests that the abstract and general terms, like the concrete and particular ones, are meant to nail down current rights, rather than aspire after future ones—that they are abstract and general references to *extant* rights and freedoms possessed under the then-current regime. The same conclusion follows from the evident purpose of the provisions. To guarantee that freedom of speech will be no less than it is today is to guarantee something permanent; to guarantee that it will be no less than the aspirations of the future is to guarantee nothing in particular at all.[72]

Scalia's Rejection of Legislative History

As a textualist, Justice Scalia totally rejects reliance on legislative history or legislative intent and invariably refuses to join any opinion (or part of an opinion) that employs it.[73] At the time of his appointment to the high bench, the Court's "traditional approach" to legislative history was, as William N. Eskridge has written, "to consider virtually any contextual evidence, especially the statute's legislative history, even when the statutory text has an apparent 'plain meaning.' "[74] And even when the meaning of the statutory text was clear, it could be "rebutted by legislative history" consisting of "committee reports, floor debates, rejected proposals, and even legislative silence."[75]

In ten major cases decided during the decade prior to Scalia joining the Court, the Court had openly acknowledged that it was displacing the plain meaning of the statute in question with what it took to be the intention of the legislature that it had gleaned from the statute's legislative history.[76] *United Steelworkers v. Weber* was perhaps the most egregious example of the Court's employment of this traditional approach. In a five-to-two ruling, Justice Brennan denied that a Kaiser–United Steelworkers affirmative action plan violated Title VII of the 1964 Civil Rights Act, despite the unambiguous language of Sections 703(a) and (d) that made it unlawful to "discriminate . . . because of . . . race" in hiring and in selecting apprentices for training programs and despite the fact that the Court majority agreed that the Kaiser–United Steelworkers plan operated to discriminate against white employees solely because they were white. Brennan told Brian Weber, a steelworker who was denied an apprenticeship opportunity because he was white, that his "reliance upon a literal construction" of Title VII was "misplaced" because, and here he quoted from *Holy Trinity Church v. United States*,[77] "a thing may be within the letter of the statute and yet not within the statute, because not within its spirit, nor within the intention of its makers." Brennan turned to floor debates in both the Senate and the House over the passage of the Civil Rights Act and to a House report to show Congress's intent to open employment opportunities for blacks—an intent that would be frustrated if employers and labor unions could not discriminate against whites and on behalf of blacks. Therefore, the act's "spirit" of providing new employment opportunities for blacks had to displace the act's clear "letter" proscribing discrimination "against any individual."[78]

During his service on the U.S. Court of Appeals for the District of Columbia, Scalia had already begun to depart from this "traditional" reliance on legislative history. In his concurrence in *Hirschey v. FERC*,[79] for example, he objected to the court's reliance on a statement in a committee report to argue that the 1985 amendments of the Equal Access to Justice Act (EAJA) "ratified" an earlier D.C. Circuit decision concerning the grant of attorney's fees under the EAJA.[80] Scalia "disassociate[d]" himself from the assumption that "the details, as opposed to the broad outlines of purpose, set forth in the committee report come to the attention of, much less are approved by, the house which enacts the committee's bill"; further, he indicated that it was "time for courts to become concerned about the fact that routine deference to the detail of committee reports, and the predictable expansion in that detail which routine deference has produced, are converting a system of judicial construction into a system of committee-staff prescription."[81] He was concerned that a judge would operate under the "false impression that elected representatives actually considered and intended the result reached by the judge."[82]

In *Gott v. Walters*,[83] Scalia argued against the use of something he held to be even more pernicious: "subsequent legislative history," or the remarks made by legislators on the meaning of a previously enacted statute. Writing for the majority, Scalia construed a statute to preclude the availability of judicial review of Veterans Administration decisions. Judge Patricia Wald dissented, arguing that judicial review was available; she cited as evidence statements senators made during debate over a subsequent veterans' benefit law that indicated their belief that judicial review was already available under the statute under review.[84] Scalia responded to what he called "the dissent's use of what has become known (with a disappointing lack of sense for the paradoxical) as 'subsequent legislative history' — i.e., legislative 'history' that postdates the statute in question."[85] He declared that the use of "self-created legislative history" by members of Congress "to achieve the result they were unable to obtain through the legislative process is precisely the sort of 'history' we should steadfastly reject."[86]

During his Senate confirmation hearings following his nomination to serve on the Supreme Court, Scalia volunteered that he was not "enamored" with the use of legislative history and reliance on committee reports. As he told Senator Charles Mathias:

> Once it was clear that the courts were going to use them [committee reports] all the time, they certainly became a device not to inform the rest of the body as to what the intent of the bill was, but rather they became avowedly a device to make some legislative history and tell the courts how to hold this way or that. Once that happens, they become less reliable as a real indicator of what the whole body thought it was voting on.[87]

And, not surprisingly, once on the high bench, he immediately threw down the gauntlet to his colleagues over their use of legislative history, writing in his concurrence in the judgment of the Court in *Immigration and Naturalization Service v. Cardoza-Fonseca*:[88]

> [T]he Court undertakes an exhaustive investigation of the legislative history of the Act. It attempts to justify this inquiry by relying upon the doctrine that if the legislative history of an enactment reveals a " 'clearly expressed legislative intention' contrary to [the enactment's] language," the Court is required to "question the strong presumption that Congress

expresses its intent through the language it chooses." Although it is true that the Court in recent times has expressed approval of this doctrine, that is to my mind an ill-advised deviation from the venerable principle that if the language of a statute is clear, that language must be given effect—at least in the absence of a patent absurdity. Judges interpret laws rather than reconstruct legislators' intentions. Where the language of those laws is clear, we are not free to replace it with an unenacted legislative intent.

Scalia invariably criticizes his colleagues for turning to "committee reports, floor speeches, and even colloquies between Congressmen" to ascertain what a law means[89] because, as he declared in *Thompson v. Thompson*, they "are frail substitutes for a bicameral vote upon the text of the law and its presentment to the President."[90] The Court's use of legislative history lends itself, he wryly observed in *Koons Buick Pontiac GMC v. Nigh*, "to a kind of ventriloquism. The *Congressional Record* or committee reports are used to make words appear to come from Congress's mouth which were spoken or written by others (individual Members of Congress, congressional aides, or even enterprising lobbyists)."[91] His extensive "inside the Beltway" experience has made him savvy to how often members of Congress will withdraw actual amendments to bills under consideration in the House because they are told by the floor leaders of the bill that they will take care of the members' concerns through the drafting of the legislative history. In *United States v. Taylor*, he perspicaciously drew out the consequences:

> By perpetuating the view that legislative history *can* alter the meaning of even a clear statutory provision, we produce a legal culture in which the following statement could be made—taken from a portion of the floor debate alluded to in the Court's opinion:

>> MR. DENNIS: "I have an amendment here in my hand which could be offered, but if we can make up some legislative history which would do the same thing, I am willing to do it."

> We should not make the equivalency between making legislative history and making an amendment so plausible. It should not be possible, or at least should not be easy, to be sure of obtaining a particular result in this Court without making that result apparent on the face of the bill which both Houses consider and vote upon, which the President approves, and which, if it becomes a law, the people must obey. I think we have an obligation to conduct our exegesis in a fashion which fosters that democratic process.[92]

When the Court departs from the text of the statute and considers the legislative history surrounding its passage, Scalia contends, its exegesis undermines rather than fosters the "democratic process" and fails to cabin the discretion of judges. As he wrote in A *Matter of Interpretation*, citing legislative history is like "look[ing] over the heads of a crowd and pick[ing] out your friends."[93] And such an exegesis removes any incentive for Congress to enact clearer statutes. Scalia believes that if Congress knows that the Court will focus only on the text of a statute and not on its legislative history, it will be more diligent and precise in its drafting. As he declared for the Court in *Finley v. United States*, "Whatever we say regarding . . . a particular statute can of course be changed by Congress. What is of paramount importance is that Congress be able to legislate against a background of clear interpretive rules, so that it may know the effect of the language it adopts."[94]

Scalia argues, therefore, that the Court is to interpret the text alone and nothing else.[95] The law should be understood to mean what it says and say what it means. Otherwise, as he noted in his Court of Appeals dissent in *Illinois Commerce Commission v. Interstate Commerce Commission*, compromise, so essential to the legislative process, "becomes impossible." "[W]hen there is no assurance that the statutory words in which [the compromise] is contained will be honored," he said, both sides to a compromise "have every reason to fear that any ambiguity will be interpreted against their interests" in subsequent litigation.[96] Likewise, if the law does not mean what it says and does not say what it means, individuals are left at a loss concerning how they should conduct themselves. As he wrote in *United States v. R.L.C.*, "It may well be true that in most cases the proposition that the words of the United States Code or the Statutes At Large give adequate notice to the citizen is something of a fiction, albeit one required in any system of law; but necessary fiction descends to needless farce when the public is charged even with knowledge of Committee Reports."[97]

Scalia insists that the Court should focus its attention on the text alone.[98] As he argued in *Wisconsin Public Intervenor v. Mortier*, "We should try to give the text its fair meaning, whatever various committees might have had to say—thereby affirming the proposition that we are a Government of laws, not committee reports."[99] He took some satisfaction in the fact that "[t]oday's decision reveals that, in their judicial application, committee reports are a forensic rather than an interpretive device, to be invoked when they support the decision and ignored when they do not. To my mind that is infinitely better than honestly giving them dispositive effect. But it would be better still to stop confusing [lower courts] and not to use committee reports at all."[100]

Scalia's attack on the use of legislative history was especially sustained and devastating in his opinion in *Crosby v. National Foreign Trade Council*.[101] Justice David Souter held for a unanimous Court that the Foreign Operations, Export

Financing, and Related Programs Appropriations Act of 1997 preempted a Massachusetts law that barred state entities from buying goods or services from companies doing business with Burma (Myanmar). He was not content, however, to
rely merely on the explicit text of the act; in a series of five footnotes, Souter cited
legislative history (statements by individual members of Congress, letters addressed
to congressional committees, proposed alternative language that Congress did not
adopt) in an apparent attempt to reinforce the act's clear text. In an opinion drip-
ping with sarcasm, Scalia utterly rejected this use of legislative history and consequently concurred only in the judgment of the Court.

In each of the first five paragraphs of his opinion addressing in turn Souter's
footnotes, Scalia began with the words "It is perfectly obvious on the face of this
statute ..." that it preempted Massachusetts' law, a conclusion that Souter's
"utterly irrelevant" employment of legislative history needlessly confirmed in his
five footnotes. Since all of this was "perfectly obvious," Scalia then repeated, also
in each of these paragraphs, that he saw "no point in [Souter] devoting" five separate footnotes invoking legislative history to establish these "interesting (albeit
unsurprising) fact[s]." These five skirmishes, however, were preliminary to the
main event. With scathing wit, Scalia declared:

> Of course even if all of the Court's invocations of legislative history were
> not utterly irrelevant, I would still object to them, since neither the state-
> ments of individual Members of Congress (ordinarily addressed to a vir-
> tually empty floor), nor Executive statements and letters addressed to
> congressional committees, nor the nonenactment of other proposed leg-
> islation, is a reliable indication of what a majority of both Houses of Con-
> gress intended when they voted for the statute before us. The *only* reliable
> indication of *that* intent—the only thing we know for sure that
> can be attributed to *all* of them—is the words of the bill that they voted to
> make law. In a way, using unreliable legislative history to confirm what the
> statute plainly says anyway (or what the record plainly shows) is less objec-
> tionable since, after all, it has absolutely no effect upon the outcome. But
> in a way, this utter lack of necessity makes it even worse—calling to mind
> St. Augustine's enormous remorse at stealing pears when he was not even
> hungry, and just for the devil of it ("not seeking aught through the shame,
> but the shame itself!"). In any case, the portion of the Court's opinion that
> I consider irrelevant is quite extensive, comprising, in total, about one-
> tenth of the opinion's size and (since it is in footnote type) even more of
> the opinion's content. I consider that to be not just wasteful (it was not pre-
> ordained, after all, that this was to be a 25-page essay) but harmful, since it
> tells future litigants that, even when a statute is clear on its face, and its

effects clear upon the record, statements from the legislative history may help (and presumably harm) the case. If so, they must be researched and discussed by counsel—which makes appellate litigation considerably more time consuming, and hence considerably more expensive, than it need be. This to my mind outweighs the arguable good that may come of such persistent irrelevancy, at least when it is indulged in the margins: that it may encourage readers to ignore our footnotes.[102]

Scalia's contempt for the use of legislative history has led him to some interesting exchanges with his colleagues. In *Chisom v. Roemer*,[103] he was provoked to declare that there is a mistaken "notion that Congress cannot be credited with having achieved anything of major importance by simply saying it, in ordinary language, in the text of a statute, 'without comment' in the legislative history." Alluding to Sir Arthur Conan Doyle's *Silver Blaze* in which Sherlock Holmes solves the mystery on the basis of the dog that did not bark—to what in *Koons Buick Pontiac GMC v. Nigh* Scalia would call "the Canon of Canine Silence"[104]—he continued: "As the Court colorfully puts it, if the dog of legislative history has not barked, nothing of great significance can have transpired. . . . We have forcefully and explicitly rejected the Conan Doyle approach to statutory construction in the past. . . . We are here to apply the statute, not legislative history, and certainly not the absence of legislative history. Statutes are the law though sleeping dogs lie."[105]

And in *United States v. Thompson/Center Arms Co.*, he ridiculed Justice Souter for resorting "to that last hope of lost interpretive causes, that St. Jude of the hagiography of statutory construction, legislative history."[106] Souter defended his antitextualist approach by quoting a passage from Justice Felix Frankfurter—a passage that perfectly encapsulates the view that Scalia rejects:

> A statute, like other living organisms, derives significance and sustenance from its environment, from which it cannot be severed without being mutilated. Especially is this true where the statute, like the one before us, is part of a legislative process having a history and a purpose. The meaning of such a statute cannot be gained by confining inquiry within its four corners. Only the historic process of which such legislation is an incomplete fragment—that to which it gave rise as well as that which gave rise to it—can yield its true meaning.[107]

Scalia's textualist critique of legislative history has produced dramatic results. In 1983, Judge Patricia Wald, Justice Scalia's onetime colleague on the U.S. Court of Appeals for the District of Columbia, noted in the *Iowa Law Review* that in its 1981–1982 term, the Supreme Court looked at legislative history in virtually every statutory case, regardless of whether it thought the statute had a clear meaning on its face.[108] In 1994, Gregory Maggs, writing in the *Public Interest Law Review*, observed that by the 1993 term of the court, legislative history was being cited in only about 40 percent of statutory cases, and no majority opinion cited legislative history as a necessary ground for its conclusion. He offered a reason:

> With Justice Scalia breathing down the necks of anyone who peeks into the *Congressional Record* or Senate reports, the other members of the Court may have concluded that the benefit of citing legislative history does not outweigh its costs. It is likely for this reason that the percentage of cases citing it has decreased dramatically. No one likes an unnecessary fight, especially not one with as formidable an opponent as Justice Scalia.[109]

Scalia has influenced members of Congress no less than his colleagues on the Supreme Court. When the House Judiciary Committee was drafting a 1991 anti-crime bill, *Congressional Quarterly* reported that "some members suggested resolving a dispute by putting compromise language into a committee report, which accompanies a bill to the floor. But Barney Frank, D-Mass., warned off his colleagues with just two words, 'Justice Scalia.'"[110]

Scalia's Originalism

Justice Scalia emphatically rejects legislative history and intent, yet he is described, and describes himself, as an originalist.[111] On the surface, this contradiction suggests a tension: If it is a mistake to consult extrinsic evidence of Congress's intentions as found in a law's legislative history, why is it appropriate for him to consult extrinsic evidence of the Framers' intentions as found, for example, in *The Federalist*?[112] The tension is heightened further as a result of Scalia's assertion in *Tome v. United States* that "the views of Alexander Hamilton (a draftsman) bear [no] more authority than the views of Thomas Jefferson (not a draftsman) with regard to the meaning of the Constitution."[113]

The answer to the question is that Scalia is a particular kind of originalist. What he means by originalism is revealed by illustration in his Holmes Lecture: "If a barn was not considered the curtilage of a house in 1791 . . . and the Fourth Amendment did not cover it then, unlawful entry into a barn today may be a trespass, but not an unconstitutional search and seizure."[114] For Scalia, *originalism* is synonymous with the doctrine of original meaning. He seeks the original meaning from the text of the document itself and from what it meant to the society that adopted it;[115] at the same time, he ignores altogether the subjective preferences or intentions of those who wrote it.[116] As he put it in *A Matter of Interpretation*:

I will consult the writings of some men who happened to be delegates to the Constitutional Convention—Hamilton's and Madison's writings in *The Federalist*, for example. I do so, however, not because they were Framers and therefore their intent is authoritative and must be the law; but rather because their writings, like those of other intelligent and informed people of the time, display how the text of the Constitution was originally understood. Thus, I give equal weight to Jay's pieces in *The Federalist*, and to Jefferson's writings, even though neither of them was a Framer. What I look for in the Constitution is precisely what I look for in a statute: the original meaning of the text, not what the original draftsmen intended.[117]

And of course, for Scalia, originalism means applying that original meaning to the case at hand. Foreshadowed in his Holmes Lecture, Scalia's application of originalism in the context of the Fourth Amendment is clearly evident in his majority opinion for the Court in *Kyllo v. United States*.[118] *Kyllo* involved the warrantless use from a public street of a thermal-imaging device aimed at a private residence occupied by someone suspected of growing marijuana. The device detected relative amounts of heat within the residence and whether high-intensity lights were being used to grow marijuana indoors. Scalia held that its warrantless use was unreasonable and therefore constituted an unlawful search within the meaning of the Fourth Amendment.[119]

[I]n the case of the search of the interior of homes—the prototypical and hence most commonly litigated area of protected privacy—there is a ready criterion, with roots deep in the common law, of the minimal expectation of privacy that *exists*, and that is acknowledged to be *reasonable*. To withdraw protection of this minimum expectation would be to permit police technology to erode the privacy guaranteed by the Fourth Amendment. We think that obtaining by sense-enhancing technology any information regarding the interior of the home that could not otherwise have been obtained without physical "intrusion into a constitutionally protected area" constitutes a search—at least where (as here) the technology in question is not in general public use. This assures preservation of that degree of privacy against government that existed when the Fourth Amendment was adopted. On the basis of this criterion, the information obtained by the thermal imager in this case was the product of a search.[120]

Scalia contrasts his "originalism" with "nonoriginalism," which he defines as a method of interpreting the Constitution "not on the basis of what the Constitution originally meant, but on the basis of what judges currently [think] it desirable for it to mean."[121] According to Scalia, the principal defect of nonoriginalism is "the impossibility of achieving any consensus on what, precisely, is to replace original meaning, once that is abandoned."[122] He notes that nonoriginalists invoke "fundamental values as the touchstone of constitutionality" but observes that "it is very difficult for a person to discern a difference between those political values that he personally thinks important, and those political values that are 'fundamental to our society.' Thus, by the adoption of such a criterion judicial personalization of the law is enormously facilitated."[123] He also observes that those values that are "fundamental to our society" can both expand and contract. Describing nonoriginalism as "a two-way street that handles traffic both to and from individual rights," he contrasts it with his originalism as displayed in *Coy v. Iowa*,[124] in which he secured the confrontation rights of a criminal defendant against legislation passed by a state less concerned with the text and tradition of the Sixth Amendment than with the "emotional frailty of children and the sensitivity of young women regarding sexual abuse."[125]

Scalia acknowledges that originalism "is also not without its warts." "Its greatest defect," he argues, "is the difficulty of applying it correctly." He continues:

> [I]t is often exceedingly difficult to plumb the original understanding of an ancient text. Properly done, the task requires the consideration of an enormous amount of material—in the case of the Constitution and its Amendments, for example, to mention only one element, the records of the ratifying debates in all the states. Even beyond that, it requires an evaluation of the reliability of that material—many of the reports of the ratifying debates, for example, are thought to be quite unreliable. And further still, it requires immersing oneself in the political and intellectual atmosphere of the time—somehow placing out of mind knowledge that we have which an earlier age did not, and putting on beliefs, attitudes, philosophies, prejudices and loyalties that are not those of our day. It is, in short, a task sometimes better suited to the historian than the lawyer.[126]

That very defect, however, is a virtue for Scalia. Because "historical research is always difficult and sometimes inconclusive," originalism will lead to "a more moderate rather than a more extreme result." Scalia argues that since judges invariably think that "the law is what they would like it to be," their errors in "judicial historiography" will be "in the direction of projecting" upon the past "current, modern values." Originalism therefore ends up as "something of a compromise, . . . not a bad characteristic for a constitutional theory."[127]

But a better argument for Scalia to have made—one consistent with his criticisms of the "Court's Constitution-making"—would be that since historical research is often inconclusive and the original understanding is unclear, there is no warrant for the Court to invalidate an act of the popular branches on the grounds that it is inconsistent with the Constitution's original meaning. After all, as Scalia writes, originalism is far more compatible than nonoriginalism with "the nature and purpose of a Constitution in a democratic system."[128]

> A democratic society does not, by and large, need constitutional guarantees to insure that its laws will reflect "current values." Elections take care of that quite well. The purpose of constitutional guarantees . . . is precisely to prevent the law from reflecting certain changes in original values that the society adopting the Constitution thinks fundamentally undesirable. Or, more precisely, to require the society to devote to the subject the long and hard consideration required for a constitutional amendment before those particular values can be cast aside.[129]

As an originalist, Scalia cites and quotes *The Federalist* to reveal constitutional history—to show how those who drafted and ratified the Constitution saw its various structural provisions and principles as means for achieving the ends the Constitution was drafted to secure. He studies the Framers, and especially *The Federalist,* not to find out what the Framers and their contemporaries, either individually or collectively, would have done if faced with a specific modern constitutional issue but rather to understand (given the words they used) how they designed the Constitution to work and, on that basis, to ascertain how, institutionally, they intended for that issue to be addressed.

What Scalia finds from his study is that seldom, if ever, was the judiciary intended to be the branch that would resolve evolving modern issues. Just how limited he regards the judicial role is apparent in his criticism of Justice Oliver Wendell Holmes's famous reply to Chief Justice John Marshall's dictum in *McCulloch v. Maryland* that "the power to tax [is] the power to destroy."[130] Holmes qualified Marshall's statement by asserting, "The power to tax is not the power to destroy while this Court sits."[131] Although he acknowledges that "the notion that predicted evils cannot occur 'while this Court sits' is comforting," Scalia sees no need for the Court to save anyone. Constitutional structure, not an activist Court, will ensure that the power to tax does not result in the destruction of the federal government: "I would have thought it a better response to Marshall's dictum that the power to tax the activities of the federal government cannot constitute the power to destroy the federal government so long as the tax is generally applicable and nondiscriminatory—because it is implausible that the state would destroy its own citizens as well."[132]

In his dissent in *Hoffmann–La Roche v. Sperling,*[133] Scalia admonished his colleagues not to "abandon" their "'passive' role in determining which claims come before them . . . which I regard as one of the natural components of a system in which courts are not inquisitors of justice but arbiters of adversarial claims." According to Scalia, the role of the Court is not to articulate a theory of justice and discover new rights based on that theory but to ensure that the majority does not contract the sphere of rights traditionally protected. If new theories of justice are to be articulated and if the sphere of protected rights is to be expanded, such expansion should be done by the will of the majority, not the Court.[134]

Scalia's Rejection of Foreign Law in the Interpretation of the U.S. Constitution

There is an increasing tendency among a number of Scalia's colleagues on the Supreme Court to turn to foreign law and practices for guidance on the meaning of various provisions of the U.S. Constitution, especially the Cruel and Unusual Punishments Clause of the Eighth Amendment. In *Trop v. Dulles*, Chief Justice Earl Warren proclaimed that since the words of that amendment were "not precise" and their scope was "not static," the justices would have to "draw its meaning from the evolving standards of decency that mark the progress of a maturing society."[135] What were those evolving standards, and where were they to be found? Though Warren did briefly invoke the views of "the civilized nations of the world" in *Trop*,[136] the Court's initial answer was, for the most part, that those evolving standards were to be discerned from a national consensus of what constitutes cruel and unusual punishment as reflected in the criminal sanctions passed by the people's elected representatives.[137]

Since Scalia's appointment to the Court, however, a majority of the justices have increasingly found those evolving standards not so much in the national consensus that has emerged among American citizens but in the views of foreign judges and legislators. For example, in 1988 in *Thompson v. Oklahoma*, Justice John Paul Stevens held for a plurality of the Court that imposing the death penalty on juveniles under the age of sixteen violated the Eighth Amendment because, inter alia, it was inconsistent with "the views of the international community."[138] In *Atkins v. Virginia* in 2002, Justice Stevens again turned to foreign opinion and relied on the fact that "within the world community, the imposition of the death penalty for crimes committed by mentally retarded offenders is overwhelmingly disapproved" to conclude, this time for a six-member majority, that the execution of criminals who were mentally retarded constitutes cruel and unusual punishment in violation of the Eighth Amendment.[139] The next year, in *Lawrence v. Texas*, Justice Kennedy invoked the "values we share with a wider civilization" and, more specifically, the decisions of the European Court of Human Rights as justification for his conclusion for a six-member majority that a Texas statute criminalizing "deviate sexual intercourse" between individuals of the same sex violated due process and the right to privacy.[140] And finally, in *Roper v. Simmons* in 2005, Justice Kennedy devoted a whole section of his opinion for a five-member majority to "the laws of other countries and to international authorities" before concluding that the Eighth Amendment forbids imposition of the death penalty on offenders who were under the age of eighteen when their crimes were committed.[141] Acknowledging "the overwhelming weight of international opinion against the juvenile death penalty" and specifically citing two amici curiae briefs (one filed by the Human Rights Committee of the Bar of England and Wales and the other by the European Union and Members of the International Community), he announced that "[o]ur determination that the death penalty is disproportionate punishment for offenders under 18 finds confirmation in the stark reality that the United States is the only country in the world that continues to give official sanction to the juvenile death penalty."[142]

Scalia has strenuously opposed any and all such references to foreign laws and traditions. In brief comments in *Thompson*, he found the plurality's reliance on the laws and practices of other countries "totally inappropriate as a means of establishing the fundamental beliefs of this Nation." He paraphrased Chief Justice John Marshall's words from *McCulloch v. Maryland*[143] that "[w]e must never forget that it is a Constitution for the United States of America that we are expounding."[144] In *Atkins*, he declared in passing that "the Prize for the Court's Most Feeble Effort to fabricate 'national consensus' must go to its appeal (deservedly relegated to a footnote) to the views of . . . the so-called 'world community.'" He found wholly irrelevant the views and practices of "'the world community,' whose notions of justice are (thankfully) not always those of our people."[145] And in *Lawrence*, he tersely observed that "[c]onstitutional entitlements do not spring into existence because . . . *foreign nations* decriminalize conduct. . . . The Court's discussion of these foreign views . . . [is] meaningless dicta. Dangerous dicta, however, since 'this Court should not impose foreign moods, fads, or fashions on America.'"[146] However, it was not until his dissent in *Simmons* that he chose to respond at length to the Court's increasing infatuation with "the views of other countries and the so-called international community."[147]

In *Simmons*, he began by criticizing Justice Kennedy's invocation of Article 37 of the United Nations Convention on the Rights of the Child, which expressly prohibits capital punishment for crimes committed by juveniles under eighteen and which, Kennedy emphasized, had been ratified by every country in the world "save for the United States and Somalia."[148] With withering criticism and devastating effect, Scalia wrote: "Unless the Court has added to its arsenal the power to join and ratify treaties on behalf of the United States, I cannot see how this evidence favors, rather than refutes, its position." Noting that under the U.S. Constitution, the Senate and the president are the "actors our Constitution empowers to enter into treaties," he concluded that their refusal to join and ratify this convention "can only suggest that *our country* has either not reached a national consensus on the question, or has reached a consensus contrary to what the Court announces."[149]

Scalia then moved on to his broader argument: "The basic premise of the Court's argument—that American law should conform to the laws of the rest of the world—ought to be rejected out of hand." He pointed out that "[i]n many significant respects the laws of most other countries differ from our law." Not only do they lack "such explicit provisions of our Constitution as the right to jury trial and grand jury indictment" but they also reject "many interpretations of the Constitution prescribed by this Court itself." He reminded his colleagues that the Supreme Court's exclusionary rule (which excludes from introduction at trial illegally seized evidence) is "distinctively American" and "has been 'universally rejected' by other countries, including those with rules prohibiting illegal searches and police misconduct." England and Canada, he noted, rarely exclude evidence, and the Court majority's favorite international institution, the European Court of Human Rights, "has held that introduction of illegally-seized evidence does not violate . . . Article 6, § 1, of the European Convention on Human Rights."[150]

Scalia was certain that the Court would be unwilling to conform to international opinion concerning the exclusionary rule; to read the First Amendment's Establishment Clause in the light of the practices of "the Netherlands, Germany, and Australia [all of which] allow direct government funding of religious schools"; to modify its abortion jurisprudence, "which makes us one of only six countries that allow abortion on demand until the point of viability"; or to "relax our double jeopardy prohibition" and "curtail our right to jury trial in criminal cases" because England now allows "the prosecution to appeal cases where an acquittal was the result of a judge's ruling that was legally incorrect" and increasingly "permits all but the most serious offenders to be tried by magistrates without a jury."[151] So why was the Court willing to invoke foreign law and court opinions with respect to the Eighth Amendment's ban on cruel and unusual punishments? For Scalia, the answer was clear: he had already given it earlier in his dissent when he accused the Court of "look[ing] over the heads of the crowd, and pick[ing] out its friends."[152] He now drove that point home. "The Court should either profess its willingness to reconsider all these matters in light of the views of foreigners, or else it should cease putting forth foreigners' views as part of the *reasoned basis* of its decisions. To invoke alien law when it agrees with one's own thinking, and ignore it otherwise, is not reasoned decisionmaking, but sophistry."[153]

Conclusions

Scalia pursues a textualist or original-meaning jurisprudence that accords primacy to the text and tradition of the document being interpreted and that regards it as the duty of the judge to apply the textual language of the Constitution or statute when it is clear or the traditional understanding of that text—what it meant to the society that adopted it—when it is not. For him, faithful adherence to the text or the traditional understanding of those who originally adopted it serves two worthy goals: it simultaneously reduces the danger that judges will substitute their beliefs and preferences for society's, and it preserves society's values by preventing any backsliding from the degree of restriction the Constitution originally imposed on the government. As a textualist, Scalia rejects the use of legislative history because, he firmly believes, the law should say what it means and mean what it says and because committee reports and debates on the floor are unacceptable substitutes for a bicameral vote upon the actual text of the law and its presentment to the president. And as an originalist, he rejects as irrelevant foreign court decisions and practices because, he is convinced, constitutional meaning is to be derived from the text itself or from what its words meant to those who originally adopted it and because alien law is a totally inappropriate means of establishing the fundamental beliefs of the people of the United States.

In *A Matter of Interpretation*, Justice Scalia acknowledged that his original-meaning jurisprudence is regarded in "some sophisticated circles" of the legal profession as "simpleminded—'wooden,' 'unimaginative,' 'pedestrian.'"[154] He rejected this characterization, though, and denied that he was "too dull to perceive the broader social purposes that a statute is designed, or could be designed to serve, or too hidebound to realize that new times require new laws"; he merely insisted that judges "have no authority to pursue those broader purposes or to write those new laws."[155] The chapters that follow assess Scalia's textualist jurisprudence as he applies it to the various structural, substantive, and procedural provisions of the Constitution.

Chapter Three

Constitutional Structure and
Separation of Powers

During a 1988 panel discussion on separation of powers, Justice Scalia assessed his legal career and remarked that "if there is anyone who, over the years, [has] had a greater interest in the subject of separation of powers [than I], he does not come readily to mind."[1] His opinions on this topic certainly support his contention. They show him to be quick to frame issues in separation-of-powers terms when his colleagues' attention is drawn elsewhere. As he remarked in *Morrison v. Olson*, many a "wolf" threatening separation of powers comes dressed in "sheep's clothing" and is discerned only by the kind of "careful and perceptive analysis" that is Scalia's forte.[2] His opinions in these cases show him to be thoroughly knowledgeable of the Framers' understanding of separation of powers and supremely confident that their understanding should be governing, not only because it is expressed in text and tradition but also because it is superior to what he derisively called in *Morrison* "the unfettered wisdom of a majority of this Court."[3] These opinions have provided him the occasion to think through, articulate, and refine the key elements of his textualist jurisprudence. They, in fact, make clear that separation of powers is the mainspring of Scalia's textualism. As he said during his Senate confirmation hearing, separation of powers makes the Constitution "work"; it "assures" that the words in the Constitution—both those spelling out procedures and those declaring rights—"are not just hollow promises"; and it assures that no branch "is able to 'run roughshod' over [either] the liberties of the people"[4] or the constitutional text as "society has adopted it."[5]

For Justice Scalia, separation of powers is a critical structural principle necessarily implicit in the text of the Constitution. As he stated in his article "The Doctrine of Standing as an Essential Element of the Separation of Powers":

> Indeed, with an economy of expression that many would urge as a model for modern judicial opinions, the principle of separation of powers is found only in the structure of the [Constitution,] which successively describes where the legislative, executive, and judicial powers shall reside. One should not think, however, that the principle was less important to the federal framers. Madison said of it, in *Federalist* No. 47, that "no political

truth is certainly of greater intrinsic value, or is stamped with the authority of more enlightened patrons of liberty." And no less than five of the *Federalist Papers* were devoted to the demonstration that the principle was adequately observed in the proposed Constitution.[6]

During his confirmation hearings, Justice Scalia was asked by Senator Strom Thurmond why he thought the Constitution had endured for so long—why he thought it had come to be "the oldest existing Constitution in the world today." Scalia responded as follows:

> I think most of the questions today will probably be about that portion of the Constitution that is called the Bill of Rights, which is a very important part of it, of course. But if you had to put your finger on what has made our Constitution so enduring, I think it is the original document before the amendments were added. Because the amendments, by themselves, do not do anything. The Russian constitution probably has better, or at least as good guarantees of personal freedom as our document does. What makes it work, what assures that those words [in the Bill of Rights] are not just hollow promises, is the structure of government that the original Constitution established, the checks and balances among the three branches, in particular, so that no one of them is able to "run roughshod" over the liberties of the people as those liberties are described in the Bill of Rights.[7]

Justice Scalia's response is most instructive. First, he said that our "liberties" are "described" (but not created or secured) by the Bill of Rights. Second and more important, Scalia identified "the structure of government that the original Constitution established, the checks and balances among the three branches, in particular," as the reason for the Constitution's protection of liberties and, hence, its longevity.

His answer to Senator Thurmond is reminiscent of James Madison's argument to the House of Representatives on June 8, 1789, when he said that the bill of rights he was proposing did no more than "expressly declare the great rights of mankind secured under this Constitution."[8] Madison believed that rights are secured not by "parchment barriers" (i.e., "thou shalt nots" written into the Constitution) but rather by governmental structure (i.e., what *Federalist* No. 51 describes as that "double security" that arises when power "is first divided between two distinct governments, and then the portion allotted to each, subdivided among distinct and separate institutions").[9] Scalia clearly agrees. As he argued in *James B. Beam Distilling Company v. Georgia*, "[T]he division of federal powers [is] central to the constitutional scheme." Moreover, he continued, "it seems to me that the fundamental nature of those powers must be preserved as that nature was understood when the Constitution was enacted."[10]

Executive Power

Morrison v. Olson

The importance of preserving the structure of the Constitution—and especially separation of powers—was central to Justice Scalia's solitary dissent in *Morrison v. Olson*,[11] the first major separation-of-powers case he heard after his elevation to the Supreme Court. Chief Justice Rehnquist held for a seven-member majority in that case[12] that the Ethics in Government Act of 1978, providing for the appointment of an independent counsel to investigate and prosecute violations of federal criminal law by high-ranking officials of the executive branch, did not violate separation of powers, even though that person was appointed by the Special Division of the Court of Appeals for the District of Columbia Circuit and could be removed by the attorney general only for "good cause." Under the act's provisions, the House Judiciary Committee charged in a 3,000-page report that Theodore Olson, at the time the assistant attorney general for the Office of Legal Counsel, had given false and misleading testimony to a House subcommittee concerning implementation of the "superfund" law; the committee requested that Attorney General Edwin Meese seek the appointment of an independent counsel to investigate these allegations. Since the act obligated the attorney general to request appointment of an independent counsel if there were "reasonable grounds" to believe further investigation was warranted, Meese did so. The Special Division then designated Alexia Morrison as independent counsel, whereupon Olson claimed that the act was an unconstitutional violation of separation of powers and that Morrison had no authority to proceed.

Chief Justice Rehnquist rejected Olson's contentions. He granted that "[t]here is no dispute that the functions performed by the independent counsel are 'executive'" in nature, but he disagreed that the act "unduly trammels on executive authority."[13] Although he acknowledged that "it is undeniable that the Act reduces the amount of control that the Attorney General and, through him, the President exercises over the investigation and prosecution of a certain class of alleged criminal activity,"[14] he denied that "this limitation as it presently stands sufficiently deprives the President of control over the independent counsel to interfere impermissibly with his constitutional obligation to ensure the faithful execution of the laws"[15] or that it "disrupts the proper balance between the coordinate branches by preventing the Executive Branch from accomplishing its constitutionally assigned functions."[16] Separation of powers, he insisted, does not require "that the three Branches of Government operate with absolute independence."[17]

Scalia vigorously dissented in what remains his most fully developed and powerful statement on his textualist understanding of the principle of separation of powers. For him, the question was not whether the act could be sustained on the basis of the majority's understanding of separation of powers but whether the act violated "the text of the Constitution and the division of power that it established."[18] That division of power—what Scalia also called "the equilibrium the Constitution sought to establish"[19]—requires that "all purely executive power must be under the control of the President," not simply those powers "the majority thinks, taking all things into account, . . . ought to be" under the president's control.[20]

Scalia's textualist jurisprudence generally demands deference to the popular branches but not in separation-of-powers cases. As he pointed out in his dissent, the "caution that we owe great deference to Congress's view that what it has done is constitutional . . . does not apply":[21]

> Where a private citizen challenges action of the Government on grounds unrelated to separation of powers, harmonious functioning of the system demands that we ordinarily give some deference, or a presumption of validity, to the actions of the political branches in what is agreed, between themselves at least, to be within their respective spheres. But where the issue pertains to separation of powers, and the political branches are (as here) in disagreement, neither can be presumed correct. The reason is stated concisely by Madison: "The several departments being perfectly co-ordinate by the terms of their common commission, neither of them, it is evident, can pretend to an exclusive or superior right to settling the boundaries between their respective powers. ..." *Federalist* No. 49. The playing field for the present case, in other words, is a level one. As one of the interested and coordinate parties to the underlying constitutional dispute, Congress, no more than the President, is entitled to the benefit of the doubt.[22]

Feeling no obligation to presume the constitutionality of the independent-counsel statute, Scalia complained that the Congress had "effectively compelled a criminal investigation of a high-level appointee of the President in connection with his actions arising out of a bitter power dispute between the President and the Legislative Branch." He further objected that the Congress also removed "the decisions regarding the scope of [any] further investigation, its duration, and finally whether or not prosecution should ensue" from "the control of the President and his subordinates,"[23] placing them instead in the hands of a "mini-Executive that is the independent counsel."[24] Quoting the language of Article II, § 1, cl. 1 of the Constitution providing that "[t]he executive Power shall be vested in the President of the United States," he declared, "[T]his does not mean some of the executive power, but all of the executive power."[25] He then proclaimed that the independent-counsel statute must be invalidated on "fundamental separation of powers principles if the following two questions are answered affirmatively: (1) Is the conduct of a criminal prosecution (and of an investigation to decide whether to prosecute) the exercise of purely executive power? (2) Does the statute deprive the President of the United States of exclusive control over the exercise of that power?" Scalia declared that even the Court majority "appears to concede an affirmative answer to both questions, but seeks to avoid the inevitable conclusion that since the statute vests some purely executive power in a person who is not the President of the United States, it is void."[26] As he noted, "[G]overnmental investigation and prosecution of crimes is a quintessentially executive function," and "the statute before us deprives the President of exclusive control over that quintessentially executive activity."[27]

The Court majority's response conceded that the statute reduced the president's control but insisted that he preserved "sufficient control" to "perform his constitutionally assigned duties" and that it did not "interfere impermissibly with his constitutional obligation to ensure the faithful execution of the laws."[28] Scalia's rejoinder was direct: "It is not for us to determine, and we have never presumed to determine, how much of the purely executive powers of government must be within the full control of the President. The Constitution prescribes that they all are."[29] He accused the majority of replacing "the clear constitutional prescription that the executive power belongs to the President with a 'balancing test'" and of abandoning the "text of the Constitution" as the "governing standard" in favor of "what might be called the unfettered wisdom of a majority of this Court, revealed to an obedient people on a case-by-case basis." Waxing indignant, Scalia proclaimed: "This is not only not the government of laws that the Constitution established, it is not a government of laws at all."[30] He chided the majority for adopting an "ad hoc approach to constitutional adjudication" whose "real attraction, even apart from its work-saving potential," is that "it is guaranteed to produce a result, in every case, that will make a majority of the Court happy with the law. The law is, by definition, precisely what the majority thinks, taking all things into account, it ought to be." For his part, however, Scalia preferred "to rely upon the judgment of the wise men who constructed our system, and of the people who approved it, and of the two centuries of history that have shown it to be sound."[31]

Scalia acknowledged that a "system of separate and coordinate powers necessarily involves an acceptance of exclusive power that can theoretically be abused."[32] He pointed out, however, that this prospect was only "theoretical," as there are two powerful "checks against any branch's actual abuse of its exclusive powers." First, there is the likely prospect of retaliation by the other branches through the use of their exclusive powers: "Congress, for example, can impeach the executive who willfully fails to enforce the laws; the executive can decline to prosecute under unconstitutional statutes; and the courts can dismiss malicious prosecutions." Second, there is an "ultimate" political check—the people can "replace those in the political branches who are guilty of abuse."[33] For Scalia, these two checks provide much greater accountability than the appointment of an independent counsel. If the judges on the Special Division are "hostile to the administration," if the independent counsel is "an old foe of the President," if the independent counsel chooses as staff "refugees from the recently defeated administration," there is, Scalia observed, *no one accountable to the public to whom the blame could be assigned*" for the launching of a politically inspired witch-hunt. By contrast, separation of powers as created by the Framers ensures that the "Chief Executive [is] accountable to the people" for any prosecutorial malfeasance by his subordinates; it ensures that "the blame can be assigned to someone who can be punished."[34]

Scalia also defended strict adherence to the Framers' conception of separation of powers because, in addition to fostering greater accountability, it ensures "that we do not lose liberty."[35] He stressed that a fundamental purpose of separation of powers and a unitary executive is "to preserve individual freedom." And, he continued, those who have held high office in the executive branch are as "entitled" to the protection of their freedom "as are the rest of us."[36] Observing that the independent counsel has one task only—to investigate and perhaps prosecute a particular individual—Scalia could not "imagine a less equitable manner of fulfilling the executive responsibility to investigate and prosecute,"[37] as he put it, than by taking some of the constitutionally assigned prosecutorial power from the president and giving it to an independent counsel who is "cut off from the unifying influence of the Justice Department, and from the perspective that multiple responsibilities provide." He noted that in the "small world" of the independent counsel, a technical violation might assume the "proportions of an indictable offense," and "an investigation that has reached the level of pursuing such picayune matters that it should be concluded" may "go on for another year."[38] The uncertainty, enormous expense, and potential loss of liberty suffered by the high-level executive branch official because of the appointment of an independent counsel were, for Scalia, the direct consequences of the act's violation of the principle of separation of powers.

Scalia elaborated on these points at length, and in the process, he displayed his keen "inside the Beltway" savvy and political acumen. He noted, for example, how critically important in "all investigative or prosecutorial decisions" is the "balancing of innumerable legal and practical considerations":

[E]ven political considerations (in the nonpartisan sense) must be considered, as exemplified by the recent decision of an independent counsel to subpoena the former Ambassador of Canada, producing considerable tension in our relations with that country. Another pre-eminently political decision is whether getting a conviction in a particular case is worth the disclosure of national security information that would be necessary. The Justice Department and our intelligence agencies are often in disagreement on this point, and the Justice Department does not always win. The present Act even goes so far as specifically to take the resolution of that dispute away from the President and give it to an independent counsel. In sum, the balancing of various legal, practical, and political considerations, none of which is absolute, is the very essence of prosecutorial discretion. To take this away is to remove the core of the prosecutorial function, and not merely "some" Presidential control.[39]

Scalia's keen grasp of how Washington politics is played was also evident when he addressed the vulnerability of a president's high-level assistants. Since these individuals "typically have no political base of support," he found it as "utterly unrealistic to think that they will not be intimidated" by the prospect of a criminal investigation by an independent counsel and "that their advice to him and their advocacy of his interests before a hostile Congress will not be affected" as it was "to think that the members of Congress and their staffs would be unaffected by replacing the Speech and Debate Clause with a similar provision." The independent-counsel provision of the Ethics in Government Act, he argued, "deeply wounds the President, by substantially reducing the President's ability to protect himself and his staff. This is the whole object of the law, of course, and I cannot imagine why the Court believes it does not succeed."[40]

Finally, he demonstrated his savvy when he explained how an independent counsel can "enfeeble" the president by "eroding his public support": "Nothing is so politically effective as the ability to charge that one's opponent and his associates are not merely wrongheaded, naive, ineffective, but, in all probability, 'crooks.' And nothing so effectively gives an appearance of validity to such charges as a Justice Department investigation and, even better, prosecution."[41]

With each of these many points, Scalia anticipated the central criticisms that would be launched against Kenneth W. Starr's investigation of the Clinton White House a decade later.[42] However, at one point in his dissent, Scalia appeared vulnerable to the suggestion that he was more naive than savvy. This occurred when he complained of the "practical compulsion" brought to bear on the attorney general to appoint an independent counsel to investigate Olson:[43]

As a practical matter, it would be surprising if the Attorney General had any choice (assuming this statute is constitutional) but to seek appointment of an independent counsel to pursue the charges against . . . Mr. Olson. Merely the political consequences (to him and the President) of seeming to break the law by refusing to do so would have been substantial. How could it not be, the public would ask, that a 3,000-page indictment drawn by our representatives over 2½ years does not even establish "reasonable grounds to believe" that further investigation or prosecution is warranted.[44]

However, as Attorney General Janet Reno repeatedly demonstrated during William Clinton's presidency and contra Scalia's predictions, it was indeed possible to withstand with impunity the "practical compulsion" of Republican lawmakers to appoint independent counsels to pursue allegations against various members of the Clinton administration. Charging Scalia with naïveté may, however, do him an injustice. He wrote when the Democrats controlled the Congress, and he was doubtless savvy enough to know what Attorney General Meese also knew, namely, the Democrats were sufficiently skilled politically to have been able to impose on Meese a very high political price had he not appointed an independent counsel in Olson's case. In her own way, Reno was equally savvy, for she knew that the inexperienced Republicans who were demanding that she appoint various independent counsels lacked the political skills and cunning to do her much harm.

At bottom, however, Scalia's dissent in *Morrison* had nothing to do with his political savvy or knowledge of how Washington operates and everything to do with his firm grasp of and abiding commitment to the constitutional principle of separation of powers. As he insisted, "[I]f to describe this case is not to decide it, the concept of a government of separate and coordinate powers no longer has meaning."[45] Scalia bitterly attacked his colleagues for their failure to abide by what "the text of the Constitution seems to require, . . . the Founders seemed to expect, and . . . our past cases have uniformly assumed."[46] He sought to preserve separation of powers because, as he noted, "without a secure structure of separated powers, our Bill of Rights would be worthless, as are the bills of rights of many nations of the world that have adopted, or even improved upon, the mere words of ours."[47] Scalia's argument is clear: by refusing in this case to defer to Congress and by steadfastly protecting constitutional structure, he can be restrained and deferential elsewhere, i.e., he is spared the need in other cases to protect constitutional rights that are better secured by structure than by judges.

Printz v. United States

Justice Scalia's argument in *Morrison*—his interest in protecting the system of separation of powers created by the Framers and his efforts to preserve all executive power in the hands of the president—was central (although discreetly soft-pedaled) in his opinion for the Court in *Printz v. United States*.[48] *Printz* is typically viewed as a federalism case because the Court used it to consider the constitutionality of those provisions of the Brady Handgun Violence Prevention Act that commanded the chief law enforcement officer (CLEO) of each local jurisdiction to conduct background checks on prospective handgun purchasers on an interim basis until a national instant background check system became operational in late 1998.[49] And, on the surface, *Printz* does deal with federalism, for Scalia held for a five-member majority that this congressional command was "fundamentally incompatible with our constitutional system of dual sovereignty" and was, therefore, unconstitutional.[50] His opinion seems to have been little more than an application of the Court's "commandeering jurisprudence" first introduced by Justice Sandra Day O'Connor in *New York v. United States*.[51] In that case, the Court held unconstitutional a key provision of the Low-Level Radioactive Waste Policy Amendments Act of 1985 requiring that if a state had failed to provide for the disposal of all its internally generated low-level radioactive waste by a particular date, it would have to take title to and possession of that waste and become liable for all damages suffered by the generator or owner of that waste as a result of the state's failure to take prompt possession. Justice O'Connor asserted for a six-member majority that "[n]o matter how powerful the federal interest involved, the Constitution simply does not give Congress the authority to require the states to regulate. The Constitution instead gives Congress the authority to regulate matters directly and to preempt contrary state regulation. Where a federal interest is sufficiently strong to cause Congress to legislate, it must do so directly; it may not conscript state governments as its agents."[52]

Why does the Congress have the authority to regulate either directly or through preemption but not through conscription or commandeering? O'Connor's provisional answer was that commandeering diminishes the "accountability of both state and federal officials." If Congress preempts state lawmaking and regulates directly, "it is the Federal Government that makes the decision in full view of the public, and it will be federal officials that suffer the consequences if the decisions turn out to be detrimental or unpopular." If, however, Congress commandeers the states to regulate, "it may be state officials who will bear the brunt of public disapproval, while the federal officials who devised the regulatory program may remain insulated from the electoral ramifications of their decision."[53] Accountability is, of course, an important consideration, but clearly, O'Connor felt uneasy about declaring commandeering unconstitutional because of its tendency to undermine accountability, and so she was obliged to move on to her final answer—that coercing the states into enacting or enforcing a federal regulatory program "infringe[s] upon the core of state sovereignty reserved by the Tenth Amendment" and "is inconsistent with the federal structure of our Government established by the Constitution."[54]

O'Connor acknowledged that the Tenth Amendment declares but "a truism that all is retained which has not been surrendered." Nonetheless, she insisted that the Tenth Amendment is as enforceable and contains limitations as identifiable as, for example, the First Amendment.

> Congress exercises its conferred powers subject to the limitations contained in the Constitution. Thus, for example, under the Commerce Clause Congress may regulate publishers engaged in interstate commerce, but Congress is constrained in the exercise of that power by the First Amendment. The Tenth Amendment likewise restrains the power of Congress, but this limit is not derived from the text of the Tenth Amendment itself, which, as we have discussed, is essentially a tautology. Instead, the Tenth Amendment confirms that the power of the Federal Government is subject to limits that may, in a given instance, reserve power to the States.[55]

How are these limits to be determined if they are not "derived from the text"? O'Connor's exposition was unclear on this matter, but the answer apparently is that they come from the Court's own sense of its responsibility to protect the "core of state sovereignty." As she asserted, "The Tenth Amendment thus directs us to determine, as in this case, whether an incident of state sovereignty is protected by a limitation on an Article I power."[56] How does a truism, a tautology, help the Court to "determine" whether that core has been penetrated by the federal government, whether the line separating constitutionality from unconstitutionality has been crossed? It is a question that O'Connor in *New York* never answered, and it is a question that Scalia in *Printz* never reached because he ultimately held the Brady Act to be unconstitutional not because it violated the principle of federalism but because it violated the principle of separation of powers.

Unlike O'Connor in *New York*, Scalia readily conceded in *Printz* that "no constitutional text," not even the Tenth Amendment, would justify Court invalidation of a commandeering statute so long as it was enacted by Congress pursuant to an express delegation of power enumerated in Article I, § 8.[57] Scalia did identify, however, three other bases for finding such a statute to be unconstitutional: historical understanding and practice, the structure of the Constitution, and the Court's past decisions.

Concerning the first basis, historical understanding and practice, Scalia reviewed the historical records of the early Congresses; observed that they had studiously "avoided use of this highly attractive power"; and concluded that, since "the power was thought not to exist" in the early Republic, it therefore does not exist now.[58] This basis is weak, however, for his conclusion cannot withstand scrutiny. Scalia equated the failure of the early Congresses to use their power to commandeer state officials with a conviction on their part that they did not possess such a power in the first place. As Justice John Paul Stevens noted in his dissent, "We have never suggested that the failure of the early Congresses to address the scope of federal power in a particular area or to exercise a particular authority was an argument against its existence."[59] Scalia did not consider the possibility that the power to commandeer may indeed have been understood by the early Congresses to exist but that the Senate, elected at the time by state legislatures and representing the interests of the states as states, simply refused to accede to its use. Contemporaneous use of a power that Congress has always had but that it has not previously exercised because the mode of electing the Senate practically prevented its use is not rendered constitutionally suspect simply because the structural impediment against its use has been removed by the adoption and ratification of the Seventeenth Amendment.[60]

Scalia then turned to his second (and fundamental) basis for finding the statute unconstitutional: the structure of the Constitution. Here, however, he largely ignored federalism and focused instead primarily on separation of powers. He noted that "[t]he Constitution does not leave to speculation who is to administer the laws enacted by Congress; the President, it says, 'shall take Care that the Laws be faithfully executed,' personally and through officers whom he appoints." The Brady Act, however, effectively transferred this responsibility to thousands of state and local law-enforcement officers in the fifty states, who were commanded to implement the program "without meaningful Presidential control." Scalia pointed out that the Framers insisted on "unity in the Federal Executive—to insure both vigor and accountability." That unity, he concluded, "would be shattered, and the power of the President would be subject to reduction, if Congress could act as effectively without the President as with him, by simply requiring state officers to execute its laws."[61] This is Scalia's central argument, and it is powerful. In fact, the argument is the same one that Scalia had made before in his dissent in *Morrison*. It is, however, most assuredly not a federalism argument; it is not an argument justifying invalidation of federal law on the grounds of preserving "our constitutional system of dual sovereignty."

The fact that Scalia felt obliged to wrap the kernels of his separation-of-powers argument in the husk of federalism shows his mastery of the persuasive arts. When he made this same separation-of-powers argument explicitly in *Morrison*, he spoke for himself alone; when he hid it in a defense of federalism, he spoke for a five-member majority. The fact that Scalia found it necessary to move the ground on which the Court's commandeering jurisprudence was based from the shifting sands of federalism to the rock-solid principles of separation of powers shows how problematic he regarded O'Connor's reasoning in *New York* to be and manifests what little faith Scalia put in the Court's past decisions—the third basis he identified for finding the commandeering provisions of the Brady Act unconstitutional. To be sure, he insisted that "the prior jurisprudence of this Court" was "conclusive,"[62] and he paid painstaking obeisance to "our constitutional system of dual sovereignty," yet it was clear that his intention was to rely on, and his goal was to vindicate, his view of separation of powers in *Morrison*, not O'Connor's view of federalism and the Tenth Amendment in *New York*.

Delegation of Legislative Power: Mistretta v. United States

Scalia's text-and-tradition jurisprudence, in service of the Take Care Clause in *Morrison* and *Printz*, was employed to defend the constitutional prohibition against the delegation of legislative power in his dissent in *Mistretta v. United States*,[63] in which an eight-member majority upheld the constitutionality of the U.S. Sentencing Commission. The Sentencing Reform Act of 1984 was designed to eliminate the wide disparity in sentences that resulted from the broad sentencing discretion then available to federal judges; it provided a system of determinate sentencing, with mandatory sentencing guidelines to ensure similar sentences for comparable offenders and offenses. It also created the U.S. Sentencing Commission, an independent commission within the judicial branch with seven voting members (three of them federal judges) appointed by the president. The commission was charged with developing sentencing guidelines, on the basis of criteria outlined in the act, that would prescribe the range of sentences for various categories of offenses and offenders. A federal judge could depart from the guidelines in particular cases because of aggravating or mitigating factors not considered by the commission but would have to give written reasons for the deviation that were subject to appellate review.

The Supreme Court upheld the constitutionality of the U.S. Sentencing Commission from the charge that Congress had delegated excessive legislative power to it and thereby violated separation of powers. Justice Harry Blackmun acknowledged in his majority opinion that "[t]he Sentencing Commission unquestionably is a peculiar institution within the framework of our Government" and that it is "an unusual hybrid in structure and authority,"[64] but, he insisted, "[o]ur constitutional principles of separated powers are not violated . . . by mere anomaly or innovation."[65] He stressed the importance of adopting a "pragmatic, flexible view of differentiated governmental power" that would not "prevent Congress from obtaining the assistance of its coordinate branches."[66]

Justice Blackmun reminded his readers that Congress's motives were lofty: Congress was attempting to resolve "the seemingly intractable dilemma of excessive disparity in criminal sentencing." And he invoked the principle of judicial deference, stating, "When this Court is asked to invalidate a statutory provision that has been approved by both Houses of the Congress and signed by the President, particularly an Act of Congress that confronts a deeply vexing national problem, it should only do so for the most compelling constitutional reasons."[67] He insisted that "separation of powers contemplates the integration of dispersed powers into a workable Government." If "workable Government" requires "statutory provisions that to some degree commingle the functions of the Branches," the Court will uphold them as long as they "pose no danger of either aggrandizement or encroachment." After all, what the Constitution requires, he continued, is "a carefully crafted system of checked and balanced power within each Branch," not "a hermetic division between the Branches."[68]

As in *Morrison*, Scalia filed a vigorous and solitary dissent. He argued that the act established a "sort of junior-varsity Congress,"[69] whose guidelines "have the force and effect of laws, prescribing the sentences criminal defendants are to receive. A judge who disregards them will be reversed." Again refusing to defer to Congress, he declared, "I can find no place within our constitutional system for an agency created by Congress to exercise no governmental power other than the making of laws."[70]

He argued that the commission's "power to make law . . . is quite naked. The situation is no different in principle from what would exist if Congress gave the same power of writing sentencing laws to a congressional agency such as the General Accounting Office, or to members of its staff."[71] He especially took exception to the Court majority's treatment of the Constitution "as though it were no more than a generalized prescription that the functions of the Branches should not be commingled too much," with the determination of "how much is too much" left, case by case, to the Court. "The Constitution is not that. Rather, as its name suggests, it is a prescribed structure, a framework, for the conduct of government. In designing that structure, the framers themselves considered how much commingling was acceptable, and set forth their conclusions in the document."[72] For Scalia, then, judgments concerning the degree of acceptable commingling were made, once and for all, by the Framers through the "carefully designed structure they created," not by the Court in contemporary decisions. He feared that Court "improvisation of a constitutional structure on the basis of currently perceived utility will be disastrous."[73]

The *Mistretta* majority denied that the act granted the commission excessive legislative discretion and therefore violated the doctrine of unconstitutional delegation of legislative authority:[74] "The statute outlines the policies which promoted establishment of the Commission, explains what the Commission should do and how it should do it, and sets out specific directives to govern particular situations."[75] Scalia fundamentally disagreed;[76] Congress, he insisted, had delegated "lawmaking authority to the Commission," giving it the power to "prescribe the law, conduct the investigations useful and necessary for prescribing the law, and clarify the intended application of the law that it prescribes."[77] These are lawmaking powers that can only be exercised by the Congress. As he noted, "The only governmental power the Commission possesses is the power to make law, and it is not the Congress."[78]

Although Scalia insisted that the doctrine of unconstitutional delegation is "unquestionably a fundamental element of our constitutional system," he recognized that "it is not an element readily enforceable by the courts." This is so because the debate over unconstitutional delegation typically is "a debate not over a point of principle but over a question of degree," and the Court has "almost never felt qualified to second guess Congress regarding the permissible degree of policy judgment that can be left to those executing or applying the law."[79] Since the Court cannot determine the permissible degree of delegation, Scalia argued that it should focus instead on rigorously preserving "the Constitution's structural restrictions that deter excessive delegation,"[80] something the Court had abandoned in *Morrison*. Until *Morrison*, Congress could delegate its lawmaking authority only to, and at the expense of increasing the power of, the president, "its primary competitor for political power."[81] The competition among the branches created by the Constitution's scheme of separation of powers,[82] though, ensured that delegations of lawmaking power to the president would have to be important enough "to induce Congress to aggrandize" its principal political rival. The risks of such delegation were further diminished because the recipient of the delegated policy-making power, the president, "would at least be politically accountable."[83] After *Morrison*, however, this important constitutional restraint on excessive delegation was removed; as Scalia complained, Congress was now free to delegate its lawmaking powers to a "mini-Executive" or a "junior-varsity Congress" with no fear of augmenting the power of a rival branch (and, in fact, perhaps in the hopes of weakening it) and with no guarantee that political accountability would be preserved. *Mistretta* thus set "an undemocratic precedent" not because of the degree or scope of the delegated power "but because its recipient is not one of the three Branches of Government."[84] *Mistretta* upheld a system for issuing sentencing guidelines that blurred political responsibility. If the public were to dislike the guidelines, there would be no branch that would be truly responsible for them, and for Scalia, that plainly transgressed the doctrine of separation of powers.[85]

Judicial Power

Plaut v. Spendthrift Farm, Inc.

Scalia was equally emphatic that Congress had violated separation-of-powers principles in *Plaut v. Spendthrift Farm, Inc.*;[86] this time, however, he spoke for a six-member majority.[87] Although the facts in *Plaut* are complicated, the constitutional question, at least for Scalia, was not. In 1987, Ed Plaut and his fellow plaintiffs alleged in a civil action that Spendthrift Farm and other defendants had committed fraud and deceit in 1983 and 1984 in the sale of stock in violation of § 10(b) of the Securities Exchange Act of 1934. The District Court for the Eastern District of Kentucky eventually dismissed Plaut's action with prejudice following the Supreme Court's 1991 decision in *Lampf, Pleva, Lipkind, Prupis & Petigrow v. Gilbertson*,[88] which replaced an array of state statutes of limitations that had governed shareholder actions under the Securities Exchange Act and required instead that suits such as Plaut's be commenced within one year after the discovery of the facts constituting the violation and within three years after such violation.

After the district court's judgment had become final, Congress enacted § 27A(b) of the Securities Exchange Act, which provided for reinstatement, on motion, of any action commenced before *Lampf* but dismissed thereafter as time-barred if the action would have been timely filed under applicable pre-*Lampf* state law. Although the district court found that the statute's terms required that Plaut's ensuing § 27A(b) motion be granted, it denied the motion on the ground that § 27A(b) unconstitutionally violated the principle of separation of powers.[89] The Court of Appeals for the Sixth Circuit affirmed,[90] and Scalia for the Supreme Court majority agreed, arguing that "Congress has exceeded its authority by requiring the federal courts to exercise 'the judicial Power of the United States' in a manner repugnant to the text, structure, and traditions of Article III."[91] In categorical terms, he declared that the "Constitution's separation of legislative and judicial powers denies [Congress] the authority" to require "an Article III court to set aside a final judgment."[92]

Plaut and the U.S. government both argued that, in § 27A(b), Congress did not review or revise any final judgments previously entered and that it did not deprive the federal courts of the power or authority to finally determine the outcome of the reopened cases or prescribe a rule for their decision. In his dissent, Justice Stevens agreed: § 27A(b) "decided neither the merits of any 10b–5 claim nor even whether any such claim should proceed to decision of the merits."[93] All it did was "remove an impediment to judicial decision on the merits,"[94] an impediment he believed was created when the Court itself "undertook a legislative function" in *Lampf* by "suppl[ying] a statute of limitations for 10b–5 actions."[95]

According to Stevens, the Court in *Lampf* had "failed to adopt the transition rules that ordinarily attend alterations shortening the time to sue."[96] These transition rules, providing a reasonable time to commence an action before the bar of the shorter period would take effect, are required by due process. As Stevens observed in a note, "Our decisions prior to *Lampf* consistently held that retroactive application of new, shortened limitation periods would violate 'fundamental notions of justified reliance and due process.'"[97] Congress, in § 27A(b), had supplied these transition rules that retroactively restored Plaut's due process rights that the Court in *Lampf* had "inadvertently or unfairly impaired."[98] For Stevens, § 27A(b) reflected "the ability of two coequal branches to cooperate in providing for the impartial application of legal rules to particular disputes."[99]

Stevens chided the Court for its "mistrust of such cooperation,"[100] and he urged his colleagues to "regard favorably, rather than with suspicious hostility, legislation that enables the judiciary to overcome impediments to the performance of its mission of administering justice impartially, even when, as here, this Court has created the impediment."[101] Noting that "judgments in areas such as the review of potential conflicts among the three coequal Branches of the federal Government partake of art as well as science" and reminding his colleagues that separation of powers is based on "interdependence" as well as "separateness" and "reciprocity" as well as "autonomy,"[102] he concluded that an "appropriate regard for the interdependence of Congress and the judiciary amply supports the conclusion that § 27A(b) reflects constructive legislative cooperation rather than a usurpation of judicial prerogatives."[103]

Scalia was unpersuaded. For him, the issue was simple:

> Article III establishes a "judicial department" with the "province and duty
> . . . to say what the law is" in particular cases and controversies. *Marbury v.
> Madison* . . . (1803). The record of history shows that the Framers crafted
> this charter of the judicial department with an expressed understanding that
> it gives the Federal Judiciary the power, not merely to rule on cases, but to
> decide them, subject to review only by superior courts in the Article III hier-
> archy—with an understanding, in short, that "the judgment conclusively
> resolves the case" because "a 'judicial Power' is one to render dispositive
> judgments." By retroactively commanding the federal courts to reopen final
> judgments, Congress has violated this fundamental principle.[104]

Scalia reviewed the instances of legislative interference with the private law judgments of the courts prior to the Constitutional Convention that instilled in the "Framers of the new Federal Constitution"[105] a "sense of a sharp necessity to separate the legislative from the judicial power."[106] Those instances of legislative interference and that "sense of a sharp necessity" had led to the creation of Article III, § 1 and its provision that "the judicial Power of the United States" shall be vested in "one supreme Court, and in such inferior Courts as Congress may from time to time ordain and establish." For Scalia, if the "need for separation of legislative from judicial power was plain," the principal effect to be accomplished by that separation "was even plainer"; Hamilton had stated the matter unambiguously in *Federalist* No. 81: "A legislature without exceeding its province cannot reverse a determination once made, in a particular case; though it may prescribe a new rule for a future case."[107] For Scalia, the conclusion was inescapable: since § 27A(b) "requires its application in a case already finally adjudicated, it does no more and no less than 'reverse a determination once made, in a particular case,'" and it was therefore "a clear violation of the separation-of-powers principle we have just discussed."[108]

Scalia recognized that Congress was motivated by good intentions when it passed § 27A(b)—the desire to assist defrauded shareholders hurt by the Court's ruling in *Lampf.* He acknowledged that this particular "legislative interference with judicial judgments" was not "prompted by individual favoritism." But, he insisted, "it is legislative interference with judicial judgments nonetheless." Then, expressing the very core of his understanding of separation of powers, Scalia declared: "Not favoritism, not corruption, but power is the object of the separation-of-powers prohibition."[109] He continued, "The prohibition is violated when an individual final judgment is legislatively rescinded for even the very best of reasons, such as the legislature's genuine conviction (supported by all the law professors in the land) that the judgment was wrong."[110] Later in his opinion, Scalia explained his refusal to be swayed by either Congress's good intentions or Justice Stevens's concern for Plaut's due process: "[T]he doctrine of separation of powers is a structural safeguard rather than a remedy to be applied only when specific harm, or risk of specific harm, can be identified. In its major features (of which the conclusiveness of judicial judgments is assuredly one) it is a prophylactic device, establishing high walls and clear distinctions because low walls and vague distinctions will not be judicially defensible in the heat of interbranch conflict."[111] For Scalia, judicial independence must be resolutely protected even when the stakes are low for fear that the Court's failure to protect "the judicial Power" from well-motivated congressional interference will (1) encourage hostile congressional forces intent on punishing the judiciary for its protection of constitutional guarantees, and (2) compromise the judiciary's efforts, at that critical juncture, to preserve the Constitution's system of separated powers.

In a 1979 article in *Regulation* magazine, Scalia called on the Supreme Court to strike down the legislative veto as a violation of separation of powers.[112] He worried about the "sick[ening] . . . spectacle of lawyers and legal scholars arguing that this or that feature of proposed legislation is contrary to the Constitution. We live in an age of 'hair-trigger unconstitutionality,' and almost no result produced by the democratic process at any level of government seems immune from attack by some Scribe or Pharisee with a law degree on the ground that it contravenes the Basic Charter of our Liberties."[113] Nonetheless, he worried even more about the effect that an unconstitutional legislative veto was having on "the constitutional balance of power between the first and second branches of government" and especially on "the balance of power between these two branches combined and the people." He argued that, counter to the popular perception, the legislative veto enhanced the power not of the Congress but rather of the president. He noted that the legislative veto encouraged "congressional delegation of vague and standardless rulemaking authority" to the agencies of the executive branch and consequently resulted in the "transfer of basic policy decisions to the agencies. It is significant in this regard that some of the most prominent examples of legislative vetoes enacted in the past were proposed by the executive branch itself—to induce the congressional transfer of power which would otherwise not have been accorded."[114]

Even worse, however, the legislative veto undermined political accountability. Scalia complained that it resulted in "an egregious subversion of the democratic process"; issues "too hot to handle" could be ducked by the "people's representatives" and handled instead by an insulated and politically irresponsible bureaucracy. It was, for Scalia, "an excellent mechanism for enabling the President and the Congress to facilitate the passage of unpopular laws by eliminating the congressional burden of having to vote for them."[115] In *Immigration and Naturalization Service v. Chadha*,[116] the Supreme Court had declared the legislative veto unconstitutional along much the same lines that Scalia had outlined in his 1979 article in *Regulation*.[117] In his majority opinion in *Plaut*, he expressed his full and continued support for *Chadha* by likening what Congress had done with its passage of § 27A(b) to its widespread use of legislative vetoes declared unconstitutional in *Chadha*, by asserting that "legislated invalidation of judicial judgments deserves the same categorical treatment accorded by *Chadha* to congressional invalidation of executive action." He concluded his extended discussion of separation of powers in his *Plaut* majority opinion by observing, "Separation of powers, a distinctively American political doctrine, profits from the advice authored by a distinctively American poet: Good fences make good neighbors."[118]

Young v. United States ex rel. Vuitton et Fils S.A.

Scalia is no less attentive to any possible trampling of the "good fences" of separation of powers by the judiciary than he is by the Congress. For example, in his concurrence in the judgment in *Young v. United States ex rel. Vuitton et Fils S.A.*,[119] he argued that the federal courts have no constitutional power to prosecute contemners for disobedience of court judgments and no power derivative of that to appoint attorneys to conduct contempt prosecutions.[120] "Prosecution of individuals who disregard court orders is not an exercise of '[t]he judicial power of the United States,'" he argued. For Scalia, the judicial power is "the power to decide, in accordance with law, who should prevail in a case or controversy"; it includes "the power to serve as a neutral adjudicator in a criminal case, but does not include the power to seek out law violators in order to punish them—which would be quite incompatible with the task of neutral adjudications."[121] Prosecution of law violators is, he insisted, "part of the implementation of the laws," and it is an "executive power, vested by the Constitution in the President."[122]

It should be noted that Scalia was referring not to the ability of courts to initiate contempt prosecutions for in-court contempts that interfere with the judicial process but only to their ability to initiate contempt prosecutions for out-of-court contempts. The latter, Scalia contended, are essentially conventional crimes that require prosecution by a party other than the court and only at the initiative of the executive branch. As he explained to his colleagues, the federal courts have those "inherent powers . . . necessary to permit the courts to function," among which is "the contempt power when used to prevent interference with the conduct of judicial business." This exception does not, however, include "the enforcement of judgments, much less of an investigative or prosecutory authority."[123]

Justice William Brennan for the majority argued that criminal contempts can be prosecuted by the courts themselves because otherwise the efficaciousness of judicial judgments would be "at the mercy" of the executive branch and "what the Constitution now fittingly calls 'the judicial power of the United States' would be a mere mockery."[124] Scalia strenuously disagreed:

> There are numerous instances in which the Constitution leaves open the theoretical possibility that the actions of one Branch may be brought to nought by the actions or inactions of another. Such dispersion of power was central to the scheme of forming a Government with enough power to serve the expansive purposes set forth in the preamble of the Constitution, yet one that would "secure the blessings of liberty" rather than use its powers tyrannically. Congress, for example, is dependent on the Executive and the courts for the enforcement of the laws it enacts. Even complete failure by the Executive to prosecute law violators, or by the courts to convict them, has never been thought to authorize congressional prosecution and trial. The Executive, in its turn, cannot perform its function of enforcing the laws if Congress declines to appropriate the necessary funds for that purpose; or if the courts decline to entertain its valid prosecutions. Yet no one suggests that some doctrine of necessity authorizes the Executive to raise money for its operations without congressional appropriations, or to jail malefactors without conviction by a court of law.[125]

Although Scalia wondered why his colleagues believed that the courts alone should be immune from this interdependence, he knew that the Framers of the Constitution, "of a certainty," thought that they were not. He considered it "instructive." to compare the Court's claim that federal courts "cannot be at the mercy of another branch in deciding whether [contempt] proceedings should be initiated" with "one of the most famous passages from *The Federalist*: '[T]he judiciary, from the nature of its functions, will always be the least dangerous to the political rights of the constitution; because it will be least in a capacity to annoy or injure them. . . . The judiciary . . . may truly be said to have neither Force nor Will but merely judgment; and *must ultimately depend upon the aid of the executive arm even for the efficacy of its judgments.*' "[126]

Scalia concluded by focusing directly on the separation-of-powers implications of this litigation. He reminded his colleagues of the "broad sweep of modern judicial decrees" and warned them of the "tyrannical" prospects,"[127] as he put it, of "permitting a judge to promulgate a rule of behavior, prosecute its violation, and adjudicate whether the violation took place." Such a "flagrant" violation of separation of powers was, for Scalia, "no less fundamental a threat to liberty than . . . deprivation of a jury trial, since 'there is no liberty if the power of judging be not separated from the legislative and executive powers.' "[128] In fact, he continued, the "impairment of judicial power produced by requiring the Executive to prosecute contempts" is less substantial than the impairment produced by requiring a jury trial. "The power to acquit is as decisive as the power not to prosecute," and the jury can abuse its power with impunity whereas the federal prosecutor "must litigate regularly before the judges whose violated judgments he ignores."[129]

United States v. Munoz-Flores

For Scalia, separation of powers requires that the judiciary be as hesitant to assume the constitutionally assigned powers of the other branches as it is vigilant to protect its own. Separation of powers also requires, as he argued in his concurrence in the judgment in *United States v. Munoz-Flores*,[130] that the judiciary accept "at face value" the "official representations" of the other branches concerning matters of their "internal process."[131] *Munoz-Flores* addressed the question whether § 3013 of the Victims of Crime Act of 1984, requiring federal courts to impose on any person convicted of a federal misdemeanor a monetary "special assessment" to be paid into the Crime Victims Fund, was passed in violation of the Origination Clause of the Constitution, which mandates that "all Bills for raising Revenues shall originate in the House of Representatives." The Ninth Circuit Court of Appeals concluded that it was; it held that § 3013 was a bill for raising revenue that had originated in the Senate (because the Senate was the first chamber to pass the assessment provision) and thus was passed in violation of the clause.[132] The Supreme Court reversed. Speaking for the Court, Justice Thurgood Marshall argued that the special-assessment statute was not a bill "for raising revenue"; he insisted that a statute that creates and raises revenues to support a particular government program—as opposed to a statute that raises revenue to support government generally—is not a bill "for raising revenue." Congress passed § 3013 in order to provide money for the Crime Victims Fund, and though it specified that any excess go to the U.S. Treasury, Justice Marshall noted that there was no evidence that Congress contemplated the possibility of a substantial excess, nor did any such excess in fact materialize. Consequently, he said, there was no violation of the Origination Clause.[133]

Justice Scalia rejected the Court's reasoning and concurred only in the judgment. He argued that the principle of separation of powers, reinforced by the "uncertainty and instability" that would result if every statute could be challenged as not having been properly passed, "leads me to conclude that federal courts should not undertake an independent investigation into the origination of the statute at issue here."[134] Scalia pointed out that the enrolled bill—which, when signed by the president, became the Victims of Crime Act of 1984—bore the indication "H.J. Res. 648," which attested that the legislation originated in the House. Such an attestation, although not explicitly required by the Constitution, was reasonably necessary because the president, if he vetoes a bill, must, according to Article I, § 7, cl. 2, "return it, with his Objections to that House in which it shall have originated." For Scalia, "[t]he enrolled bill's indication of its house of origin establishes that fact as officially and authoritatively as it establishes the fact that its recited text was adopted by both Houses. With respect to either fact a court's holding, based on its own investigation, that the representation made to the President is incorrect would . . . manifest a lack of respect due a coordinate Branch and produce uncertainty as to the state of the law."[135]

Scalia declared that he could not imagine the Court entertaining the contention that a purportedly vetoed bill is valid law because, although the president returned the vetoed measure to the house of origination as indicated on the enrolled bill, that body was not the real house of origination. If it would not entertain such a contention, he argued, it ought not entertain the contention in the instant case.

> We should no more gainsay Congress' official assertion of the origin of a
> bill than we would gainsay its official assertion that the bill was passed by
> the requisite quorum; or any more than Congress or the President would
> gainsay the official assertion of this Court that a judgment was duly con-
> sidered and approved by our majority vote. Mutual regard between the
> coordinate Branches, and the interest of certainty, both demand that offi-
> cial representations regarding such matters of internal process be accepted
> at face value.[136]

Lujan v. Defenders of Wildlife

Scalia's concern for trampling on the good fences of separation of powers is also manifest in his scholarly writings and judicial opinions on standing. Standing was described by the Supreme Court, in *Sierra Club v. Morton*,[137] as "a sufficient stake in an otherwise justiciable controversy to obtain judicial resolution of that controversy." To have standing, parties invoking judicial power must show that they have sustained, or are in immediate danger of sustaining, some direct injury as a result of the enforcement of some statute or regulation. Article III, § 2 limits the jurisdiction of the federal courts to "cases" and "controversies," and the doctrine of standing holds that there is no case or controversy when there are no adverse parties with personal interests in the matter.

Until the Warren Court era, the alleged injury suffered by the complainant had to be a particularized one that set the complainant apart from the populace at large; as the Court held in *Frothingham v. Mellon*,[138] it was not enough for the complainant to show that "he suffers in some indefinite way in common with people generally." The Warren Court, however, worked what Scalia called a "seachange . . . in the judicial attitude towards the doctrine of standing."[139] That change was perhaps most apparent in *Flast v. Cohen*[140] and *United States v. Students Challenging Regulatory Agency Procedures* [SCRAP].[141]

Flast gave a federal taxpayer standing to challenge, on Establishment Clause grounds, federal expenditures authorized under the Elementary and Secondary Education Act of 1965 that would assist denominational schools in the purchase of textbooks. Never before had an improper expenditure of federal funds been held to injure a federal taxpayer in such a fashion as to confer standing to sue, but Chief Justice Earl Warren wrote for the Court that federal taxpayers would be allowed to challenge congressional spending if the legislation in question emanated from the Taxing and Spending Clause of Article 1, § 8 and if the taxpayers could show a nexus between their status as taxpayers and a specific constitutional limitation upon the exercise of the spending power (in this case, the Establishment Clause of the First Amendment).[142]

The Court in *SCRAP* held that a group of law students at George Washington University had standing to challenge the failure of the Interstate Commerce Commission to prepare an environmental impact statement before it permitted a railroad freight surcharge to take effect. The students claimed standing to sue based on their assertions that they used parks and forests, that these areas would be less desirable if littered, that litter would increase if there was a reduction in the use of recycled goods, that a reduction in their use would result if the cost of these goods increased, and that the cost of these goods would increase if the freight surcharge went into effect. They further claimed standing by asserting that they breathed the air within the Washington metropolitan area and that this air would suffer from increased pollution caused by the modified rate structure. After the Supreme Court held that the alleged injuries sustained by the plaintiffs in *Flast* and *SCRAP* were adequate to support their suits, any claim that standing still required particularized injury rang hollow. Further, any restraint that standing had once imposed on the federal courts to keep them from trampling on the good fences of separation of powers and from assuming the constitutionally assigned powers of the other branches evanesced.

Scalia has devoted considerable thought and energy to revitalizing the doctrine of standing by reconnecting it to the principle of separation of powers. In 1983, soon after his appointment to the Court of Appeals for the District of Columbia Circuit, he delivered the Donahue Lecture at Suffolk University Law School on the doctrine of standing. In it, he argued that "the judicial doctrine of standing is a crucial and inseparable element" of the principle of separation of powers, "whose disregard will inevitably produce—as it has during the past few decades—an overjudicialization of the process of self-governance."[143] In particular, he stressed the importance of having the federal courts reestablish "concrete injury" as "the indispensable prerequisite of standing."[144] When the law of standing is understood to demand "concrete injury," Scalia observed, it "roughly restricts courts to their traditional undemocratic role of protecting individuals and minorities against impositions of the majority." However, when the law of standing is understood to permit, as in *SCRAP*, "all who breathe air" to complain to the court that an agency has failed "to impose a requirement or prohibition of someone else," it involves the courts in "the even more undemocratic role of prescribing how the other two branches should function in order to serve the interest *of the majority itself.*" Failure of another branch or agency to perform "harms the plaintiff, by depriving him, as a citizen, of governmental acts which the Constitution or laws require." But, Scalia continued, "that harm alone is, so to speak, a *majoritarian one.*" The plaintiff may "*care* more" about the failure to perform than his fellow citizens; he may be "a more ardent proponent of constitutional regularity or of the necessity of the governmental act that has been wrongfully omitted" than others. That, however, does not establish, Scalia continued, "that he has been harmed distinctively—only that he assesses the harm as more grave, which is a fair subject for democratic debate in which he may persuade the rest of us." And "since our readiness to be persuaded is no less than his own (we are harmed just as much) there is no reason to remove the matter from the political process and place it in the courts."[145]

A decade later, Scalia was able to express these same sentiments in his opinion for the Court in *Lujan v. Defenders of Wildlife.*[146] In *Lujan*, various wildlife conservation and environmental groups brought an action against the secretary of the interior, challenging a regulation promulgated by his department implementing § 7 of the Endangered Species Act (ESA) of 1973 and arguing that it had failed to follow Congress's intentions.

In § 7, Congress sought to protect endangered species by requiring that all federal agencies consult with the secretary of the interior to ensure that any action funded by the agency did not jeopardize the continued existence or habitat of any endangered or threatened species. Through its regulations implementing § 7, the Interior Department extended the ESA's coverage to federally funded projects in the United States and on the high seas but did not apply it to actions funded in foreign countries—for example, to financial support by the U.S. Agency for International Development (USAID) for the construction of the Aswan High Dam in Egypt, which the plaintiffs claimed threatened the endangered Nile crocodile, and for the Mahaweli Project in Sri Lanka, which they claimed threatened "endangered species such as the Asian elephant and the leopard."[147] The plaintiffs filed an action in federal district court seeking a declaratory judgment that these regulations erred as to § 7's geographic scope and an injunction requiring the secretary of the interior to promulgate new rules extending § 7's coverage to actions taken in foreign nations. The issue that eventually came before the Supreme Court was whether the plaintiffs had standing to seek judicial review of these rules.

Scalia held for a six-member majority that they did not. He began by arguing that, consistent with the "essential and unchanging part of the case-or-controversy requirement of Article III," there are three elements to the "irreducible constitutional minimum of standing": (1) the plaintiffs must establish that they have "suffered an 'injury in fact' "—an invasion of a legally protected interest that is concrete, particularized, and actual or imminent as opposed to conjectural or hypothetical; (2) they must show causation between the challenged action and the injury; and (3) they must establish that it is likely (as opposed to merely "speculative") that the injury will be redressed by a decision in their favor.[148] The plaintiffs invoking federal jurisdiction bear the burden of establishing these three elements, and, he continued, in the instant case, they had failed to bear that burden.

To begin with, they had failed to establish that they had been injured in fact. In affidavits, two members of the Defenders of Wildlife claimed that they had visited Egypt and Sri Lanka in the past, where they had observed the habitats of the Nile crocodile and the Asian elephant and leopard; they also indicated that they intended at some time in the future to return to these countries, with the hope of observing these animals directly. They contended that they would be injured and therefore had standing to sue if USAID funds were used to assist in the completion of these development projects and, therefore, in the alleged destruction of the habitats of those animals they were planning to see "one day." Scalia briskly dismissed this contention: "[A]ssum[ing] for the sake of argument that these affidavits contain facts showing that certain agency-funded projects threaten listed species—though that is questionable, [t]hey plainly contain no facts showing how damage to the species will produce 'imminent' injury" to the two members.[149]

The Defenders of Wildlife did not rely solely on the contention of its two members; it also proposed what Scalia described as "a series of novel standing theories," including the "animal nexus approach," whereby anyone who has an interest in studying or seeing an endangered animal anywhere on the globe has standing, and the "vocational nexus approach," under which anyone with a professional interest in such animals can sue. Under these theories, as Scalia pointed out, "anyone who goes to see Asian elephants in the Bronx Zoo, and anyone who is a keeper of Asian elephants in the Bronx Zoo has standing to sue" the secretary of the interior because his regulations do not require the director of USAID to consult with him before funding projects in Sri Lanka. Scalia found this preposterous: "This is beyond all reason. Standing is not 'an ingenious academic exercise in the conceivable.'"[150]

The plaintiffs showed no injury in fact and, Scalia continued, no causal connection between their alleged injury and the conduct of which they complained. USAID had provided only a small fraction of the funding of the development projects at issue; it had, for example, provided less than 10 percent of the funding for the Mahaweli Project in Sri Lanka. Scalia noted that the Defenders of Wildlife had "produced nothing to indicate that the projects they have named will either be suspended, or do less harm to listed species, if that fraction is eliminated." He found it "entirely conjectural" whether these development projects (and the destruction of endangered-species habitat they were alleged to cause) would be altered or affected by a Department of Interior regulation requiring the director of USAID to consult with the secretary prior to funding foreign projects.[151]

Scalia held that the plaintiffs failed to meet the third element of standing as well; they failed to demonstrate redressability. Enjoining the secretary of the interior to revise his regulations would not remedy the plaintiffs' alleged injury "unless the funding agencies were bound by the Secretary's regulations, which is very much an open question."[152] He pointed out that both the funding agencies themselves and the solicitor general of the United States denied that the secretary's regulations were binding.

Having shown that the plaintiffs failed to meet all three elements of the "irreducible constitutional minimum of standing," Scalia was nonetheless obliged to address still another reason recognized by the Eighth Circuit for why the plaintiffs could proceed with their suit: they had suffered a "procedural injury."[153] The ESA contains a "citizen-suit" provision that states: "[A]ny person may commence a civil suit on his own behalf to enjoin any person, including the United States and any other governmental instrumentality or agency . . . who is alleged to be in violation of any provision of this chapter."[154] The Eighth Circuit had held that since § 7 requires interagency consultation, the citizen-suit provision creates a "procedural right" to consultation in all persons, so that anyone can file suit in federal court to challenge the failure of the secretary or any other government official to follow the assertedly correct consultative procedure, even in the absence of any concrete injury resulting from that failure.

Scalia's response to this argument was blunt: "We reject this view."[155] He began by reminding his colleagues that plaintiffs who raise grievances about government that claim harm to them and every other person's interest in the proper application of the Constitution and law and who seek relief that benefits them no more directly or tangibly than the public at large "do not state an Article III case or controversy."[156] He then declared that in the ESA, Congress had no more power to violate the Article III concrete injury requirement than did the Court itself. Vindicating the public interest in government observance of the Constitution and laws was, Scalia asserted, "the function of the Congress and the Chief Executive."[157] Absent evidence of a particularized injury to a plaintiff caused by government failure to observe the Constitution and law, there was no case or controversy and therefore no function for the courts to perform. Providing a lesson on separation of powers, Scalia continued:

> To permit Congress to convert the undifferentiated public interest in executive officers' compliance with the law into an "individual right" vindicable in the courts is to permit Congress to transfer from the President to the courts the Chief Executive's most important constitutional duty, to "take care that the laws be faithfully executed." It would enable the courts, with the permission of Congress, "to assume a position of authority over the governmental acts of another and co-equal department," and to become "virtually continuing monitors of the wisdom and soundness of Executive action." We have always rejected that vision of our role.[158]

Franklin v. Massachusetts

Interestingly enough, however, though Scalia was able to carry a six-member majority in establishing and elaborating upon his three-element standing test in *Lujan*, within two weeks, he wrote for himself alone when he applied this same standing test in his opinion concurring in the judgment in *Franklin v. Massachusetts*.[159] *Franklin* presented a complaint by the Commonwealth of Massachusetts about the way in which the secretary of commerce (in whose department is located the Bureau of the Census) and the president (acting upon the secretary's recommendation) had allocated overseas employees of the Defense Department to particular states for reapportionment purposes in the 1990 census. Massachusetts complained that the "usual residence" allocation mechanism recommended by the secretary and employed by the president, which resulted in the shift of a representative from Massachusetts to the state of Washington, violated Article I, § 2, cl. 3 of the Constitution, which requires that the decennial apportionment of representatives be determined by an "actual enumeration" of persons "in each State." A three-judge panel of the District Court of Massachusetts agreed, directed the secretary to eliminate overseas military personnel from the apportionment count, and directed the president to recalculate the number of representatives each state was to receive and to submit the new calculations to the Congress.[160]

The Supreme Court unanimously reversed, although the justices differed among themselves as to the reasons for reversing. Justice O'Connor wrote for all the justices save Scalia when she held that, although Massachusetts had standing to challenge the Census Bureau's allocation of representatives, its claims were baseless. She argued that the allocation of overseas military personnel to their designated home states was consistent with the "usual residence" standard used from the first census on, and it served the purpose of making representation in the Congress more equal.[161]

Scalia concurred only in the judgment to reverse the district court, for he disputed that Massachusetts had standing to sue.[162] He restated the three requirements for standing he had enunciated only a few days before in *Lujan* and concluded that Massachusetts "founder[ed] on the third," i.e., redressability. Justice O'Connor and her colleagues concluded that had they ruled in favor of Massachusetts, "declaratory relief directed at the Secretary alone would be sufficient to redress" the commonwealth's injury. But Scalia declared, "I do not agree. Ordering the Secretary to recalculate the final census totals will not redress [Massachusetts'] injury unless the President accepts the new numbers, changes his calculations accordingly, and issues a new reapportionment statement to Congress."[163] Scalia denied that the president's role in this scenario was purely ministerial; he denied that, for purposes of the Article III redressability requirement, courts are "ever entitled to assume, no matter how objectively reasonable the assumption may be, that the President (or, for that matter, any official of the Executive or Legislative Branches) in performing a function that is not wholly ministerial, will follow the advice of a subordinate official." Redressability, he continued, is based on a court's ability "to afford relief through the exercise of its powers," not on its assumption that "everyone (including those who are not proper parties to an action) will honor the legal rationales" that underlie its decree.[164]

He decried the district court's arrogance and constitutional ignorance in providing Massachusetts with the relief it sought. "It is a sad commentary upon the level to which judicial understanding—indeed, even judicial awareness—of the doctrine of separation of powers has fallen, that the District Court entered this order against the President without blinking an eye. I think it clear that no court has authority to direct the President to take an official act."[165] Since the Court could not remedy Massachusetts' injury without ordering declaratory and injunctive relief against the president and since the Court, under the constitutional scheme of separation of powers, has no power to do that, Scalia argued that Massachusetts' claims should be dismissed for lack of standing.[166]

Scalia's redressability argument in turn led him into a pointed discussion on the limits of the judicial power, in which he revisited a theme he introduced in *Morrison,* namely, that the ultimate check on the popular branches is not the courts but the people who, through the electoral process, can replace those who are guilty of abuse. An "unbroken historical tradition supports the view, which I think implicit in the separation of powers established by the Constitution, that the principals in whom the executive and legislative powers are ultimately vested— viz., the President and the Congress (as opposed to their agents)—may not be ordered to perform particular executive or legislative acts at the behest of the Judiciary."[167] Because the Constitution subordinates the president and the Congress to the will of the people, not the will of the Court, "we cannot direct the President to take a specified executive act or the Congress to perform particular legislative duties."[168]

The Line-Item Veto: Clinton v. City of New York

In April 1996, Congress enacted the Line Item Veto Act of 1996,[169] which gave the president of the United States authority to cancel certain spending and tax benefit measures after the president had signed such measures into law. The act became effective on January 1, 1997, and the following day, six members of Congress who had voted against the measure brought suit in the District Court for the District of Columbia, challenging its constitutionality. On April 10, 1997, the district court, in *Byrd v. Raines,* entered an order holding the act to be unconstitutional.[170] The Supreme Court, however, reversed, holding that the members of Congress did not have standing to sue because they had not "alleged a sufficiently concrete injury to have established Article III standing."[171]

That ruling, however, did not end constitutional challenges to the act, as the measure contained an expedited-review provision that authorized any individual adversely affected by the Line Item Veto Act to bring a declaratory judgment action alleging that any provision of the act violated the Constitution. After President Bill Clinton exercised his authority under the Line Item Veto Act to cancel certain measures—including the section of the Balanced Budget Act of 1997 that waived the federal government's statutory right to recoup certain taxes levied by

the state of New York on Medicaid providers and the provision of the Taxpayer
Relief Act of 1997 that permitted owners of certain food refiners and processors
to defer recognition of capital gains from sales of their stock to eligible farmers'
cooperatives, the city of New York and a potato farmers' cooperative in Idaho successfully secured declaratory relief from the District Court for the District of
Columbia. They had claimed that the Line Item Veto Act was unconstitutional
because it violated the Constitution's Presentment Clause (Article I, § 7, cl. 2)
and the doctrine of separation of powers. The Supreme Court, in *Clinton v. New
York*,[172] affirmed the judgment of the District Court, finding that the parties had
been adversely affected by President Clinton's cancellation of these budgetary and
tax relief provisions and that the act's cancellation procedures violated the Presentment Clause. Scalia's opinion, in which he concurred in part and dissented
in part, offers additional insight into his understanding of standing and separation
of powers.

Scalia concurred in the part of Justice Stevens's majority opinion that concluded the city of New York had standing because President Clinton's cancellation order deprived the federal government of the power to waive recoupment of
certain taxes levied by the state of New York on Medicaid providers, and, as a consequence, New York State law would automatically require the city of New York to
make retroactive tax payments to the state of about $4 million for each of the years
at issue. Scalia stated, "The tax liability they will incur under New York law is a
concrete and particularized injury, fairly traceable to the President's action, and
avoided if that action is undone."[173]

Scalia dissented from the part of Stevens's opinion that found the Snake River
Potato Growers to have suffered a similar "legally cognizable injury"[174] because
President Clinton's line-item veto allegedly prevented them from acquiring a pro-
cessing plant that the Idaho Potato Packers (IPP) was willing to sell to them only
on a tax-deferred basis. Scalia found this putative injury to be "conjectural" and
"hypothetical" and therefore insufficient for Article III standing.[175]

> [A]ll we know from the record is that Snake River had two discussions with
> IPP concerning the sale of its processing facility on the tax deferred basis
> the Act would allow; that IPP was interested; and that Snake River ended
> the discussions after the President's action. We do not know that Snake
> River was prepared to offer a price—tax deferral or no—that would cross
> IPP's laugh threshold. We do not even know for certain that the tax defer-
> ral was a significant attraction to IPP; we know only that . . . [Snake River]
> thought it was. On these facts—which never even bring things to the *point*
> of bargaining—it is pure conjecture to say that Snake River suffered an
> impaired bargaining position.[176]

Scalia flatly rejected the majority's contention that there was "a sufficient likelihood of economic injury on the Snake River appellees to establish standing under this Court's precedents."[177] "All we know," he insisted, "is that a potential seller was 'interested' in talking about the subject before the President's action, and that after the President's action Snake River itself decided to proceed no further." This, however, did not establish that it was likely that Snake River "would have made a bargain purchase but for the President's action" nor that it was likely that the President's action "rendered 'more difficult' a purchase that was realistically within Snake River's grasp." If these conjectures are sufficient to establish "likelihood," he continued, "then we must adopt for our standing jurisprudence a new definition of likely: 'plausible.' "[178] And so he concluded that Snake River's "allegations do not establish an injury in fact, attributable to the Presidential action it challenges, and remediable by this Court's invalidation of that Presidential action."[179]

Scalia also dissented on the more immediate separation-of-powers issue: "I do not believe that Executive cancellation of . . . direct spending violates the Presentment Clause."[180] He faulted the Court for being "faked out" by the title of the Line Item Veto Act. The title was designed, he insisted, merely to "simplify for public comprehension" what the act practically accomplished and to "comply with the terms of a campaign pledge."[181] In fact, the act did not provide for a line-item veto; it did not authorize the president to veto parts of a bill and sign others into law but rather authorized him to "cancel" certain parts of statutes that had been duly enacted. As Scalia emphasized, "It was only *after* the requirements of the Presentment Clause had been satisfied [in the enactment of the Balanced Budget Act] that the President exercised his authority under the Line Item Veto Act to cancel the spending item" in question.[182]

Scalia agreed that the Presentment Clause prevented the president from canceling a law that Congress had not authorized him to cancel, but that clearly was not the case here. And, he insisted, Article I, § 7 "no more categorically prohibits the Executive *reduction* of congressional dispositions in the course of implementing statutes that authorize such reduction, than it categorically prohibits the Executive *augmentation* of congressional dispositions in the course of implementing statutes that authorize such augmentation—generally known as substantive rulemaking." What limited these congressional authorizations for Scalia was the doctrine of unconstitutional delegation of legislative authority. As he put it, "When authorized Executive reduction or augmentation is allowed to go too far, it usurps the nondelegable function of Congress and violates the separation of powers." For Scalia, then, the crucial question was whether Congress's authorization in the Line Item Veto Act of presidential cancellation of an item of spending went "too far by transferring to the Executive a degree of political, law-making power that our traditions demand be retained by the Legislative Branch."[183]

His answer was direct: "[T]here is not a dime's worth of difference" in terms of transferring legislative power to the executive "between Congress's authorizing the President to *cancel* a spending item, and Congress's authorizing money to be spent on a particular item at the President's discretion. And the latter has been done since the Founding of the Nation."[184] With the crucial question concerning unconstitutional delegation thus answered, Scalia concluded that the Line Item Veto Act did not in fact "authorize a line-item veto and thus did not violate the Presentment Clause," did not go beyond "what Congress has permitted the President to do since the formation of the Union," and did not violate the Constitution.[185]

The War on Terror

On June 28, 2004, the Supreme Court handed down three separate decisions on military detentions arising out of what has come to be known as the War on Terror. In *Rumsfeld v. Padilla*, the Court dismissed on procedural grounds the habeas corpus petition of Jose Padilla, an American citizen being held in a navy brig in South Carolina as an "enemy combatant"; it held that his petition had been improperly filed in the wrong federal district court.[186] By so ruling, the Court did not reach the merits of Padilla's case, in which he contended that neither the president's power as commander-in-chief nor Congress's Authorization for Use of Military Force Resolution (AUMF)—which included authorization for the president to use "all necessary and appropriate force" against "nations, organizations, or persons" associated with the September 11, 2001, attacks on the United States—authorized military detentions of American citizens captured in the United States. Scalia joined in the majority opinion in this five-to-four decision.

In *Rasul v. Bush*, the Court held that federal district courts have jurisdiction under the habeas corpus provisions of 28 USC § 2241 to review the legality of detentions by the U.S. military of foreign nationals captured during the military campaign against al Qaeda and the Taliban regime in Afghanistan and incarcerated at the Guantanamo Bay Naval Base in Cuba.[187] Scalia dissented in this six-to-three decision on the grounds that these foreign nationals were not within the territorial jurisdiction of the federal courts. In *Hamdi v. Rumsfeld*, Justice O'Connor held for a plurality of the Court that although Congress had effectively suspended the writ of habeas corpus when it authorized the detention of enemy combatants in its AUMF resolution, due process demanded that a citizen held in the United States as an enemy combatant had to be given a meaningful opportunity to contest the factual basis for that detention before a neutral decision maker.[188] Scalia again dissented, this time on the grounds that in the absence of a formal suspension of the writ of habeas corpus by Congress, a citizen held in the United States and accused of being an enemy combatant was entitled either to a criminal trial or to a judicial decree requiring the citizen's release. Both of Scalia's dissents perfectly reflect his text-and-tradition approach to resolving the difficult separation-of-powers questions posed by the way in which the popular branches have responded to terrorism after September 11.

Rasul v. Bush

In *Rasul*, the Court majority read the habeas corpus provisions of § 2241 in what Scalia called a "clumsy, countertextual" manner.[189] The Court held that since the statute authorizes federal courts, "within their respective jurisdictions," to entertain habeas applications by persons claiming to be held in violation of the laws of the United States, it therefore gives them jurisdiction to hear petitions from aliens held at the Guantanamo Bay Naval Base, a territory over which the United States "exercises plenary and exclusive jurisdiction, but not 'ultimate sovereignty.' "[190] Scalia charged that by "largely ignor[ing]" the text of § 2241, the Court "irresponsibl[y] overturn[ed]"[191] settled law and elevated federal judges to the position of "oversee[ing]" a crucial "aspect of the Executive's conduct of a foreign war."[192]

Scalia argued that "[e]ven a cursory reading of the habeas statute shows that it presupposes a federal district court with territorial jurisdiction over the detainee." He pointed out that the text of § 2241 states that "[w]rits of habeas corpus may be granted by the Supreme Court, any justice thereof, the district courts and any circuit judge *within their respective jurisdictions*"; requires that "[t]he order of a circuit judge shall be entered in the records of *the* district court of *the district wherein the restraint complained of is had*"; and provides that a petition "addressed to the Supreme Court, a justice thereof or a circuit judge . . . shall state the reasons for not making application to *the* district court of *the district in which the applicant is held*." For Scalia, the text was clear: "No matter to whom the writ is directed, custodian or detainee, the statute could not be clearer that a necessary requirement for issuing the writ is that *some* federal district court have territorial jurisdiction over the detainee." And since the Court conceded that the Guantanamo Bay detainees were not located within the territorial jurisdiction of any federal district court, Scalia concluded that "one would think that is the end of this case."[193]

But for the Court majority, it was not. The majority read the territorial requirement out of the federal courts' habeas jurisdiction and, according to Scalia, in a "breathtaking" blow of the proper relations that should exist among the branches, "sprung a trap on the Executive, subjecting Guantanamo Bay to the oversight of the federal courts even though it has never before been thought to be within their jurisdiction—and thus making it a foolish place to have housed alien wartime detainees."[194] The Court's nontextualist reading of the reach of federal habeas relief would, he feared, have "a potentially harmful effect upon the Nation's conduct of a war. The Commander in Chief and his subordinates had every reason to expect that the internment of combatants at Guantanamo Bay would not have the consequence of bringing the cumbersome machinery of our domestic courts into military affairs." For Scalia, results such as these "should not be brought about lightly, and certainly not without a textual basis in the statute."[195] And in a further reminder to his colleagues of the separation-of-powers implications of the Court's decision, he observed that "Congress is in session. If it wished to change federal judges' habeas jurisdiction from what this Court had previously held that to be, it could have done so." Moreover, he was convinced, it would have done so by an "intelligent revision of the statute" and thereby avoided the perverse consequence of the Court's nontextualist interpretation that ended up conferring upon "wartime prisoners greater habeas rights than domestic detainees."[196]

> The latter must challenge their present physical confinement in the district of their confinement, whereas under today's strange holding Guantanamo Bay detainees can petition in any of the 94 federal judicial districts. The fact that extraterritorially located detainees lack the district of detention that the statute requires has been converted from a factor that precludes their ability to bring a petition at all into a factor that frees them to petition wherever they wish—and, as a result, to forum shop. For this Court to create such a monstrous scheme in time of war, and in frustration of our military commanders' reliance upon clearly stated prior law, is judicial adventurism of the worst sort.[197]

Hamdi v. Rumsfeld

In *Rasul*, Scalia argued on textualist grounds against granting habeas relief to the Guantanamo Bay detainees; the text of § 2241, he insisted, did not give the federal courts habeas jurisdiction outside U.S. sovereign territory. In *Hamdi*, he argued on textualist grounds that an American citizen held on American soil and accused of being an enemy combatant is entitled to a habeas decree requiring his release unless criminal proceedings are promptly brought against him; the text of Article I, § 9 of the Constitution authorizes only Congress to suspend the writ of habeas corpus, and the text of its AUMF resolution contained no such suspension.[198]

The plurality in *Hamdi* disagreed, reading the AUMF resolution as authorizing the president to detain enemy combatants (even if they are citizens) for the duration of hostilities.[199] Justice O'Connor noted that in its AUMF resolution, Congress authorized "the President to use 'all necessary and appropriate force' against 'nations, organizations, or persons' associated with the September 11, 2001, terrorist attacks," and she concluded "that detention of individuals falling into the limited category we are considering, for the duration of the particular conflict in which they were captured, is so fundamental and accepted an incident to war as to be an exercise of the 'necessary and appropriate force' Congress has authorized the President to use."[200] Yaser Esam Hamdi had no grounds to object to his detention under Article I, § 9; however, O'Connor continued, he did have grounds under the Due Process Clause of the Fifth Amendment: "[A] citizen-detainee seeking to challenge his classification as an enemy combatant must receive notice of the factual basis for his classification, and a fair opportunity to rebut the Government's factual assertions before a neutral decision-maker."[201]

In his dissent, Scalia powerfully rejected the plurality's reliance on the AUMF resolution to justify Hamdi's continued imprisonment: "This is not remotely a congressional suspension of the writ."[202] Article I, § 9 "would be a sham" if it could be so easily evaded. If it "does not guarantee the citizen that he will either be tried or released, unless the conditions for suspending the writ exist and the grave action of suspending the writ has been taken; if it merely guarantees the citizen that he will not be detained unless Congress by ordinary legislation says he can be detained," then, Scalia concluded, it "guarantees him very little indeed."[203]

The plurality, Scalia charged, had "discarded the categorical procedural protection" of Article I, § 9 and replaced it with those due process protections "it thinks appropriate." The major effect of this "constitutional improvisation" was, he observed, to "increase the power of the Court."[204] And as he does so often, Scalia tied his criticism of the Court's departure from the constitutional text to an attack on judicial activism—to what he described on this occasion as "an approach that reflects what might be called a Mr. Fix-it Mentality."[205]

> The plurality seems to view it as its mission to Make Everything Come Out Right, rather than merely to decree the consequences, as far as individual rights are concerned, of the other two branches' actions and omissions. Has the Legislature failed to suspend the writ in the current dire emergency? Well, we will remedy that failure by prescribing the reasonable conditions that a suspension should have included. And has the Executive failed to live up to those reasonable conditions? Well, we will ourselves make that failure good, so that this dangerous fellow (if he is dangerous) need not be set free. The problem with this approach is not only that it steps out of the courts' modest and limited role in a democratic society; but that by repeatedly doing what it thinks the political branches ought to do it encourages their lassitude and saps the vitality of government by the people.[206]

Conclusions

In *Democracy in America*, Alexis de Tocqueville observed that "[m]en living in democratic ages do not readily comprehend the utility of forms: they feel an instinctive contempt for them." He explained the reason: they "commonly aspire to none but easy and present gratifications, they rush onwards to the object of their desires, and the slightest delay exasperates them." Since forms and institutions "perpetually retard and arrest them in some of their projects," their "contempt and often their hatred" are to be expected. Yet, as Tocqueville continued, these very objections to forms and institutions make them all the more necessary. "Their chief merit is to serve as a barrier between the strong and the weak, the ruler and the people, to retard the one and give the other time to look about him," he stated. Their merit and service to freedom continue to increase, for, as the perceptive Tocqueville also observed, "[f]orms become more necessary in proportion as the government becomes more active and more powerful, while private persons are becoming more indolent and more feeble. Thus, democratic nations are naturally more in need of forms than other nations, and they naturally respect them less."[207]

As the cases considered in this chapter indicate, Scalia's approach to separation of powers is much like Tocqueville's approach to forms. He understands the utility of, and need for, separation of powers, especially now that the federal government has become "more active and more powerful." He also recognizes that many of his colleagues on the Court have come to respect separation of powers "less" and even seem to have "an instinctive contempt" for it.

He understands the sense of necessity that leads the popular branches to trample the good fences of separation of powers in various ways: by adopting the independent-counsel statute to deal with alleged criminal misconduct by high-ranking officials of the executive branch; by creating the Sentencing Commission to deal with the inability of Congress and the judges to eliminate sentencing disparities; by providing relief for aggrieved shareholders through instructing federal courts to reopen final judgments; and by attempting to protect endangered species by passing a citizen-suit provision in the ESA that allows individuals who have suffered no concrete injury to sue and thereby compel the act's enforcement but that, by so doing, transfers the president's "Take Care" power to the judiciary. Scalia also understands, however, that a firm adherence to the constitutional principles of separation of powers requires that these measures be "retard[ed] and arrest[ed]," and he has voted accordingly.

He also understands that an instinctive contempt for separation of powers can occur as equally when the good fences are moved by the Court as when they are trampled by the Congress. For Scalia, it was as wrong for the Court in *Mistretta* to ignore an unconstitutional delegation of legislative power as it was for it to find in *Clinton v. City of New York* that Congress had unconstitutionally authorized the president to cancel an item of spending. And it was equally wrong for the

Court to conclude in *Hamdi* that Congress had implicitly suspended the writ of habeas corpus in its Authorization for Use of Military Force Resolution even when it had failed explicitly to do so.

Scalia understands that, in order for the Court to avoid the "contempt and often the hatred" that results from its interference with the wishes of the popular branches, his colleagues have adopted (to use Justice Blackmun's words again) a "pragmatic, flexible view of differentiated governmental power" that permits members of Congress to obtain (in Tocqueville's words) the "object of their desires." Thus, *Morrison*, *Mistretta*, *Plaut*, and *Lujan* are filled with language arguing that the principle of separation of powers is only a "generalized prescription" that the functions of the three branches should not be "commingled too much." Since the justices on the Court understand that they themselves will determine how much commingling is too much, they can claim to be faithful to the principle of separation of powers while winking at the "anomal[ies]" and "innovation[s]" introduced by the popular branches. Against this disregard for separation of powers, Scalia argues that the question of how governmental powers were to be commingled (and how much) was answered once and for all by the Framers and that the duty of the Court is, as he described it in *James B. Beam Distilling Company*, to preserve the division of federal powers as it was "understood when the Constitution was enacted."[208]

And he understands how his colleagues bristle at the way that such "an essential ingredient of separation and equilibration of powers" as standing can "retard and arrest" them in their efforts to reach the merits of a case and "pronounce upon the meaning or the constitutionality of a state or federal law,"[209] as well as why they are so easily persuaded to ignore the three elements that he described in *Lujan* as constituting the "irreducible constitutional minimum of standing."

Scalia also understands that separation of powers is to "serve as a barrier between the strong and the weak." In *Morrison*, he dramatically expressed Tocqueville's insight :

> How frightening it must be to have your own independent counsel and staff appointed, with nothing else to do but to investigate you until investigation is no longer worthwhile — with whether it is worthwhile not depending upon what such judgments usually hinge on, competing responsibilities. And to have that counsel and staff decide, with no basis for comparison, whether what you have done is bad enough, willful enough, and provable enough, to warrant an indictment. How admirable the constitutional system that provides the means to avoid such a distortion. And how unfortunate the judicial decision that has permitted it.[210]

In *Young v. United States ex rel. Vuitton et Fils*, Scalia expressed a similar concern, although this time against the tyrannical potential of judges once freed from the restraints of separation of powers and permitted to hold litigants in contempt as a means of enforcing their judgments: "[P]ermitting a judge to promulgate a rule of behavior, prosecute its violation, and adjudicate whether the violation took place . . . is no less fundamental a threat to liberty than is deprivation of a jury trial, since 'there is no liberty if the power of judging be not separated from the legislative and executive powers.' "[211]

The barrier between the strong and weak that separation of powers is to preserve even exists, Scalia insists, during the War on Terror. "The very core of liberty secured by our Anglo-Saxon system of separated powers has been freedom from indefinite imprisonment at the will of the Executive,"[212] he has stated. That freedom can be suspended only by Congress's formal suspension of the writ of habeas corpus. As he declared in *Hamdi*: "If the situation demands it, the Executive can ask Congress to authorize suspension of the writ—which can be made subject to whatever conditions Congress deems appropriate." The Constitution limits suspension to "cases of rebellion or invasion," but, he noted, "whether the attacks of September 11, 2001, constitute an 'invasion,' and whether those attacks still justify suspension several years later, are questions for Congress rather than this Court."[213]

Scalia clearly has a Tocquevillian appreciation for the utility and need of forms, of separation of powers, of good fences. When Scalia quoted Robert Frost's famous passage that good fences make good neighbors in his majority opinion in *Plaut*, Justice Stephen Breyer, who concurred only in the judgment, was provoked to respond in kind: "As the majority invokes the advice of an American poet, one might consider as well that poet's caution, for he not only notes that 'Something there is that doesn't love a wall,' but also writes, 'Before I built a wall I'd ask to know / What I was walling in or walling out.' "[214] Breyer's selection of these particular passages from Frost highlights the chasm that exists between him and Scalia—and more generally between a majority of the Court and Scalia—concerning separation of powers. Unlike most of his colleagues, including Breyer, Scalia loves the wall of separation of powers. He loves it because, as he said in his *Morrison* dissent, "without a secure structure of separated powers, our Bill of Rights would be worthless." He loves this wall and wants it kept high and strong because, as he noted in *Plaut*, "low walls . . . will not be judicially defensible in the heat of interbranch conflict." He also loves the wall of separation of powers because, as he said in *Morrison*, it was built by and reflects the "judgment of the wise men who constructed our system, and of the people who approved it, and of the two centuries that have shown it to be sound." Additionally, unlike Breyer and those others, Scalia would never quote a passage that implies that it is his job to build the wall and, therefore, his task to decide what to wall in or wall out. True to his text-and-tradition jurisprudence, Scalia would argue that the justices are to secure the wall of separation of powers built by the Framers, not wonder whether it is worthy of their love and certainly not replace it with one of judicial design. The decisions of the Framers concerning constitutional structure are for the justices to secure, not to alter or to second-guess.

Chapter Four

Constitutional Structure and Federalism

When Scalia indicated to Senator Strom Thurmond during his confirmation hearing that the Constitution's longevity was the result of "the structure of government that the original Constitution established,"[1] he was referring not only to separation of powers but also to federalism. Together, these two structural features formed what Madison, in *Federalist* No. 51, had described as that "double security" that arises when power "is first divided between two distinct governments, and then the portion allotted to each, subdivided among distinct and separate institutions."[2] Scalia's textualist understanding and ardent defense of separation of powers were explored in Chapter Three. This chapter examines his understanding and defense of federalism. As the discussion will reveal, his understanding of federalism is less often textually based, and as a consequence, his defense of this structural feature is occasionally inconsistent with his broader jurisprudential principles.[3]

A case presenting a federalism question requires the Court to determine whether a power has been delegated by the Constitution to the federal government or has been reserved to the states. The Court's task is to draw the line between the powers of the federal government and those of the states. This line of demarcation, however, cannot be fixed permanently or precisely. As Chief Justice John Marshall remarked in *McCulloch v. Maryland*, "The question respecting the extent of the powers actually granted, is perpetually arising, and will probably continue to arise, as long as our system shall exist."[4] The answers given by the Court to this perpetually arising question have varied over time but have generally helped to maintain a balance of power between the states and the federal government.

Initially, under Marshall's leadership, the Court drew the line between the powers of these two levels of government in such a way as to benefit the fledgling federal government.[5] Marshall systematically interpreted the Necessary and Proper Clause in *McCulloch*, the Commerce Clause in *Gibbons v. Ogden*,[6] and Article III (creating the federal judiciary) in *Martin v. Hunter's Lessee*[7] and *Cohens v. Virginia*[8] so as to render secure the power and authority of the federal government. His efforts in fact proved so successful and the federal government over time grew so considerably in power that the concern of many justices since the 1930s has been directed toward drawing the line in a manner that will maintain a balance of power between the federal and state governments and ensure the independent existence and agency of the states.

Scalia is no exception in this regard. However, it should be noted from the outset that his interest in protecting federalism has not matched his interest in protecting separation of powers.[9] To begin with, he believes that the principal branch responsible for protecting federalism is the Congress. As he announced during his confirmation hearing, Congress is the "primary defender of the constitutional balance" between the federal government and the states: "It is a principle of the Constitution that there are certain responsibilities that belong to the States and some that belong to the Federal Government, but it is essentially the function of the Congress—the Congress, which takes the same oath to uphold and defend the Constitution that I do as a judge—to have that constitutional prescription in mind when it enacts the laws."[10] Additionally, he understands (even if he does not always act consistently with this understanding) that if the people and their representatives in Congress want the federal government to grow at the expense of the states, there is little the Court can or should do to prevent this growth.[11] As he wrote in *Regulation* magazine in 1979: "[C]onstitutional provisions subsist only as long as they remain not merely imprinted on paper, but also embedded in the thinking of the people. When our people ceased to believe in a federal government of narrowly limited powers, Congress's constitutional interpretation disregarded such limitations, and the courts soon followed."[12]

This chapter focuses on five areas of constitutional law where Scalia has sought to defend federalism by protecting the states from federal control: the negative Commerce Clause, federal preemption of state regulations, federal commandeering of state officials, the state sovereign immunity doctrine, and Congress's enforcement power under § 5 of the Fourteenth Amendment. The discussion begins with areas of law where Scalia's textualism is on full display and moves to areas where his textualism all but disappears, allowing him to write, as he does in *Blatchford v. Native Village of Noatak*, that the Eleventh Amendment "stand[s] not so much for what it says, but for the presupposition . . . which it confirms."[13]

The "Negative" Commerce Clause

From his first term on the Court, Scalia has consistently opposed what he calls the Court's "'negative' Commerce Clause jurisprudence,"[14] which holds that the Commerce Clause of Article I, § 8 not only grants power to Congress to regulate commerce among the states but also confers power on the Court to protect the "right to engage in interstate trade free from restrictive state regulation."[15] This jurisprudence holds that "the very purpose of the Commerce Clause was to create an area of free trade among the several States" and that the clause "by *its own force* created an area of trade free from interference by the States."[16] Therefore, irrespective of whether Congress has itself acted on the basis of its delegated power to prohibit this interference, the Court's negative Commerce Clause jurisprudence holds that the Court is constitutionally authorized to protect this area of free trade and to vindicate this right to engage in interstate commerce free from state interference by weighing the burdens that state regulation of commerce imposes against the benefits it provides and invalidating all discriminatory burdens it concludes are unjustified.[17]

Scalia has opposed this negative Commerce Clause jurisprudence, which serves as a major limitation on the power of the states. He has opposed it, first and foremost, because it has "no foundation in the text of the Constitution."[18] As he declared in *American Trucking Association v. Smith,*

> The text from which we take our authority to act in this field provides only
> that "Congress shall have Power . . . to regulate Commerce . . . among the
> several States." It is nothing more than a grant of power to Congress, not
> the courts; and that grant to Congress cannot be read as being exclusive
> of the States, as even a casual comparison with other provisions of Article
> I will reveal. The Commerce Clause, therefore, may properly be thought
> to prohibit state regulation of commerce only indirectly — that is, to the
> extent that Congress' exercise of its Commerce Clause powers pre-empts
> state legislation under the Supremacy Clause, Art. VI, cl. 2.[19]

He has opposed the negative Commerce Clause as well because it takes the Court, "self-consciously and avowedly, beyond the judicial role itself" and casts it in an "essentially legislative role." It requires the justices to weigh "the imponderable" and balance "the importance of the State's interest in this or that (an importance that different citizens would assess differently) against the degree of impairment of commerce."[20] This weighing and balancing by the Court, he argues, is often impossible, for the political interests on the opposite sides of the scale are often "incommensurate." As he noted in *Bendix Autolite Corp. v. Midwesco Enterprise,* the Court is often asked to judge "whether a particular line is longer than a particular rock is heavy," a role inconsistent with its "function as the nonpolitical branch." Weighing "the governmental interests of a State against the needs of interstate commerce is," he insists, "a task squarely within the responsibility of Congress."[21]

Scalia argues that the Supreme Court initially alluded to the doctrine of the negative Commerce Clause in 1852 in *Cooley v. Board of Wardens of the Port of Philadelphia*[22] and formally adopted it twenty-one years later in the *Case of the State Freight Tax.*[23] In that 1873 case, Justice William Strong, speaking for a seven-member majority, declared that preventing "embarrassing restrictions" on "the transportation of articles of trade from one State to another was the prominent idea in the minds of the framers of the Constitution, when to Congress was committed the power to regulate commerce among the several States,"[24] and that, therefore, even in the absence of congressional legislation regulating interstate commerce, "no State can impose a tax upon freight transported from State to State" and any attempt to do so provides grounds for the Court to declare it "unconstitutional and void."[25] Once adopted, the doctrine would go largely unquestioned for well over a century,[26] until Scalia in *Tyler Pipe Industries v. Washington State Department of Revenue*—his first negative Commerce Clause case during his first term on the Court—launched a comprehensive and well-thought-out attack against it, declaring that it made "no sense."[27] His many subsequent opinions on the doctrine have invariably cited *Tyler Pipe* and served primarily to elaborate on themes he introduced in it.

In *Tyler Pipe*, the Court found that a Washington State manufacturing tax imposed only on in-state goods sold to out-of-state purchasers discriminated against interstate commerce, in violation of the Commerce Clause. Scalia dissented on two grounds. First, he denied that this particular tax had a discriminatory effect. As he put it, "An in-state manufacturer selling in-state pays one tax to Washington; an in-state manufacturer selling out-of-state pays one tax to Washington; and an out-of-state manufacturer selling in-state pays one tax to Washington. The State collects the same tax whether interstate or intrastate commerce is involved."[28] But second and more important, he attacked the very idea of a negative Commerce Clause, for even if the tax did have a discriminatory effect on interstate commerce, he argued that it was up to Congress (and not the Court) to prohibit such discrimination because the Framers gave the power to regulate interstate commerce to the Congress (and not the Court).[29]

In elaborating upon this second point, Scalia directed his readers to the text of Article I, § 8, which states that "Congress shall have Power . . . to regulate Commerce with foreign Nations, and among the several States, and with the Indian Tribes." This language, he noted, provides no support "for judicial 'enforcement' of the Commerce Clause," for "on its face, this is a charter for Congress, not the courts, to ensure 'an area of trade free from interference by the States.'"[30]

Scalia then set about systematically to refute the arguments made by those who endorsed the doctrine of the negative Commerce Clause. He began by addressing the contention that the Court's power to apply its negative Commerce Clause jurisprudence "automatically follow[s]" because the Constitution's grant of power to Congress to regulate interstate commerce is "exclusive." Scalia conceded that this was an argument that "John Marshall at one point [in *Gibbons v.*

Ogden[31]] seemed to believe";[32] it was also the argument that Justice Strong made for the Court when it formally adopted the idea of the negative Commerce Clause in the *Case of the State Freight Tax.* As Strong wrote:

> In the earlier decisions of this court it was said to have been so entirely vested in Congress that no part of it can be exercised by a State. It has, indeed, often been argued, and sometimes intimated, by the court that, so far as Congress has not legislated on the subject, the States may legislate respecting interstate commerce. Yet, if they can, why may they not add regulations to commerce with foreign nations beyond those made by Congress, if not inconsistent with them, for the power over both foreign and interstate commerce is conferred upon the Federal legislature by the same words. And certainly it has never yet been decided by this court that the power to regulate interstate, as well as foreign commerce, is not exclusively in Congress.[33]

Scalia demonstrated, however, that the argument for an exclusive Commerce Clause simply cannot be sustained. Turning first to the constitutional text, he noted that, "unlike the District Clause, which empowers Congress 'to exercise exclusive Legislation,' Article I, § 8, cl. 17, the language of the Commerce Clause gives no indication of exclusivity." Many of Congress's Article I powers "plainly coexist with concurrent authority in the States," and as he observed, "there is no correlative denial of power over commerce to the States in Art. I, § 10, as there is, for example, with the power to coin money or make treaties."[34]

He turned next to the "historical record" and found that it provided no more support for an exclusive Commerce Clause than the text of the Constitution itself. "The strongest evidence," he contended, "in favor of a negative Commerce Clause—that version of it which renders federal authority over interstate commerce exclusive—is Madison's comment during the Convention: 'Whether the States are now restrained from laying tonnage duties depends on the extent of the power to regulate commerce. These terms are vague but seem to exclude this power of the States.'" But as Scalia observed, this comment came during discussion of what became part of Article I, § 10: "No State shall, without the Consent of Congress, lay any Duty on Tonnage." This prompted him to remark: "The fact that it is difficult to conceive how the power to regulate commerce would *not* include the power to impose duties; and the fact that, despite this apparent coverage, the Convention went on to adopt a provision prohibiting States from levying duties on tonnage without congressional approval; suggest that Madison's assumption of exclusivity of the federal commerce power was ill considered and not generally shared."[35]

Against this "mere shadow of historical support," he pointed to "the over-whelming reality that the Commerce Clause, in its broad outlines, was not a major subject of controversy, either during the constitutional debates or in the rat-ifying conventions." The records, he continued, "disclose no constructive criti-cisms by the states of the commerce clause as proposed to them." Scalia quoted Madison in *Federalist* No. 45, who described the Commerce Clause as an addi-tion to the powers of the national government "which few oppose and from which no apprehensions are entertained," and he concluded that "I think it beyond ques-tion that many 'apprehensions' would have been 'entertained' if supporters of the Constitution had hinted that the Commerce Clause, despite its language, gave this Court the power it has since assumed."[36]

Finally, he concluded by noting that "the exclusivity rationale is infinitely less attractive today" than it was at the time of the Constitution's adoption and ratifi-cation. He stated, "Now that we know interstate commerce embraces such activ-ities as growing wheat for home consumption, *Wickard v. Filburn*,[37] and local loan sharking, *Perez v. United States*,[38] it is more difficult to imagine what state activ-ity would survive an exclusive Commerce Clause than to imagine what would be precluded."[39]

Scalia then turned to the "theoretical justification for judicial enforcement of the Commerce Clause," asserted as dicta in *Cooley v. Board of Wardens*, that "whatever subjects of this power are in their nature national, or admit only of one uniform system, or plan of regulation, may justly be said to be of such a nature as to require exclusive legislation by Congress." He acknowledged that this "would perhaps be a wise rule to adopt," but, he continued, "it is hard to see why judges rather than legislators are fit to determine what areas of commerce 'in their nature' require national regulation."[40] As he would later elaborate in *American Trucking Association v. Smith*, the doctrine that judges should enforce the Commerce Clause requires that they ask "what would a reasonable federal regulator of com-merce intend—which is no different from the question a legislator himself must ask." And when judges ask these questions, they render the negative Commerce Clause "inherently unpredictable"—not just because its "standards" have been poorly and inconsistently applied but also because it requires "courts to accom-modate, like a legislature, the inevitably shifting variables of a national economy." As he continued, "Whatever it is that we are expounding in this area, it is not a Constitution."[41]

Finally, Scalia addressed in *Tyler Pipe* what he termed "the least plausible the-oretical justification of all," namely, "that in enforcing the negative Commerce Clause the Court is not applying a constitutional command at all, but is merely interpreting the will of Congress, whose silence in certain fields of interstate commerce (but not in others) is to be taken as a prohibition of regulation." As he pointed out, "There is no conceivable reason why congressional inaction under the Commerce Clause should be deemed to have the same pre-emptive effect elsewhere accorded only to congressional action."[42] He elaborated on this matter as well in his concurrence in *American Trucking Association v. Smith*: "When we prohibit a certain form of state regulation that does not conflict with any federal statute we are saying, in effect, that we presume from Congress' silence that, in the exercise of its commerce-regulating function, it means to prohibit state regulation." However, presuming law from congressional silence is "quite different from the normal judicial task of interpreting and applying text, or determining and applying common-law tradition."[43] Moreover, as he reminded his colleagues in *Tyler Pipe*, Congress can act only by an affirmative vote of both houses, and it is a "recurring fallacy" to treat congressional inaction as the equivalent of either "permissive or prohibitory legislation."[44]

Scalia concluded his attack on the negative Commerce Clause in *Tyler Pipe* by declaring that "the Court for over a century has engaged in an enterprise that it has been unable to justify by textual support or even coherent nontextual theory, that it was almost certainly not intended to undertake, and that it has not undertaken very well." For him, there is no "national free market" unless Congress affirmatively employs its Commerce Clause powers to create one,[45] and therefore, the Court on its own is never constitutionally authorized to keep interstate trade free from discriminatory state regulation. He did not deny that the Court had a limited power to guard against one state engaging in "rank discrimination against citizens of other states," but, he insisted, its power to do so "is regulated not by the Commerce Clause but by the Privileges and Immunities Clause, U.S. Const., Art. IV, § 2, cl. 1 ('The Citizens of each State shall be entitled to all Privileges and Immunities of Citizens in the several States.')."[46]

At that moment, his textualist approach to constitutional interpretation was clearly evident. The text of the Commerce Clause expressly gives Congress the power to regulate interstate commerce if and to the extent it chooses to do so; it is found in Article I, § 8, which begins with the words "Congress shall have power." By contrast, the text of the Privileges and Immunities Clause authorizes the Court, among other matters, to prohibit one state from "imposing unreasonable burdens on citizens of other states in their pursuit of common callings within the state."[47] But, consistent with Scalia's conviction that textualism is a means of constraining judicial discretion,[48] it does not extend to the Court the same invitation to assume a legislative role that the negative Commerce Clause does. As Justice Bushrod Washington noted in *Corfield v. Coryell*, the first major consideration of the Privileges and Immunities Clause, the Court is limited by its terms to invalidating burdens that are unreasonable, and, he concluded, it was not unreasonable for New Jersey to favor its own residents and to limit harvesting oyster beds in New Jersey waters to residents of New Jersey.[49] The only economic discriminations that justify judicial invalidation are those that, in the words of Justice Blackmun in *Baldwin v. Montana Fish and Game Commission*, touch on "basic and essential activities, interference with which would frustrate the purposes of the formation of the Union,"[50] or those, in the words of Scalia in *Tyler Pipe*, that are "rank discriminations."[51]

Scalia's sustained attack on the negative Commerce Clause has had little or no impact thus far. His criticisms of it have typically occurred in solitary dissents or concurrences in the judgments of the Court.[52] He has been unable to convince his colleagues that the Court has been mistaken since 1873 when it began reading the Commerce Clause as containing a "self-operative prohibition upon the states' regulation of commerce."[53] Given his failure to reverse the Court's direction and given his commitment to stare decisis, he has been forced to be content with attempting to restrict any further expansion of the doctrine. In *Itel Containers International Corporation v. Huddleston*, he announced that "on *stare decisis* grounds," he would "enforce a self-executing, 'negative' Commerce Clause in two circumstances."[54] The first would be "against a state law that facially discriminates against interstate commerce,"[55] and the second would be "against a state law that is indistinguishable from a type of law previously held unconstitutional by this Court."[56]

But even here, his efforts have been unavailing, as his dissent in *Camps Newfound/Owatonna v. Harrison* so clearly shows.[57] In this 1997 case, a five-member majority of the Court held that a Maine property tax exemption for charitable institutions that excluded organizations operating principally for the benefit of nonresidents violated the negative Commerce Clause. In a passionate dissent, joined by Chief Justice Rehnquist and Justices Thomas and Ginsburg, Scalia proclaimed that "the Court's negative-commerce-clause jurisprudence has drifted far from its moorings." He was especially angered that the Court had expanded the doctrine to such an extent that it could now reach a state's tax exemption that excused from taxation "only that property used to relieve the state of its burden of caring for its residents." Once the doctrine was employed only "to create a national market for commercial activity," but "it is today invoked to prevent a state from giving a tax break to charities that benefit the state's inhabitants."[58]

Scalia denied that Maine's tax exemption had anything to do with interstate commerce or "economic protectionism."[59] All it did was to allow the state "to provide some of its social services indirectly—by compensating or subsidizing private charitable providers." And since "a state that provides social services directly may limit its largesse to its own residents," he saw no reason why it could not impose the same limitation indirectly.[60] And even if it did "indirectly affect" interstate commerce, he denied that it was facially discriminatory: "Disparate treatment constitutes discrimination only if the objects of the disparate treatment are, for the relevant purposes, similarly situated." However, he observed, "for purposes of entitlement to a tax subsidy from the State, it is certainly reasonable to think that property gratu-itously devoted to relieving the State of some of its welfare burden is not similarly situated to property used 'principally for the benefit of persons who are not residents of [the state].' "[61]

Scalia was angered and frustrated not only by the Court's expansion of the reach of the negative Commerce Clause but also by its elimination of any need on its part to consider the grounds on which a statute (in this case, Maine's tax exemption) that it has concluded facially discriminates against interstate com-merce could be justified. Until *Camps Newfound/Owatonna*, facially discrimina-tory statutes were not regarded as per se invalid but had been analyzed by the Court's use of the "strict scrutiny" test; in this case, however, the Court did not proceed to inquire "whether the purposes of the tax exemption *justify* its favoritism."[62] Had members of the majority engaged in this analysis, Scalia argued, they would have concluded that the tax exemption "is supported by such tradi-tional and important state interests that it survives scrutiny . . . or on the ground that there is a 'domestic charity' exception (just as there is a 'public utility' excep-tion) to the negative Commerce Clause."[63]

Federal Preemption

When Congress enters a field in which it is authorized by the Constitution to act, its legislation supersedes or preempts all incompatible state regulations under the Supremacy Clause.[64] This rule of statutory construction is simple to state but dif-ficult for the Court to apply, and how the Court and its individual justices apply it can affect the balance of power between the federal government and the states.

This rule is difficult to apply because, in the first place, a state may deny that its regulation is incompatible with federal law. In *California Coastal Commission v. Granite Rock Co.*, for example, California insisted that its statute requiring a permit from the California Coastal Commission for anyone who undertakes min-ing in a designated coastal zone was not preempted by the Mining Act of 1872 (which preempted state regulation of mining on federal land) because the state was regulating the environment and not land use.[65] Likewise, in *City of Colum-bus v. Ours Garage and Wrecker Service*, Columbus, Ohio, maintained that its safety regulation of tow-truck operators was not preempted by a federal trans-portation law because the statute had excepted from preemption the safety regu-lations of motor vehicles of "a State" and that term should be understood to include its political subdivisions (even though elsewhere but not here, the same statute had specifically excepted from preemption other specified transportation regulations by "a State or a political subdivision of a State").[66] And in *Kentucky Association of Health Plans, Inc. v. Miller*, the state of Kentucky argued that its "any willing provider" (AWP) statutes, prohibiting health insurers from discriminating against health-care providers who were willing to meet the insurers' conditions,[67] were not preempted by the Employee Retirement Income Security Act of 1974 (ERISA), a federal statute that regulates employee welfare benefit plans and generally preempts state laws related to such plans because it specifically excepts from preemption state laws regulating insurance.[68]

This rule of statutory construction is also difficult to apply because, alternatively, a state may argue that its regulation does not contradict but rather goes beyond what Congress requires and that, in the absence of clear language by Congress expressly preempting states from entering the field altogether, its supplementary regulation is not incompatible. An example is *Wisconsin Public Intervenor v. Mortier,* in which Wisconsin argued that the Federal Insecticide, Fungicide, and Rodenticide Act (FIFRA), a comprehensive regulatory statute, did not preempt the regulation of pesticides by local governments because it contained no explicit language preempting local regulation of pesticide use.[69] *Morales v. Trans World Airlines* provides another example: Texas argued that a provision of the Airline Deregulation Act of 1978, which prohibited states from enforcing laws "relating to rates, routes, or services" of any air carrier, did not preempt it from enforcing, through its consumer protection laws, restrictions on deceptive advertising and other trade practices by the airlines concerning fares, fare availability, disclosure of round-trip fares, inclusion of taxes and surcharges, and the like.[70]

Scalia invariably applies this rule of statutory construction by employing a textualist approach. As he declared in his opinion for the Court in *Morales,* Congress's decision to preempt can be stated "explicitly" in the statute's text or contained "implicitly" in "its structure and purpose." The goal for him in all preemption cases is neither to enhance federal power nor to protect state power; rather, it is to identify "statutory intent," which he does by beginning with "the language employed" by either the federal or state lawmakers as well as with "the assumption that the ordinary meaning of that language accurately expresses the legislative purpose."[71]

His textualist approach is obvious in cases where the question for the Court concerns whether a state regulation is in fact incompatible with federal regulation. Thus, in *Granite Rock,* Scalia turned to the language of the California Coastal Act. He found that the permit in question was to be granted "if the proposed development is in conformity with a state-approved local coastal program," and he noted that "the 'local coastal programs' to which these provisions refer consist of two parts: (1) a land use plan, and (2) zoning ordinances, zoning maps, and other implementing efforts."[72] For Scalia, that resolved the matter: "[I]t could hardly be clearer that the California Coastal Act is land use regulation." Moreover, the fact that California had designated its Coastal Act as its coastal management plan for purposes of complying with the federal Coastal Zone Management Act "com-pound[ed] the certainty" because the requirements of such a program include "a definition of what shall constitute permissible land uses and water uses within the coastal zone."[73] He therefore filed a sharp dissent, declaring that "we should not allow California to claim, in the teeth of the plain language of its legislation, . . . [that] its Coastal Act . . . [imposes] only environmental controls."[74] The language of the act made it clear for him that the "permit requirement constitutes a regu-lation of land use of federal land and is therefore pre-empted by federal law."[75]

Likewise, in *Ours Garage*, Scalia sought his answer to the key question — whether Congress intended its transportation statute to except from preemption the safety regulations not only of "a State" but also of "a political subdivision of a State"—by carefully reading the language of the statute. When he did so, he found that "[i]t is impossible to read this text without being struck by the fact that the term 'political subdivision of a State' is *added* to the term 'State' in some of the exceptions but *not* in the exception at issue here."[76] He concluded that the "only conceivable reason for this specification of 'political subdivision' apart from 'State' is *to establish*, in the rule, the two *separate categories* of state power—state power exercised through political subdivisions and state power exercised by the State directly—that are later treated differently in the exceptions to the rule."[77] Yet, unlike the Congress that had intended these two categories to be treated differ-ently, the Court majority treated them as the same, causing "the text's crystal-clear distinction between state and local authority to disappear" and prompting Scalia to dissent.[78] He offered the following analogy to drive his point home:

> The situation is comparable to the following hypothetical using the term "football" (which may be used to include soccer): Assume a statute which says that "football and soccer shall not be played on the town green," except that "football and soccer may be played on Saturdays," "football and soccer may be played on summer nights," and "football may be played on Mondays." In today's opinion, the Court says soccer may be played on Mondays. I think it clear that soccer is not to be regarded as a subset of football but as a separate category. And the same is true of "politi-cal subdivision" here.[79]

Scalia's criticism of the Court majority for engaging in a statutory construc-tion of the statute that rendered "utterly superfluous"[80] Congress's use of the term *political subdivision of a state* necessitated that the majority "invoke federalism concerns to justify its decision." Scalia remained unpersuaded. Given Congress's "clear and manifest" intention not to except the "political subdivisions of a State" from preemption concerning safety regulations of motor vehicles and given the fact that there was a long history of the federal government's interference with the power of the states to control the relationship between themselves and their political subdivisions, Scalia found the Court's "federalism concerns . . . overblown"[81] and, in fact, "absurd."[82]

Similarly, in *Kentucky Association of Health Plans, Inc. v. Miller,* Scalia turned to the text of ERISA to determine whether Kentucky's AWP statutes were incompatible with its language. If the statutes in question were understood to be related to employee benefit plans, then they were incompatible because § 1144(a) of ERISA specifically preempts all state laws "insofar as they may now or hereafter relate to any employee benefit plan." If, by contrast, they were understood to regulate insurance, they were not incompatible because § 1144(b) of ERISA specifically excepts from preemption all state laws "which regulate insurance." The petitioners—several health maintenance organizations—argued that Kentucky's AWP statutes did not regulate insurance because they did not regulate an insurance practice. For a unanimous Court, Scalia provided a "common sense" construction of the word *regulate* by reasoning as follows:[83]

> Suppose a state law required all licensed attorneys to participate in 10 hours of continuing legal education (CLE) each year. This statute "regulates" the practice of law—even though sitting through 10 hours of CLE classes does not constitute the practice of law—because the state has *conditioned* the right to practice law on certain requirements, which substantially affect the product delivered by lawyers to their clients. Kentucky's AWP laws operate in a similar manner with respect to the insurance industry: Those who wish to provide health insurance in Kentucky (any "health insurer") may not discriminate against any willing provider.[84]

Scalia's textualism is no less apparent in cases where the state argues that its regulation does not supplant but rather supplements federal law and is therefore not preempted because it is not incompatible. In *Mortier,* for example, Scalia concurred with the Court majority that "FIFRA does not pre-empt the local regulation" because "the terms of the statute do not alone manifest a pre-emption of the entire field of pesticide regulation."[85] For him, nothing more needed to be said.[86]

In *Morales,* he concluded for a five-member majority that Texas' efforts to prohibit allegedly deceptive airline fare advertisements through the enforcement of its general consumer protection statutes did not supplement the Airline Deregulation Act of 1978 but rather contradicted it by violating § 1305 (a)(1) of the act, which prohibited states from "enacting or enforcing any law, rule, regulation, standard, or other provision having the force and effect of law relating to rates, routes, or services of any air carrier."[87] The "key phrase," as Scalia pointed out, was "relating to." And "the ordinary meaning of these words is a broad one—'to stand in some relation; to have bearing or concern; to pertain; refer; to bring into association with or connection with,' *Black's Law Dictionary* 1158 (5th ed. 1979)—and the words thus express a broad pre-emptive purpose."[88] Texas had argued that the act only preempted the states from actually prescribing rates, routes, or services. But as Scalia pointed out, "This simply reads the words 'relating to' out of the statute. Had the statute been designed to pre-empt state law in such a limited fashion, it would have forbidden the States to '*regulate* rates, routes, and services.'"[89] And since Scalia's textualism focuses on what is not only explicit in the text's language but also implicit in its structure, he continued, declaring: "[I]f the pre-emption effected by § 1305(a)(1) were such a limited one, no purpose would be served by the very next subsection, which preserves to the States certain proprietary rights over airports."[90]

As is apparent from the cases reviewed thus far, Scalia's textualist approach to preemption is not biased toward either the federal government or the states; rather, it is designed to determine, to use his memorable words in *Puerto Rico Department of Consumer Affairs v. Isla Petroleum Corp.*, whether there is "a pre-emptive grin" on Congress's "statutory cat."[91]

In reaching that determination, he consistently refuses to consider legislative history, and his refusal to do so works to the advantage of the states.[92] He repeatedly reminds his colleagues that "unenacted approvals, beliefs, and desires are not laws" and that "[t]here is no federal pre-emption *in vacuo*, without a constitutional text or a federal statute to assert it."[93] Put another way, the grin must be on the lawmakers' statutory cat, not on the lawmakers themselves. Thus, in *Isla Petroleum*, after concluding that the test for federal preemption of the law of Puerto Rico is the same as the test for the preemption of the law of a state,[94] he wrote that, in the absence of textual language, "excerpts from the legislative history" of a statute can never provide the Court with grounds for preempting state law.[95] And in *Mortier*, he objected to "the practice of utilizing legislative history for the purpose of giving authoritative content to the meaning of a statutory text,"[96] which led the Court majority in that case to question whether FIFRA's clear text excepting local pesticide regulation from preemption could be trumped by comments in Senate committee reports.

Scalia's most extensive criticism of the use of legislative history in a preemption case came in his concurrence in *Mortier*. In determining that FIFRA did not preempt the regulation of pesticides by local governments, the Court majority relied heavily on the fact that none of the three congressional committees that had jurisdiction over the bill asserted in their committee reports that FIFRA preempted the field of pesticide regulation. Scalia faulted his colleagues for "failing to recognize how unreliable Committee Reports are—not only as a genuine indicator of congressional intent but as a safe predictor of judicial construction. We use them when it is convenient, and ignore them when it is not."[97] He also faulted them for relying on action on the Senate floor. In reaching its conclusion concerning the preemptive effect of FIFRA, the majority also found it significant that the full Senate rejected an amendment offered by the Commerce Committee that would have "changed the result of the supposed interpretation." But as Scalia observed,

> the full Senate could have rejected that *either* because a majority of its Members disagreed with the Commerce Committee's proposed policy; *or* because they disagreed with the Commerce Committee's . . . interpretation (and thus thought the amendment superfluous); *or* because they were blissfully ignorant of the entire dispute and simply thought that the Commerce Committee, by asking for recommittal and proposing 15 amendments, was being a troublemaker; *or* because three different minorities (enough to make a majority) had each of these respective reasons. We have no way of knowing.[98]

"All we know for sure," he continued, "is that the full Senate adopted the text that we have before us here, as did the full House, pursuant to the procedures prescribed by the Constitution; and that that text, having been transmitted to the President and approved by him, again pursuant to the procedures prescribed by the Constitution, became law."[99] And it was on that text, and on that text alone, that Scalia wanted to focus his (and the Court's) attention.

When, however, Scalia determines that the statutory cat is sporting a preemptive grin,[100] he will give it full preemptive effect, and that, of course, works to the advantage of the federal government.[101] For example, he dissented vigorously in *Cipollone v. Liggett Group, Inc.*, when the Court held that federal cigarette labeling and advertising statutes did not preempt all state-law damage claims with respect to cigarette smoking because even express preemptive provisions must occasionally be given "the narrowest possible construction" in order not to supersede "the historic police powers of the states."[102] In his view, there was "no merit to this newly crafted doctrine of narrow construction. Under the Supremacy Clause, our job is to interpret Congress's decrees of pre-emption neither narrowly nor broadly, but in accordance with their apparent meaning."[103] Moreover, the Court's narrow construction yielded "extraordinary" results: "The statute that says *anything* about pre-emption must say *everything*; and it must do so with great exactitude, as any ambiguity concerning its scope will be read in favor of preserving state power. If this is to be the law, surely only the most sporting of Congresses will dare to say anything about pre-emption."[104]

Finally, on those occasions when Scalia is unable to determine definitively whether the statutory cat has a preemptive grin or not, he will deny the statute any preemptive effect. As he said in *BFP v. Resolution Trust Corporation,* "Where the intent to override is doubtful, our federal system demands deference to long-established traditions of state regulation."[105]

Federal Commandeering of State Officials

In 1992, for the first time in U.S. history, the Supreme Court in *New York v. United States* declared a federal law to be unconstitutional because it commanded state officials to execute its provisions.[106] The Court did so on the grounds that "commandeering" or "conscripting"[107] state officials "infringe[s] upon the core of state sovereignty reserved by the Tenth Amendment" and is "inconsistent with the federal structure of our Government established by the Constitution."[108] Scalia joined Justice O'Connor's majority opinion, although her argument must have offended his textualist sensibilities. After all, she found the statute in question to be unconstitutional either because it was "outside Congress's enumerated powers" or because it was "inconsistent with the federal structure of our Government established by the Constitution."[109] She saw no need to decide which it was because, "[i]n the end, just as a cup may be half empty or half full, it makes no difference whether one views the question at issue in the case as one of ascertaining the limits of the power delegated to the Federal Government under the affirmative provisions of the Constitution or one of discerning the core of sovereignty retained by the States under the Tenth Amendment."[110] And to make matters worse, after she announced that the Tenth Amendment is no more than a "truism" and "essentially a tautology" and that no "limit" on Congress's power can be derived from its "text," she nonetheless insisted that it "directs us to determine, as in this case, whether an incident of state sovereignty is protected by a limitation on an Article I power."[111]

The issue of commandeering state officials surfaced again in *Printz v. United States,*[112] as the Court considered the constitutionality of that provision of the Brady Handgun Violence Prevention Act of 1993 that commanded state and local law-enforcement officers temporarily to conduct background checks on prospective handgun purchasers. In a five-to-four decision, Scalia found this congressional command to be "fundamentally incompatible with our constitutional system of dual sovereignty" and therefore unconstitutional.[113] On the surface, he appears to have simply embraced O'Connor's arguments in *New York.* However, a closer reading of his opinion makes it clear that his understanding of commandeering is quite different and much narrower; though he gains the votes of his colleagues by writing of state sovereignty and proclaiming the Court's decision in *New York* to be "conclusive,"[114] he ultimately limits Congress's power to commandeer state officials not to protect federalism but because the text of the Constitution clearly prohibits it.

As a textualist, he readily acknowledged in *Printz* that there was "no constitutional text" specifically prohibiting Congress from commandeering state officials; it was free to do so as long as it was acting pursuant to an express delegation of power enumerated in Article I, § 8.[115] There was, however, the "constitutional text" of Article II, § 3, which declares that the president "shall take Care that the Laws be faithfully executed." And for Scalia, it was that text that required the Court to invalidate the commandeering provision of the Brady Act.

As has already been discussed at some length in Chapter Three, Scalia employed in *Printz* an argument that came directly from his dissent in *Morrison v. Olson*.[116] He found Congress's commandeering of state and local law-enforcement officers to conduct background checks to be unconstitutional because Congress effectively had transferred the president's textually explicit constitutional duty to "take Care that the Laws be faithfully executed" to thousands of state and local law-enforcement officers. For him, the tautological Tenth Amendment provided the Court with no warrant to protect the sovereignty of the states and limit Congress's ability to commandeer, but the text of Article II, § 3 and the critical structural principle of separation of powers implicit in that text did;[117] they obliged the Court to invalidate all measures that allowed the Congress to "act as effectively without the President as with him, by simply requiring state officers to execute its laws,"[118] for such measures would "shatter" unity in the executive, "reduce" the powers of the president, and thereby fundamentally alter the structural principle of separation of powers.[119]

Scalia sugarcoated his separation of powers argument (with its textualist reliance on Article II, § 3) with a defense of federalism. This, however, was the price he was willing to pay to transform his solitary defense of separation of powers in his *Morrison* dissent into the opinion of the Court in *Printz*. And proof that his rhetorical defense of federalism was only that—rhetorical—is found in his textualist approach to commandeering in *Branch v. Smith*.[120] This 2003 decision dealt with the consequences of the 2000 census (reducing Mississippi's seats in the U.S. House of Representatives from five to four) and the failure of the state to pass a new congressional redistricting plan. Mississippi law provided, in pertinent part, that if an election of representatives occurred after the number of representatives to which the state was entitled had been diminished as a result of a new apportionment—and before the state's districts had been changed to conform to the new apportionment—then the representatives would be elected at large. However, a 1967 federal law provided the contrary; it declared that in each state entitled to more than one representative under an apportionment, a number of districts, equal to the number of representatives to which the state was entitled, would be established "by law," and representatives would be elected only from districts so established, with no district electing more than one representative. Scalia held for the majority that a federal district court had acted properly when it enjoined a Mississippi court's congressional redistricting plan (because it had not been precleared under § 5 of the Voting Rights Act) and then proceeded to fashion its own plan rather than ordering at-large elections.

In her dissent, Justice O'Connor invoked the "Court's anti-commandeering jurisprudence," specifically mentioning *New York* and *Printz*; she argued that Congress lacked the power to pass the 1967 statute directly compelling a state to elect representatives from single-member districts.[121] Scalia responded that Congress's enactment of the 1967 statute was supported by a clear constitutional text: Article I, § 4, cl. 1, which obligates states to prescribe the "Times, Places, and Manner" of holding congressional elections and authorizes Congress "at any time" to "make or alter such regulations."[122] O'Connor replied that "Article I, § 8 uses similar language when it authorizes Congress to 'regulate Commerce . . . among the several States'"; she thereby raised the question "[w]hether the anticommandeering principle of *New York* and *Printz* is as robust in the Article I, § 4 context (the font of congressional authority here) as it is in the Article I, § 8 context (the source of congressional authority in those cases)."[123]

Although she quickly withdrew the question and announced that it need not "be definitively resolved here," Scalia did so nonetheless and, in the process, dismissed her "anticommandeering" argument as a "straw man."[124] His answer was this: a statute commandeering state officials will be affirmed, as in *Branch*, if the Constitution gives Congress express power to do so, as it did in Article I, § 4, and it will be struck down, as in *Printz*, if it interferes with the president's specific "Take Care" power as found in Article II, § 3. Any concerns the Court might have concerning the impact of these statutes on federalism are irrelevant, as the Framers of the Constitution clearly determined in both instances that other principles (uniformity in the manner of elections or unity in the executive) have priority and expressly wrote them into the text of the Constitution. Only in an instance such as *New York*, in which Congress was relying on its broadly enumerated powers under Article I, § 8 and in which there was no constitutional language specifically authorizing commandeering of state officials, may the Court invalidate a commandeering statute, but even then, it can do so only if the statute reduces the residuary sovereignty of the states in ways that go beyond what the Framers of the Constitution had expressly authorized in its text.

The State Sovereign Immunity Doctrine

The Court's doctrine of state sovereign immunity, i.e., the doctrine that a state cannot be sued in federal court without its consent, has developed against the backdrop of four key documents: Article III, § 2 of the Constitution, the Judiciary

Act of 1789, the Supreme Court's decision in *Chisholm v. Georgia*,[175] and the Eleventh Amendment. A brief consideration of the texts of these key documents is necessary to appreciate Scalia's nontextual approach to this doctrine.

The relevant provisions of Article III, § 2 declare that the "judicial Power of the United States shall extend to all cases, in Law and Equity, arising under this Constitution, the Laws of the United States, and Treaties made, or which shall be made under their authority," as well as "to Controversies . . . between a State and Citizens of another State." It proceeds to give the federal judiciary jurisdiction to hear such cases "with such exceptions and under such regulations as the Congress shall make."[126] Jurisdiction in cases "arising under" the Constitution, federal law, and treaties is commonly referred to as "arising under" or "federal question" or "subject matter" jurisdiction. Jurisdiction in cases involving a state and citizens of another state is known as "state citizen diversity" jurisdiction.[127]

Article III, § 2 is utterly silent on the question of whether federal courts have state citizen diversity jurisdiction only in cases "where a State is Plaintiff, but not where it is Defendant."[128] Nowhere in the Constitution is there announced a principle of state sovereign immunity. The Framers may have taken the principle for granted and thought there was no need to specify that the federal courts would provide states a forum in which to sue, but not reciprocally to be sued by, citizens of other states, foreign nations, or aliens. This clearly was the view expressed in *Federalist* No. 81 by Alexander Hamilton, who found the idea that Article III, § 2 implied the destruction of the principle of state sovereign immunity to be "altogether forced and unwarrantable."[129]

By contrast, the Framers may have understood that the very idea of state sovereign immunity had its origins in feudalism and was therefore inconsistent with the principles of the American Revolution. As Chief Justice John Jay (along with Hamilton and James Madison, one of the authors of *The Federalist*) wrote in his opinion in *Chisholm*, the English common-law notion of sovereign immunity was based "on feudal principles. That system considers the Prince as the sovereign, and the people as his subjects; it regards his person as the object of allegiance, and excludes the idea of his being on an equal footing with a subject, either in a Court of Justice or elsewhere." In a system that contemplated the prince "as being the fountain of honor and authority" and from whose grace "all franchises, immunities and privileges" are derived, "it is easy to perceive that such a sovereign could not be amenable to a Court of Justice, or subjected to judicial control and actual constraint. It was of necessity, therefore, that suability became incompatible with such sovereignty." As Jay continued, "The same feudal ideas run through all their jurisprudence, and constantly remind us of the distinction between the Prince and the subject." But, he asserted, "[n]o such ideas obtain here; at the Revolution, the sovereignty devolved on the people; and they are truly the sovereigns of the country." There is no need for sovereign immunity because sovereignty (i.e., "the right to govern") "rests with the people." "Our Governors are the agents of the people," he said, and do not "partake in the sovereignty otherwise, or in any other capacity, than as private citizens."[130]

This ambiguity concerning the reach of the federal courts' state citizen diversity jurisdiction continued when Congress passed the Judiciary Act of 1789,[131] as its § 13, which actually granted the federal judiciary state citizen diversity jurisdiction, largely repeated the words of Article III, § 2.[132] The Senate was wholly responsible for the drafting of the Judiciary Act; the House approved it with "no material alterations."[133] Nonetheless, the Senate—despite the fact that it was then elected by state legislators and clearly understood itself as existing in large part to protect the interests of the states as states[134] and despite the many ways in which it had otherwise ensured that the act was "permeated"[135] with the principles of federalism,[136]—failed to include any language in § 13 making clear that the states could not be sued in federal court without their consent. The reason, again, may be that the Senate took the principle of state sovereign immunity for granted and that, though it displayed an abundance of caution in protecting the interests of the states as states elsewhere in the act, it saw no threat to the principle on the horizon that required state sovereignty to be protected expressly.

The threat was there, however, and imminent. Just four years later, in *Chisholm v. Georgia*,[137] the Supreme Court held, four-to-one, that (1) the language in Article III, § 2, conferring on the federal courts jurisdiction in cases involving a state and citizens of another state, abrogated any sovereign immunity the states might have enjoyed in their own courts,[138] and (2) Georgia was therefore subject to federal judicial power in a common-law assumpsit action by a South Carolina citizen suing to collect a debt.[139] By implication, the *Chisholm* majority also rejected the claim that states were immune from suit in cases in which the federal courts were exercising federal question jurisdiction. After all, Article III, § 2 was as devoid of language recognizing or protecting state sovereign immunity when it was providing the federal courts with federal question jurisdiction as it was when it was providing them with state citizen diversity jurisdiction.

Two years later, the Congress repudiated the Supreme Court's holding in *Chisholm* by adopting the Eleventh Amendment to the U.S. Constitution: "The judicial power of the United States shall not be construed to extend to any suit in law or equity commenced or prosecuted against one of the United States by citizens of another State, or by the Citizens or Subjects of any Foreign State." Three years later, in 1798, the amendment was ratified by the requisite three-fourths of the state legislatures. Both the text and the history of the Eleventh Amendment show conclusively, however, that it was meant to bar only suits against the states brought in the federal courts under their state citizen diversity jurisdiction.

The text tracks precisely the state citizen diversity language of Article III, § 2. Had the Framers of the amendment meant it to bar federal question suits as well, they could have expressed their intentions easily and clearly by simply adopting the first post-*Chisholm* proposed amendment, introduced in 1793 in the House of Representatives by Theodore Sedgwick of Massachusetts on instructions from the legislature of his commonwealth. Its provisions would have had exactly that effect: "No state shall be liable to be made a party defendant, in any of the judicial courts, established, or which shall be established under the authority of the United States, at the suit of any person or persons, whether a citizen or citizens, or a foreigner or foreigners, or of any body politic or corporate, whether within or without the United States."[140]

Sedgwick's proposed amendment, with its references to suits by citizens as well as noncitizens, clearly reached beyond the federal courts' state citizen diversity jurisdiction for a reason that would have been obvious to the people of the time. As Justice David Souter pointed out in his dissent in *Seminole Tribe of Florida v. Florida*, "Sedgwick sought such a broad amendment because many of the States, including his own, owed debts subject to collection under the Treaty of Paris. Suits to collect such debts would 'arise under' that Treaty and thus be subject to federal-question jurisdiction under Article III." Such suits were, in fact, already pending against Massachusetts, including one by "Christopher Vassal, an erstwhile Bostonian whose move to England on the eve of revolutionary hostilities had presented his former neighbors with the irresistible temptation to confiscate his vacant mansion."[141] But Sedgwick's proposed amendment went even further: it would have barred all "arising under" or federal question suits as well. It declared, after all, that "[n]o state shall be liable to be made a party defendant" in any federal court in an action brought against it by "any body politic or corporate, whether within or without the United States." The proposed amendment would have conferred on the states complete sovereign immunity, which could not be abrogated even by Congress.

Congress, however, took no action on Sedgwick's proposal, and two years later, it withdrew from the federal courts only state citizen diversity jurisdiction. In *Cohens v. Virginia*, Chief Justice John Marshall stated for a unanimous Court its understanding of the meaning of the Eleventh Amendment. The amendment had, he declared, no effect on the federal courts' federal question jurisdiction, and he concluded that "a case arising under the constitution or laws of the United States, is cognizable in the Courts of the Union, whoever may be the parties to that case."[142] He utterly rejected the suggestion that the Eleventh Amendment was meant "to strip the [federal] government of the means of protecting, by the instrumentality of its courts, the constitution and laws from active violation [by the states]."[143]

Early in his tenure on the Supreme Court and at the very time he was otherwise employing and articulating the reasons for a textualist approach to the interpretation of constitutional provisions, Scalia was adopting a decidedly nontextualist approach to the Eleventh Amendment and the principle of state sovereign immunity. In his 1989 dissent in *Pennsylvania v. Union Gas Co.*,[144] he asserted that "the Eleventh Amendment was important not merely for what it said but for what it reflected: a consensus that the doctrine of sovereign immunity . . . was part of the understood background against which the Constitution was adopted, and which its jurisdictional provisions did not mean to sweep away."[145]

Scalia began his *Union Gas* dissent by embracing completely the Court's argument in the 1890 case of *Hans v. Louisiana*,[146] in which it had concluded that the Eleventh Amendment precludes individuals from bringing damages suits against states in federal court even if the asserted basis of jurisdiction is not state citizen diversity but rather the existence of a federal question.[147] Scalia quoted approvingly from Justice Joseph Bradley's opinion in *Hans* that "the cognizance of suits and actions [against nonconsenting states] was not contemplated by the Constitution when establishing the judicial power of the United States"[148] and that *Chisholm* "created . . . a shock of surprise throughout the country" that led to the Eleventh Amendment.[149] He agreed with the finding in *Hans* that although the amendment "by its precise terms repudiated that decision," it "reflected as well a repudiation of the premise upon which that decision was based, namely, that Article III's jurisdictional grants over the States are unlimited by the doctrine of sovereign immunity."[150]

So enamored was Scalia with *Hans* that he found the following passage from Justice Bradley's opinion persuasive: "Suppose that Congress, when proposing the Eleventh Amendment, had appended to it a proviso that nothing therein contained should prevent a State from being sued by its own citizens in cases arising under the Constitution or laws of the United States: can we imagine that it would have been adopted by the States? The supposition that it would is almost an absurdity on its face."[151] But of course, Justice Bradley's "imaginary horrible" is exactly the consequence that Representative Sedgwick's proposed amendment would have prevented, and the Congress rejected it. Scalia, however, appeared unaware of Sedgwick's proposal because he was content to rely on Justice Bradley's rhetorical question rather than on solid historical research. Scalia has argued that textualism, i.e., an original-meaning approach, is "a task sometimes better suited to the historian than the lawyer" because it "requires the consideration of an enormous amount of material" and immersion "in the political and intellectual atmosphere of the time."[152] When he abandoned his textualist approach to the Eleventh Amendment, he abandoned as well his commitment to engaging in careful historical research.

Scalia then turned to the equally nontextualist argument of Chief Justice Charles Evans Hughes in *Monaco v. Mississippi,* in which the Court held that, despite Article III's express grant of jurisdiction over suits "between a State . . . and foreign States" and despite the absence of an express grant of sovereign immunity in the Eleventh Amendment, a state could not be sued by a foreign state in federal court: "Manifestly, we cannot rest with a mere literal application of the words of § 2 of Article III, or assume that the letter of the Eleventh Amendment exhausts the restrictions upon suits against non-consenting States." For Hughes, the "postulates" that stood "behind the words of the constitutional provisions . . . which limit and control" were more important. One was the "postulate that States of the Union, still possessing attributes of sovereignty, shall be immune from suits, without their consent, save where [as Hamilton wrote in *Federalist* No. 81] there has been 'a surrender of this immunity in the plan of the convention.' "[153] Scalia seized on Hughes's use of Hamilton's language and proceeded to investigate to what extent there had been a surrender of state sovereign immunity in the plan of the convention. His investigation, however, was not textually based.

A textualist reading of Article III, § 2 would have led Scalia to conclude that all state sovereign immunity had been surrendered in the plan of the convention. The resulting Constitution had given the federal judiciary both federal question and state citizen diversity jurisdiction over the states, and the only exceptions would be those "that the Congress shall make," not that the Court shall invent. To the extent that Congress would want to protect states from suits against them in federal court, it could do so by excepting such suits from the federal courts' jurisdiction, either when it initially passed the Judiciary Act of 1789 or subsequently. Under the plan of the convention, the Senate, elected by state legislatures and therefore especially interested in protecting the interests of the states as states, could have insisted on express language in either the Judiciary Act or the Eleventh Amendment (or both) to protect the states from suits without their consent. A textualist or original-meaning reading of the Eleventh Amendment would lead one to conclude that Congress intended to provide the states with sovereign immunity only in cases involving state citizen diversity and that, consistent with the plan of the convention, all other aspects of state immunity remained surrendered.

Such a textualist reading would have allowed Scalia to avoid what he described in "Originalism: The Lesser Evil" as "the main danger in judicial interpretation of the Constitution"—that the judge "will mistake [his] own predilections for the law."[154] But having in this instance abandoned the text for his own view of what the Framers must have implicitly intended, he fell prey to viewing the question of state sovereign immunity through the eyes of a policymaker and to judging on the basis of what made sense to him. Thus, he found it reasonable (and therefore consistent with the plan of the convention) that the Framers would have abrogated state sovereign immunity in Article III, § 2 in "disputes between the Union and the individual States, and between the individual States themselves" because of the "inherent necessity of a tribunal for peaceful resolution" of such disputes. But he found it far less reasonable that the Framers would have abrogated state sovereign immunity in "disputes on federal questions between individuals and the States." These disputes were of much less constitutional significance, and he concluded that the necessity for federal courts to have jurisdiction to resolve the former "is incomparably greater, in my view," than the jurisdiction to resolve the latter.[155]

When he became untethered from his textualist moorings, Scalia also lost his appreciation for another aspect of the plan of the convention, namely, the moderating effects brought about by the Constitution's establishment of an extended republic. James Madison had explained all of this in *Federalist* No. 10. The smaller the republic, "the fewer probably will be the distinct parties and interests composing it; the fewer the distinct parties and interests, the more frequently will a majority be found of the same party; and the smaller the compass within which they are placed, the more easily will they concert and execute their plans of oppression." In contrast, the larger the republic, the greater the variety of interests, parties, and sects present within it and the more moderate and diffused the conflict. In the words of *Federalist* No. 10, "Extend the sphere, and you take in a greater variety of parties and interests; you make it less probable that a majority of the whole will have a common motive to invade the rights of other citizens; or if such a common motive exists, it will be more difficult for all who feel it to discover their own strength, and to act in unison with each other."[156] Because of the greater variety of economic, geographic, religious, political, cultural, and ethnic interests that the extended republic created by the Constitution takes in, politics is moderated. As Madison observed in *Federalist* No. 51, this diversity of interests assures that "a coalition of a majority of the whole society" will seldom take place "on any other principles than those of justice and the common good."[157] The advantages of an extended republic thus helped to make it possible for the Framers to give the national government sufficient power to "control the governed" while simultaneously obliging it to "control itself."[158]

Scalia demonstrates repeatedly throughout his writings that he is intimately familiar with *The Federalist,* including this argument from *Federalist* No. 10.[159] However, his nontextualist interest in protecting state sovereign immunity led him to deny that the small-republic states could pose a greater threat to liberty (and should therefore be more subject to suit by private individuals in federal courts) than the large federal republic itself and to conclude that it was "impossible to find in the scheme of the Constitution a necessity that private remedies be expanded . . . to include a remedy not available, for a similar infraction, against the United States itself."[160]

For purposes of argument in his *Union Gas* dissent, he conceded that he might be "wrong" about "the original meaning of the Constitution, or the assumption adopted by the Eleventh Amendment, or the structural necessity for federal-question suits against the States," but, he insisted, "it cannot possibly be denied that the question is at least close." And so, he concluded that "the mere venerability" of *Hans*, which had been "consistently adhered to for almost a century, and the difficulty of changing, or even clearly identifying, the intervening law" that had been based on *Hans* "strongly argue against a change."[161]

The nontextualist Scalia of the state sovereign immunity cases was far more concerned with the venerability of precedent than the textualist Scalia of the negative Commerce Clause cases. The *Case of the State Freight Tax* predated *Hans* by seventeen years, but since the negative Commerce Clause doctrine it formally announced was not grounded in the text of the Constitution, Scalia sought in *Tyler Pipe* to reverse it outright; when he failed in that effort, he sought thereafter to restrict any further expansion of the doctrine. By contrast, *Hans* was decided later and without constitutional language on which to ground its prohibition of suits against the states in cases under the federal courts' subject matter jurisdiction, yet Scalia not only declined the invitation in *Union Gas* to overrule it but has also written subsequent opinions that have extended considerably the doctrine of state sovereign immunity.

His opinion for the Court in *Blatchford v. Native Village of Noatak* is especially noteworthy in this respect.[162] To begin with, Scalia held that the Eleventh Amendment bars suits by Native American tribes against the states without their consent, even though the tribes clearly are neither citizens of another state nor citizens or subjects of any foreign state within the meaning of the Eleventh Amendment. And more important, he departed even further from his textualist principles than he had in *Union Gas* by declaring that the Eleventh Amendment stands "not so much for what it says, but for the presupposition of our constitutional structure which it confirms."[163] This expansive language has subsequently provided the basis for the same five-member majority of the Supreme Court[164] to find unconstitutional seven federal laws on the grounds that they violate the "presupposition" of the Eleventh Amendment that the states enjoy state sovereign immunity and cannot be sued without their consent.[165]

Thus, in *Seminole Tribe of Florida v. Florida*,[166] Chief Justice Rehnquist specifically quoted Scalia's language in *Blatchford* as the basis for proclaiming that a "blind reliance upon the text of the Eleventh Amendment" would be "overly exacting"[167] and for finding unconstitutional that provision of the Indian Gaming Regulatory Act of 1988 mandating the states to negotiate in good faith with Native American tribes to form compacts governing certain gaming activities and authorizing them to be sued by the tribes in federal court if they fail to do so. In *Florida*

Prepaid Postsecondary Education Expense Board v. College Savings Bank,[168] Chief Justice Rehnquist then cited *Seminole Tribe* as precedent for invalidating the 1992 amendments to the Patent Remedy Act expressly abrogating state sovereign immunity in patent cases.

In *College Savings Bank v. Florida Prepaid Postsecondary Education Expense Board*,[169] Scalia declared that, although "its precise terms bar only federal jurisdiction over suits brought against one State by citizens of another State or foreign state, . . . the Eleventh Amendment accomplished much more"[170] and on that basis voided the Trademark Remedy Clarification Act of 1992 subjecting states to suit under the Trademark Act of 1946.[171] In *Alden v. Maine*,[172] Justice Kennedy invoked Scalia's words in *Blatchford* and found unconstitutional those 1974 amendments to the Fair Labor Standards Act authorizing private actions against the states in their own courts without their consent. In *Kimel v. Florida Board of Regents*,[173] Justice O'Connor cited Scalia's language in *Blatchford* when she invalidated the provisions of the Age Discrimination in Employment Act of 1967 subjecting states to suits filed by state employees for age discrimination. In *Trustees of the University of Alabama v. Garrett*,[174] Rehnquist cited *Kimel* to invalidate the provisions of the Americans with Disabilities Act of 1990 allowing suits in federal court by state employees seeking to recover money damages by reason of a state's failure to comply with the act's provisions. And in *Federal Maritime Commission v. South Carolina State Ports Authority*,[175] Justice Thomas specifically mentioned Scalia's language in *Blatchford* when he voided the provisions of the Shipping Act of 1984 allowing the Federal Maritime Commission to adjudicate complaints filed by private parties against state port authorities. In that case, the consequences of Scalia's expansive, nontextual reading of the Eleventh Amendment were fully apparent. An amendment whose text bars federal courts from hearing cases against the states under their state citizen diversity jurisdiction was eventually applied even to the adjudicatory procedures of federal administrative agencies.

Congress's Power under § 5 of the Fourteenth Amendment

In *City of Boerne v. Flores*,[176] the Supreme Court, by a vote of six to three, struck down the Religious Freedom Restoration Act of 1993 (RFRA), a measure that had passed unanimously in the House of Representatives and by a vote of ninety-seven to three in the Senate before being enthusiastically signed into law by President Bill Clinton. The Court did so because it claimed that RFRA upset "the federal balance."[177]

RFRA was a direct response to *Employment Division, Department of Human Resources of Oregon v. Smith*,[178] in which Scalia held for a five-member majority that the Free Exercise Clause of the First Amendment "does not relieve an individual of the obligation to comply with a 'valid and neutral law of general application on the ground that the law proscribes (or prescribes) conduct that his religion prescribes (or proscribes).'"[179] In so ruling, he declined to apply the balancing test, previously set forth by Justice Brennan in *Sherbert v. Verner*,[180] that asks whether the law at issue substantially burdens a religious practice and, if so, whether the burden is justified by a compelling government interest. In effect, the Court in *Smith* held that the Free Exercise Clause protects individuals only from intentional state discrimination on the basis of religion, not from state action that incidentally has a burdensome effect on religious exercise.

Smith was greeted with an overwhelming storm of protest that united fundamentalist religious groups on the right with the American Civil Liberties Union, Americans United for the Separation of Church and State, and the People for the American Way on the left. And so Congress enacted RFRA, which forbade "[g]overnment" from "substantially burden[ing] a person's exercise of religion," even if the burden results from a law of general applicability, unless it could demonstrate that the burden was "in furtherance of a compelling governmental interest" and was "the least restrictive means of furthering that interest." RFRA's mandate applied to any branch of federal or state government and to all officials acting under color of law. Its coverage was universal, including "all Federal or State law, and the implementation of that law, whether statutory or otherwise, and whether adopted before or after [RFRA's] enactment."[181] In effect, RFRA declared that religious exercise was to be protected from incidental burdens no less than from intentional discrimination.

Congress presented RFRA as merely restoring the balancing test that the Court had been using in free exercise cases after *Sherbert* but that it had abandoned in *Smith*. In truth, however, RFRA went much further and mandated that the *Sherbert* balancing test be applied in all free exercise controversies, not merely in the two areas of law where the Court had previously applied it and to which Congress expressly referred in the statute itself, i.e., in unemployment compensation cases and in *Wisconsin v. Yoder*,[182] where the Court exempted the Amish from the need to comply with a state's mandatory school attendance law. RFRA was, in many ways, an ill-conceived measure;[183] nevertheless, a bad law is not necessarily an unconstitutional law, and the Court's invalidation of RFRA was much more problematic than the act itself.

In imposing RFRA's requirements on the states, Congress had relied on its power under § 5 of the Fourteenth Amendment "to enforce, by appropriate legislation," the amendment's guarantee that no state shall deprive any person of "life, liberty, or property, without due process of law" or deny any person the "equal protection of the laws." RFRA's sponsors contended that the act was permissible enforcement legislation under § 5 because it was enforcing the constitutional right

to free exercise of religion, made applicable to the states by the Court itself in
Cantwell v. Connecticut.[184]

Justice Kennedy held for the majority, however, that Congress in this instance
lacked the power to enforce such a prohibition against the states. He argued that
Congress's enforcement power under § 5 is merely "preventive" or "corrective"
or "remedial" and does not extend to decreeing the substance of the amendment's
restrictions on the states.[185] And, he continued, when Congress exercises that
power, "there must be a congruence and proportionality between the injury to be
prevented or remedied and the means adopted to that end. Lacking such a connection, legislation may become substantive in operation and effect."[186] Additionally, the Congress is limited to remedying only those problems that the Court
itself considers sufficiently serious to justify intervention. Religious bigotry in the
United States, he continued, was not serious enough to justify congressional reme-
diation. He dismissed congressional hearings on the need for RFRA as focusing
only on "incidental burdens of religion. Much of the discussion centered upon
anecdotal evidence of autopsies performed on Jewish individuals and Hmong
immigrants in violation of their religious beliefs."[187] Convinced that there was no
"widespread pattern of religious discrimination in this country" sufficient to make
RFRA an "appropriate" response, he declared that "RFRA is so out of proportion
to a supposed remedial or preventive object that it cannot be understood as respon-
sive to, or designed to prevent, unconstitutional behavior."[188]

City of Boerne was a clear break with precedent. To begin with, it rejected the
Court's seminal construction of § 5 in *Ex Parte Virginia* in 1880,[189] in which the
Court upheld a provision of the Civil Rights Act of 1875 that made it a crime for
state officials to exclude any citizen from serving as a juror based on the citizen's
race, color, or previous condition of servitude. The act "created a sword for persons discriminatorily excluded from juries," thereby going beyond the Constitution, which had only provided "a shield for defendants against prosecution in a
court with a discriminatorily chosen jury."[190] Nonetheless, Justice William Strong
wrote for a seven-member majority when he declared that § 5 provided Congress
with full power to legislate on this matter. Proclaiming that the post–Civil War
amendments "derive[d] much of their force" from their enforcement sections, he
narrowed his focus to the Fourteenth Amendment and continued: "It is not said
[in § 5 that] the judicial power of the general government shall extend to enforcing the prohibitions and to protecting the rights and immunities guaranteed. It is
not said that this branch of the government [i.e., the judiciary] shall be authorized
to declare void any action of a State in violation of the prohibitions." Rather, he
noted, "[i]t is the power of Congress which has been enlarged. Congress is authorized to enforce the prohibitions by appropriate legislation."[191] Strong's words left

little doubt concerning the meaning of § 5: the responsibility for enforcing the protections of the Fourteenth Amendment (or, for that matter, the other post–Civil War amendments) was assigned to Congress, not the Court. And should doubt remain, Strong removed it later in the same opinion when he insisted that "[w]ere it not for the fifth section of the amendment, there might be room for argument that the first section is only declaratory of the moral duty of the States."[192]

Strong emphasized that the post–Civil War amendments were not self-executing and that "[s]ome legislation is contemplated to make the[m] . . . fully effective." That legislation, he insisted, ought to be treated most deferentially by the Court: "Whatever legislation is appropriate, that is, adopted to carry out the objects the amendments have in view, whatever tends to enforce submission to the prohibitions they contain, and to secure to all persons the enjoyment of perfect equality of civil rights and the equal protection of the laws against State denial or invasion, if not prohibited, is brought within the domain of congressional power."[193]

The Court in *City of Boerne* also repudiated an entire series of recent cases based on *Ex Parte Virginia* and on which the Court's own modern voting rights and civil rights jurisprudence had been built. These cases include *Katzenbach v. Morgan*,[194] *Jones v. Alfred H. Mayer Company*,[195] *Oregon v. Mitchell*,[196] *Fitzpatrick v. Bitzer*,[197] and *City of Rome v. United States*.[198] In these five cases together, the Court held that, under the enforcement sections of the post–Civil War amendments, Congress may independently interpret the Constitution and that, when it does so, the Court will defer to these congressional judgments even if it is not persuaded that, acting independently, it would have reached the same conclusion.[199]

Scalia joined Kennedy's majority opinion in *City of Boerne,* and he joined the majority in *United States v. Morrison*[200] when Chief Justice Rehnquist employed *City of Boerne* to conclude that Congress lacked the constitutional authority to enact a key provision of the Violence against Women Act (VAWA) of 1994 under § 5 of the Fourteenth Amendment, which Congress had explicitly identified as a source of its authority to legislate in this area.[201]

The U.S. government had asserted in *Morrison* that there was "pervasive bias" in various state justice systems against victims of gender-motivated violence, an assertion it said was supported by a voluminous congressional record. It argued that Congress had received evidence that many state justice systems were perpetuating an array of erroneous stereotypes and assumptions and that Congress had concluded on the basis of this evidence that these discriminatory stereotypes often resulted in insufficient investigation and prosecution of gender-motivated crime, inappropriate focus on the behavior and credibility of the victims of that crime, and unacceptably lenient punishments for those who were actually convicted of gender-motivated violence. It argued that this bias, in turn, denied victims of gender-motivated violence the equal protection of the laws and that Congress there-fore had acted appropriately and in keeping with *City of Boerne* when it enacted VAWA to remedy the states' bias and deter future instances of discrimination in the state courts.

Chief Justice Rehnquist responded for a five-member majority, however, that the Framers of the Fourteenth Amendment placed "limitations" on Congress's power to attack discriminatory conduct in order "to prevent the Fourteenth Amendment from obliterating the Framers' carefully crafted balance of power between the States and the National Government"; further, he stated that "fore-most among these limitations" is the "time honored principle that the Fourteenth Amendment, by its very terms, prohibits only state action."[202] He noted that VAWA's civil remedies were not directed at "gender-based disparate treatment by state authorities" but "at individuals who have committed criminal acts motivated by gender bias." The remedies visited "no consequences on any . . . public offi-cial" but rather reached only private conduct. As a consequence, he concluded, "Congress's power under § 5 does not extend to the enactment" of VAWA.[203]

Scalia also joined a five-member majority in a series of cases[204] that relied on *City of Boerne* to invalidate various congressional measures that had expressly abrogated state sovereign immunity, on the ground that the remedy of abrogation was excessive (and not congruent and proportional) to the injury Congress was seeking to prevent and therefore exceeded Congress's enforcement power under § 5.[205] In *Nevada Department of Human Resources v. Hibbs*[206] and *Tennessee v. Lane*,[207] however, Scalia broke ranks with his colleagues when they began employ-ing *City of Boerne* to affirm (rather than invalidate) congressional abrogations and allow states to be sued without their consent.

In *Hibbs*, Rehnquist held for a six-member majority that a state can be sued in federal court without its consent by its state employees to recover money dam-ages for its failure to comply with the family-care provisions of the Family and Medical Leave Act of 1993 (FMLA). *City of Boerne*, he noted, allowed Congress to enact, in the exercise of its § 5 power, so-called prophylactic legislation that proscribes facially constitutional conduct in order to prevent and deter unconsti-tutional conduct. He concluded that this was what Congress was doing when it passed FMLA. It had before it significant evidence of a long and extensive history of sex discrimination with respect to the administration of leave benefits by the states, and that was adequate to justify the enactment of prophylactic § 5 legisla-tion. Moreover, Congress's chosen remedy, FMLA's family-care provision, was "congruent and proportional to the targeted violation" because Congress had already tried unsuccessfully to address this problem through Title VII of the Civil Rights Act of 1964 and the Pregnancy Discrimination Act. When previous legis-lative attempts have failed, such problems may justify added prophylactic measurcs in response. And, Rehnquist continued, by creating an across-the-board, routine employment benefit for all eligible employees, Congress was able to ensure that family-care leave would no longer be stigmatized as an inordinate drain on the workplace caused by female employees and that employers could not evade leave obligations simply by hiring men.[208]

Scalia dissented. He argued that "the constitutional violation that is a prerequisite to 'prophylactic' congressional action to 'enforce' the Fourteenth Amendment is a violation *by the State against which the enforcement action is taken.* There is no guilt by association, enabling the sovereignty of one State to be abridged under § 5 of the Fourteenth Amendment because of violations by another State, or by most other States, or even by 49 other States."[209] There was no evidence that Nevada had discriminated against its women employees, and so he complained that the Court, in finding that the enactment of this prophylactic legislation was justifiable, treated the states "as some sort of collective entity which is guilty . . . of unconstitutional participation in, and fostering of, gender-based discrimination." This, he objected, "will not do. Prophylaxis in the sense of extending the remedy beyond the violation is one thing; prophylaxis in the sense of extending the remedy beyond the violator is something else."[210]

In *Lane*, Justice Stevens held for a five-member majority that a state can be sued in federal court without its consent for violating Title II of the Americans with Disabilities Act of 1990 (ADA), which provides that "[n]o qualified individual with a disability shall, by reason of such disability, be excluded from participation or denied the benefits of the services, programs or activities of a public entity." George Lane was a paraplegic who sued Tennessee for damages and equitable relief on the ground that one of its counties had denied him physical access to its courts. Stevens wrote that Title II constituted a valid exercise of Congress's authority under § 5 of the Fourteenth Amendment to enforce that amendment's Due Process Clause and its substantive guarantee of the fundamental right of access to the courts.

Congress, Stevens maintained, enacted Title II against a backdrop of pervasive unequal treatment of persons with disabilities in the administration of state services and programs, including systematic deprivations of fundamental rights. With respect to the particular services at issue in *Lane*, he pointed out that Congress had learned many individuals in many states were being excluded from courthouses and court proceedings by reason of their disabilities. He referred to a U.S. Civil Rights Commission report that showed that more than three-fourths of public services and programs housed in state-owned buildings were inaccessible to and unusable by such persons, and he noted that a congressionally appointed task force had heard numerous examples of their exclusion from state judicial services and programs, including the failure to make courtrooms accessible to witnesses with physical disabilities.[211]

Title II was, therefore, according to Stevens, an appropriate response to this history and pattern of unequal treatment and valid § 5 legislation as applied to the class of cases implicating the accessibility of judicial services.

Moreover, Congress's chosen remedy for the pattern of exclusion and discrimination at issue, Title II's requirement of program accessibility, was congruent and proportional to its object of enforcing the right of access to the courts for two reasons.[212] First, this long history of unequal treatment of disabled persons in the administration of judicial services had persisted despite several state and federal legislative efforts to remedy the problem; discrimination warranted added prophylactic measures. Second, the remedy that Congress chose was a limited one because Congress did not require states to employ any and all means to make judicial services accessible or to compromise essential eligibility criteria for public programs; it required only "reasonable modifications" that would not fundamentally alter the nature of the service provided and only when the individual seeking modification is otherwise eligible for the service.[213] Title II was, therefore, "a reasonable prophylactic measure, reasonably targeted to a legitimate end."[214]

Scalia again dissented—this time, not perfunctorily, as in *Hibbs*, but in a thoughtful opinion spelling out comprehensively his understanding of Congress's enforcement power under § 5. He began by invoking the Court's opinions in *Ex Parte Virginia* and *Katzenbach v. Morgan*, cases in which the Court had declared that the standard for determining what constitutes "appropriate legislation" under § 5 was the flexible "necessary and proper" standard of *McCulloch v. Maryland*.[215] That standard, he noted, led to such an "inevitable expansion" of Congress's power under the Fourteenth Amendment that the Court was forced to replace it in *City of Boerne* with its congruence-and-proportionality test. He declared that he "signed on" to the Court's opinion in that case and "adhered to it in later cases" but "with some misgiving" because, as he said, he generally rejects "tests based on such malleable standards as 'proportionality,' because they have a way of turning into vehicles for the implementation of individual judges' policy preferences."[216]

Hibbs and *Lane*, however, had convinced him of the error of his previous ways. "I yield to the lessons of experience," he said. He denounced the congruence-and-proportionality standard for being "like all such flabby tests," namely, "a standing invitation to judicial arbitrariness and policy-driven decisionmaking."[217] Even worse, he declared, the standard cast the Court "in the role of Congress's taskmaster. Under it, the courts (and ultimately this Court) must regularly check Congress's homework to make sure that it has identified sufficient constitutional violations to make its remedy congruent and proportional." Displaying his judicial-restraintist colors, he reminded his colleagues that "we are ill advised to adopt or adhere to constitutional rules that bring us into constant conflict with a coequal branch of Government. And when conflict is unavoidable, we should not come to do battle with the United States Congress armed only with a test ('congruence and proportionality') that has no demonstrable basis in the text of the Constitution and cannot objectively be shown to have been met or failed."[218]

He announced that he would replace the nontextual congruence-and-proportionality test with a textual one—"one that provides a clear, enforceable limitation" on Congress "supported by the text of § 5," i.e., by the words "enforce by appropriate legislation." In typical textualist fashion, he turned to dictionaries of the era for guidance. "The 1860 edition of Noah Webster's *American Dictionary of the English Language*, current when the Fourteenth Amendment was adopted, defined 'enforce' as: 'To put in execution; to cause to take effect; as, to *enforce* the laws.' *Id.*, at 396. See also J. Worcester, *Dictionary of the English Language* 484 (1860) ('To put in force; to cause to be applied or executed; as, to *enforce* a law')." For Scalia, the conclusion was clear: the word *enforce* does not authorize "Congress to go *beyond* the provisions of the Fourteenth Amendment" and to enact prophylactic legislation that proscribes, prevents, or remedies "conduct that does not *itself* violate any provision of the Fourteenth Amendment." He offered the following illustration: "One does not, for example, 'enforce' a 55-mile-per-hour speed limit by imposing a 45-mile-per-hour speed limit—even though that is indeed directed to the same end of automotive safety and will undoubtedly result in many fewer violations of the 55-mile-per-hour limit." And, addressing the particulars of *Lane*, he continued: "[O]ne does not 'enforce' the right of access to the courts at issue in this case by requiring that disabled persons be provided access to *all* of the 'services, programs, or activities' furnished or conducted by the State."[219]

Scalia acknowledged that stare decisis was a "major impediment" to his textualist test: "A lot of water has gone under the bridge since *Morgan*, and many important and well-accepted measures, such as the Voting Rights Act, assume the validity of *Morgan* and *South Carolina*." But, he noted, all of the major cases from *Ex Parte Virginia* forward in which the Court had given an expansive interpretation of *enforce* had, with the exception of *Hibbs*, "involved congressional measures that were directed exclusively against, or were used in the particular case to remedy, *racial discrimination*."[220] The Court's expansive reading of § 5 with respect to Congress's power to combat racial discrimination not only comported with "the principal purpose of the Fourteenth Amendment" but also had begun before "the guarantee of equal protection had . . . been extended beyond race to sex, age, and the many other categories it now covers" (what is often called "substantive equal protection"), before the development of "the incorporation doctrine" (which holds that the Fourteenth Amendment incorporates and applies against the states the Bill of Rights), and before the adoption of "the doctrine of so-called 'substantive due process'" (which holds that the Fourteenth Amendment's Due Process Clause protects unenumerated liberties). Since the Fourteenth Amendment did not initially "include the many guarantees that it now provides," it did not appear to be a "massive expansion of congressional power" when the Court interpreted § 5 broadly to allow Congress to bar racial discrimination.[221]

Therefore, Scalia announced that, "principally for reasons of *stare decisis*, I shall henceforth apply the permissive *McCulloch* standard to congressional measures designed to remedy racial discrimination by the States."[222] However, he also announced that in the future, "I shall also not subject to 'congruence and proportionality' analysis congressional action under § 5 that is *not* directed to racial discrimination." Rather than second-guessing Congress, "I shall give full effect to that action when it consists of 'enforcement' of the provisions of the Fourteenth Amendment, within the broad but not unlimited meaning of that term I have described above." Prophylactic measures were, for him, another matter: when congressional action "goes beyond enforcement to prophylaxis, however, I shall consider it ultra vires." And for Scalia, the legislation at issue in *Lane* was "plainly of the latter sort," for "[r]equiring access for disabled persons to all public buildings cannot remotely be considered a means of 'enforcing' the Fourteenth Amendment."[223]

Scalia's dissent in *Lane* was a conscientious attempt on his part to scuttle the congruence-and-proportionality test and put a textualist foundation (albeit after the fact) under his previous opinions and votes with respect to the meaning of § 5 (including *City of Boerne*) and, by implication, his opinions and votes in the state sovereign immunity cases. His effort, however, ultimately failed.

To begin with, his dictionary definitions of *enforce* were unhelpful and circular. How does the phrase "to put into execution, to cause to take effect; as, to enforce the laws" limit Congress from enforcing the Due Process Clause right of the disabled to have access to the courts or the Equal Protection Clause right of female workers to be protected from sex discrimination? Scalia is never clear in this regard.[224] His dictionary definitions also do not explain why the Congress was wrong when, during its passage of RFRA, it defined *enforce* to mean "implement." The Senate report on RFRA observed that "congressional power under § 5 to enforce the 14th Amendment includes congressional power to enforce the free exercise clause. Because the Religious Freedom Restoration Act is clearly designed *to implement* the free exercise clause—to protect religious liberty and eliminate laws 'prohibiting the free exercise' of religion—it falls squarely within Congress's § 5 enforcement powers."[225] How is Congress's use of *implement* inconsistent with Scalia's reliance on "to put in execution; to cause to take effect; as, to enforce the laws" or "to put in force; to cause to be applied or executed; as, to *enforce* a law"?

Likewise, Scalia's speed-limit illustration raises more questions than it answers. A 45-mile-per-hour speed limit would, in fact, "cause to be applied" (to use one of his dictionary definitions of *enforce*) a 55-mile-per-hour speed limit. Moreover, as Scalia admits, it has the "same end of automobile safety." Since the Fourteenth

Amendment is written in the language of ends—due process and equal protection—not means—such as access to the courts or avoiding the stigmatization of women—Congress would seem to have the power to achieve those ends and by the means it considers "necessary and proper."

Scalia's attempt to limit "the flexible 'necessary and proper' standard" of *McCulloch v. Maryland* to "congressional measures designed to remedy racial discrimination by the states" also is problematic, especially for a textualist. The full text of Article I, § 8, cl. 18 states: "Congress shall have power . . . to make all Laws which shall be necessary and proper for carrying into Execution the foregoing Powers, and all other Powers vested by this Constitution in the Government of the United States, or in any Department or Officer thereof." That language clearly includes Congress's power under § 5 of the Fourteenth Amendment, and it gives Congress the same flexible enforcement powers whether it is addressing racial discrimination or securing the other ends or purposes of the amendment.

There is still another problem in Scalia's dissent: it is simply not true that all of the major cases except for *Hibbs* in which the Court had given an expansive interpretation of the word *enforce* involved congressional measures addressing racial discrimination. To begin with, *Katzenbach v. Morgan,* the first major case of the modern Court's § 5 jurisprudence and one that Scalia mentions repeatedly, dealt not with racial discrimination but with Congress's power to prohibit a state from barring any person from voting solely on grounds of English literacy if that person could demonstrate that he had been educated in an American-flag school "in which the predominant classroom language was other than English"; in short, it dealt with Congress's power to prohibit New York from barring Puerto Ricans from voting. Of perhaps even greater importance, however, is *Fitzpatrick v. Bitzer,* in which the Court held that Congress could abrogate state sovereign immunity and authorize class-action suits against the states by male employees claiming discrimination in their state retirement benefit plans. Scalia had discussed at some length the *Fitzpatrick* decision in both his *Pennsylvania v. Union Gas* dissent[226] and his *Blatchford v. Noatak* majority opinion,[227] and Stevens underscored its importance for the *Lane* majority,[228] but Scalia here treated it as an inconvenient fact and studiously ignored it.

Finally, Scalia's argument that the Court can no longer tolerate its initial expansive reading of Congress's enforcement powers under § 5 because of the emergence of the doctrines of substantive equal protection, incorporation, and substantive due process is simply unpersuasive. The Court itself has been responsible for the emergence of all three of these doctrines. Since the emergence of these doctrines, the major threat to the continued independent existence and agency of the states has been the Court itself, not the Congress; yet Scalia argues that Congress's enforcement powers against the states, expressly granted in § 5 and originally affirmed in *Ex Parte Virginia,* must be limited because otherwise the massive expansion of federal powers over the states unleashed by these three doctrines that the Court itself has devised will imperil federalism.

Ultimately, Scalia's dissent in *Lane* is an attempt to preserve for the Court alone the power and prerogative to protect the states from congressional enactments. Neither the text nor the context of the Fourteenth Amendment supports such an attempt.[229] If ever there was an amendment intended to enhance the power of Congress at the expense of the Court, it was the Fourteenth Amendment. After all, it begins in § 1 by explicitly repudiating the Supreme Court's outrageous assertion in *Dred Scott* that blacks could not be citizens of the United States, and it concludes in § 5 by giving to the Congress, and not to the Court, the power to enforce its provisions.[230] Additionally, if ever there was an amendment consciously intended to strengthen the power of Congress at the expense of the states, it was also the Fourteenth Amendment. The Civil War established on the fields of battle that the United States was indeed a nation, not a confederacy, and the Fourteenth Amendment ratified that fact both in how it limited the states and in how it empowered the Congress. Scalia's ardent textualist defense of federalism in the negative Commerce Clause and federal preemption cases appears to carry over and make him an equally ardent defender of federalism in the state sovereign immunity and § 5 cases, where his textualism provides no reason to do so and where his implicit embrace of the nontextualist doctrines of substantive equal protection, incorporation, and substantive due process undercut his textualist premises.

Conclusions

This chapter has explored five areas of constitutional law in which Scalia has defended federalism by protecting the states from federal control. In the first three areas (the negative Commerce Clause, federal preemption of state regulations, and federal commandeering of state officials), Scalia has faithfully adhered to his textualist approach to constitutional and statutory interpretation.

He has opposed the Court's negative Commerce Clause jurisprudence, which serves as a major limitation on the power of the states, because it has "no foundation in the text of the Constitution." He argues that the Commerce Clause of Article I, § 8 is an express grant of power to Congress, not to the Court; if the federal government is to eliminate state burdens on interstate commerce, it must be by an affirmative act of the Congress exercising its enumerated power to do so, not by the Court, proceeding on the nontextualist premise that the Commerce Clause has also delegated to it the power to keep interstate trade free from restrictive state regulation. Scalia relies on the text of the Supremacy Clause to justify Congress's power to preempt all state regulations that are incompatible with federal law, and he carefully studies the text of the federal law in question to determine whether the statutory cat has a preemptive grin. If it does, he will give it full preemptive effect. But if it does not or if it cannot be determined definitively from its text that it does, he will permit the states to regulate as they choose. And he relies on such specific constitutional texts as Article 1, § 4 or Article II, § 3 to determine whether federal commandeering statutes will be affirmed or struck, protecting federalism only when doing so is not incompatible with the words of these texts.

In the fourth area (the state sovereign immunity doctrine), Scalia has clearly departed from his textualist moorings. He has adopted a decidedly nontextualist approach to the Eleventh Amendment, declaring that it is important "not so much for what it says" but for the "presupposition" of state sovereign immunity it "confirms." When proceeding as a textualist, he readily rejects an 1873 precedent establishing the negative Commerce Clause as inconsistent with the language of Article I, § 8, but when proceeding as a nontextualist, he warmly embraces as venerable an 1890 precedent that established state sovereign immunity not only in cases involving the federal courts' state citizen diversity jurisdiction (consistent with the text of the Eleventh Amendment) but also in cases involving the federal courts' subject matter jurisdiction (inconsistent with the text of the amendment and contrary to Congress's actions at the time of its adoption).

And in the fifth area (Congress's enforcement powers under § 5 of the Fourteenth Amendment), although Scalia initially accepted the Court's nontextualist congruence-and-proportionality test to protect federalism, he abandoned it when it proved unreliable. However, his attempt to put a textualist foundation under his opinions and votes was clearly flawed. His argument that the Court should read Congress's power under § 5 to enforce the Equal Protection Clause broadly to allow Congress to bar racial discrimination but that it should read Congress's same power to enforce the Due Process Clause narrowly to prohibit it from protecting free exercise of religion is not textually based—nothing in the text of the Fourteenth Amendment (and certainly nothing in any opinion Scalia has ever written) suggests that its scope is limited to matters of race. Likewise, his dictionary definitions of *enforce* are circular, and the conclusions he draws from them are contrary to his advice in *A Matter of Interpretation*—that "context is everything" in textual interpretation and that the context of the Constitution requires words and phrases to be given "an expansive rather than a narrow interpretation."[231]

Scalia's nontextualist approach to the state sovereign immunity doctrine and his flawed textualist efforts to protect the states from congressional power are clear departures from his generally consistent textualist jurisprudence. They are also departures from his comments during his Senate confirmation hearing that the protection of federalism is the primary responsibility of the Congress and from his

pre-judicial observations in *Regulation* that the principle that the federal government is a government of limited powers no longer has a "living effect" because
society no longer has "an abiding belief in it." These departures can be explained
in part by the way he described federalism in *Printz*:[232] he quoted approvingly
Madison's words from *Federalist* No. 51 that federalism and separation of powers
together constitute a "double security" for the rights of the people. Scalia appears
so committed to preserving this double security that he will protect federalism as
vigorously as he protects separation of powers, whether or not the text requires
him to do so. These departures therefore offer an important concluding insight:
when Scalia fails to abide by his textualist premises, he ends up acting like the
activist justice he routinely criticizes.

Chapter Five

Scalia's Textualism
Applied to Substantive Rights

In answering Senator Thurmond's question during his Senate confirmation hearings on why the U.S. Constitution had endured for so long, Scalia gave primacy to "the structure of government that the original Constitution created."[1] Chapters Three and Four focused on his understanding of constitutional structure and his textualist defense of separation of powers and federalism and the "double security"[2] they provide for ensuring that the government cannot "'run roughshod' over the liberties of the people."[3] In his response to the senator's question, Scalia did not discount the Bill of Rights and subsequent amendments; in fact, he described them as being "very important" to the preservation of "personal freedom."[4] This chapter focuses on his textualist approach to those substantive rights spelled out in the First Amendment, the Takings Clause of the Fifth Amendment, and the Equal Protection Clause of the Fourteenth Amendment. Chapter Six discusses procedural rights and explores his textualist approach to the Due Process Clauses of the Fifth and Fourteenth Amendments and the various criminal procedural provisions of Amendments Four through Eight.

As the chapters make clear, Scalia's understanding and textualist defense of these provisions is strikingly different from his textualist defense of constitutional structure. By actively and aggressively defending federalism and especially separation of powers, he can be restrained and deferential elsewhere, i.e., he is spared the need in other cases to protect constitutional rights that are better secured by structure than by judges. And he is protected from the temptation to expand constitutional rights to "progressively higher degrees." His textualism requires only that he "preserve our society's values" as they have been traditionally understood; it requires only that he "prevent backsliding"[5] by "restrain[ing] transient majorities from impairing long-recognized personal liberties."[6] It does not authorize him to "revise" or expand them.[7] If the public wants rights to evolve and to mean more now than when they were written into the constitutional text, he argues that the appropriate way for such an evolution to take place is through the people via their elected state legislatures and Congress. As he said in *Burnham v. Superior Court*, the difference between his textualist approach and the approach of those who feel themselves unconstrained by the words of the Constitution "has nothing to do with whether 'further progress [is] to be made' in the 'evolution of our legal system.' It has to do with whether changes are to be adopted as progressive by the American people or decreed as progressive by the Justices of this Court."[8]

The First Amendment's Religion Clauses

The First Amendment's Religion Clauses state that "Congress shall make no law respecting an establishment of religion, or prohibiting the free exercise thereof." As construed by the contemporary Court, these two clauses are made to work at cross-purposes: actions that are demanded by some justices to ensure free exercise of religion constitute an establishment of religion according to others. As a consequence, for any governmental action touching on religion to survive constitutional scrutiny, it must successfully negotiate, in Scalia's words, the "narrow channel between the Scylla of what the Free Exercise Clause demands and the Charybdis of what the Establishment Clause forbids."[9] The "vise between the Establishment Clause on one side and the . . . Free Exercise Clause on the other" in which policymakers find themselves,[10] he has stated, has been tightened considerably as a result of Court decisions holding that the Fourteenth Amendment incorporates these clauses to apply to the states no less than to the federal government.[11]

Since his appointment to the Court, Scalia has employed his textualist approach to harmonize these two clauses. In the light of the text of the First Amendment and "the long-standing traditions of our people,"[12] he has consistently read them to mean that no religion should be preferred to any other religion and that no person should enjoy privileges or suffer penalties because of his religious beliefs.[13]

His textualist, "no preferences, no privileges, no penalties" approach leads him to a narrow construction of the Establishment Clause. For Scalia, an establishment of religion means preferring one religion over others by giving it alone official status,[14] by providing its members with special privileges, by imposing burdens on those who are not its members, or by granting it financial support not available on a nondiscriminatory basis to other religions. And as he confidently declared in *Kiryas Joel v. Grumet*, "I have always believed, and all my opinions are consistent with the view, that the Establishment Clause prohibits the favoring of one religion over others."[15]

In his dissent in *Lee v. Weisman*, Scalia declared that the Establishment Clause was adopted not only to "prohibit an establishment of religion [such as the Church of England] at the federal level" but also "to protect state establishments of religion from federal interference."[16] He was clearly focusing on the words *respecting* and *an establishment*. His textual reading of *respecting* led him to appreciate the dual purposes the word served: he read it to prohibit not only laws respecting (i.e., tending toward) a national establishment of religion but also laws respecting (i.e., with respect to) existing or future state establishments. And his textual reading of *an establishment* led him to conclude that nondiscriminatory aid to religion was perfectly constitutional.[17] The text prohibits "an establishment" of religion and therefore bars only those official activities that tend to promote the interests of a particular sect; it does not prohibit "the establishment" of religion and therefore does not proscribe official preferences of religion over nonreligion.[18] As he argued in his concurrence in the judgment in *Lamb's Chapel v. Center Moriches Union Free School District*, "As for the asserted Establishment Clause justification, I would hold, simply and clearly, that giving Lamb's Chapel nondiscriminatory access to school facilities cannot violate that provision because it does not signify state or local embrace of a particular religious sect."[19]

Interestingly, however, though Scalia has acted consistently with his textualist reading of the Establishment Clause when it comes to prohibiting an establishment of religion at the federal level, he has unquestioningly accepted the incorporation doctrine and its application of the Establishment Clause to apply to the states and has thereby failed to act consistently with his textualist premises when it comes to protecting state establishments of religion from federal interference. He has never written an opinion that asks the unanswerable question of how it is that the Establishment Clause, intended by the words used by its Framers in the First Congress to prevent the federal government from tampering with state establishments of religion,[20] can possibly be construed to mandate precisely such tampering.[21]

Given his narrow textualist reading of the Establishment Clause, it is not surprising that Scalia has never written the majority opinion in any case addressing that clause.[22] This, however, has left him free to express his no preferences, no privileges, no penalties understanding of the Establishment Clause clearly and without the need to accommodate the views of others. In particular, it has allowed him to engage in systematic critiques of the three major tests the Supreme Court has from time to time applied to determine whether acts of the federal or state governments constitute an establishment of religion: the three-prong *Lemon* test, the endorsement test, and the coercion test.

In *Lemon v. Kurtzman* in 1971, the Court spelled out a three-prong test to determine whether a statute conforms to the requirements of the Establishment Clause: "First, the statute must have a secular legislative purpose; second, its principal or primary effect must be one that neither advances nor inhibits religion; and finally, the statute must not foster 'an excessive government entanglement with religion.'"[23] Since Scalia understands the Establishment Clause to prohibit only "the favoring of one religion over others,"[24] he has, of course, consistently refused to apply the *Lemon* test.

He has attacked in particular *Lemon*'s "purpose" prong. To begin with, he denies that "the 'purpose' requirement of *Lemon* is a proper interpretation of the

Constitution."[25] As he declared in *Church of Lukumi Bababu Aye v. City of Hialeah*,[26] "The First Amendment does not refer to the purposes for which legislators enact laws, but to the effects of the law enacted."

Further, he contends that by allowing the justices to substitute their determination of what the purpose of a law is for that of the popular branches, the purpose test simply transfers power to the Court. In *Edwards v. Aguillard*, the test allowed the justices to dismiss Louisiana's claim that the secular purpose behind its passage of the Balanced Treatment Act (requiring the state's public schools to give a "balanced treatment" to "creation science" and "evolution science") was to protect academic freedom, and it allowed them to conclude instead that the state's purpose was to advance religion. Not only was this an improper role for the Court to play, according to Scalia, but it also wrongly allowed the Court subjectively to invalidate a law "on the basis of its visceral knowledge regarding what must have motivated the legislators."[27] In a strongly worded dissent in *Aguillard*, he reminded his colleagues that the Establishment Clause does not forbid legislators from acting upon "their religious convictions. We surely would not strike down a law providing money to feed the hungry or shelter the homeless if it could be demonstrated that, but for the religious beliefs of the legislators, the funds would not have been approved." Turning to tradition, he argued that "political activism by the religiously motivated is part of our heritage." And he flatly rejected the presumption "that the sole purpose of a law is to advance religion merely because it was supported strongly by organized religions or by adherents of particular faiths." Doing so would violate what he considers the "no penalties" injunction of the Religion Clauses, for it "would deprive religious men and women of their right to participate in the political process." He concluded, "Today's religious activism may give us the Balanced Treatment Act, but yesterday's resulted in the abolition of slavery, and tomorrow's may bring relief for famine victims."[28]

Because of its flaws, *Lemon*'s purpose prong has resulted in what Scalia has described as a "strange Establishment Clause geometry of crooked lines and wavering shapes."[29] As he declared in *Aguillard*, it has

> made such a maze of the Establishment Clause that even the most conscientious governmental officials can only guess what motives will be held unconstitutional. We have said essentially the following: Government may not act with the purpose of advancing religion, except when forced to do so by the Free Exercise Clause (which is now and then); or when eliminating existing governmental hostility to religion (which exists sometimes); or even when merely accommodating governmentally uninhibited religious practices, except that at some point (it is unclear where) intentional

accommodation results in the fostering of religion, which is of course unconstitutional.[30]

Because of these serious deficiencies and because of the presence of competing tests for determining violations of the Establishment Clause, the *Lemon* test has only been used intermittently. Nonetheless, it is occasionally invoked, and when it was in *Lamb's Chapel*, it served to bring out one of the best of Scalia's rhetorical flourishes:

> Like some ghoul in a late-night horror movie that repeatedly sits up in its grave and shuffles abroad, after being repeatedly killed and buried, *Lemon* stalks our Establishment Clause jurisprudence once again, frightening the little children and school attorneys of Center Moriches Union Free School District. . . . Over the years, no fewer than five of the currently sitting Justices have, in their own opinions, personally driven pencils through the creature's heart and a sixth has joined an opinion doing so.
>
> The secret of the *Lemon* test's survival, I think, is that it is so easy to kill. It is there to scare us (and our audience) when we wish it to do so, but we can command it to return to the tomb at will. When we wish to strike down a practice it forbids, we invoke it; when we wish to uphold a practice it forbids, we ignore it entirely. Such a docile and useful monster is worth keeping around, at least in a somnolent state; one never knows when one might need him.[31]

The flaws in the *Lemon* test have led other justices to develop other tests for determining whether official acts conform to the Establishment Clause. One such test, "government endorsement or disapproval of religion," was first enunciated by Justice Sandra Day O'Connor in her concurrence in *Lynch v. Donnelly*.[32] "Endorsement," she declared, "sends a message to nonadherents that they are outsiders, not full members of the political community, and an accompanying message to adherents that they are insiders, favored members of the political community. Disapproval sends the opposite message." For her, it is "the evil of government endorsement or disapproval of religion"[33] ("whether intentionally or unintentionally"[34] and whether of a particular religion or religions in general) that the Establishment Clause condemns, not whether it advances or inhibits religion.[35]

Again, because the endorsement test departs from his own textualist no preferences, no privileges, no penalties understanding of the Religion Clauses, Scalia has simply refused to join any opinion employing it. In *Lamb's Chapel*, for instance, he declared, "I cannot join [the majority opinion] for yet another reason:

the Court's statement that the proposed use of the school's facilities is constitutional because (among other things) it would not signal endorsement of religion in general." In his concurrence in the judgment, he trenchantly remarked: "What a strange notion, that a Constitution which *itself* gives 'religion in general' preferential treatment (I refer to the Free Exercise Clause) forbids endorsement of religion in general." He observed that New York's attorney general "not only agrees with that strange notion, he has an explanation for it: 'Religious advocacy,' he writes, 'serves the community only in the eyes of its adherents and yields a benefit only to those who already believe.'" But, Scalia continued, "[t]hat was *not* the view of those who adopted our Constitution, who believed that the public virtues inculcated by religion are a public good." He offered an example: "[D]uring the summer of 1789, when it was in the process of drafting the First Amendment, Congress enacted the Northwest Territory Ordinance that the Confederation Congress had adopted in 1787—Article III of which provides: 'Religion, morality, and knowledge, *being necessary to good government and the happiness of mankind,* schools and the means of education shall forever be encouraged.'" For him, the conclusion was obvious: endorsement of religion in general is a good thing, not something to be rooted out by the Supreme Court. As he put it, "Indifference to 'religion in general' is *not* what our cases, both old and recent, demand."[36]

His refusal to employ the endorsement test meant that he was reduced from writing the opinion of the Court to writing only the judgment of the Court in *Capitol Square v. Pinette.* Although O'Connor (and David Souter and Stephen Breyer, who joined her opinion) found that there was no government endorsement of religion present in allowing the Ku Klux Klan to display an unattended cross on the statehouse square, she insisted that the endorsement test "asks the right question about governmental practices challenged on Establishment Clause grounds,"[37] and she objected to Scalia's efforts to limit the test to "expression *by the government itself.*"[38] Scalia, however, insisted to the contrary and made the textualist argument that "[b]y its terms that Clause applies only to the words and acts of *government.* It was never meant, and has never been read by this Court, to serve as an impediment to purely *private* religious speech connected to the State only through its occurrence in a public forum."[39] To read the Establishment Clause as restricting private religious speech would, he declared, make the First Amendment "more hospitable to private expletives than to private prayers," more protective of "pornography" than "piety." This reading, he continued, "would be merely bizarre were religious speech simply *as* protected by the Constitution as other forms of private speech; but it is outright perverse when one considers that private religious expression receives *preferential* treatment under the Free Exercise Clause."[40] O'Connor contended, however, that "an impermissible message of endorsement can be sent in a variety of contexts, not all of which involve direct government speech or outright favoritism." And wanting to preserve her freedom to employ the endorsement test to invalidate even "private speech endorsing religion" should the need arise,[41] she clung to her endorsement test.

In *Lee v. Weisman*, Justice Anthony Kennedy introduced still another test for determining whether official acts constitute an establishment of religion. He held for a five-member majority that exposing junior high students to an officially invited nondenominational prayer at a graduation ceremony violated the Establishment Clause because it psychologically coerced the students to participate in a formal religious exercise.[42] Students at graduation who want "to avoid the fact or appearance of participation" in the invocation or benediction are, Kennedy proclaimed, psychologically obligated by state-induced "public pressure as well as peer pressure . . . to stand as a group or, at least, maintain respectful silence."[43]

Kennedy's opinion provided Scalia with the opportunity to elaborate on the no penalties dimension of his no preferences, no privileges, no penalties approach. Consistent with this text-and-tradition jurisprudence, he began by looking at the "history and tradition of our Nation," which, he noted, "are replete with public ceremonies featuring prayers of thanksgiving and petition."[44]

He observed how "the Declaration of Independence, the document marking our birth as a separate people, 'appealed to the Supreme Judge of the world for the rectitude of our intentions' and avowed 'a firm reliance on the protection of divine Providence'"; how George Washington, "after swearing his oath of office on a Bible," prayed in his first inaugural address and thereby "deliberately made a prayer a part of his first official act as President"; how Thomas Jefferson and James Madison prayed in their inaugural addresses; how "our national celebration of Thanksgiving . . . dates back to President Washington"; how "congressional sessions have opened with a chaplain's prayer ever since the First Congress"; and how the Supreme Court's "own sessions have opened with the invocation 'God save the United States and this Honorable Court' since the days of Chief Justice Marshall."[45] He also pointed out that "[i]n addition to this general tradition of prayer at public ceremonies, there exists a more specific tradition of invocations and benedictions at public school graduation exercises." He informed his colleagues that "the first public high school graduation ceremony took place in Connecticut in July 1868—the very month, as it happens, that the Fourteenth Amendment (the vehicle by which the Establishment Clause has been applied against the States) was ratified" and that, at this ceremony, "15 seniors from the Norwich Free Academy marched in their best Sunday suits and dresses into a church hall and waited through majestic music and long prayers."[46] And he argued that the Court's approach to prayer at public school graduation exercises should be governed by this tradition, not by a "psycho-coercion test, which suffers the double disability of having no roots whatever in our people's historic practice, and being as infinitely expandable as the reasons for psychotherapy itself."[47]

According to Scalia, the Court was wrong not only because it laid waste "a tradition that is as old as public school graduation ceremonies themselves, and that is a component of an even more longstanding American tradition of nonsectarian prayer to God at public celebrations generally" but also because it departed from the traditional constitutional understanding of what constitutes coercion and therefore a penalty. "The coercion that was a hallmark of historical establishments of religion was coercion of religious orthodoxy and of financial support *by force of law and threat of penalty.*" He noted that in the colony of Virginia, for example, where the Church of England had been established, "ministers were required by law to conform to the doctrine and rites of the Church of England; and all persons were required to attend church and observe the Sabbath, were tithed for the public support of Anglican ministers, and were taxed for the costs of building and repairing churches." It was that kind of coercion that the Establishment Clause prohibited, not the "ersatz, 'peer-pressure' psycho-coercion" that obliges a student to appear to take part in the invocation and benediction at graduation ceremonies.[48] And it was that kind of coercion, "backed by threat of penalty," that the members of the Court actually knew something about because, as he noted, they "have made a career of reading the disciples of Blackstone rather than Freud."[49]

The Court had invented "a boundless, and boundlessly manipulable, test of psychological coercion,"[50] and Scalia would have none of it. Attacking with all the wit and sarcasm he could muster, he declared:

> I find it a sufficient embarrassment that our Establishment Clause jurisprudence regarding holiday displays has come to "require scrutiny more commonly associated with interior decorators than with the judiciary." But interior decorating is a rock-hard science compared to psychology practiced by amateurs. A few citations of "research in psychology" that have no particular bearing upon the precise issue here cannot disguise the fact that the Court has gone beyond the realm where judges know what they are doing.[51]

Scalia's textualist, no preferences, no privileges, no penalties approach also leads him to a narrow construction of the Free Exercise Clause. His no privileges reading is most clearly on display in *Employment Division, Department of Human Resources of Oregon v. Smith,*[52] in which he held for a five-member majority that the Free Exercise Clause permits the state of Oregon to prohibit the use of peyote for sacramental purposes and therefore to deny unemployment benefits to individuals discharged for such use. He declared that the free exercise of religion "means, first and foremost, the right to believe and profess whatever religious doctrine one desires" and thus excludes "all governmental regulation of religious *beliefs* as such" and prohibits the government from "compel[ling] affirmation of religious belief, punish[ing] the expression of religious doctrines it believes to be false, impos[ing] special disabilities on the basis of religious views or religious status, or lend[ing] its power to one or the other side in controversies over religious authority or dogma."[53] It does not, however, prohibit the government from enforcing "a generally applicable law that requires (or forbids) the performance of an act that his religious belief forbids (or requires). As a textual matter, we do not think the words must be given that meaning."[54]

Scalia analogized one part of the First Amendment with another, arguing that it is no more necessary to read the Free Exercise Clause as prohibiting the collection of a general tax from citizens "who believe support of organized government is sinful" than it is to read the Free Press Clause as prohibiting the collection of the same tax from "publishing companies that must pay the tax as a condition of staying in business." "It is a permissible reading of the text, in the one case as in the other," he contended, "to say that if prohibiting the exercise of religion (or burdening the activity of printing) is not the object of the tax but merely the incidental effect of a generally applicable and otherwise valid provision, the First Amendment has not been offended." Neither text nor tradition required a different outcome: "We have never held that an individual's religious beliefs excuse him from compliance with an otherwise valid law prohibiting conduct that the State is free to regulate. On the contrary, the record of more than a century of our free exercise jurisprudence contradicts that proposition."[55]

The respondents argued that even though exemption from generally applicable criminal laws need not automatically be extended to religiously motivated actors, the claim for a religious exemption must be evaluated under the balancing test previously set forth in the unemployment compensation case of *Sherbert v. Verner*,[56] which asks whether the law at issue substantially burdens a religious practice and, if so, whether the burden is justified by a compelling governmental interest. Scalia disagreed. "Even if we were inclined to breathe into *Sherbert* some life beyond the unemployment compensation field, we would not apply it to require exemptions from a generally applicable criminal law."[57] To begin with, such a requirement would put the justices in the position of having to make judgments concerning matters of faith, as it would compel them to "determine the 'centrality' of religious beliefs before applying a 'compelling interest' test in the free exercise field."[58] Moreover, making "an individual's obligation to obey . . . a law contingent upon the law's coincidence with his religious beliefs, except where the state's interest is 'compelling'" would permit him, "by virtue of his beliefs, 'to become a law unto himself' " and thereby threaten the society with "anarchy," a danger that "increases in direct proportion to the society's diversity of religious beliefs, and its determination to coerce or suppress none of them." In short, it would "contradict constitutional tradition and common sense."[59]

Conscious that courts are not the only means by which rights can be protected, Scalia reminded his colleagues that the Oregon legislature was free to make an exception (as a number of other states had already done) for the sacramental use of peyote. (He was quick to note, however, that "to say that a nondiscriminatory religious-practice exemption is permitted, or even that it is desirable, is not to say that it is constitutionally required, and that the appropriate occasions for its creation can be discerned by the courts.")[60] States, he argued, are free, if they choose, to grant exemptions. But what if they were constitutionally proscribed from doing so, as they might have been regarding the exemption of sacramental wine during Prohibition had the drafters of the Eighteenth Amendment been less precise in their drafting than they were?

Scalia has danced around the issue of the use of sacramental wine in Christian services. He said in *Smith* that a state would violate the Free Exercise Clause if it banned the use of wine only for religious purposes.[61] And he would say later in *Kiryas Joel* that even though "not every religion uses wine in its sacraments," making "an exemption from Prohibition for sacramental wine" was an appropriate accommodation and did not constitute an establishment of religion.[62] But what if there were a flat prohibition by the federal government on the use of wine for any purpose, thereby rendering the states unable to grant exemptions? Would the Court be justified under the Free Exercise Clause in granting them?

The drafters of the Eighteenth Amendment clearly did not believe so. They did not assume that the Free Exercise Clause by itself would be sufficient to ensure the use of sacramental wine during Prohibition. This is clear from the amendment's text, and Scalia could have cited this language to strengthen his no privileges interpretation of the Free Exercise Clause. In the amendment, § 1 states: "After one year from the ratification of this article the manufacture, sale, or transportation of intoxicating liquors within, the importation thereof into, or the exportation thereof from the United States and all territory subject to the jurisdiction thereof *for beverage purposes* is hereby prohibited."[63]

The drafters of the Eighteenth Amendment understood that it was a neutral law of general application and that, as such, its prohibition on the "manufacture, sale, and transportation of intoxicating liquors" would apply to sacramental wine. Not wanting that consequence and not believing that the traditional understanding of the Free Exercise Clause would prevent it, they drafted a precise text that limited its prohibition to "intoxicating liquors" used "for beverage purposes," not for sacramental purposes. Instead of dancing around the issue of sacramental wine and Prohibition, Scalia in *Smith* could have quoted the amendment directly and strengthened his already powerful textualist argument.

As noted at the beginning of this chapter, Scalia understands that the principal role of the Court in the area of civil liberties is to prevent the government from "backsliding" in its protection of long-recognized personal liberties. He concluded his majority opinion in *Smith* by observing that

> [v]alues that are protected against government interference through enshrinement in the Bill of Rights are not thereby banished from the political process. Just as a society that believes in the negative protection accorded to the press by the First Amendment is likely to enact laws that affirmatively foster the dissemination of the printed word, so also a society that believes in the negative protection accorded to religious belief can be expected to be solicitous of that value in its legislation as well.[64]

Congress took up Scalia's suggestion and adopted legislation to protect "religious belief" beyond what *Smith* required. Employing its enforcement powers under § 5 of the Fourteenth Amendment, Congress enacted the Religious Freedom Restoration Act (RFRA). RFRA was discussed at length in Chapter Four, as was the Court's declaration in *City of Boerne v. Flores* that it was unconstitutional on the grounds that Congress lacked power under § 5 to enact it.[65] Scalia concurred in all of the *City of Boerne* majority opinion save for the portion that addressed the legislative history of the passage of the Fourteenth Amendment. He concurred separately to rebut Justice O'Connor's use of historical materials that she argued established beyond peradventure that the Free Exercise Clause is "best understood as an affirmative guarantee of the right to participate in religious practices and conduct without impermissible governmental interference, even when such conduct conflicts with a neutral, generally applicable law."[66]

Scalia announced that he was limiting his response to "the new items of 'historical evidence'" brought forward in O'Connor's dissent; nonetheless, he concluded his concurrence by returning to the same theme he had introduced at the end of his *Smith* opinion: namely, "whether the people, through their elected representatives, or rather this Court, shall control the outcome of th[ese] concrete cases." His answer was unequivocal: "It shall be the people."[67] Yet he had just voted with the Court majority to declare unconstitutional what the people, through their elected representatives, had passed, based on Congress's clear enforcement powers delegated to it under § 5 of the Fourteenth Amendment. How these objectives can be accomplished by "a society that believes in the negative protection accorded to religious belief,"[68] that rejects "backsliding,"[69] and that prefers instead to be affirmatively "solicitous of that value"[70] by enacting legislation that adds to its protection is a question Scalia never answers.[71]

As *Smith* displayed Scalia's no privileges approach to the Free Exercise Clause, so *Locke v. Davey* displayed his no preferences and no penalties approach.[72] At issue in this case was the Promise Scholarship Program established by the state of Washington to assist academically gifted students with postsecondary education expenses. In accordance with what are known as the Blaine Amendments to the state's constitution, the program barred students from using the scholarship to pursue a degree in devotional theology. In a seven-to-two opinion written by Chief Justice William Rehnquist, the Court held that "such an exclusion from an otherwise inclusive aid program does not violate the Free Exercise Clause of the First Amendment."[73] Scalia filed an impassioned dissent.

Joshua Davey, the respondent in this case, had relied heavily on *Church of Lukumi Babalu Aye, Inc. v. Hialeah*,[74] in which the Court had held that "[a] law burdening religious practice that is not neutral" is presumptively unconstitutional and "must undergo the most rigorous of scrutiny" and that "the minimum requirement of neutrality is that a law not discriminate on its face."[75] Rehnquist rejected Davey's argument: "To do otherwise would extend the *Lukumi* line of cases well beyond not only their facts but their reasoning. In *Lukumi*, the city of Hialeah made it a crime to engage in certain kinds of animal slaughter. We found that the law sought to suppress ritualistic animal sacrifices of the Santeria religion. In the present case, the state's disfavor of religion (if it can be called that) is of a far milder kind." It did not impose "criminal or civil sanctions on any type of religious service or rite," did not "deny to ministers the right to participate in the political affairs of the community," and did not "require students to choose between their religious beliefs and receiving a government benefit." It merely refused to "fund a distinct category of instruction."[76]

Rehnquist further distinguished *Lukumi* from the facts before him. Far from evincing hostility toward religion, he stated, "the Promise Scholarship Program goes a long way toward including religion in its benefits." It evinced no "animus toward religion," as it permitted students to attend "pervasively religious schools, so long as they are accredited," including Davey's school, Northwest College, which advertised that its "concept of education is distinctly Christian in the evangelical sense" and that it "prepares *all* of its students, 'through instruction, through modeling, [and] through [its] classes, to use . . . the Bible as their guide, as the truth,' no matter their chosen profession." Rehnquist also noted that "under the Promise Scholarship Program's current guidelines, students are still eligible to take devotional theology courses" and that all students at Northwest College "are required to take at least four devotional courses, 'Exploring the Bible,' 'Principles of Spiritual Development,' 'Evangelism in the Christian Life,' and 'Christian Doctrine,' and some students may have additional religious requirements as part of their majors."[77]

Scalia began his dissent by quoting from *Everson v. Board of Education,* more famous for having incorporated the Establishment Clause to apply to the states than for its reflections on the free exercise of religion: "New Jersey cannot hamper its citizens in the free exercise of their own religion. Consequently, it cannot exclude individual Catholics, Lutherans, Mohammedans, Baptists, Jews, Methodists, Non-believers, Presbyterians, or the members of any other faith, because of their faith, or lack of it, from receiving the benefits of public welfare legislation."[78] For Scalia, *Everson* articulated the no penalties principle that should govern in *Davey,* and that governing principle could lead to only one conclusion: when a state "makes a public benefit generally available, that benefit becomes part of the baseline against which burdens on religion are measured," and, therefore, when a state "withholds that benefit from some individuals solely on the basis of religion, it violates the Free Exercise Clause no less than if it had imposed a special tax."[79]

Withdrawing the benefit of the Promise Scholarship from Davey because he wanted to study devotional theology clearly imposed on him a burden, and Scalia contested Rehnquist's characterization of it as being "relatively minor."[80] To begin with, he said, the "indignity of being singled out for special burdens on the basis of one's religious calling is so profound that the concrete harm produced can never be dismissed as insubstantial. The Court has not required proof of 'substantial' concrete harm with other forms of discrimination." And of course, Davey was burdened financially. "The First Amendment, after all, guarantees *free* exercise of religion, and when the State exacts a financial penalty of almost $3,000 for religious exercise—whether by tax or by forfeiture of an otherwise available benefit—religious practice is anything *but* free."[81]

It should be noted that Scalia did not argue that the state of Washington had to provide scholarship support for those wanting to study devotional theology; to do so would run afoul of his no privileges understanding of the Free Exercise Clause. He merely argued that the state could not penalize these students by excluding them from scholarship support. Indeed, Scalia actually suggested ways the state of Washington could constitutionally structure its Promise Scholarship Program so as to conform with the dictates of the Free Exercise Clause: "It could make the scholarships redeemable only at public universities (where it sets the curriculum), or only for select courses of study. Either option would replace a program that facially discriminates against religion with one that just happens not to subsidize it."[82]

Davey reflects not only Scalia's no penalties approach to Free Exercise but also his no preferences approach. He reviewed the possible reasons the state of

Washington might have had for excluding students of devotional theology from scholarship support. He concluded that it could not be "protecting the pocket-books of its citizens" because, "given the tiny fraction of Promise Scholars who would pursue theology degrees, the amount of any citizen's tax bill at stake is *de minimis*"; nor could it be "preventing [the] mistaken appearance of endorsement" because, if the state "merely declines to penalize students for selecting a religious major, no reasonable observer is likely to draw an inference that the state itself is endorsing a religious practice or belief"; nor could it be that this is "a means of assuring that the State will neither favor nor disfavor Davey in his religious calling."[83] Rather, he concluded that it was "a pure philosophical preference" on the part of the state that "it would violate taxpayers' freedom of conscience *not* to discriminate against candidates for the ministry."[84]

By limiting the Promise Scholarship Program in the way it did, the state was preferring those who wished to discriminate against religion over those who wished to practice it; the state was preferring the "freedom of conscience" of those imbued with "a trendy disdain for deep religious conviction"[85] to the "freedom of conscience" of those with such deep convictions. And, Scalia worried, this preference for "secularism"[86] over religion has "no logical limit and can justify the singling out of religion for exclusion from public programs in virtually any context."[87] It could, he feared, justify denying "priests and nuns their prescription-drug benefits on the ground that taxpayers' freedom of conscience forbids medicating the clergy at public expense." Scalia acknowledged that his concerns might "seem fanciful," but he reminded his colleagues that "France has proposed banning religious attire from schools," invoking secular interests "no less benign than those the Court embraces today."[88] For Scalia, in a secular age, only a strong no preferences approach that treats secularism as being a religion can ensure that those who freely exercise their religious beliefs will enjoy no privileges and suffer no penalties.

The First Amendment's Free Speech and Free Press Clauses

After the Religion Clauses come the First Amendment's Free Speech and Free Press Clauses, declaring that "Congress shall make no law . . . abridging the freedom of speech, or the press." In his many opinions on these clauses, Scalia has consistently argued that "the bedrock principle" underlying them "is that government may not prohibit the expression of an idea simply because society finds the idea itself offensive or disagreeable"[89] and that their language "guarantees that you and I can say and believe whatever we like (subject to a few tradition-based exceptions, such as obscenity and 'fighting words') without going to jail or being fined."[90]

As a textualist, Scalia limits freedom of speech and press to "oral and written speech—not 'expressive conduct.'"[91] He therefore argues, along the same lines he argued in the Free Exercise Clause case of *Smith*,[92] that "a general law not specifically targeted at expressive conduct" does not implicate the First Amendment.[93] But, as he insisted in *Barnes v. Glen Theatre, Inc.*, "this is not to say that the First Amendment affords no protection to expressive conduct"; in those instances in which the government has prohibited "conduct *precisely because of its communicative attributes*," he has consistently found the prohibition to be unconstitutional.[94]

For Scalia, the Free Speech and Free Press Clauses, at their core, protect political speech[95] that can be restricted only under the strict-scrutiny test, by which the government must prove that its restriction is narrowly tailored and serves a compelling state interest.[96] They protect especially the statements of political candidates and, he insists, flatly bar the government from "prohibit[ing] candidates from communicating relevant information to voters during an election."[97]

Thus, he wrote the majority opinion in *Republican Party of Minnesota v. White*, striking down a rule of the Minnesota Supreme Court prohibiting candidates for judicial election in that state from announcing their views on disputed legal and political issues.[98] Declaring that "the notion that the special context of electioneering justifies an *abridgment* of the right to speak out on disputed issues sets our First Amendment jurisprudence on its head,"[99] he attacked the state supreme court rule as utterly failing the strict-scrutiny test. Since judges "make law themselves" and "set aside the laws enacted by the legislature,"[100] there was certainly no compelling state interest in keeping the voters ignorant of the views of judicial candidates on disputed legal and political issues, and since the state supreme court rule prohibited "judges (and would-be judges)" from discussing these matters "only at certain times and in certain forums,"[101] it was not narrowly tailored to serve its objective of securing impartial judges.

> The short of the matter is this: In Minnesota, a candidate for judicial office may not say "I think it is constitutional for the legislature to prohibit same-sex marriages." He may say the very same thing, however, up until the very day before he declares himself a candidate, and may say it repeatedly (until litigation is pending) after he is elected. As a means of pursuing the objective of open-mindedness that respondents now articulate, the announce clause is so woefully underinclusive as to render belief in that purpose a challenge to the credulous.[102]

According to Scalia, the Free Speech and Free Press Clauses protect political parties and corporations no less than candidates.[103] In *California Democratic Party v. Jones*,[104] Scalia wrote the majority opinion protecting the right of political parties to determine for themselves who can vote in their primary elections and striking down on First Amendment grounds California's "blanket" primary system.

Under that system, every voter received a ballot listing every candidate for every office regardless of party affiliation and was allowed to choose freely among them; the candidate of each party who received the greatest number of votes became that party's nominee.

The state defended its blanket primary on the grounds that it would produce less partisan, more moderate, and more representative candidates in the general election. The messages they would communicate to voters would be "closer to the median policy positions of their districts" than would those of candidates selected only by party members. Scalia argued, however, that it violated the free speech and free press rights of the parties. Opening up a party's primary election to "persons wholly unaffiliated with the party" has "the likely outcome—indeed, in this case the *intended* outcome—of changing the parties' message."[105] Only evidence that California's blanket primary was "narrowly tailored to serve a compelling state interest" could save it. As Scalia continued, however, even if the Court were to agree that all the interests proffered by the state were compelling, the blanket primary law was "not a narrowly tailored means of furthering them." He finished by remarking that "[r]espondents' legitimate state interests and petitioners' First Amendment rights are not inherently incompatible"[106] and could be reconciled "by resorting to a *nonpartisan* blanket primary" under which the state would determine "what qualifications it requires for a candidate to have a place on the primary ballot—which may include nomination by established parties and voter-petition requirements for independent candidates"—and would then permit "[e]ach voter, regardless of party affiliation, [to] vote for any candidate," with "the top two vote getters (or however many the State prescribes) then mov[ing] on to the general election."[107]

And in his opinion in *McConnell v. Federal Elections Commission*, Scalia dissented from the Court's opinion generally upholding the constitutionality of the Bipartisan Campaign Reform Act of 2002 (BCRA), popularly known as the McCain-Feingold Act. According to Scalia, the BCRA violated the First Amendment because, even though "we are governed by Congress," it prohibits "the criticism of Members of Congress by those entities most capable of giving such criticism loud voice: national political parties and corporations." Its "most offensive provisions" forbid "national-party use of 'soft' money to fund 'issue ads' that incumbents find so offensive" and "pre-election criticism of incumbents by corporations, even not-for-profit corporations, by use of their general funds."[108]

Scalia engaged in a text-and-tradition analysis of what he described as the "three fallacious propositions" embraced by those who defended the constitutionality of the BCRA. The first is that "money is not speech." This proposition holds that raising and spending money is conduct, not speech, and may therefore be regulated as other forms of conduct, such as burning draft cards.[109] "Until today," Scalia, observed, "that view has been categorically rejected by our jurisprudence," and "our traditional view was correct."[110] The traditional view was correct, he insisted, for, although raising and spending money was, indeed, conduct, it was expressive conduct, and the BCRA specifically targeted it for the messages it could communicate.[111] Scalia acknowledged that not "*any* regulation of money is a regulation of speech," and he readily conceded that "[t]he government may apply general commercial regulations to those who use money for speech if it applies them even-handedly to those who use money for other purposes." But, he insisted, "where the government singles out money used to fund speech as its legislative object, it is acting against speech as such, no less than if it had targeted the paper on which a book was printed or the trucks that deliver it to the bookstore."[112]

Moreover, the traditional view was correct because "[i]n any economy operated on even the most rudimentary principles of division of labor, effective public communication requires the speaker to make use of the services of others. An author may write a novel, but he will seldom publish and distribute it himself. A freelance reporter may write a story, but he will rarely edit, print, and deliver it to subscribers." Scalia drilled his point home:

> To a government bent on suppressing speech, this mode of organization presents opportunities: Control any cog in the machine, and you can halt the whole apparatus. License printers, and it matters little whether authors are still free to write. Restrict the sale of books, and it matters little who prints them. Predictably, repressive regimes have exploited these principles by attacking all levels of the production and dissemination of ideas. . . . The right to speak would be largely ineffective if it did not include the right to engage in financial transactions that are the incidents of its exercise.[113]

The founding generation saw such practices as "grievous incursions on the freedom of the press," he noted, and until its validation of BCRA, the Court had "kept faith with the Founders' tradition."[114] He concluded his analysis of the first proposition:

> [A] law limiting the amount a person can spend to broadcast his political views is a direct restriction on speech. That is no different from a law limiting the amount a newspaper can pay its editorial staff or the amount a charity can pay its leafletters. It is equally clear that a limit on the amount a candidate can *raise* from any one individual for the purpose of speaking is also a direct limitation on speech. That is no different from a law limiting the amount a publisher can accept from any one shareholder or lender, or the amount a newspaper can charge any one advertiser or customer.[115]

The second fallacious proposition, according to Scalia, is that "the First Amendment right to spend money for speech does not include the right to combine with others in spending money for speech." He declared that the freedom to associate with others for the dissemination of ideas is part of the freedom of speech and that this freedom extends not just to "singing or speaking in unison" but to "pooling financial resources for expressive purposes."[116] Otherwise, he insisted, "Congress would be empowered to enact legislation requiring newspapers to be sole proprietorships, banning their use of partnership or corporate form." Since that sort of restriction "would be an obvious violation of the First Amendment," he found it "incomprehensible why the conclusion should change when what is at issue is the pooling of funds for the most important (and most perennially threatened) category of speech: electoral speech." And, he concluded, without full First Amendment protection for such financial association, the very existence of all political parties is threatened.[117]

For Scalia, the third fallacious proposition explaining the Court's "casual abridgment of free speech rights" is that "the particular form of association known as a corporation does not enjoy full First Amendment protection." He noted, first of all, that "the text of the First Amendment does not limit its application in this fashion, even though 'by the end of the eighteenth century the corporation was a familiar figure in American economic life.'"[118] He then turned to the Court's traditional understanding of corporate speech, expressed in *First National Bank of Boston v. Belloti*: "The inherent worth of the speech in terms of its capacity for informing the public does not depend upon the identity of its source, whether corporation, association, union, or individual."[119]

In *Austin v. Michigan Chamber of Commerce*,[120] in which the Court upheld a state prohibition of independent corporate expenditures in support of candidates for state office, Scalia had dissented from the Court's departure from this traditional understanding. He indicated that he was convinced that the Founders would have endorsed Tocqueville's argument in *Democracy in America* for the need for strong private associations, including corporations, to check the power of democratic governments. In aristocratic countries, Tocqueville observed, the nobility stand upon such a lofty platform that they are able to introduce their opinions and sentiments into the minds and hearts of the multitude. In democratic countries, however (and here Scalia quoted Tocqueville), "the governing power alone is naturally in a condition to act in this manner," allowing it to "exercise, even unintentionally, an insupportable tyranny." Tocqueville's worry was Scalia's: "Worse still will be the case if the government really believes itself interested in preventing all circulation of ideas; it will then stand motionless and oppressed by the heaviness of voluntary torpor." And Tocqueville's solution to this problem was, Scalia believed, the Founders' solution—and accordingly, his as well: "Governments, therefore, should not be the only active powers; associations ought, in democratic nations, to stand in lieu of those powerful private individuals whom the equality of conditions has swept away."[121]

In his *McConnell* opinion, Scalia picked up where he had left off in *Austin*. He clearly saw the BCRA as allowing the federal government and especially incumbents in Congress to silence the opposition: "In the modern world, giving the government power to exclude corporations from the political debate enables it effectively to muffle the voices that best represent the most significant segments of the economy and the most passionately held social and political views."[122] He noted that people who pool their financial resources for purposes of economic enterprise "overwhelmingly do so in the corporate form." Moreover, he continued, with increasing frequency, incorporation is chosen by those who "associate to defend and promote particular ideas—such as the American Civil Liberties Union and the National Rifle Association, parties to these cases." He gave a hypothetical example:

> Imagine . . . a government that wished to suppress nuclear power—or oil and gas exploration, or automobile manufacturing, or gun ownership, or civil liberties—and that had the power to prohibit corporate advertising against its proposals. To be sure, the individuals involved in, or benefited by, those industries, or interested in those causes, could (given enough time) form political action committees or other associations to make their case. But the organizational form in which those enterprises already *exist*, and in which they can most quickly and most effectively get their message across, is the corporate form.[123]

The First Amendment, he insisted, "does not . . . permit the restriction of that political speech," and, he continued, "the same holds true for corporate electoral speech: A candidate should not be insulated from the most effective speech that the major participants in the economy and major incorporated interest groups can generate."[124]

Scalia was willing to "stipulate that all those who voted for the Act believed they were acting for the good of the country" by attempting to make campaigns "fairer."[125] But, as he proclaimed in *Austin*, "government cannot be trusted to assure, through censorship, the 'fairness' of political debate."[126] Those who voted for the BCRA were concerned about the "amassed wealth" of for-profit and not-for-profit corporations, but Scalia noted that the "most direct threat from that source comes in the form of undisclosed favors and payoffs to elected officials—which have already been criminalized, and will be rendered no more discoverable by the legislation at issue here." Moreover, he argued, the use of corporate wealth to speak to the electorate is unlikely to distort elections, *"especially* if disclosure requirements *tell* the people where the speech is coming from." For Scalia, the premise of the First Amendment is that "the American people are neither sheep nor fools, and hence fully capable of considering both the substance of the speech presented to them and its proximate and ultimate source." If that premise is wrong, he averred, "our democracy has a much greater problem to overcome than merely the influence of amassed wealth. Given the premises of democracy, there is no such thing as *too much* speech."[127]

The defenders of the BCRA also argued that corporate speech in the form of contributions to a candidate's campaign "engenders an obligation which is later paid in the form of greater access to the officeholder, or indeed in the form of votes on particular bills." Scalia observed that "any *quid-pro-quo* agreement for votes would of course violate criminal law, and actual payoff *votes* have not even been claimed by those favoring the restrictions on corporate speech."[128] He admitted that "corporate (like noncorporate) allies will have greater access to the officeholder, and that he will tend to favor the same causes as those who support him (which is usually *why* they supported him)." But, he continued, that is "the nature of politics—if not indeed human nature—and how this can properly be considered 'corruption' (or 'the appearance of corruption') with regard to corporate allies and not with regard to other allies is beyond me." With his textualist foundations showing, he continued: "If the Bill of Rights had intended an exception to the freedom of speech in order to combat this malign proclivity of the officeholder to agree with those who agree with him, and to speak more with his supporters than his opponents, it would surely have said so. It did not do so, I think, because the juice is not worth the squeeze."[129] For Scalia, "corporate . . . influences are well enough checked (so long as adequate campaign-expenditure disclosure rules exist) by the politician's fear of being portrayed as 'in the pocket' of so-called moneyed interests." Moreover, he insisted, the "incremental benefit obtained by muzzling corporate speech is more than offset by loss of the information and persuasion that corporate speech can contain. That, at least, is the assumption of a constitutional guarantee which prescribes that Congress shall make no law abridging the freedom of speech."[130]

For Scalia, the First Amendment protects not only candidates, parties, and corporations but also those who protest public policies in public forums.[131] His colleagues would say they are in full agreement with him, but he would demur and point out that, under the Court's "relentlessly pro-abortion jurisprudence,"[132] the free speech rights of antiabortion protestors have been repeatedly suppressed "in stark contradiction of the constitutional principles we apply in all other contexts."[133] And, he would continue, none of this "should come as a surprise" because when the right to an abortion is involved, the Court has set in motion an *"ad hoc nullification machine"* that "push[es] aside whatever doctrines of constitutional law stand in the way of that highly favored practice."[134]

In *Hill v. Colorado*,[135] the Court affirmed the constitutionality of a Colorado statute that made it a criminal offense knowingly to approach within 8 feet of another person on the public way or sidewalk area within 100 feet of the entrance door of a health-care facility for the purpose of passing a leaflet or displaying a sign to or engaging in oral protest, education, or counseling with that person without that person's consent. To begin with, the Court held that the statute was content-neutral, restricting neither a particular viewpoint nor any subject matter that may be discussed by a speaker. Rather, it simply established "a minor place restriction on an extremely broad category of communications with unwilling listeners. Instead of drawing distinctions based on the subject that the approaching speaker may wish to address, the statute applies equally to used car salesmen, animal rights activists, fundraisers, environmentalists, and missionaries. Each can attempt to educate unwilling listeners on any subject, but without consent may not approach within eight feet to do so."[136] As such, it was simply a valid time, place, and manner regulation, narrowly tailored to serve the state's interest in preserving unimpeded access to abortion facilities.

Scalia vigorously dissented. The statute was, he insisted, "obviously and undeniably content-based." He noted that a speaker can approach another for the purpose of communicating any message except one of protest, education, or counseling without the need of first securing the other's consent, and thus, "[w]hether a speaker must obtain permission before approaching within eight feet—and whether he will be sent to prison for failing to do so—depends entirely on *what he intends to say* when he gets there." He had "no doubt that this regulation would be deemed content-based *in an instant* if the case before us involved antiwar protesters, or union members seeking to 'educate' the public about the reasons for their strike." But, he regretted, "the jurisprudence of this Court has a way of changing when abortion is involved."[137] He marveled at the Court's "confident assurance" that the statute posed no special First Amendment threat because it applied alike to "used car salesmen, animal rights activists, fundraisers, environmentalists, and missionaries." He pointed out that it was a "wonderful replication (except for its lack of sarcasm) of Anatole France's observation that 'the law, in its majestic equality, forbids the rich as well as the poor to sleep under bridges. ...' This Colorado law is no more targeted at used car salesmen, animal rights activists, fund raisers, environmentalists, and missionaries than French vagrancy law was targeted at the rich." He turned to the text of the statute for confirmation of his argument: "We know what the Colorado legislators, by their careful selection of content ('protest, education, and counseling'), were taking aim at, for they set it forth in the statute itself: the 'right to protest or counsel *against* certain medical procedures' on the sidewalks and streets surrounding health care facilities."[138]

For Scalia, the Court's refusal to see the Colorado statute as a content-based regulation of speech was, by itself, bad enough, but as he noted, it was only "one of many aggressively pro-abortion novelties announced by the Court" in its decision, and, in fact, it was not the worst. Worse still was the Court's apparent willingness to regard protecting people from "unwelcomed communications" as a compelling state interest.[139] Justice John Paul Stevens, writing for the majority, declared that "the unwilling listener's interest in avoiding unwanted communication has been repeatedly identified in our cases. It is an aspect of the broader 'right to be let alone' that one of our wisest Justices [Louis Brandeis] characterized as 'the most comprehensive of rights and the right most valued by civilized men.' *Olmstead v. United States.*[140] The right to avoid unwelcome speech has special force in the privacy of the home and its immediate surroundings, but can also be protected in confrontational settings."[141]

Scalia could hardly contain himself. To begin with, he observed that the Court had "elevated the abortion clinic to the status of the home."[142] But more fundamentally and "amusing[ly]," the "slim reed" supplied by the Court's invocation of Brandeis contradicted rather than supported its own position. Scalia reminded the Court that the right to be let alone that Justice Brandeis had identified "was a right the Constitution 'conferred, *as against the* government,'" not as against one's fellow citizens, and thus, "[t]o the extent that there can be gleaned from our cases a 'right to be let alone' in the sense that Justice Brandeis intended, it is the right of the *speaker* in the public forum to be free from government interference of the sort Colorado has imposed here."[143] All of this supported his basic conclusion: "Suffice it to say that if protecting people from unwelcome communications is a compelling state interest, the First Amendment is a dead letter."[144]

For Scalia, the First Amendment also protects from criminal prosecution those who engage in even "constitutionally proscribable"[145] speech (e.g., cross burning or "fighting words") if the government's efforts to regulate that speech are "based on hostility . . . towards the underlying message expressed."[146] He elaborated upon this argument at some length in his opinion for the Court in *R.A.V. v. City of St. Paul.* St. Paul, Minnesota, had passed a "bias-motivated crime ordinance" that made it a misdemeanor to display a symbol "including, but not limited to, a burning cross or Nazi swastika, which one knows or has reasonable grounds to know arouses anger, alarm or resentment in others on the basis of race, color, creed, religion or gender." Scalia found it to be "facially unconstitutional in that it prohibits otherwise permitted speech solely on the basis of the subjects the speech addresses."[147]

Scalia argued that, although content-based regulations of speech are presumptively invalid, the First Amendment permits restrictions upon the content of speech in a few limited areas, including obscenity, defamation, and so-called fighting words, because they "are 'of such slight social value as a step to truth that any benefit that may be derived from them is clearly outweighed by the social interest in order and morality.'" As he continued, "We have recognized that 'the freedom of speech' referred to by the First Amendment does not include a freedom to disregard these traditional limitations."[148] But, he elaborated, that does not mean that the government can restrict these categories of speech for reasons "unrelated to their distinctively proscribable content." Thus, though the government may proscribe libel, "it may not make the further content discrimination of proscribing *only* libel critical of the government." He rejected the view that the First Amendment "imposes no obstacle whatsoever to regulation of particular instances of such proscribable expression, so that the government may regulate them freely." Were that the case, it "would mean that a city council could enact an ordinance prohibiting only those legally obscene works that contain criticism of the city government or, indeed, that do not include endorsement of the city government. Such a simplistic, all-or-nothing-at-all approach to First Amendment protection is at odds with common sense and with our jurisprudence as well."[149]

Scalia drew a comparison between proscribable forms of speech and "a noisy sound truck." Both are modes of speech that can be used to convey an idea, he contended, but they do not have, in and of themselves, a claim upon the First Amendment. However, as with the sound truck, so too with fighting words, "[t]he government may not regulate use based on hostility—or favoritism—towards the underlying message expressed."[150]

When he applied these principles to St. Paul's ordinance, he concluded that it was facially unconstitutional. He noted that it applied only to fighting words that insulted or provoked violence "on the basis of race, color, creed, religion or gender," not to fighting words that expressed hostility, for example, "on the basis of political affiliation, union membership, or homosexuality."[151] It allowed one to hold up a sign saying that "all 'anti-Catholic bigots' are misbegotten but not that all 'papists' are, for that would insult and provoke violence 'on the basis of religion.'" The First Amendment, he insisted, "does not permit St. Paul to impose special prohibitions on those speakers who express views on disfavored subjects." Even speech subject to content regulation cannot be subjected to viewpoint discrimination. Or, as Scalia so colorfully put it, "St. Paul has no such authority to license one side of a debate to fight freestyle, while requiring the other to follow Marquis of Queensberry rules."[152]

St. Paul had defended its ordinance on the grounds that it wished to display the city council's special hostility toward the particular biases singled out. But, as

Scalia underscored, "[t]hat is precisely what the First Amendment forbids."[153] The city council was entitled to express that hostility in many ways, including, for example, through the adoption of resolutions condemning racial, religious, and gender bias. However, it was forbidden by the First Amendment from doing so "through the means of imposing unique limitations upon speakers who (however benightedly) disagree."[154]

Scalia limits the meaning of the text of the Free Speech and Free Press Clauses to "oral and written speech" traditionally covered by their protection. As a consequence, he has refused to participate in the Court's "invent[ion]" of new First Amendment rights such as the right to be free from politically motivated hiring, firing, or contracting by government.[155]

In *Rutan v. Republican Party of Illinois,*[156] the Court held that the First Amendment forbids governmental officials from promoting, transferring, recalling after layoff, or hiring public employees on the basis of party affiliation and support. Justice William Brennan, writing for the Court majority, relied heavily on its 1976 decision in *Elrod v. Burns*[157] and its 1980 decision in *Branti v. Finkel,*[158] which had found that the patronage practice of discharging public employees on the basis of their political affiliation violated the First Amendment. Scalia dissented, arguing that *Elrod* and *Branti* should be "overruled," not extended.[159] When in *Board of County Commissioners, Wabaunsee County, Kansas v. Umbehr*[160] and *O'Hare Truck Service Inc. v. City of Northlake*[161] the Court went further still and, in Scalia's words, "extended" these patronage precedents "*far* beyond *Rutan* to the massive field of all governmental contracting," he filed a searing combined dissent. Declaring that "the cases before the Court today set the blood boiling,"[162] he accused the majority of displaying a "fickle" commitment to the Constitution by "proscribing as unconstitutional practices that do not violate any explicit text of the Constitution and that have been regarded as constitutional ever since the framing."[163]

He argued in his dissent in *Rutan* that the Constitution treats the government differently in its "capacity as lawmaker, i.e., as a regulator of private conduct" than in its "capacity as employer."[164] He noted, for example, that "[p]rivate citizens cannot be punished for refusing to provide the government information that may incriminate them, but government employees can be dismissed when the incriminating information that they refuse to provide relates to the performance of their jobs." What is true of the Constitution generally, he observed, is also true for the First Amendment, which "does not apply to laws enacted in the government's capacity as employer in the same way that it does to laws enacted in the government's capacity as regulator of private conduct." Otherwise, he pointed out, the Court could not have upheld, in a whole series of opinions,[165] the federal Hatch Act and similarly drafted state statutes that provide for the dismissal of federal and state employees for engaging in partisan political activity.[166]

Scalia suggested in *Rutan* that the First Amendment is implicated not in cases where the government is employer but only in those cases where government, as lawmaker, can "impose criminal penalties."[167] In his combined dissent in *Umbehr* and *O'Hare Truck Service*, he made this argument explicitly: "The First Amendment guarantees that you and I can say and believe whatever we like (subject to a few tradition-based exceptions, such as obscenity and 'fighting words') without going to jail or being fined."[168] Since there were no criminal penalties (no jail time, no fines) involved in any of these patronage cases, Scalia argued that the First Amendment was not implicated, and hence, there was no justification for the Court's use of strict scrutiny to invalidate hiring, firing, and contracting policies by politicians that "reward one's allies" and "refuse to reward one's opponents."[169] The appropriate test to determine the constitutionality of patronage schemes was, he insisted in *Rutan*, the rational-basis test: "Can the governmental advantages of th[ese] employment practice[s] reasonably be deemed to outweigh [their] 'coercive' effects?" And the "*dispositive*" answer to that question was, he declared, found in "the clear and continuing tradition of our people."[170] The American people have traditionally found the advantages of patronage to outweigh their coercive effects (and thus to be rational) because patronage helps maintain "party discipline" and thereby "stabilizes political parties," because it "prevents excessive political fragmentation" and thereby fosters the two-party system, and because it is "a powerful means of achieving social and political integration."[171] These traditional reasons were, for Scalia, sufficient to allow the question of whether patronage should continue or end "to be left to the judgment of the people's elected representatives."[172]

For the same reasons that he argues the First Amendment does not ban political patronage in hiring, firing, or contracting, Scalia contends it does not prohibit government from refusing to subsidize political viewpoints with which it disagrees. He concurred in the judgment in the Court's decision in *National Endowment of the Arts* [NEA] *v. Finley*,[173] which concluded that a federal statute directing the NEA to consider standards of decency and respect for the diverse beliefs and values of the American public when it judged applications for arts grants was not facially invalid under the First Amendment. However, he found the Court's reasoning so poor that he began his concurrence by declaring: " 'The operation was a success, but the patient died.' What such a procedure is to medicine, the Court's opinion in this case is to law."[174] Justice O'Connor argued for the Court majority that the statute somehow did not engage in content or viewpoint discrimination, but Scalia disagreed. It did discriminate on the basis of content and viewpoint, but, he argued, that discrimination was entirely permissible because the First Amendment is "inapplicable" when it comes to government funding programs.[175] The Free Speech and Free Press Clauses have no application because the withholding of federal funds is not an abridgment of speech.

Scalia cited Thomas Sheridan's definition of *abridge* from the 1796 edition of *The Complete Dictionary of the English Language*: "To abridge is 'to contract, to diminish; to deprive of.' "[176] With that contemporaneous definition of the First Amendment's use of the word *abridge* before him, the textualist Scalia declared: "Congress did not *abridge* the speech of those who disdain the beliefs and values of the American public, nor did it *abridge* indecent speech. Those who wish to create indecent and disrespectful art are as unconstrained now as they were before the enactment of this statute. *Avant-garde artistes* such as respondents remain entirely free to *epater les bourgeois*; they are merely deprived of the additional satisfaction of having the bourgeoisie taxed to pay for it."[177]

The government is "not constitutionally required to fund" indecent or disrespectful speech.[178] Rather, Scalia argued, it is "the very business of government to favor and disfavor points of view on (in modern times, at least) innumerable subjects—which is the main reason we have decided to elect those who run the government." And, he insisted, revealing his logical-positivist premises, it makes no difference insofar as the Constitution is concerned whether the government furthers its "favored point of view by achieving it directly (having government-employed artists paint pictures, for example, or government-employed doctors perform abortions); or by advocating it officially (establishing an Office of Art Appreciation, for example, or an Office of Voluntary Population Control); or by giving money to others who achieve or advocate it (funding private art classes, for example, or Planned Parenthood)."[179] None of these actions, he was adamant, "has anything to do with abridging anyone's speech."[180]

Scalia also limits the meaning of the text of the Free Speech and Free Press Clauses to conduct that can clearly be identified as undertaken for no other reason than to communicate an idea.[181] In his view, "a general law regulating conduct and not specifically directed at expression . . . is not subject to First Amendment scrutiny at all."[182] The government, therefore, faces no constitutional limitations in banning such conduct as, for example, nude dancing.

Scalia acknowledged that "virtually *every* law restricts conduct, and virtually *any* prohibited conduct can be performed for an expressive purpose—if only expressive of the fact that the actor disagrees with the prohibition."[183] But, he insisted, the First Amendment is implicated only if the government bans the conduct in question "*precisely because of its communicative attributes.*"[184] Cases involving nude dancing raise no First Amendment questions because the conduct is banned not for the message it communicates but because "of moral opposition to nudity," which "supplies a rational basis for its prohibition."[185]

Finally, Scalia sees no First Amendment problems when public officials seek to ban obscenity[186] or to regulate the conduct of businesses engaged in what he has called the "marketing of obscenity."[187] They can do so because these businesses are "commercial entities" engaged in "the sordid business of pandering by deliberately emphasizing the sexually provocative aspects of their nonobscene products, in order to catch the salaciously disposed."[188]

His fullest discussion of this matter is found in his dissenting opinion in *FW/PBS, Inc. v. Dallas*,[189] a case in which the Court found unconstitutional on First Amendment grounds Dallas's ordinance regulating sexually oriented businesses, i.e., adult bookstores and video stores, escort agencies, nude model studios, and so forth. The First Amendment does not, he insisted, "require a state or municipality to permit a business that intentionally specializes in, and holds itself forth to the public as specializing in, performance or portrayal of sex acts, sexual organs in a state of arousal, or live human nudity."[190] Although it does require public officials to "tolerate" "individual works," i.e., "any particular book, film, or entertainment,"[191] even when they "have marginal communicative context beyond raw sexual appeal," he insisted that it does not require them "to tolerate businesses that hold themselves forth as specializing in such material."[192] Businesses that offer "live nudity or hard-core sexual material as a constant, intentional objective of their business" are engaged not in the communication of ideas but in "pandering,"[193] an activity traditionally unprotected by the First Amendment and specifically recognized as unprotected by the Court in the "dispositive case" of *Ginzburg v. United States*.[194] As he described it in *United States v. Playboy Entertainment Group, Inc.*, pandering is no more than the "commercial exploitation of erotica solely for the sake of their prurient appeal."[195] It is therefore subject to regulation by public officials because "it is clear from the context in which exchanges between such businesses and their customers occur that neither the merchant nor the buyer is interested in the work's literary, artistic, political, or scientific value."[196] It is, in short, "constitutionally unprotected behavior."[197]

The Takings Clause

The Takings Clause of the Fifth Amendment to the Constitution states, "Nor shall private property be taken for public use, without just compensation." This language tacitly recognizes the federal government's inherent power of eminent domain; as the Court said in *Boom Co. v. Patterson*, this power "appertains to every independent government. It requires no constitutional recognition; it is an attribute of sovereignty."[198]

Prior to the adoption of the Fourteenth Amendment, the power of eminent domain of state governments was unrestrained by any federal authority. In *Barron v. Baltimore*, the Court held that the Takings Clause of the Fifth Amendment did not apply to the states.[199] In *Chicago, Burlington, & Quincy Railroad Co. v. Chicago*,[200] however, the Court embraced the argument that the Due Process

Clause of the Fourteenth Amendment afforded property owners the same measure of protection against the states as the Fifth Amendment did against the federal government. The Court ruled that, although a state "legislature may prescribe a form of procedure to be observed in the taking of private property for public use, . . . it is not due process of law if provision be not made for compensation. . . . The mere form of the proceeding instituted against the owner . . . cannot convert the process used into due process of law, if the necessary result be to deprive him of his property without compensation."[201]

When a government itself initiates a condemnation proceeding against someone's property, the question whether that property has been "taken," with the consequent requirement of just compensation, does not arise. However, questions do arise when regulatory action limits activity on the property or otherwise deprives it of value. Regulation may deprive owners of most or all beneficial use of their property or may destroy the value of the property for the purposes to which it is suited. Does such regulation also constitute a taking? Initially, the Court flatly denied the possibility of compensation for this diminution of property value; however, in *Pennsylvania Coal Co. v. Mahon*, it established as a general principle that "if regulation goes too far it will be recognized as a taking."[202] But how far is too far?

As late as 1978 in *Penn Central Transportation Co. v. City of New York*, the Court confessed that it had failed to develop a "set formula" for determining where regulation ends and taking begins.[203] However, by the time Scalia joined the Court just eight years later, it had responded to increasing governmental regulation of property in terms of zoning and land-use controls, environmental regulations, and the like, by formulating four general principles for determining whether a regulatory taking had occurred. One guideline was spelled out in *Penn Central* itself: courts must consider the economic impact of the regulation on the claimant and, particularly, the extent to which the regulation has interfered with reasonable investment-backed expectations.[204] A second guideline, announced in *Loretto v. Teleprompter Manhattan CATV Corp.*, involves physical invasions: when government permanently occupies or authorizes someone else to occupy property, the action constitutes a taking, and compensation must be paid regardless of the public interests served by the occupation or the extent of damage to the parcel as a whole.[205] A third guideline was spelled out by the Court in *Agins v. City of Tiburon*: a land-use regulation must "substantially advance legitimate state interests."[206] A fourth guideline was also announced in *Agins*: the regulation cannot deny a property owner "economically viable use of his land."[207]

Once on the Court, Scalia quickly began employing these guidelines to demand just compensation for regulatory takings and to argue for their invalidation in cases where such compensation was not provided. In 1987—his first year on the high bench—he wrote in *Nollan v. California Coastal Commission*,[208] for the

Court majority, that the extraction from a landowner of a public-access easement across a strip of beach as a condition for a permit to enlarge a beachfront home did not "substantially advance" the state's legitimate interest in preserving the public's view of the beach from the street in front of the lot and therefore constituted a taking of property without just compensation in violation of the Takings Clause. The next year, he contended in his dissent in *Pennell v. City of San Jose* that the tenant-hardship provision of San Jose's rent-control ordinance effected an unconstitutional regulatory taking.[209] And in 1992, he again wrote for the Court majority in *Lucas v. South Carolina Coastal Council* that land-use regulations that deny the property owner all economically viable use of his land constitute a taking requiring just compensation.[210]

Since in none of these cases was property physically taken, a question can be raised whether Scalia's vigorous use in them of the Takings Clause is not inconsistent with his textualist jurisprudence. When Justice Harry Blackmun raised this very question in his dissent in *Lucas*,[211] Scalia had a ready response, and it was one he considered entirely consistent with his original-meaning approach. He observed that James Madison, in his June 8, 1789, speech to the First Congress (in which he introduced a series of amendments that eventually became the Bill of Rights), had originally proposed the following language: "No person shall be . . . obliged to relinquish his property, where it may be necessary for public use, without a just compensation." Scalia pointed out that the First Congress declined to adopt Madison's original language, which clearly limited its scope solely to physical deprivations, and he continued, "We decline to do so as well." The First Congress's modification of Madison's proposed language convinced him that the text of the Takings Clause is to "be read to encompass regulatory as well as physical deprivations."[212]

Scalia is convinced that the text of the Takings Clause applies to regulatory takings no less than actual physical takings; he is also convinced that its "guiding principle" is to ensure that public burdens are "borne by the public as a whole."[213] He expressed that guiding principle in *Nollan* when he declared that, even if the California Coastal Commission was right in its belief that the public interest would be served by a continuous strip of publicly accessible beach along the coast, "that does not establish that the Nollans alone can be compelled to contribute to its realization." The commission was free to serve this public interest, if it wished, "by using its power of eminent domain for this 'public purpose,' " but, he insisted, if it wanted "an easement across the Nollans' property, it must pay for it."[214] The California Coastal Commission justified its extraction from the Nollans of a public-access easement across a strip of their beach, as a condition for granting them a permit to enlarge their beachfront home, on the grounds that it could have simply denied them a permit altogether. Scalia employed a very creative analogy to demolish the commission's argument.

The evident constitutional propriety disappears, however, if the condition substituted for the prohibition utterly fails to further the end advanced as the justification for the prohibition. When that essential nexus is eliminated, the situation becomes the same as if California law forbade shouting fire in a crowded theater, but granted dispensations to those willing to contribute $100 to the state treasury. While a ban on shouting fire can be a core exercise of the State's police power to protect the public safety, and can thus meet even our stringent standards for regulation of speech, adding the unrelated condition alters the purpose to one which, while it may be legitimate, is inadequate to sustain the ban. Therefore, even though, in a sense, requiring a $100 tax contribution in order to shout fire is a lesser restriction on speech than an outright ban, it would not pass constitutional muster. Similarly here, the lack of nexus between the condition and the original purpose of the building restriction converts that purpose to something other than what it was. The purpose then becomes, quite simply, the obtaining of an easement to serve some valid governmental purpose, *but without payment of compensation.* Whatever may be the outer limits of "legitimate state interests" in the takings and land-use context, this is not one of them. In short, unless the permit condition serves the same governmental purpose as the development ban, the building restriction is not a valid regulation of land use but *"an out-and-out plan of extortion."*[215]

In the rent-control case of *Pennell,* Scalia expanded on the theme he introduced in *Nollan* that public burdens must be borne by the public as a whole, and he offered a text-and-tradition explanation for why the state must address social problems with taxes, not uncompensated takings. As he put it, "The traditional manner in which American government has met the problem of those who cannot pay reasonable prices for privately sold necessities" — housing, food, clothing — "has been the distribution to such persons of funds raised from the public at large through taxes, either in cash (welfare payments) or in goods (public housing, publicly subsidized housing, and food stamps)."[216] A regulatory taking, however, undermines that traditional approach; it "permits wealth transfers to be achieved . . . 'off budget,' with relative invisibility and thus relative immunity from normal democratic processes."[217] It operates contrary to "our governmental system," which requires that these "wealth transfers" be openly agreed upon "through the process of taxing and spending, where both economic effects and competing priorities are more evident." The "fostering of an intelligent democratic process is," he concluded, "one of the happy effects of the [Takings Clause's] constitutional prescription — perhaps accidental, perhaps not." But whatever its effects, its "essence" remains "the unfairness of making one citizen pay, in some fashion other than taxes, to remedy a social problem that is none of his creation."[218]

Equal Protection

The Fourteenth Amendment declares that "no state shall . . . deny to any person within its jurisdiction the equal protection of the laws."[219] Unlike the phrase *due process of law*, which can be traced back to the Magna Carta, the phrase *equal protection of the laws* has no similar common-law lineage and appears as constitutional language for the first time in 1868, thanks to the work of the Thirty-ninth Congress. The Equal Protection Clause received its seminal construction by the Court in Justice Samuel Miller's majority opinion in the 1873 *Slaughterhouse Cases:* "In the light of [its] history . . . and pervading purpose, . . . it is not difficult to give a meaning to this clause. The existence of laws in the states where the newly emancipated negroes resided, which discriminated with gross injustice and hardship against them as a class, was the evil to be remedied by this clause, and by it such laws are forbidden."[220]

Miller's opinion was important and clarifying, but it raised other questions. What about laws that do not discriminate against blacks "with gross injustice and hardship" but merely segregate on a "separate but equal" basis or laws that discriminate on the basis of race in order to ameliorate the effects of past discrimination or laws that discriminate on some basis other than race—are they also forbidden? Scalia brings his text-and-tradition approach to his answers to these difficult questions.

In *Rutan v. Republican Party of Illinois,* Scalia made it clear that he believed there is nothing ambiguous about the text of the Equal Protection Clause and that, therefore, there is no need for him to accept the traditional understanding that it tolerates racial segregation as it prevailed prior to *Brown v. Board of Education.*[221] "I argue for the role of tradition in giving content only to *ambiguous* constitutional text; no tradition can supersede the Constitution," and, he continued, "[i]n my view the Fourteenth Amendment's requirement of 'equal protection of the laws,' combined with the Thirteenth Amendment's abolition of the institution of black slavery, leaves no room for doubt that laws treating people differently because of their race are invalid." Acknowledging that the Fourteenth Amendment is not necessarily "crystal clear on this point," he nonetheless insisted that "a tradition of *unchallenged* validity did not exist with respect to the [segregationist practices challenged] in *Brown.*" And he emphasized that the tradition that accepted "in the 19th century the principle of 'separate-but-equal' had been vigorously opposed on constitutional grounds, litigated up to this Court, and upheld only over the dissent of one of our historically most respected Justices. See *Plessy v. Ferguson* (1896) (Harlan, J., dissenting)."[222]

Scalia's argument in *Rutan* is revelatory in several respects. He invoked Justice John Marshall Harlan and by so doing associated himself with Harlan's argument in *Plessy* that the Constitution is "color-blind," something he had done expressly the year before in *City of Richmond v. Croson*.[223] But Scalia also invoked the Thirteenth Amendment as helping to make "crystal clear" for him the meaning of the Equal Protection Clause. And by invoking both Harlan and the Thirteenth Amendment, he also thereby associated himself with Harlan's argument in *Plessy* that the Thirteenth Amendment bans all "badges of slavery,"[224] an argument that Harlan had unsuccessfully advanced in both *Plessy* and the *Civil Rights Cases*[225] and that Justice Stewart revived for the Warren Court in *Jones v. Mayer*.[226] As a logical positivist, Scalia cannot invoke the principles of the Declaration of Independence[227] and conclude, as did Justice Clarence Thomas in *Adarand Constructors v. Pena*,[228] that since "all men are created equal," racial discrimination of any kind is unconstitutional because it is contrary to the principles on which the Constitution is based. However, as a textualist, he is able to reach the same conclusion by reading the Thirteenth and Fourteenth Amendments together and declaring invalid on that basis "laws treating people differently because of their race."[229]

For a long time, of course, laws did treat people differently because of their race, and blacks were the victims of discrimination. That reality posed the question the Court was obliged to confront in *Croson*: are there circumstances under which governments can "discriminate on the basis of race in order (in a broad sense) 'to ameliorate the effects of past discrimination' "?[230] For Scalia, the answer is an unequivocal no. As he declared in his concurrence in the judgment in *Adarand*, "In my view, government can never have a 'compelling interest' in discriminating on the basis of race in order to 'make up' for past racial discrimination in the opposite direction."[231]

His reason is, again, textually based: "Individuals who have been wronged by unlawful racial discrimination should be made whole; but under our Constitution there can be no such thing as either a creditor or a debtor race. That concept," he noted, "is alien to the Constitution's focus upon the individual" (Scalia quoted the words of the Fourteenth Amendment that "nor shall any State . . . deny *to any person*" the equal protection of the laws) "and its rejection of dispositions based on race . . . or blood" (he quoted the words of the Fifteenth Amendment prohibiting abridgment of the right to vote "on account of race," the words of Article III, § 3 declaring that "no Attainder of Treason shall work Corruption of Blood," and the words of Article I, § 9, cl. 8 prohibiting the granting of "Title[s] of Nobility"). That concept, he continued, is also pernicious in that, even when it is pursued "for the most admirable and benign of purposes," it inevitably "reinforce[s] and preserve[s] for future mischief the way of thinking that produced race slavery, race privilege and race hatred" in the first place.[232]

Scalia is committed to making whole individuals who have been wronged by unlawful racial discrimination. But "where injustice is the game," he insisted in *Croson*, "turnabout is not fair play."[233] For him, "there is only one circumstance in which the states may act *by race* to 'undo the effects of past discrimination': where that is necessary to eliminate their own maintenance of a system of unlawful racial classification." He provided a concrete example to show precisely what he meant: if "a state agency has a discriminatory pay scale compensating black employees in all positions at 20% less than their nonblack counterparts, it may assuredly promulgate an order raising the salaries of 'all black employees' to eliminate the differential."[234]

Scalia was quick to point out that there are "many permissible ways" in which the states can act "to undo the effects of past discrimination" that do not involve classification by race. Since the Court in *Croson* addressed governmental contracting, he gave two examples in this arena. First, the states can adopt a contracting preference "for small businesses, or even for new businesses—which would make it easier for those previously excluded by discrimination to enter the field." Although such programs would doubtless have a racially disproportionate impact, "they are not based on race." And second, the states can accord "a contracting preference to identified victims of discrimination. While most of the beneficiaries might be black, neither the beneficiaries nor those disadvantaged by the preference would be identified *on the basis of their race*." He also gave an example from the employment arena: a state can give to "the identified victim of state discrimination that which it wrongfully denied him." A state can, for example, give to "a previously rejected black applicant the job that, by reason of discrimination, had been awarded to a white applicant, even if this means terminating the latter's employment." As Scalia was at pains to note, "In such a context, the white jobholder is not being selected for disadvantageous treatment because of his race, but because he was wrongfully awarded a job to which another is entitled. That is worlds apart from [a system] in which those to be disadvantaged are identified solely by race."[235] Only programs such as these, and not those that operate on the basis of race, are, he insisted, "in accord with the letter and the spirit of our Constitution."[236]

And just as government can never have a compelling interest in discriminating on the basis of race in order to "make up" for past racial discrimination, so it can never have a compelling interest in discriminating on the basis of race in order to promote diversity. In his dissent in *Grutter v. Bollinger*, Scalia openly mocked the Court majority's conclusion that the University of Michigan Law School had a compelling interest in attaining a diverse student body and in engaging in racial discrimination to do so because of the "educational benefits" that result from such diversity, including cross-racial understanding and preparing students for work and citizenship.

> This is not, of course, an "educational benefit" on which students will be graded on their Law School transcript (Works and Plays Well with Others: B+) or tested by the bar examiners (Q: Describe in 500 words or less your cross-racial understanding). For it is a lesson of life rather than law—essentially the same lesson taught to (or rather learned by, for it cannot be "taught" in the usual sense) people three feet shorter and twenty years younger than the full-grown adults at the University of Michigan Law School, in institutions ranging from Boy Scout troops to public-school kindergartens. If properly considered an "educational benefit" at all, it is surely not one that is either uniquely relevant to law school or uniquely "teachable" in a formal educational setting. *And therefore:* If it is appropriate for the University of Michigan Law School to use racial discrimination for the purpose of putting together a "critical mass" that will convey generic lessons in socialization and good citizenship, surely it is no less appropriate—indeed, *particularly* appropriate—for the civil service system of the State of Michigan to do so. There, also, those exposed to "critical masses" of certain races will presumably become better Americans, better Michiganders, better civil servants. And surely private employers cannot be criticized—indeed, should be praised—if they also "teach" good citizenship to their adult employees through a patriotic, all-American system of racial discrimination in hiring. The nonminority individuals who are deprived of a legal education, a civil service job, or any job at all by reason of their skin color will surely understand.[237]

For Scalia, the Equal Protection Clause bans only laws that treat "people differently because of their race."[238] On that basis, he rejects the view that it prevents the use of peremptory challenges on the basis of any group characteristic. As he wrote in his dissent in *J.E.B. v. Alabama ex rel. T.B.*: "Since all groups are subject to the peremptory challenge (and will be made the object of it, depending upon the nature of the particular case), it is hard to see how any group is denied equal protection. That explains why peremptory challenges coexisted with the Equal Protection Clause for 120 years."[239]

And continuing, he stated that since the Equal Protection Clause bans only laws that treat people differently because of race, it does not ban treating people differently in other respects, so long as that differential treatment is consistent with "longstanding national traditions."[240] As Scalia declared in his dissent in *United States v. Virginia*, the assertion that a "constant and unbroken national tradition"[241] has been unconstitutional through the centuries "is not law, but politics-smuggled-into-law."[242] He understands that "the function of the Court is to *preserve* our society's values regarding (among other things) equal protection, not to *revise* them"—in short, to "prevent backsliding" by rejecting those "new restrictions that a changing society constantly imposes upon private conduct" that trench on those protections "our society has always accorded in the past."[243]

The Equal Protection Clause, therefore, does not, in his judgment, prohibit Virginia from adhering to its traditional, male-only admission policy at the Virginia Military Institute.[244] As he noted, "The tradition of having government-funded military schools for men is as well rooted in the traditions of this country as the tradition of sending only men into military combat." The people, of course, could "decide to change the one tradition, like the other, through democratic processes," but that was their job, not the Court's. He found the Court's "assertion that either tradition" was unconstitutional to be an example of judicial policy-making at its worst.[245]

For the same reason, he argued, the Equal Protection Clause did not ban Colorado from passing a constitutional amendment preventing all levels of state government from bestowing special protections upon homosexual conduct.[246] As he began his impassioned dissent in *Romer v. Evans:* "The constitutional amendment before us here is not the manifestation of a 'bare . . . desire to harm' homosexuals, but is rather a modest attempt by seemingly tolerant Coloradans to preserve traditional sexual mores against the efforts of a politically powerful minority to revise those mores through use of the laws."[247] The Court majority found that Colorado's Amendment 2 violated equal protection because it did not bear a rational relationship to any legitimate governmental purpose. Scalia vehemently disagreed: "The people of Colorado have adopted an entirely reasonable provision which . . . merely denies [homosexuals] preferential treatment." The amendment was "designed to prevent piecemeal deterioration of the sexual morality favored by a majority of Coloradans," and Scalia found it to be "not only an appropriate means to that legitimate end, but a means that Americans have employed before. Striking it down is an act, not of judicial judgment, but of political will."[248]

Along the same lines, Scalia does not understand the Equal Protection Clause to forbid Texas from discriminating against homosexuality by criminalizing homosexual sodomy.[249] In *Lawrence v. Texas,* the Court majority held that there was no rational basis for Texas' statute because it furthered no legitimate state interest that could justify the statute's intrusion into the personal and private life of the individual. The Court found "the fact that the governing majority in a State has traditionally viewed a particular practice as immoral is not a sufficient reason for upholding a law prohibiting the practice." In his dissent, Scalia defended his reliance on tradition. "The Texas statute undeniably seeks to further the belief of its citizens that certain forms of sexual behavior are 'immoral and unacceptable.' "[250] What Texas had chosen to do, Scalia insisted, was "well within the range of traditional democratic action, and its hand should not be stayed . . . by a Court that is impatient of democratic change." He noted that later generations may come to see that "laws once thought necessary and proper in fact serve only to oppress," and, he declared, when they do, they "can repeal those laws. Moreover, their decision to do so will be consistent with "the premise of our system that those judgments are to be made by the people," not imposed by judges.[251]

And finally, Scalia does not understand the Equal Protection Clause to bar state laws prohibiting either polygamy or same-sex marriage. In *Romer v. Evans*, he noted that a close parallel existed between Colorado's Amendment 2 and the constitutions of the states of Arizona, Idaho, New Mexico, Oklahoma, and Utah, which "*to this day* contain provisions stating that polygamy is 'forever prohibited.'" Since these constitutional provisions involved "precisely the [same] effort by the majority of citizens [in these states] to preserve its view of sexual morality" as was expended by the citizens of Colorado in their passage of Amendment 2, Scalia suggested that the Court would also find "these provisions are unconstitutional . . . , unless, of course, polygamists for some reason have fewer constitutional rights than homosexuals."[252] He "suspected" that, on this question as well, the Court would "take sides in the culture war" and conclude that, indeed, polygamists did have fewer rights because, in its judgment, "the perceived social harm of polygamy is a legitimate concern of government," whereas "the perceived social harm of homosexuality is not." But, he insisted, these questions were not "the business of the courts" but rather of "the political branches," and they should be free in their answers to "adhere to traditional attitudes."[253]

Likewise, in *Lawrence v. Texas*, Scalia argued that the logic of the Court's majority opinion would lead inevitably to judicial imposition of same-sex marriage. Although the Court assured the public that the case before it did "not involve whether the government must give formal recognition to any relationship that homosexual persons seek to enter," Scalia sternly warned, "Do not believe it." He found "more illuminating than this bald, unreasoned disclaimer . . . the progression of thought displayed by an earlier passage in the Court's opinion, which notes the constitutional protections afforded to 'personal decisions relating to *marriage*, procreation, contraception, family relationships, child rearing, and education,' and then declares that 'persons in a homosexual relationship may seek autonomy for these purposes, just as heterosexual persons do.'" The Court, he noted, had just dismantled "the structure of constitutional law that has permitted a distinction to be made between heterosexual and homosexual unions." And since moral disapprobation of homosexual conduct was no longer considered by the Court to be a legitimate reason for proscribing that conduct, he was convinced that the Court would inevitably confer "the benefits of marriage to homosexual couples."[254] For Scalia, the public would remain in the grasp of this "governing caste that knows best"[255] on this and many other issues concerning public morality so long as the Court refused to acknowledge that the Equal Protection Clause bans only laws that treat people differently because of race, not laws that treat people differently in other respects based on "longstanding national traditions."

The Court has seen matters differently and has not felt itself restrained from invalidating traditionally recognized nonracial classifications and discriminations. Rather, it has, in Scalia's terms, established an "equal protection jurisprudence which regards this Court as free to evaluate everything under the sun by applying one of three tests": rational-basis scrutiny, intermediate scrutiny, or strict scrutiny. These tests, he insists, "are no more scientific than their names suggest, and a further element of randomness is added by the fact that it is largely up to us which test will be applied in each case."[256] They result in what Scalia has called "our ad-hocery"[257]—the Court's tendency to determine which test to apply based on its preference for or opposition to the policy issue under review.

Scalia has attempted to discipline the Court's applications of these tests by reserving strict scrutiny for state classifications based on race or those that affect fundamental rights, by which he means "interest[s] traditionally protected by our society."[258] The Court, however, has not acceded to his understanding, and so, he complains, strict scrutiny "is applied to the deprivation of whatever sort of right we consider 'fundamental.'" He notes that the Court also has no established criteria for when it should apply intermediate scrutiny, prompting him to declare that it appears to invoke this test "when it seems like a good idea to load the dice."[259] He complains that even rational-basis scrutiny is now randomly applied by his activist colleagues, allowing them to conclude in *Lawrence* that "the enforcement of traditional notions of sexual morality" is "not a sufficient reason for upholding a law" prohibiting particular practices.[260]

These "made-up tests," he insists, "cannot displace longstanding traditions as the primary determinant of what the Constitution means."[261] Yet his colleagues disagree, and so Scalia has himself had to employ these tests and argue that they, in fact, support the conclusions he has reached by employing his text-and-tradition approach concerning the constitutionality of the various laws under review. In *United States v. Virginia*, he maintained that "Virginia's election to fund one public all-male institution and one on the adversarial model—and to concentrate its resources in a single entity that serves both these interests in diversity—is substantially related to the Commonwealth's important educational interests,"[262] and it therefore withstands intermediate scrutiny—the test the Court applies in cases concerning discrimination on the basis of sex. And in *Lawrence v. Texas*, he argued that Texas' traditional interest "in protecting order and morality" provided a rational basis to "criminalize homosexual acts."[263] But of course, he uses these tests, to paraphrase his language from *Wisconsin Public Intervenor v. Mortier*, for "forensic" rather than "interpretive" purposes[264] and in an attempt to discourage their use because he understands that, when the Court uses them in its decision making, it is no longer engaged in "the interpretation of a Constitution but the creation of one."[265]

Conclusions

As this chapter illustrates, Scalia's textualist jurisprudence leads him to seek to understand the original meaning of the rights found in the First Amendment, the Takings Clause, and the Equal Protection Clause and thereafter faithfully to apply that meaning to the facts in the cases before him. He understands his duty as a justice is not to expand them and say that they mean more than they have traditionally been understood to mean; that is the job of the people and their elected representatives, through either the passage of legislation or the adoption of constitutional amendments. As he declared during his debate with Justice Stephen Breyer at American University Law School in January 2005, "I am chained, because of my theory of the Constitution," to what each provision of the Constitution meant to those who adopted it. "That's what it is today," he said, "unless you amend it."[266] Accordingly, Scalia has adopted a no preferences, no privileges, no penalties approach to the Establishment and Free Exercise Clauses, has limited the Free Speech and Free Press Clauses to "oral and written speech" and not to "expressive conduct" unless the government has prohibited the conduct precisely because of its "communicative attributes," and has interpreted the Equal Protection Clause to ban only racial discrimination (in all its forms—invidious or otherwise).

Rather, Scalia understands his duty as a justice is to ensure that these rights do not come to mean less than they have traditionally meant. He has therefore vigorously dissented from the Court's acquiescence to such backsliding by the popular branches as Washington State's Promise Scholarship Program and its withholding of benefits for some students solely on the basis of religion, Congress's passage of the Bipartisan Campaign Reform Act and its ban on political parties from using soft money to fund issue ads and on for-profit and nonprofit corporations from using their funds to purchase preelection ads critical of incumbents, Colorado's law prohibiting antiabortion protestors from positioning themselves within 100 feet of the entrance of an abortion clinic, San Jose's rent-control statute and its regulatory taking of a landlord's property, and the University of Michigan's policy of discriminating on the basis of race in order to achieve a diverse student body.

As a textualist, Scalia views the substantive rights found in the Constitution as establishing a floor, and he views his job as ensuring that the floor does not collapse under the weight of majority sentiment and political expediency—i.e., to prevent backsliding. He faults his colleagues no less when they allow the floor to sag (as in *Locke v. Davey* when Chief Justice Rehnquist characterized the burden on Davey as being "relatively minor") as when they allow it to collapse altogether (as in *McConnell v. FEC* or *Grutter v. Bollinger*). And he also faults them when they decide it is their job to add new floors—what he called elsewhere adding "new stories to the temples of constitutional law."[267] Thus, he has objected to the Court's construction of the right to be free from nondenominational prayer at public graduation ceremonies; the right to be free from patronage considerations in public hiring, firing, and contracting; and the right to be free from laws criminalizing homosexual sodomy.

In a constitutional democracy, Scalia is convinced, it is necessary and altogether appropriate for the Court to protect vigilantly those rights long recognized by the people and specified in the Constitution. However, he is equally convinced that it is contrary to democratic principle and therefore altogether inappropriate for the Court—a committee of nine attorneys appointed for good behavior—to create new rights for individuals and groups. Such rights invariably come at the cost of the most important right of the people, which is to govern themselves and to make their own decisions through their elected representatives about when and how much to add to the Constitution's original substantive protections.

Chapter Six

Scalia's Textualism
Applied to Procedural Rights

This chapter shifts the focus from substantive rights to procedural rights and explores Scalia's textualist approach to the Due Process Clauses of the Fifth and Fourteenth Amendments and the various criminal procedural provisions of Amendments Four through Eight. As with the previous chapter, the discussion here will highlight Scalia's efforts to understand the original meaning of these rights (based on the words of the text when they are clear and on the traditional understanding of the text when they are not) and thereafter faithfully apply that meaning to the facts in the cases before him. He believes his duty as a justice lies not in expanding these rights by saying that they mean more than they have traditionally been understood to mean; in a democracy, the people, through their elected representatives, can expand these rights whenever they wish either by statute or by constitutional amendment. Rather, his duty is to prevent those rights from meaning *less* than they have traditionally meant, or, as he wrote in his dissent in *United States v. Virginia*, to "prevent backsliding from the degree of restriction the Constitution imposed upon democratic government."[1]

Due Process

The Due Process Clauses of the Fifth and Fourteenth Amendments declare that neither the federal government nor the states shall deprive any person "of life, liberty, or property, without due process of law." These clauses have been employed by the Supreme Court to incorporate most of the provisions of the Bill of Rights to apply to the states and to invalidate various federal and state laws held by the justices to trench on economic and civil liberties.[2] Even though the clauses speak of "process" and would seem therefore to authorize the Court to review only how, procedurally, the federal and state governments act when they deprive a person of life, liberty, or property ("procedural due process"), the Court has, for more than a century, construed them to mean that it is authorized as well to review what, substantively, these governments have done and to invalidate as arbitrary, irrational, and unjust acts by these governments with which a majority of the Court disagrees ("substantive due process"). Consistent with his text-and-tradition

166

approach, Scalia rejects substantive due process, rightly calling it an "oxymoron";[3] it is, he asserted in *Burnham v. Superior Court,* nothing more than "each Justice's subjective assessment of what is fair and just."[4]

For Scalia, the Due Process Clauses are simply the "embodiment of common-law tradition."[5] As he said in his concurrence in the judgment in *Pacific Mutual Life Insurance Co. v. Haslip,* "[A] process approved by the legal traditions of our people is 'due' process."[6] Leaving no doubt as to his understanding, he continued, "If the government chooses to follow a historically approved procedure, it necessarily *provides* due process."[7] He therefore looks to see whether the particular procedure in question was acceptable at the time of the adoption of the Fifth and Fourteenth Amendments;[8] if it was, it is part of the traditional "law of the land"[9] and therefore constitutional — at least on due process grounds.[10]

Scalia does not argue that every historically approved procedure is constitutional because it does not violate due process; it may violate some other provision of the Constitution — the Equal Protection Clause, for example.[11] And he also does not argue that a departure from historical practice necessarily denies due process. The people are free to demand from government, through their elected representatives, more protection of their rights to life, liberty, and property.[12] But, he insists, the decisions concerning whether to expand rights and by how much are reserved for the popular branches, not the courts.[13] And if the popular branches should decide not to expand these rights, their judgment is final and is not to be gainsaid by the justices. Thus, when Congress passed the Military Justice Act of 1968, allowing military judges for courts-martial to serve without fixed terms of office, he pointed out in his concurrence in the judgment that "a fixed term of office for a military judge has never been a part of the military justice tradition" and that Congress had given "members of the military at least as much procedural protection, in the respects at issue here, as they enjoyed when the Fifth Amendment was adopted and have enjoyed ever since. That is enough," and, he added, "to suggest otherwise arrogates to this Court a power it does not possess."[14]

For Scalia, the Due Process Clauses permit the Court to ban only practices unacceptable at the time the Fifth and Fourteenth Amendments were adopted, thereby preventing society from backsliding in its protection of "long-recognized personal liberties."[15] Cases in which such practices are at issue rarely come before the Court, but when they do, Scalia is quick to object, even if his colleagues are not. His dissent in *Rogers v. Tennessee*[16] is an excellent example of how Scalia's original-meaning jurisprudence led him to declare a practice unconstitutional because "it was unheard-of at the time the original Due Process Clause was adopted."[17]

After a stabbing incident that caused the death of the victim fifteen months later, Wilbert Rogers was tried and convicted of second-degree murder. Even though the statute under which he was convicted made no mention of any exceptions based on the length of time between the incident causing the death and the death itself, Rogers argued on appeal that his conviction was precluded by the common-law year-and-a-day rule, under which no defendant could be convicted of murder unless the victim died as a result of the defendant's act within a year and a day of the act. The Tennessee Supreme Court rejected his argument. Although it acknowledged that the year-and-a-day rule had long been recognized in the state, it announced that it was retroactively abolishing the rule, finding that the reasons for recognizing it at common law no longer existed. The court disagreed with Rogers's contention that the application of its decision abolishing the rule in his case would violate the Ex Post Facto Clause, observing that the provision referred only to legislative acts.

In a six-to-three decision, the U.S. Supreme Court affirmed the decision of the Tennessee Supreme Court and held that its retroactive application of its decision abolishing the year-and-a-day rule violated neither the Ex Post Facto Clause (in her majority opinion, Justice Sandra Day O'Connor agreed with the Tennessee Supreme Court that the provision applied only to legislatures) nor Rogers's due process rights (in her opinion, O'Connor found the Tennessee Supreme Court's decision to be a routine exercise of common-law decision making in which the law was being brought "into conformity with reason and common sense").[18] Scalia filed a strident dissent: "The Court today approves the conviction of a man for a murder that was not murder (but only manslaughter) when the offense was committed. It thus violates a principle . . . which 'dates from the ancient Greeks' and has been described as one of the most 'widely held value-judgments in the entire history of human thought.' "[19] He declared that the Court's opinion produced "a curious constitution that only a judge could love. One in which (by virtue of the *Ex Post Facto* Clause) the elected representatives of all the people cannot retroactively make murder what was not murder when the act was committed; but in which unelected judges can do precisely that." He continued: "I do not believe this is the system that the Framers envisioned — or, for that matter, that any reasonable person would imagine."[20]

Scalia declared that the Tennessee Supreme Court had written "a judicial opinion acknowledging that under prior law, for reasons that used to be valid, the accused could not be convicted, but decreeing that, because of changed circumstances, 'we hereby abolish the common law rule,' and upholding the conviction by applying the new rule to conduct that occurred before the change in law was announced." He then spent six pages reviewing the writings of such legal giants as Francis Bacon and William Blackstone, Edward Coke and Nathaniel Chipman, in order to establish that the Tennessee Supreme Court's "retroactive revision of a concededly valid legal rule" was "unheard-of" in criminal cases in the late eighteenth century and therefore "contrary to the judicial traditions embraced within the concept of due process of law."[21]

O'Connor accused Scalia of "circumvent[ing] the clear constitutional text" of the Ex Post Facto Clause, which, "by its own terms, does not apply to courts."[22] Scalia responded that he was neither circumventing the text nor extending the clause to the courts; he was only "determining what due judicial process consists of—and it does not consist of retroactive creation of crimes." The Ex Post Facto Clause was relevant to his argument, he insisted, "only because it demonstrates beyond doubt that, however much the acknowledged and accepted role of common-law courts could evolve (as it has) in other respects, retroactive revision of the criminal law was regarded as so fundamentally unfair that an alteration of the judicial role which permits *that* will be a denial of due process."[23] Quoting James Madison from *Federalist* No. 44 that ex post facto laws "are contrary to the first principles of the social compact, and to every principle of social legislation," Scalia found it "impossible to believe, as the Court does, that this strong sentiment attached only to retroactive laws passed by the legislature, and would not apply equally (or indeed with even greater force) to a court's production of the same result through disregard of the traditional limits upon judicial power." He closed by noting that "[t]he injustice to the individuals affected is no less."[24]

Though Scalia generally understands due process to ban only practices unacceptable at the time the Fifth and the Fourteenth Amendments were adopted, he has nonetheless accepted the proposition that it also incorporates, through the Fourteenth Amendment, certain explicit protections of the Bill of Rights.[25] The incorporation doctrine is difficult to square with Scalia's textualist approach, however. The Fourteenth Amendment simply does not say that no state shall deprive any person of specific protections found in Amendments One through Eight. Language in *Barron v. Baltimore* is critical here.[26] In that decision, Chief Justice John Marshall expressly rejected John Barron's claim that the provisions of the Bill of Rights (in this case, the Takings Clause of the Fifth Amendment) applied equally to the states as to the federal government. The basis of Marshall's reasoning was the following: "Had Congress engaged in the extraordinary occupation of improving the constitutions of the several states by affording the people" the additional protections found in the Bill of Rights, "they would have declared this purpose in plain and intelligible language."[27] Those who drafted the Fourteenth Amendment were therefore on notice that if they wanted the Bill of Rights to apply to the states, they had to state their intention expressly in the text rather than implicitly by simply including the Due Process Clause in the Fourteenth Amendment. As Scalia well knows, they did not.

The incorporation doctrine is supported neither by the constitutional text nor by the traditional understanding of it.[28] Nevertheless, Scalia has accepted it without complaint. In his concurring opinion in *Albright v. Oliver*, he explained why: "I accept [incorporation] because it is both long established and narrowly limited."[29]

As he explained in *Haslip,* what was "important enough to have been included within the Bill of Rights has good claim to being an element of 'fundamental fairness' [and thus protected by the Due Process Clause], whatever history may say; and as a practical matter, the invalidation of traditional state practices achievable through the Bill of Rights is at least limited to enumerated subjects."[30]

Scalia is, therefore, willing to apply to the states, through the Due Process Clause of the Fourteenth Amendment, the "enumerated subjects" of Amendments One through Eight. The provisions of the Bill of Rights, he accepts, were meant to bar traditional governmental practices that could infringe on rights considered as so important by its drafters that they specifically mentioned them in the text. By the time of the ratification of the Fourteenth Amendment in 1868, these specifically enumerated rights had become part of those "long-recognized personal liberties" its Due Process Clause was to secure.[31] But Scalia declared in *TXO Production Corp. v. Alliance Resources Corp.*, "I do not accept the proposition that [the Due Process Clause of the Fourteenth Amendment] is the secret repository of all sorts of . . . unenumerated, substantive rights."[32]

A decade later in *Chavez v. Martinez,* he made much the same point, indicating his unwillingness to engage in substantive due process and to make "unlawful certain government conduct regardless of whether the procedural guarantees of the Fifth Amendment (or the guarantees of any of the other provisions of the Bill of Rights) have been violated."[33] Thus, he has consistently rejected the argument that due process contains within it a substantive right not to be subjected to excessive punitive damages.[34] His reading, he notes, "adheres to the text of the Due *Process* Clause."[35] It also adheres to tradition, "[s]ince it has been the traditional practice of American courts to leave punitive damages (where the evidence satisfies the legal requirements for imposing them) to the discretion of the jury; and since in my view a process that accords with such a tradition and does not violate the Bill of Rights necessarily constitutes 'due' process."[36] And in a nice bit of textual analysis, he also shows that his reading is necessary to avoid rendering part of the Eighth Amendment "superfluous": "It is particularly difficult to imagine that 'due process' contains the substantive right not to be subjected to excessive punitive damages, since if it contains *that* it would surely also contain the substantive right not to be subjected to excessive fines, which would make the Excessive Fines Clause of the Eighth Amendment superfluous in light of the Due Process Clause of the Fifth Amendment."[37]

He has also consistently rejected the argument that due process contains within it the right to an abortion, and as a consequence, he has sought to overturn *Roe v. Wade.*[38] As he argued in his concurring opinion in *Ohio v. Akron Center for Reproductive Health,* "[T]he Constitution contains no right to abortion. It is not to be found in the longstanding traditions of our society, nor can it be logically deduced from the text of the Constitution."[39] In *Planned Parenthood of Southeastern Pennsylvania v. Casey*, he acknowledged that the right to an abortion was a liberty interest "of great importance to many women." But, he declared, the proper issue for the Court is whether that liberty interest is constitutionally protected. Denying that it is, he explained that he did not reach that conclusion "because of anything so exalted as [his] views concerning the 'concept of existence, of meaning, of the universe, and of the mystery of human life'"—these, of course, being the grounds on which the joint opinion of Justices O'Connor, Anthony Kennedy, and David Souter was based upholding the essential finding of *Roe v. Wade*—but rather "because of two simple facts: (1) the Constitution says absolutely nothing about [abortion], and (2) the longstanding traditions of American society have permitted it to be legally proscribed."[40]

In *Hodgson v. Minnesota*, a badly fragmented Court held that Minnesota's two-parent notification requirement for a minor to receive an abortion without a judicial-bypass provision was unconstitutional but that such a requirement *with* judicial bypass was valid. In an opinion in which he concurred in part and dissented in part, Scalia made it clear why, as a textualist, he believed the Court has no business involving itself in the abortion controversy:

> As I understand the various opinions today: One Justice holds that two-parent notification is unconstitutional (at least in the present circumstances) without judicial bypass, but constitutional with bypass; four Justices would hold that two-parent notification is constitutional with or without bypass; four Justices would hold that two-parent notification is unconstitutional with or without bypass, though the four apply two different standards; six Justices hold that one-parent notification with bypass is constitutional, though for two different sets of reasons; and three Justices would hold that one-parent notification with bypass is unconstitutional. One will search in vain the document we are supposed to be construing for text that provides the basis for the argument over these distinctions; and will find in our society's tradition regarding abortion no hint that the distinctions are constitutionally relevant, much less any indication how a constitutional argument about them ought to be resolved. The random and unpredictable results of our consequently unchanneled individual views make it increasingly evident, Term after Term, that the tools for this job are not to be found in the lawyer's—and hence not in the judge's—workbox. I continue to dissent from this enterprise of devising an Abortion Code, and from the illusion that we have authority to do so.[41]

Scalia stressed in *Casey* that the states "may, if they wish, permit abortion on demand." His only point in all of these cases was that "the Constitution does not *require* them to do so."[42] The questions whether to permit abortions and under what circumstances are, he insisted, "to be resolved like most important questions in our democracy: by citizens trying to persuade one another and then voting."[43] As he observed in *Akron Center,* leaving these questions to the political process "is not only legally correct, it is pragmatically so," for that alone can "produce compromises satisfying a sufficient mass of the electorate that this deeply felt issue will cease distorting the remainder of our democratic process."[44]

For the same reasons, Scalia has rejected the argument that due process contains within it the right of parents to rear their own children and the right of individuals to commit suicide. In *Troxel v. Granville,*[45] when the Supreme Court struck down a statute of the state of Washington that allowed visitation rights to paternal grandparents on the grounds that it violated the Due Process Clause of the Fourteenth Amendment by interfering with parents' fundamental right to make decisions concerning the care, custody, and control of their children, Scalia dissented. He described the right of parents to direct the upbringing of their children as among the "unalienable rights" of the Declaration of Independence and as among the unenumerated rights of the Ninth Amendment, but, he insisted, "I do not believe that the power which the Constitution confers upon me *as a judge* entitles me to deny legal effect to laws that (in my view) infringe upon what is (in my view) that unenumerated right."[46] Family law in the United States had traditionally been decided by the states, not by the federal government and certainly not by federal judges, and Scalia concluded by observing, "I have no reason to believe that federal judges will be better at this than state legislatures; and state legislatures have the great advantages of doing harm in a more circumscribed area, of being able to correct their mistakes in a flash, and of being removable by the people."[47]

And in *Cruzan v. Director, Missouri Department of Health,*[48] when the Supreme Court affirmed as consistent with due process a Missouri living-will statute requiring that an incompetent's wish to have life-sustaining measures withdrawn be established by clear and convincing evidence, Scalia joined the Court majority and wrote a separate concurring opinion. American law, he noted, "has always accorded the state the power to prevent, by force if necessary, suicide — including suicide by refusing to take appropriate measures necessary to preserve one's life."[49] He rejected the petitioner's claim that Missouri had violated the Due Process Clause by depriving her of the liberty of ending her life, observing that this was never "a right historically and traditionally protected against state interference."[50] Whether the state should interfere (and under what circumstances) was a different question, as Scalia saw it, and one for "the citizens of Missouri to decide, through their elected representatives."[51] He was comfortable leaving this decision with them, for "[o]ur salvation is the Equal Protection Clause, which requires the democratic majority to accept for themselves and their loved ones what they impose on you and me. This Court need not, and has no authority to, inject itself into every field of human activity where irrationality and oppression may theoretically occur, and if it tries to do so it will destroy itself."[52]

Scalia's insistence that due process protects only those rights present when the Fifth and Fourteenth Amendments were ratified and that the creation of new rights is the responsibility of the people, not the Court, found its most passionate expression to date in his dissent in *Lawrence v. Texas,*[53] the 2003 decision in which the Court held that Texas' statute making it a crime to engage in homosexual sodomy violated the Due Process Clause of the Fourteenth Amendment. Homosexual sodomy, he argued, "is not a fundamental right 'deeply rooted in this Nation's history and tradition'";[54] as such, it is a liberty interest that the state can deprive a person of "so long as 'due process of law' is provided,"[55] i.e., so long as the restraint on liberty is rationally related to a legitimate state interest.

The Court majority agreed with Scalia—up to that point. But it then proceeded to declare that "[t]he Texas statute furthers no legitimate state interest which can justify its intrusion into the personal and private life of the individual."[56] Simply because the people have "traditionally viewed a particular practice as immoral is not a sufficient reason for upholding a law prohibiting the practice,"[57] Justice Kennedy observed for the majority. He continued in a passage that contrasted sharply with Scalia's original-meaning approach to constitutional interpretation and that fully displayed what Scalia had elsewhere described as "the conventional fallacy that the Constitution is a living document [whose text] means from age to age whatever the society (or perhaps the Court) thinks it ought to mean."[58] Kennedy asserted that "those who drew and ratified the Due Process Clauses of the Fifth Amendment or the Fourteenth Amendment" knew that "times can blind us to certain truths and later generations can see that laws once thought necessary and proper in fact serve only to oppress. As the Constitution endures, persons in every generation can invoke its principles in their own search for greater freedom."[59]

Scalia assailed this position, arguing that the Texas statute served the legitimate state interest of "further[ing] the belief of its citizens that certain forms of sexual behavior are 'immoral and unacceptable,'—the same interest furthered by criminal laws against fornication, bigamy, adultery, adult incest, bestiality, and obscenity."[60] If this is not a legitimate state interest, he argued, the Court's decision "effectively decrees the end of all morals legislation. If, as the Court asserts, the promotion of majoritarian sexual morality is not even a *legitimate* state interest, none of the above-mentioned laws can survive rational-basis review."[61]

Scalia insisted that "it is the premise of our system" that judgments concerning morals legislation are to be made by the people, not imposed by judges.[62] That premise yields, he emphasized, one enormous benefit: leaving regulation of homosexual sodomy to the people rather than to the courts means "that the people, unlike judges, need not carry things to their logical conclusion. The people may feel that their disapprobation of homosexual conduct is strong enough to disallow homosexual marriage, but not strong enough to criminalize private homosexual acts—and may legislate accordingly." Not so for the Court: "Today's opinion dismantles the structure of constitutional law that has permitted a distinction to be made between heterosexual and homosexual unions, insofar as formal recognition in marriage is concerned. If moral disapproval of homosexual conduct is 'no legitimate state interest' for purposes of proscribing that conduct," there is, he warned, no logical reason "for denying the benefits of marriage to homosexual couples exercising 'the liberty protected by the Constitution.' "[63]

Criminal Procedural Guarantees

Of the twenty-three rights enumerated in the first eight amendments of the Bill of Rights, thirteen relate to the treatment of criminal defendants. The Fourth Amendment guarantees the right of the people to be secure "in their persons, houses, papers, and effects" against unreasonable searches and seizures and prohibits the issuance of warrants without probable cause. The Fifth Amendment requires prosecution by grand jury indictment for all capital crimes and prohibits placing a person "twice in jeopardy of life or limb" for the same offense or compelling him to be a "witness against himself." The Sixth Amendment lists several rights that the accused shall enjoy "in all criminal prosecutions": a speedy and public trial by an impartial jury, notice of the "nature and cause of the accusation," confrontation of hostile witnesses, compulsory process for obtaining favorable witnesses, and assistance of counsel. The Eighth Amendment adds prohibitions against the imposition of excessive bail and fines and the infliction of cruel and unusual punishments. And in addition to these specific guarantees, the Fifth Amendment adds the general prohibition against the deprivation of life, liberty, or property without due process of law.

To each of these provisions, Scalia has brought his text-and-tradition approach to constitutional interpretation, and he has sought to give them "the meaning ascribed to them at the time of their ratification."[64] His job, as he understands it, is not to expand these rights—he prefers to leave "further expansion to the good judgment, not of this Court, but of the people through their representatives in the legislature."[65] Rather, his job is to secure these rights from "all sorts of intrusion" that "a later, less virtuous age" may consider necessary or appropriate.[66] Scalia is therefore especially critical when the Court itself is responsible for these "intrusions," as he claims it is when it creates rules that exclude reliable and probative evidence.

As he declared in his dissent in *Jaffee v. Redmond,* these rules often result in "injustice" for those individuals who are "prevented from proving a valid claim—or (worse still) prevented from establishing a valid defense. The latter is particularly unpalatable for those who love justice, because it causes the courts of law not merely to let stand a wrong, but to become themselves the instruments of wrong."[67]

Unreasonable Searches and Seizures

Accordingly, Scalia attempts to construe the Fourth Amendment "in the light of what was deemed an unreasonable search and seizure when it was adopted."[68] And so, when his colleagues concluded in *County of Riverside v. McLaughlin* that it was not unreasonable to seize an individual and delay a judicial determination of the probable cause grounds for that person's warrantless arrest for up to forty-eight hours, excluding weekends and holidays, Scalia dissented, proclaiming that the majority had "eliminate[d] a very old right indeed."[69] The Court viewed its task as one of "balancing [the] competing concerns" of "protecting public safety," on the one hand, and avoiding "prolonged detention based on incorrect or unfounded suspicion," on the other, and of striking a "practical compromise" between these concerns.[70] Scalia declared there was no room for such an approach to resolve questions "on which a clear answer already existed in 1791 and has been generally adhered to by the traditions of our society ever since." On those matters, the balance had already been struck and the practical compromise reached, and, he continued, "it is the function of the Bill of Rights to *preserve* that judgment."[71]

He reminded his colleagues that the "Fourth Amendment's prohibition of 'unreasonable seizures,' insofar as it applies to the seizure of the person, preserves for our citizens the traditional protections against unlawful arrest afforded by the common law," the most important of which is that a person arresting a suspect without a warrant must deliver the arrestee to a magistrate "as soon as he reasonably can."[72] Yet the Court majority was willing to sacrifice the arrestee's traditional right "to have a *prompt* impartial determination that there was reason to deprive him of his liberty" to "the state's convenience in piggybacking various [judicial] proceedings."[73] Scalia reviewed the practices of the federal government and the states and concluded that it was "unreasonable" to allow delaying a probable cause hearing for more than twenty-four hours.[74] He ended with an original-meaning argument that perfectly reflects his understanding of the proper role of the Court:

> One hears the complaint, nowadays, that the Fourth Amendment has become constitutional law for the guilty; that it benefits the career criminal (through the exclusionary rule) often and directly, but the ordinary citizen remotely if at all. By failing to protect the innocent arrestee, today's

opinion reinforces that view. The common-law rule of *prompt* hearing had as its primary beneficiaries the innocent—not those whose fully justified convictions must be overturned to scold the police; nor those who avoid conviction because the evidence, while convincing, does not establish guilt beyond a reasonable doubt; but those so blameless that there was not even good reason to arrest them. While in recent years we have invented novel applications of the Fourth Amendment to release the unquestionably guilty, we today repudiate one of its core applications so that the presumptively innocent may be left in jail. Hereafter a law-abiding citizen wrongfully arrested may be compelled to await the grace of a Dickensian bureaucratic machine, as it churns its cycle for up to two days—never once given the opportunity to show a judge that there is absolutely no reason to hold him, that a mistake has been made. In my view, this is the image of a system of justice that has lost its ancient sense of priority, a system that few Americans would recognize as our own.[75]

Scalia's same objection to backsliding on the Fourth Amendment is also apparent in his opinion for the Court in *Kyllo v. United States.*[76] When the federal government engaged in the warrantless use of a thermal-imaging device to detect heat within the house that suggested the use of halide lights to grow marijuana indoors, Scalia found the search "unreasonable" because it violated "that degree of privacy against government that existed when the Fourth Amendment was adopted."[77] The Court's duty is, he insisted, to prevent "advancing technology" capable of "discern[ing] all human activity in the home"[78] from "shrink[ing] the realm of guaranteed privacy."[79]

For Scalia, the "ultimate measure of the constitutionality of a governmental search is 'reasonableness.' "[80] He regards a search as reasonable or unreasonable based on whether it was regarded as reasonable or unreasonable in 1791 when the Fourth Amendment was ratified. There are, however, cases in which there is "no clear practice, either approving or disapproving the type of search at issue, at the time the constitutional provision was enacted";[81] in those cases, the answer for him in regard to what is reasonable "depends largely upon the social necessity that prompts the search."[82]

The standard of social necessity may seem vague and appear to invite the very exercise of judicial discretion that the textualist Scalia is at pains to cabin. But of course, the text of the Fourth Amendment is itself vague in the same respect: it does not ban all searches and seizures, only those that are unreasonable. And, to appropriate language from Justice Oliver Wendell Holmes, whether a search or seizure is reasonable "depends upon the circumstances in which it is done."[83] Judges are left with no alternative but to assess the circumstances of a search or scizure—to judge its reasonableness, and for Scalia, a measure of reasonableness is social necessity. Judgment involves weighing things, and Scalia reminds us that the symbol of the judiciary is the scales of justice. Social necessity adds a stabilizing weight to the scales. It ensures that governmental intrusions on privacy and deprivations of liberty are balanced against a consistent and weighty standard. It ensures, in Scalia's words, "that the symbol of our profession may remain the scales, not the seesaw."[84]

Applying the test of social necessity in *National Treasury Employees Union v. Von Raab*, Scalia found the implementation by the U.S. Customs Service of a drug-screening program, which required urinalysis tests of its employees seeking transfer or promotion to positions having a direct involvement in drug interdiction or requiring the incumbent to carry firearms or to handle "classified" material, to be "particularly destructive of privacy and offensive to personal dignity" and therefore unreasonable.[85] Scalia was willing to consider "social necessity," but, as he noted, "[w]hat is absent in the Government's justifications—notably absent, revealingly absent, and as far as I am concerned dispositively absent—is the recitation of *even a single instance* in which . . . the cause of bribetaking, or of poor aim, or of unsympathetic law enforcement, or of compromise of classified information [by Customs Service employees], was drug use."[86] He insisted that it was not social necessity but "symbolic opposition to drug use" that explained the government's imposition of this drug-testing regime.[87] And for Scalia, that justification was "unacceptable": "[T]he impairment of individual liberties cannot be the means of making a point; that symbolism, even symbolism for so worthy a cause as the abolition of unlawful drugs, cannot validate an otherwise unreasonable search."[88]

When "social necessity" can be shown, Scalia will find the searches reasonable.[89] In *Vernonia School District v. Acton*, he balanced the intrusion on the Fourth Amendment interests of student athletes against the government's legitimate interests in preventing drug use and found a school district's policy authorizing urinalysis of students who participated in the school's athletics programs to be reasonable. He found the students' privacy interests to be insubstantial. "Traditionally at common law, and still today, unemancipated minors lack some of the most fundamental rights of self-determination—including even the right of liberty in its narrow sense, *i.e.*, the right to come and go at will." Students are subject, "even as to their physical freedom, to the control of their parents or guardians" and to the custodial control of their schools through compulsory school attendance laws.[90] Student athletes must submit to mandatory physical examinations and "suit up" and shower in locker rooms "not notable for the privacy they afford."[91] By contrast, he found the school district's interest in preventing drug use, especially by student athletes who serve as "role models" for the other students and who in a drug-induced state could injure themselves and others, to be great.[92]

He concluded that, taking all of these factors into account, the school district's policy was "reasonable and hence constitutional."[93]

Scalia has also found reasonable searches pursuant to valid warrants issued wholly independently of initially illegal searches[94] and warrantless searches based upon the consent of third parties whom the police, at the time of the entry, reasonably but incorrectly believed to possess common authority over the premises.[95] And he has argued in a series of opinions that warrantless searches of containers within automobiles and of passengers (and their personal belongings) either in or recently in automobiles are always reasonable.[96]

Double Jeopardy

Scalia relies on the text-and-tradition understanding of the Double Jeopardy Clause when he concludes that it guarantees the right not to be twice put in jeopardy for the same offense, as opposed to the right not to be twice put in jeopardy for the same conduct. In *Grady v. Corbin*,[97] when the Court departed from "clear text and clear precedent" and held that a drunk driver, who had weaved across the double-yellow line and fatally injured the driver of an oncoming car, was protected by the Double Jeopardy Clause from being prosecuted for vehicular manslaughter because he had already pleaded guilty to driving while intoxicated before the driver died, Scalia filed a furious dissent:[98] "Even if we had no constitutional text and no prior case law to rely upon, rejection of today's opinion is adequately supported by the modest desire to protect our criminal legal system from ridicule."[99] And when he was given the opportunity three years later in *United States v. Dixon*,[100] he triumphantly announced for the Court majority that "*Grady* must be overruled"; its "same conduct" rule was, he proclaimed, "wholly inconsistent with earlier Supreme Court precedent and the clear common-law understanding of double jeopardy."[101]

His text-and-tradition approach also leads Scalia to hold that the clause prohibits only "successive prosecution, not successive punishment."[102] In his dissent in *Department of Revenue of Montana v. Kurth Ranch*,[103] he laid out a textualist argument concerning the meaning of double jeopardy, reminiscent of the textualist argument he laid out in *Lucas* concerning the meaning of the Takings Clause:

> "To be put in jeopardy" does not remotely mean "to be punished," so by its terms this provision prohibits, not multiple punishments, but only multiple prosecutions. Compare the proposal of the House of Representatives [during the First Congress], for which the Senate substituted language similar to the current text of the Clause: "No person shall be subject, except in cases of impeachment, to more than one punishment or one trial for the same offence."[104]

He regarded his reading of the text to be confirmed by history, noting that it was quite common for the very Congress that framed the Fifth Amendment to pass legislation that provided two sanctions for the same misconduct, enforceable in separate proceedings—one a conventional criminal prosecution and the other a forfeiture proceeding or a civil action, as upon a debt. His understanding that the clause prohibits only successive prosecutions, not successive punishments, led him to conclude in a series of cases that there were no double jeopardy barriers to the assessment by Montana of a tax on the possession and storage of dangerous drugs on an individual already successfully prosecuted for possession of marijuana,[105] to the prosecution of an individual on federal cocaine charges even though the conduct that gave rise to these charges had previously been considered in determining his sentence for a federal marijuana offense,[106] or to the prosecution of an individual for illegal lending transactions when that individual had stipulated to sanctions in a prior administrative hearing involving those transactions.[107]

Self-Incrimination

Scalia's textualist reading of the Self-Incrimination Clause leads him to regard *Miranda v. Arizona*[108] and its prophylactic restrictions on in-custody police interrogation as "a milestone of judicial overreaching."[109] The Fifth Amendment abhors only "compelled confessions," but Scalia has complained that in *Miranda*, the Court displayed a "palpable hostility" toward confessions per se.[110]

"It is wrong and subtly corrosive of our criminal justice system," he argued in his dissent in *Minnick v. Mississippi*, "to regard an honest confession as a 'mistake.'" Conceding that every person is entitled to stand silent, he nevertheless insisted that "it is more virtuous for the wrongdoer to admit his offense and accept the punishment he deserves." An admission of guilt, "if not coerced," is "inherently desirable," not only for society but also "for the wrongdoer himself" because it advances the goals of both "justice *and* rehabilitation." Thus, he concluded, "[w]e should rejoice at an honest confession, rather than pity the 'poor fool' who has made it; and we should regret the attempted retraction of that good act, rather than seek to facilitate and encourage it." *Miranda*, he argued, is based "on premises contrary to these," and it undercuts the public's "belief in either personal responsibility or the moral claim of just government to obedience."[111]

Given his views that *Miranda* represents "an illegitimate exercise" of the Court's authority,[112] Scalia has attempted to confine what he regards as its pernicious consequences whenever the occasion presents itself. One such occasion was *McNeil v. Wisconsin*,[113] when Scalia held that an accused's invocation of the Sixth Amendment's right to counsel during a judicial proceeding did not constitute an invocation of the right to counsel derived by *Miranda* from the Fifth Amendment's guarantee against compelled self-incrimination. The accused claimed that his request for a court-appointed attorney in a case against him for armed robbery constituted as well a request for an attorney when he was subsequently interviewed about a murder. Although he was repeatedly advised of and signed forms waiving his *Miranda* rights before he went on to admit his involvement in the murder, he subsequently sought to suppress his incriminating statements on the grounds that, since he had requested an attorney in the armed robbery case, any statements he had made to the police in the murder case were obtained in violation of his right to remain silent and to be free from repeated requests by the police to waive that right.

Scalia, however, drew a distinction between the Sixth Amendment's "offense-specific" right to counsel, which, he argued, "cannot be invoked once for all future prosecutions, for it does not attach until a prosecution is commenced,"[114] and *Miranda*'s different "nonoffense-specific" right to counsel "relating to the Fifth Amendment guarantee that 'no person . . . shall be compelled in any criminal case to be a witness against himself.' "[115] These rights, he observed, serve different purposes. The purpose of the Sixth Amendment guarantee of the right to counsel "is to protect the unaided layman at critical confrontations with his expert adversary, the government, *after* the adverse positions of government and defendant have solidified with respect to a particular alleged crime." By contrast, the purpose of the *Miranda* guarantee "is to protect a quite different interest: the suspect's desire to deal with the police only through counsel." This *Miranda* right, he continued, is both narrower than the Sixth Amendment guarantee in that it relates only to custodial interrogation and broader in that it relates to "interrogation regarding *any* suspected crime and attaches whether or not the adversarial relationship produced by a pending prosecution has yet arisen." To invoke the former is, therefore, not to invoke the latter, and as a consequence, he concluded that the accused in this case suffered no violation of his *Miranda* rights when the police questioned him about the murder.[116]

Scalia also tried to restrict *Miranda* and its prophylactic rules by urging the federal government to rely on § 3501 of the Omnibus Safe Streets and Crime Control Act of 1968 when it was accused of having obtained a voluntary confession not in conformity with *Miranda*. That provision, passed by Congress in direct response to *Miranda*, declared that "a confession . . . shall be admissible in evidence if it is voluntarily given" and that voluntariness shall be determined on the basis of "all the circumstances surrounding the giving of the confession, including whether or not [the] defendant was advised or knew that he was not required to make any statement, whether or not [the] defendant had been advised prior to questioning of his right to the assistance of counsel; and whether or not [the] defendant was without the assistance of counsel when questioned." To remove all doubt, the provision stated: "The presence or absence of any of the above-mentioned factors . . . need not be conclusive on the issue of voluntariness of the confession." In his concurring opinion in *Davis v. United States*, Scalia pointed out that § 3501 had been "studiously avoided by every Administration, not only in this Court but in the lower courts, since its enactment more than 25 years ago."[117] He noted that "[t]he United States' repeated refusal to invoke § 3501, combined with the courts' traditional (albeit merely prudential) refusal to consider arguments not raised, has caused the federal judiciary to confront a host of '*Miranda*' issues that might be entirely irrelevant under federal law. Worse still," he added, "it may have produced—during an era of intense national concern about the problem of runaway crime—the acquittal and the nonprosecution of many dangerous felons, enabling them to continue their depredations upon our citizens. There is no excuse for this."[118] He therefore announced that he would "no longer be open to the argument that this Court should continue to ignore the commands of § 3501 simply because the Executive declines to insist that we observe them."[119]

Scalia's wish to consider the commands of § 3501 was finally realized in *Dickerson v. United States* but with a result not at all to his satisfaction. Chief Justice Rehnquist held for a seven-member majority that "*Miranda*, being a constitutional decision of this Court, may not be in effect overruled by an Act of Congress, and we decline to overrule *Miranda* ourselves. We therefore hold that *Miranda* and its progeny in this Court govern the admissibility of statements made during custodial interrogation in both state and federal courts."[120] Scalia was reduced to composing a spirited dissent revealing his profound disagreement not only with the majority's holding but also with its sense of its own power:

One will search today's opinion in vain, however, for a statement (surely simple enough to make) that what 18 U.S.C. § 3501 prescribes—the use at trial of a voluntary confession, even when a *Miranda* warning or its equivalent has failed to be given—violates the Constitution. The reason the statement does not appear is . . . that it would be absurd, inasmuch as § 3501 excludes from trial precisely what the Constitution excludes from trial, viz., compelled confessions. . . . And so, to justify today's agreed-upon result, the Court must adopt a significant *new*, if not entirely comprehensible, principle of constitutional law. As the Court chooses to describe that principle, statutes of Congress can be disregarded, not only when what they prescribe violates the Constitution, but when what they prescribe contradicts a decision of this Court that "announced a constitutional rule." . . . [T]he only thing that can possibly mean in the context of this case is that this Court has the power, not merely to apply

the Constitution but to expand it, imposing what it regards as useful "prophylactic" restrictions upon Congress and the States. That is an immense
and frightening antidemocratic power, and it does not exist.[121]

As the preceding makes clear, what outraged Scalia most was the Court's decision to exclude Congress entirely from the policy arena concerning how to protect the right against self-incrimination. It was in *Miranda* that the Court had first
interjected itself into the policymaking process: it announced there that it would
no longer proceed retrospectively as courts had previously done, judging on a case-
by-case basis whether a particular defendant's confession was voluntary based on
the totality of circumstances; rather, it would thereafter proceed prospectively as
a policymaking body and exclude in all future cases confessions obtained without *Miranda* warnings or waivers. At that juncture, however, it did not completely
exclude Congress from fashioning its own policies but actually invited it to do so,
which Congress did in its passage of § 3501.[122] But now in *Dickerson*, the Court
simply monopolized all policymaking power concerning how best to secure the
protection against self-incrimination and found § 3501 to be unconstitutional not
because it violated any provision of the Constitution but because it conflicted with
the policies the Court had decided to put in place.

Right to Confrontation

The Confrontation Clause of the Sixth Amendment guarantees the accused the
right "to be confronted with witnesses against him." It is one of two clauses (the
Compulsory Process Clause being the other) that explicitly address the right of
criminal defendants to elicit evidence in their defense from witnesses at trial. As
Justice Potter Stewart wrote in *Faretta v. California*, "[W]hen taken together, these
clauses guarantee that a criminal charge may be answered in a manner now considered fundamental to the fair administration of American justice. . . . [They]
constitutionalize the right in an adversary criminal trial to make a defense as we
know it."[123]

In *Crawford v. Washington*, Scalia brought his text-and-tradition approach to
constitutional interpretation to bear on the meaning of the Confrontation Clause
and concluded, in an opinion of the Court, that it flatly bars "testimonial statements of a witness who did not appear at trial unless he was unavailable to testify,
and the defendant had had a prior opportunity for cross examination."[124] The text
of the clause alone did not compel this conclusion; as he noted, "One could plausibly read 'witnesses against' a defendant to mean those who actually testify at
trial."[125] But when the text was supplemented by the "historical background of the
Clause," the conclusion became obvious, and he therefore reversed the assault

and attempted murder convictions of the defendant because the trial court had allowed the state to play for the jury a tape-recorded statement in which the defendant's wife (who did not testify at trial because of the state's marital privilege barring one spouse from testifying against the other without the other's consent) had described, during a police interrogation, her husband's stabbing of the victim.[126] The state insisted that her statement should not be barred because it bore "particularized guarantees of trustworthiness,"[127] but Scalia declared, "Where testimonial statements are at issue, the only indicium of reliability sufficient to satisfy constitutional demands is the one the Constitution actually prescribes: confrontation."[128]

Scalia employs his textualist approach no less assiduously when witnesses actually appear at trial; when they do, he insists, the defendant has a right to confront them "face to face" and to subject them to cross-examination. After Iowa sought to reduce the trauma experienced by child victims of sexual abuse who testify in court by passing a law that allowed for a large screen to be placed between them and their alleged assailants, Scalia wrote the majority opinion in *Coy v. Iowa* striking it down as a violation of the defendant's right to face-to-face confrontation. The text, he was adamant, was unequivocal and governing.[129]

Scalia conceded that "face-to-face presence may, unfortunately, upset the truthful rape victim or abused child," but, he insisted, "by the same token it may confound and undo the false accuser, or reveal the child coached by a malevolent adult. It is a truism that constitutional protections have costs."[130] He elaborated on this theme two years later in his dissent in *Maryland v. Craig*,[131] when the Court upheld Maryland's law permitting the use of one-way closed-circuit television for juries to hear the testimony of child witnesses who were alleged to be the victims of child abuse—a procedure less prejudicial to the defendant than the use of the screen in *Coy* but, according to Scalia, no less violative of the Confrontation Clause:

> The Court characterizes the State's interest which "outweigh[s]" the explicit text of the Constitution as an "interest in the physical and psychological well-being of child abuse victims," an "interest in protecting" such victims "from the emotional trauma of testifying." That is not so. A child who meets the Maryland statute's requirement of suffering such "serious emotional distress" from confrontation that he "cannot reasonably communicate" would seem entirely safe. Why would a prosecutor want to call a witness who cannot reasonably communicate? And if he did, it would be the State's own fault. Protection of the child's interest—as far as the Confrontation Clause is concerned—is entirely within Maryland's control. The State's interest here is in fact no more and no less than what the State's interest

always is when it seeks to get a class of evidence admitted in criminal proceedings: more convictions of guilty defendants. That is not an unworthy
interest, but it should not be dressed up as a humanitarian one.[132]

Trial by Jury

Scalia gives an original-meaning interpretation of the right to trial by jury as well.
The right is clearly mentioned in the text of both Article III, § 2 and the Sixth
Amendment. As he declared in his dissent in *Neder v. United States*, it is the only
guarantee "to appear in both the body of the Constitution and the Bill of Rights"
and is nothing less than "the *spinal column* of American democracy."[133] It also
reflects "that healthy suspicion of the power of government which possessed the
Framers" and led them "to reserve the function of determining criminal guilt to
[the people] themselves, sitting as jurors."[134] As he declared in his opinion for the
Court in *Blakely v. Washington*, "Just as suffrage ensures the people's ultimate
control in the legislative and executive branches, jury trial is meant to ensure their
control in the judiciary."[135]

For Scalia, the right to trial by jury in a criminal case means the right of a
defendant "to have the jury determine his guilt of the crime charged [and that]
necessarily means his commission of *every element* of the crime charged."[136] It also
means that, "absent a voluntary waiver of the jury right, the Constitution does not
trust judges to make determinations of criminal guilt."[137] The judges, after all, are
"officers of the Government";[138] as he said in his concurring opinion in *Apprendi
v. New Jersey*, they "are part of the state—and an increasingly bureaucratic part of
it, at that."[139] When it comes to depriving an individual of his liberty or life, the
Framers were of the view that "the state should suffer the modest inconvenience
of submitting its accusations to 'the unanimous suffrage of twelve of his equals
and neighbors' rather than a lone employee of the state."[140]

In *Apprendi v. New Jersey*, Scalia applied these principles and held unconstitutional New Jersey's "hate-crime" statute authorizing a twenty-year sentence
instead of the usual ten-year maximum if a judge found the crime to have been
committed "with a purpose to intimidate . . . because of race, color, gender, hand-
icap, religion, sexual orientation, or ethnicity," since the Sixth Amendment
requires that "all the facts which must exist in order to subject the defendant to a
legally prescribed punishment *must* be found by the jury."[141] In his concurring
opinion in *Ring v. Arizona*, he applied his argument in *Apprendi* to an Arizona
law that authorized the death penalty if the judge found that one of ten possible
aggravating factors was present in the case, and he concluded that the defendant's
constitutional rights had been violated because the aggravating factor had been
neither admitted by the defendant nor found by the jury and because the judge

had imposed a sentence greater than the maximum he could have imposed without the challenged factual finding. Scalia observed an "accelerating propensity of both state and federal legislatures to adopt 'sentencing factors' determined by judges that increase punishment beyond what is authorized by the jury's verdict." He interjected that several of his colleagues believed "this novel practice is perfectly OK" and concluded "that our people's traditional belief in the right of trial by jury is in perilous decline." Although this trend was troubling in any case, it was especially disturbing in death penalty cases: "That decline is bound to be confirmed, and indeed accelerated, by the repeated spectacle of a man's going to his death because *a judge* found that an aggravating factor existed. We cannot preserve our veneration for the protection of the jury in criminal cases if we render ourselves callous to the need for that protection by regularly imposing the death penalty without it."[142]

Apprendi and *Ring* were merely preliminary rounds to the main event: *Blakely v. Washington.* Scalia's 2004 opinion for the Court in that case gave him the opportunity to try to accomplish on Sixth Amendment grounds what in *Mistretta v. United States* he was unable to accomplish on separation-of-powers grounds, namely, having the U.S. Sentencing Commission declared unconstitutional. In his opinion for a five-member majority, Scalia struck down Washington's sentencing process because it allowed judges, not juries, to decide facts that resulted in enhanced sentences. As he put it, when the judge sentenced the defendant who had been found guilty by a jury of kidnapping his estranged wife to 90 months (37 months more than the 53-month statutory maximum of the standard range of Washington's sentencing guidelines) because the judge found the defendant to have acted with "deliberate cruelty," the judge ordered a punishment "that the jury's verdict alone does not allow" and "exceed[ed] his proper authority."[143]

In his dissent in *Monge v. California,* Scalia had explained why it is so important that all facts—all elements of the crime—be found by the jury. He offered a hypothetical: "Suppose that a State repealed all of the violent crimes in its criminal code and replaced them with only one offense, 'knowingly causing injury to another,' bearing a penalty of 30 days in prison, but subject to a series of 'sentencing enhancements' authorizing additional punishment up to life imprisonment or death on the basis of various levels of *mens rea*, severity of injury, and other surrounding circumstances." If the state provided the defendant a jury trial, with the requirement of proof beyond a reasonable doubt, solely on the question whether the defendant "knowingly caused injury to another" but then left it up to the judge to enhance the thirty-day sentence based on the judge's own findings whether the defendant acted intentionally or accidentally and whether the victim ultimately died from the injury the defendant inflicted, would, Scalia asked, the Sixth Amendment be violated? For him, the answer was obvious, and he declared:

"If the protections extended to criminal defendants by the Bill of Rights can be so easily circumvented, most of them would be . . . 'vain and idle enactments,'" and the Court, by upholding such a procedure, would have pointed the way to that "El Dorado sought by many in vain since the beginning of the Republic: a means of dispensing with inconvenient constitutional 'rights.'"[144]

The four dissenting justices in *Blakely* (and especially Justice O'Connor) objected that Scalia's reading of the Sixth Amendment would effectively eliminate all determinate sentencing schemes, including the federal sentencing guidelines.[145] Scalia first responded, in a footnote, that "[t]he Federal Guidelines are not before us, and we express no opinion on them."[146] But he continued, and what he said could have given O'Connor little comfort: "This case is not about whether determinate sentencing is constitutional, only about how it can be implemented in a way that respects the Sixth Amendment."[147] Every defendant, Scalia insisted, has the right under the Sixth Amendment to compel the prosecutor to prove to a jury "all facts legally essential to the punishment."[148] Yet, he scolded colleagues, under the federal sentencing guidelines, a defendant with "no warning in either his indictment or plea" can "see his maximum potential sentence balloon from as little as five years to as much as life imprisonment based not on facts proved to his peers beyond a reasonable doubt, but on facts extracted after trial from a report compiled by a probation officer who the judge thinks more likely got it right than got it wrong. . . . Suffice it to say that, if such a measure exists, it is not the one the Framers left us with."[149]

What the dissenters predicted in *Blakely* came to pass in *United States v. Booker*:[150] A five-member majority of the Court (which included Scalia) concluded that the Sixth Amendment as construed in *Blakely* applied to the federal sentencing guidelines.[151] What no one could have predicted, however, was that the guidelines would escape unscathed. A different five-member majority (Justice Ruth Bader Ginsburg switched sides) concluded that what made the guidelines unconstitutional was not that they allowed judges rather than juries to decide facts that resulted in enhanced sentences but that the guidelines were mandatory; the majority therefore severed those provisions of the Sentencing Reform Act that made them mandatory and saved their constitutionality by making them advisory—i.e., by requiring only that a sentencing court consider the guidelines but permitting it to tailor the sentence in light of other statutory concerns.[152] But, of course, the second majority opinion in *Booker* was a non sequitur: a judge who consults the guidelines (whether they are mandatory or not) and proceeds to enhance the sentence of a defendant on the basis of facts not found to be true beyond a reasonable doubt by a jury is still, according to *Blakely*, violating the defendant's Sixth Amendment rights. Justice John Paul Stevens pointed this out in his dissent, which (on this issue) Scalia joined.[153] In his own dissent to the second majority opinion, Scalia found it "wonderfully ironic: In order to rescue from nullification a statutory scheme designed to eliminate discretionary sentencing, it discards the provisions that eliminate discretionary sentencing."[154]

Surprisingly, the very day that Scalia held in *Blakely* that the Sixth Amendment requires that all of the facts that go into a sentencing decision must be established by a jury, he held in *Schriro v. Summerlin*[155] that *Ring v. Arizona* did not apply retroactively to cases already final on direct review. He declared that under *Teague v. Lane*[156]—the controlling opinion spelling out the Court's prevailing understanding of when its decisions must be retroactively applied not only to cases still under direct review but also to cases that are final and subject only to collateral challenge—the rule announced in *Ring* was not substantive (which requires retroactive effect) but merely procedural (which does not apply retroactively, unless it is a "watershed" ruling that implicates the fundamental fairness and accuracy of the criminal proceeding). But did not *Ring*, with its refusal to allow judges to impose the death penalty by considering aggravating factors that had not been found by the jury, implicate fundamental fairness? Was not *Ring* a "watershed" ruling? According to Scalia, it was not.

Scalia's conclusion that, according to *Teague*, *Ring* did not implicate a fundamental right is surprising, given his insistence in *Neder* that the right to trial by jury, and with it the right to have the jury determine every element that goes to the punishment of the crime, is the very "spinal column of American democracy."[157] However, what is even more surprising, given his understanding of the role of the judiciary, is Scalia's willingness to follow *Teague*.[158] The traditional, common-law understanding of retroactivity present when the Bill of Rights was ratified in 1791 and which *Teague*, based as it is on *Linkletter v. Walker*,[159] rejects was well stated by Justice Tom Clark in *Linkletter*: new constitutional rules invariably must be applied "to cases finalized before the promulgation of the rule."[160]

The traditional understanding held that judges do not make law but merely declare it. The classic formulation and intellectual justification of this declaratory theory was found in Blackstone's *Commentaries on the Laws of England*: "[As] it is an established rule to abide by former precedents," it is the duty of the Court not to "pronounce new law, but to maintain and expound the old one."[161] Consequently, in deciding a case, a judge is bound to find the law as it existed when the controversy arose and to declare it as the controlling principle of the case. As Blackstone wrote, it is not "in the breast of any subsequent judge to alter or vary from [precedent] according to his private judgment but according to the known laws and customs of the land." Blackstone recognized that this rule did "admit of exceptions, where the former determination is most evidently contrary to reason."[162] But even in those cases, Blackstone insisted, "subsequent judges do not pretend to make a new law, but to vindicate the old one from misrepresentation. For if it be found that the former decision is manifestly absurd or unjust, it is declared, not that such a sentence was *bad law*, but that it was *not law*; that it is not the established custom of the realm, as has been erroneously determined."[163]

On the basis of this declaratory theory, Blackstone believed it necessary that judicial decisions have unlimited retroactive effect. A decision does no more than declare what the law always has been in the pending case. If it subsequently becomes necessary to overrule a previous interpretation, it was clear to Blackstone that the overruling decision also does no more than declare the law, albeit in a more enlightened manner. In the locution that Blackstone was fond of using, the first decision had been merely an "evidence" of the law. As the law changed, the former decision became an erroneous "evidence."

Blackstone's declaratory theory expressed the understanding not only of the Framers but also of the American legal community well into the 1960s, allowing Professor Herman Schwartz to declare in the *University of Chicago Law Review* in 1966: "New constitutional doctrines are not new conceptions but rather reflections of principles of 'ordered liberty' fundamental to our legal system. Such principles are equally applicable to past and present trials, for an ethical society cannot seek to retain the fruits of past defaults."[164] Scalia's willingness to give *Ring* only prospective effect not only contradicts the traditional common-law understanding of rights he embraces in other contexts but also encourages the very policymaking tendencies of the colleagues he elsewhere attacks. Ineluctable retroactivity is an automatic check—an inherent restraint—on judicial policymaking because it compels the Court to confront, in a most direct way, the possible undesirable consequences of its adoption of a new rule, i.e., it must apply to everyone already convicted, requiring new hearings, new trials, and possibly outright reversal of convictions. As Justice Hugo Black noted in *James v. United States,*

> In our judgment, one of the great restraints upon this Court's departure from the field of interpretation to enter that of law-making has been the fact that its judgments could not be limited to prospective application. This Court and in fact all departments of the government have always heretofore realized that prospective law-making is a function of Congress rather than the Courts. We continue to think this function should be exercised only by Congress under our constitutional system.[165]

As Justice John Marshall Harlan noted for the Court in *Mackey v. United States,* questions of retroactivity ought to be determined only upon "principles that comport with the judicial function, and not upon considerations that are appropriate enough for a legislative body."[166] Scalia's opinion in *Schriro* showed no awareness of this important aspect of the traditional understanding of the Bill of Rights or of the role of the Court he otherwise prides himself in defending.

Cruel and Unusual Punishments

The Eighth Amendment bans excessive bail and fines as well as cruel and unusual punishments. In *Austin v. United States,* his only opinion on the subject, Scalia concurred in the Court's judgment that the Excessive Fines Clause applied to a drug-related forfeiture of property.[167] In scores of cases addressing the Cruel and Unusual Punishments Clause, Scalia has consistently employed his text-and-tradition approach to hold that the clause, lifted directly out of the English Declaration of Rights, has a limited meaning and only "disables the Legislature from authorizing particular forms or 'modes' of punishment"[168] such as "breaking on the wheel, flaying alive, rending asunder with horses, various species of horrible tortures inflicted in the inquisition, maiming, mutilating, and scourging to death."[169] For Scalia, the clause, as introduced into American law through the Eighth Amendment, merely bars "cruel methods of punishment" that were not "regularly or customarily employed" when the amendment was ratified in 1791;[170] it does not give the justices the power to ban punishments inconsistent with the "abiding convictions of a majority of the small and unrepresentative segment of our society that sits on this Court."[171]

Because the Cruel and Unusual Punishments Clause bans "only certain *modes* of punishment,"[172] Scalia refuses to read into it a proportionality principle. In *Harmelin v. Michigan,*[173] he held that it did not prohibit the imposition of a mandatory term of life in prison without the possibility of parole for possessing more than 650 grams of cocaine. Announcing the judgment of the Court, he rejected the defendant's contention that his sentence was unconstitutional because it was "significantly disproportionate" to the crime he had committed. Scalia noted that "this claim has no support in the text and history of the Eighth Amendment."[174]

Concerning the amendment's "text," he observed that "to use the phrase 'cruel and unusual punishment' to describe a requirement of proportionality would have been an exceedingly vague and oblique way of saying what Americans were well accustomed to saying more directly."[175] He pointed out, for example, that proportionality provisions had been included in several state constitutions, including the Pennsylvania Constitution of 1776 and the South Carolina Constitution of 1778 (both of which declared that punishments should be "in general more proportionate to the crimes") and the New Hampshire Bill of Rights of 1784 (which declared that "All penalties ought to be proportioned to the nature of the offence"). He concluded, "There is little doubt that those who framed, proposed, and ratified the Bill of Rights were aware of such provisions, yet chose not to replicate them."[176]

And concerning the amendment's "history," Scalia surveyed English constitutional history since the promulgation of the English Declaration of Rights as well as the debates over the adoption and ratification of both the Constitution and the Bill of Rights to show that the "Cruel and Unusual Punishments Clause was directed at prohibiting certain *methods* of punishment."[177] He gave great weight to "[t]he actions of the First Congress, which are of course persuasive evidence of what the Constitution means" and which belied "any doctrine of proportionality."[178] He pointed out that, shortly after the First Congress proposed the Bill of Rights, it promulgated the nation's first penal code; yet, contrary to the "didactic instruction" provided in the extant New Hampshire Constitution's proportionality provision, which declared that " 'no wise legislature'—that is, no legislature attuned to the principle of proportionality—'will affix the same punishment to the crimes of theft, forgery and the like, which they do to those of murder and treason,' " the Congress chose "to punish forgery of United States securities, 'running away with [a] ship or vessel, or any goods or merchandise to the value of fifty dollars,' treason, and murder on the high seas with the same penalty: death by hanging." And, he also reported, "the lawbooks of the time are devoid of indication that anyone considered these newly enacted penalties unconstitutional by virtue of their disproportionality."[179]

Scalia did not deny that, in principle, some punishments might be so disproportionate as to raise important questions; he acknowledged that "there are no absolutes" and that "one can imagine extreme examples that no rational person, in any time or place, could accept." But, he continued, "for the same reason these examples are easy to decide, they are certain never to occur." Then, returning to his constant refrain, he remarked: "The real function of a constitutional proportionality principle, if it exists, is to enable judges to evaluate a penalty that *some* assemblage of men and women *has* considered proportionate—and to say that it is not. For that real-world enterprise, the standards seem so inadequate that the proportionality principle becomes an invitation to the imposition of subjective values."[180] As a result, he was led to argue for a plurality of the Court that *Solem v. Helms*,[181] in which the Court had held that the Eighth Amendment does contain a proportionality guarantee, was "wrong" and should be overturned.[182]

In his concurrence in the judgment in *Ewing v. California*, in which the Court upheld on proportionality principles California's "three-strikes" law imposing a sentence of twenty-five years to life on defendants convicted of a felony who have been previously convicted of two or more serious or violent felonies, Scalia offered another explanation for why the Eighth Amendment contains no proportionality principle: proportionality, i.e., the notion that the punishment should fit the crime, is "inherently a concept tied to the penological goal of retribution. It becomes difficult even to speak intelligently of proportionality once deterrence and rehabilitation are given significant weight—not to mention giving weight to the purpose of California's three strikes law: incapacitation." Since the Constitution does not mandate the adoption of any one penological theory, the "classic description of the proportionality principle (alone and in itself quite resistant to policy-free, legal analysis) now becomes merely the 'first' step of the inquiry" and must be followed by an analysis that shows that the sentence "is justified by the state's public-safety interest in incapacitating and deterring recidivist felons."[183]

Because the Eighth Amendment simply bars "cruel methods of punishment" that were not "regularly or customarily employed" when that amendment was ratified in 1791,[184] Scalia also refuses to accept all aspects of what he calls the "death-is-different" jurisprudence that he charges his colleagues are in the "continuous process" of establishing and that is making "a practical impossibility" of "this unquestionably constitutional sentence."[185] To begin with, since the amendment was originally understood to contain no proportionality principle, he denies that murder is the only crime for which the death penalty can be imposed. As noted earlier, he pointed out in *Harmelin* that the very same Congress that adopted the Eighth Amendment also imposed a sentence of death on those convicted of forging U.S. securities.[186]

On proportionality grounds, the Court held in *Coker v. Georgia*,[187] that it was a violation of the Cruel and Unusual Punishments Clause to impose capital punishment for the rape of an adult woman, and in *Enmund v. Florida*,[188] the Court held that it violated the Eighth Amendment to impose the death penalty upon a participant in a felony that results in murder without any inquiry into the participant's intent to kill. Scalia is willing to treat these decisions as controlling precedents, but he clearly believes they depart from the text and tradition of the Eighth Amendment,[189] and he seizes on every occasion to criticize the assumptions on which they were based.

Thus, in his majority opinion in *Stanford v. Kentucky*, he noted that the dissenters quoted *Enmund's* assertion that "it is for *us* ultimately to judge whether the Eighth Amendment permits imposition of the death penalty."[190] He went on to declare that "to mean that as the dissent means it, *i.e.*, that it is for *us* to judge," displays a belief that the justices are not merely "judges of the law" obliged to decide "on the basis of what we perceive the Eighth Amendment originally prohibited, or on the basis of what we perceive the society through its democratic processes now overwhelmingly disapproves," but are instead august members of "a committee of philosopher-kings" free to pronounce "on the basis of what we think 'proportionate' and 'measurably contributory to acceptable goals of punishment.'"[191] In his dissent in *Atkins v. Virginia*, he pointed out how the Court majority made a similar argument concerning its power, this time quoting from *Coker*: "The Constitution contemplates that in the end *our own judgment* will be brought to bear on the question of the acceptability of the death penalty under the Eighth Amendment."[192] Scalia suggested that "the unexpressed reason for this unexpressed 'contemplation' of the Constitution" was the Court's belief "that really good lawyers have moral sentiments superior to those of the common herd, whether in 1791 or today. The arrogance of this assumption of power takes one's breath away."[193] And in his dissent in *Roper v. Simmons*, when the Court again quoted the "our own judgment" passage from *Coker*, Scalia exclaimed: "The Court thus proclaims itself sole arbiter of our Nation's moral standards." By "what conceivable warrant," he wondered, "can nine lawyers presume to be the authoritative conscience of the Nation?"[194]

Scalia also denies that the Eighth Amendment places limits, based on age or mental retardation, on whom the death penalty can be imposed. "Like all of [the Court's death-is-different] jurisprudence," he argues, such limitations "find no support in the text or history of the Eighth Amendment."[195] In his dissent in *Thompson v. Oklahoma*,[196] he argued that the imposition of the death penalty on a defendant convicted of murder who was fifteen years old at the time of the offense but who was tried as an adult did not violate the Cruel and Unusual Punishments Clause: the historical evidence was "unusually clear and unequivocal" that the clause was not "originally understood to prohibit capital punishment for crimes committed by persons under the age of 16." The age at which juveniles could be subjected to capital punishment was, he noted, "explicitly addressed in Blackstone's *Commentaries on the Laws of England*, published in 1769 and widely accepted at the time the Eighth Amendment was adopted as an accurate description of the common law. According to Blackstone, not only was 15 above the age (viz., 7) at which capital punishment could theoretically be imposed; it was even above the age (14) up to which there was a rebuttable presumption of incapacity to commit a capital (or any other) felony."[197]

Since most of his colleagues were operating from the "Living Constitution" perspective and not employing his original-meaning approach, Scalia proceeded to show that imposing the death penalty on a fifteen-year-old was not contrary to "the evolving standards of decency that mark the progress of a maturing society."[198] He did so by reviewing the "most reliable objective signs" of these evolving standards, namely, "the legislation the society has enacted."[199] His review of "the work product of state legislatures" showed that a majority of the states with death penalty statutes were "of the view that death is not different insofar as the age of juvenile criminal responsibility is concerned" and that "what Oklahoma has done here is precisely what the majority of capital-punishment states would do."[200] Failing to persuade a majority of his colleagues who ordered Thompson's death sentence vacated, he complained in disgust: "On its face, the phrase 'cruel and unusual punishments' limits the evolving standards appropriate for our consideration to those entertained by the society rather than those dictated by our personal consciences."[201]

The next year, in *Stanford v. Kentucky*,[202] Scalia repeated many of these same arguments but this time in a majority opinion upholding the imposition of the death penalty on offenders sixteen years of age and older. He again cited Blackstone and again found that the public, reflecting society's evolving standards of decency, still approved of the death penalty for sixteen- and seventeen-year-old offenders; of the 37 states whose laws permitted capital punishment, only 15 declined to impose it on sixteen-year-old offenders and only 12 declined to impose it on seventeen-year-old offenders.[203] He also flatly rejected attempts by the petitioners to have the justices consider other evidence of "a revised national consensus" on the death penalty for juveniles, such as public opinion polls, the views of interest groups, and the positions adopted by various professional associations. The imposition of capital punishment "is either 'cruel and unusual' (i.e., society has set its face against it) or it is not. The audience for these arguments, in other words, is not this Court but the citizenry of the United States. It is they, not we, who must be persuaded." The Court's job, he insisted, "is to *identify* the 'evolving standards of decency'; to determine, not what they *should* be, but what they *are*."[204]

Sixteen years later in *Roper v. Simmons*, however, the Court reversed itself and overturned *Stanford*, and Scalia again found himself dissenting in a juvenile death penalty case. Justice Kennedy held for a five-member majority that the Eighth Amendment forbids the imposition of the death penalty on offenders who were under the age of eighteen when their crimes were committed. He did so because he found that a national consensus had arisen opposed to executing offenders who committed murder before their eighteenth birthday. His evidence was the fact that four death penalty states since *Stanford* had legislatively abolished the juvenile death penalty and that a total of "18 States—or 47% of States that permit capital punishment—now have legislation prohibiting the execution of offenders under 18."[205]

Scalia was incensed: "Words have no meaning if the views of less than 50% of death penalty States can constitute a national consensus. Our previous cases have required overwhelming opposition to a challenged practice, generally over a long period of time."[206]

Kennedy was stung by this criticism and attempted to bulwark his argument that there was a national consensus opposed to the juvenile death penalty by adding to his numbers those states that had eliminated the death penalty altogether. But Scalia ridiculed his effort: "Consulting States that bar the death penalty concerning the necessity of making an exception to the penalty for offenders under 18 is rather like including old-order Amishmen in a consumer-preference poll on the electric car. Of *course* they don't like it, but that sheds no light whatever on the point at issue." For Scalia, "that 12 States favored *no* executions said something about a possible consensus against the death penalty, but absolutely nothing about a consensus against the juvenile death penalty." As he pointed out, "In repealing the death penalty, those 12 States considered *none* of the factors that the Court puts forth as determinative of the issue before us today—lower culpability of the young, inherent recklessness, lack of capacity for considered judgment, etc." He derisively characterized Kennedy's attempt to turn a "minority consensus into a faux majority by counting Amishmen" as "an act of nomological desperation."[207]

In *Penry v. Lynaugh* in 1989, when the Supreme Court held that the Eighth Amendment did not categorically prohibit the execution of criminal defendants who suffered from mild mental retardation, Scalia concurred in part.[208] When the Court reversed itself in *Atkins v. Virginia* in 2002 and held that a national consensus had developed against such executions and that they therefore violated the Cruel and Unusual Punishments Clause, Scalia dissented. The Court asserted the presence of a national consensus because 18 states had recently enacted legislation barring execution of the mentally retarded. But, as Scalia pointed out, those states were "less than *half* (47%) of the 38 states that permit capital punishment (for whom the issue exists),"[209] and their combined population was "only 44% of the population of all death-penalty states."[210] It was, he objected, "quite absurd" to describe an agreement among a minority of the death penalty jurisdictions as constituting a consensus.[211] He labeled the Court's opinion as "the pinnacle of our Eighth Amendment death-is-different jurisprudence" and insisted that it was supported by neither text and tradition nor "current social attitudes regarding the conditions that render an otherwise just death penalty inappropriate." Seldom, he fumed, "has an opinion of this Court rested so obviously upon nothing but the personal views of its members."[212] The *Atkins* majority opinion added simply "one more to a long list" of requirements that did not "exist when the Eighth Amendment was adopted" impeding the imposition of the death penalty. Although he acknowledged "there is something to be said for popular abolition of the death penalty," he insisted that "there is nothing to be said for its incremental abolition by this Court."[213]

Because the Eighth Amendment bars only "cruel methods of punishment" not "regularly or customarily employed" when it was ratified,[214] Scalia has opposed its use to limit the introduction of victim impact statements at the sentencing phase of capital murder trials. As he declared during his first year on the Court in his dissent in *Booth v. Maryland*,[215] in which the Court for the first time banned such statements on Eighth Amendment grounds:

> Many citizens have found one-sided and hence unjust the criminal trial in which a parade of witnesses comes forth to testify to the pressures beyond normal human experience that drove the defendant to commit his crime, with no one to lay before the sentencing authority the full reality of human

suffering the defendant has produced—which is one of the reasons society deems his act worthy of the prescribed penalty. Perhaps these sentiments do not sufficiently temper justice with mercy, but that is a question to be decided through the democratic processes of a free people, and not by the decrees of this Court. There is nothing in the Constitution that dictates the answer, no more in the field of capital punishment than elsewhere.[216]

In *South Carolina v. Gathers* in 1989, he refused to follow *Booth* as precedent, thinking it "a violation of my oath to adhere to what I consider a plainly unjustified intrusion upon the democratic process in order that the Court might save face."[217] Two years later in *Payne v. Tennessee*,[218] he cast his vote with the majority to overturn *Booth*, thereby allowing states once again to introduce evidence of the victim's personal characteristics and the emotional impact of the murder on the victim's family. Nothing in the text or traditional understanding of the Eighth Amendment, he declared in his concurrence, prohibits the people from deciding "what is a crime and what constitutes aggravation and mitigation of a crime."[219]

And, likewise, because he believes the Eighth Amendment "does not, by its terms, regulate the procedures of sentencing as opposed to the substance of punishment,"[220] Scalia denies that it prohibits mandatory death sentences.[221] As he declared in his concurrence in the judgment in *Walton v. Arizona*, "The mandatory imposition of death—without sentencing discretion—for a crime which states have traditionally punished with death cannot possibly violate the Eighth Amendment."[222] But of course, not all death penalty states have passed mandatory death penalty statutes, and those that by 1976 had done so had them declared unconstitutional by the Court in *Woodson v. North Carolina*.[223]

What limitations, if any, does Scalia believe the Eighth Amendment imposes on states that enact discretionary death penalty statutes? If, "by its terms," the amendment deals only with "the substance of punishment" and not "the procedures of sentencing," his answer would necessarily have to be "none"; however, it is not. Even though he insists that the "text [of the Eighth Amendment] did not originally prohibit a traditional form of punishment that is rarely imposed, as opposed to a form of punishment that is not traditional," he declared in *Walton* that "the critical opinions" of Justice Stewart and Justice Byron White in *Furman v. Georgia*[224] were "arguably supported by this text" when they concluded that "discretionary capital sentencing had made the death sentence such a random and infrequent event among capital offenders ('wanton and freakish,' as Justice Stewart colorfully put it) that its imposition had become cruel and unusual."[225] He therefore declared himself "willing to adhere to the precedent established by our *Furman* line of cases, and to hold that when a state adopts capital punishment for a given crime but does not make it mandatory, the Eighth Amendment bars it from giving the sentencer unfettered discretion to select the recipients, but requires it to establish in advance, and convey to the sentencer, a governing standard."[226] That governing standard, however, is met for Scalia if the sentencer—be it judge or jury—finds at least one aggravating factor, such as the murder was "especially heinous, cruel, or depraved" or the defendant had been "previously convicted of a felony in the United States involving the use or threat of violence on another person."[227] That governing standard does not require, however, that the "sentencer consider mitigating evidence."[228] And it most certainly does not require the sentencer to have "unchanneled discretion" to "give full consideration and full effect" to all relevant mitigating evidence.[229] As he said in his dissent in *Tennard v. Dretke,* not only does a " 'right' to unchanneled sentencer discretion [have] no basis in the Constitution" but also "requiring unchanneled discretion to say *no* to death cannot rationally be reconciled with our prior decisions requiring canalized discretion to say *yes.*"[230]

Conclusions

Scalia is often described as a judicial conservative who favors the government over the individual when the Due Process Clauses and criminal procedural protections are involved, and there is certainly some truth to that description. However, as this chapter makes clear, that description is not simply true—perhaps not even generally true.

By pursuing a text-and-tradition approach that seeks to understand the original meaning of these rights and then faithfully apply that meaning to the facts in the cases before him, he often comes down solidly on the side of the individual. His powerful dissent on behalf of the defendant in the due process case of *Rogers v. Tennessee*; his strong Fourth Amendment opinions on behalf of criminal defendants in *County of Riverside v. McLaughlin* and *Kyllo v. United States* and customs employees in *National Employees Union v. Von Raab*; his forceful Confrontation Clause opinions in *Crawford v. Washington, Coy v. Iowa,* and *Maryland v. Craig*; and his passionate commitment to a defendant's right to have every element of the crime charged determined by a jury in *Apprendi v. New Jersey* and *Blakely v. Washington* are all examples.

With regard to other provisions, however, his textualist approach leads him to favor the government. Thus, he finds that the government can pass laws that allow for unlimited punitive damages, prohibit abortion, grant visitation rights to grandparents, prevent suicide, and criminalize homosexuality without violating due process. And the government can have laws and procedures in place that impose successive punishments (so long as it does not engage in successive prosecutions), encourage confessions (so long as it does not compel them), impose punishments that are disproportional to the offense (so long as it does not inflict certain cruel methods of punishment not regularly employed when the Eighth Amendment was ratified), and impose the death penalty on those convicted of murder regardless of age or mental retardation (so long as the defendant is subject to the jurisdiction of the adult courts and the punishment is either mandatory or the sentencing judge or jury has found at least one aggravating factor).

Scalia is aware, however, that just because the text-and-tradition understanding of these provisions means that the government can pass such laws and adopt such procedures, it does not mean that it must. If the people want the courts to favor the individual over the government, if they want procedural rights to evolve and to mean more now than when they were written into the constitutional text, they are free to pursue those ends. But, he argues, the appropriate way for that evolution to take place is through the enactment of new laws and the adoption of new constitutional amendments—i.e., through the people via their elected representatives in the state legislatures and Congress. Thus, when Scalia decides against the individual because his fidelity to the original meaning of the right in question requires him to do so, he is paying homage to the principle of democracy. His textualist commitment to original meaning "has nothing to do with whether 'further progress [is] to be made' in the 'evolution of our legal system.'" Rather, as he proclaimed in *Burnham v. Superior Court*, it has everything "to do with whether changes are to be adopted as progressive by the American people or decreed as progressive by the Justices of this Court."[231]

Chapter Seven

The Impact of Scalia's Textualism
on His Colleagues

Scalia is approaching twenty years of service on the Supreme Court, making this a timely occasion to assess the impact of his text-and-tradition approach on his colleagues. In a word, the impact has been mixed. As discussed at some length in Chapter Two, his textualist critique of the use of legislative history has produced a major change in their decision making. But in the realm of constitutional interpretation, his original-meaning jurisprudence has generally failed to win converts, even among his conservative colleagues.

Voting Alignments and Patterns

Over the years, Scalia has certainly been a consistent vote in the Court's conservative bloc, consisting of Scalia, Chief Justice William Rehnquist, and Justices Sandra Day O'Connor, Anthony Kennedy, and Clarence Thomas.[1] From the time of his elevation to the Supreme Court, he has served with thirteen different colleagues. His voting alignments with these justices are presented in Table 7.1, which records the number of opinions in which Scalia and the other justices joined, including majority, concurring, and dissenting opinions; the total number of cases in which they participated together; and the percentages of these cases in which they joined the same opinions. The table shows, most dramatically, that he has joined in the same opinions with Justice Clarence Thomas 86.3 percent of the time, but it also shows that over the years, he has joined the same opinions with each member of the conservative bloc no less than 71.3 percent of the time.[2]

Nonetheless, his adherence to textualism makes him the least consistent member of the Court's conservative bloc and the least likely either to join the opinion of the Court or to concur in the disposition of the case. This is apparent in Tables 7.2 and 7.3.

Table 7.2 shows the voting alignments of the entire Court in nonunanimous cases since the publication of *A Matter of Interpretation*, in which Scalia's mature reflections of textualism were so clearly laid out. This table reveals that Chief Justice Rehnquist and Justices O'Connor and Kennedy (and even Justice Thomas)

Table 7.1. Voting Alignments: Scalia and His Colleagues
(1986–2003 terms of the Court)

Justice	Number of Opinions*	Total Number of Cases**	Percentage Agreement†
Thomas	956	1108	86.3
Rehnquist	1433	1824	78.6
Kennedy	1031	1393	74.1
Powell	108	147	73.5
O'Connor	1287	1804	71.3
White	644	913	70.5
Souter	734	1243	59.1
Ginsburg	494	908	54.4
Breyer	421	814	51.7
Blackmun	495	996	49.7
Brennan	268	565	47.4
Stevens	857	1818	47.1
Marshall	308	685	45.0

*Total number of opinions in which both Scalia and the justice joined, including majority, concurring, and dissenting opinions

**Total number of cases in which both Scalia and the justice participated

†Percentage of all cases in which both Scalia and the justice joined the same majority, concurring, or dissenting opinions

Source: Information compiled from the *Harvard Law Review*'s annual review and statistical analysis of the work of the Supreme Court, in its November issues. See vol. 101 (for the 1986 term of the Court) through vol. 118 (for the 2003 term of the Court).

consistently have joined the same majority, concurring, and dissenting opinions far more frequently than Scalia has.

Table 7.3 compares how often, in these same nonunanimous cases, Scalia, as opposed to the other members of the conservative bloc, has either joined the opinion of the Court or merely concurred in the disposition of the case. In contrast with Justice O'Connor, who has joined the opinion of the Court in 80.8 percent of all nonunanimous cases and who has concurred in the disposition of the case in 85.5 percent of them, Scalia has joined the opinion of the Court only 56.7 percent of the time and concurred in the disposition of the case only 57.9 percent of the time. This is a direct result of his textualism, which keeps him from joining opinions that rely on legislative history or that expand the words of the Constitution beyond what they meant to those who drafted and ratified it.

Not surprisingly, as Table 7.4 shows, he writes more opinions than any of the

Table 7.2. Voting Alignments: Nonunanimous Cases (1996–2003 terms of the Court)*

Justice**	Rehnquist	Stevens	O'Connor	Scalia	Kennedy	Souter	Thomas	Ginsburg	Breyer
Rehnquist		25.4	71.6	63.2	76.5	40.4	65.5	40.8	43.2
Stevens	25.4		33.1	14.0	32.5	65.7	17.0	66.3	61.9
O'Connor	71.6	33.1		51.2	65.7	50.1	51.3	46.1	55.5
Scalia	63.2	14.0	51.2		56.1	27.6	75.0	25.4	23.4
Kennedy	76.5	32.5	65.7	56.1		45.8	58.9	43.7	44.1
Souter	40.4	65.7	50.1	27.6	45.8		29.4	80.0	69.8
Thomas	65.5	17.0	51.3	75.0	58.9	29.4		25.0	23.6
Ginsburg	40.8	66.3	46.1	25.4	43.7	80.0	25.0		73.0
Breyer	43.2	61.9	55.5	23.4	44.1	69.8	23.6	73.0	

*Percentage of all cases in which both justices have joined the same majority, concurring, or dissenting opinions

**The justices are listed with the chief justice first, followed by the most senior associate justice down to the most junior associate justice

Source: Information compiled from the *Harvard Law Review's* annual review and statistical analysis of the work of the Supreme Court, in its November issues. See vol. 111 (for the 1996 term of the Court) through vol. 118 (for the 2003 term of the Court).

Table 7.3.   Voting Patterns: Nonunanimous Cases (1996–2003 terms of the Court)

Justice	Joins Opinion of the Court	Concurs in Disposition of Case
O'Connor	80.8	85.5
Kennedy	77.4	83.3
Rehnquist	76.7	78.5
Thomas	57.8	68.0
Scalia	56.7	57.9

Source: Information compiled from the *Harvard Law Review*'s annual review and statistical analysis of the work of the Supreme Court, in its November issues. See vol. 111 (for the 1996 term of the Court) through vol. 118 (for the 2003 term of the Court).

Table 7.4.   Total Number of Opinions Written by Each Justice (1994–2003 terms of the Court)

Justice*	Number of Opinions
Rehnquist	148
Stevens	313
O'Connor	181
Scalia	270
Kennedy	175
Souter	190
Thomas	222
Ginsburg	185
Breyer	220
Total	1904

*The justices are listed with the chief justice first, followed by the most senior associate justice down to the most junior associate justice

Source: "Nine Justices, Ten Years: A Statistical Retrospective," 118 *Harvard Law Review* (November 2004): 519.

other members of the conservative bloc and more opinions than any other justice except for Justice John Paul Stevens.

Not only is Scalia the least likely member of the conservative bloc to join the opinion of the Court or to concur in the disposition of the case, he is also the least likely member of that bloc to vote with the majority in a five-to-four decision. As Table 7.5 shows, in the 175 five-to-four decisions handed down during the ten-year period of 1994 to 2003—a period during which all nine justices served

Table 7.5.   Five-to-Four Decisions: Voting with the
Majority (1994–2003 terms of the Court)

Justice*	Number of Votes Cast with the Majority in Five-to-Four Decisions
Rehnquist	111
Stevens	73
O'Connor	135
Scalia	106
Kennedy	128
Souter	73
Thomas	111
Ginsburg	68
Breyer	70

The total number of 5–4 decisions during these terms was 175.

*The justices are listed with the chief justice first, followed by the most
senior associate justice down to the most junior associate justice

Source: "Nine Justices, Ten Years: A Statistical Retrospective," 118 *Harvard
Law Review* (November 2004): 520.

together—Scalia joined the majority only 106 times, whereas Justice O'Connor
voted with the majority 135 times.

And, as Table 7.6 demonstrates, Scalia is also the most likely member of the
conservative bloc to write a dissenting opinion. Over the ten-year period from 1994
to 2003, he wrote 188 dissents, compared with Justices O'Connor and Kennedy,
for example, who wrote only 91 and 88, respectively.

As these tables make clear, Scalia's voting is most closely aligned with that of
Justice Thomas—despite the fact that Scalia, operating on logical-positivist assumptions, rejects Thomas's natural-rights premises and insistence that the Constitution
is to be read in the light of the principles of the Declaration of Independence. In
86.3 percent of all the cases they have heard together and in 75 percent of all recent
nonunanimous cases, Scalia and Thomas have joined the same opinions. Over
their fourteen years together on the Court, in only 38 cases has one written a dissenting opinion when the other has voted with the majority;[3] in only two cases has
one written the opinion of the Court and the other joined the dissent;[4] and, most
remarkable of all, in only six cases has one written the majority opinion and the
other written a dissent.[5] Not surprisingly, all six of those cases involved statutory
construction, and what split them was Scalia's insistence on pursuing a textualist
approach. Thomas dissented from Scalia's majority opinions in *AT&T v. Iowa Util-*

Table 7.6. Total Number of Dissenting Opinions Written by Each Justice (1994–2003 terms of the Court)

Justice*	Number of Dissenting Opinions
Rehnquist	124
Stevens	251
O'Connor	91
Scalia	188
Kennedy	88
Souter	162
Thomas	186
Ginsburg	178
Breyer	178
Total	1446

**The justices are listed with the chief justice first, followed by the most senior associate justice down to the most junior associate justice

Source: "Nine Justices, Ten Years: A Statistical Retrospective," 118 *Harvard Law Review* (November 2004): 520.

ities Board, construing the Federal Communications Act; *United States v. McDermott,* construing a federal tax-lien statute; and in *Clark v. Martinez,* construing detention language in an immigration statute. Scalia dissented from Thomas's majority opinions in *United States v. Rodriguez-Moreno,* construing a federal statute authorizing prosecution for "using or carrying a gun" during the commission of a crime;[6] in *Olympic Airways v. Husain,* holding that the death of a passenger who died on an airplane after a flight attendant refused to move him away from the airplane's smoking section constituted an "accident" within the meaning of Article 17 of the Warsaw Convention; and in *National Cable & Telecommunications Association v. Brand X Internet Services,* holding that the Federal Communications Commission's conclusion that broadband cable modem companies are exempt from mandatory common-carrier regulations is a lawful construction of the Federal Communications Act under *Chevron U.S.A., Inc., v. Natural Resources Defense Council,* 467 U.S. 837 (1984) and the Administrative Procedure Act.

The Impact of Scalia's Textualism on the Broader Legal Community

Scalia is criticized for the fact that he has not been able to build a coalition among his conservative colleagues to support his textualist approach to constitutional interpretation.[7] The criticism is unjustified.

It is simply not possible for Scalia—who argues that judges are to be governed only by the "text and tradition of the Constitution," not by their "intellectual, moral, and personal perceptions"[8]—to build a strong, lasting, and principled coalition that includes Justices O'Connor and Kennedy. They, after all, jointly authored the plurality opinion in *Planned Parenthood v. Casey* (along with Justice Souter), asserting perhaps the most antitextualist argument ever uttered by members of the Supreme Court, namely, that the Due Process Clause prohibits states from interfering with a person's "right to define one's own concept of existence, of meaning, of the universe, and of the mystery of human life."[9] O'Connor and Kennedy may occasionally join in a Scalia opinion on the meaning of due process, but they will never find persuasive his textualist conclusions that due process is simply the "embodiment of common-law tradition" and that "[i]f the government chooses to follow a historically approved procedure, it necessarily *provides* due process,"[10] for that understanding of due process can never justify the more activist role they have assigned to themselves.

A textualist jurisprudence constrains judicial discretion; therefore, O'Connor and Kennedy will refuse to follow Scalia's textualist lead on any issue important to them because it will prevent them from doing what they consider to be the right thing. Thus, O'Connor rejected Scalia's textualist reading in *Coy v. Iowa* that the Confrontation Clause literally requires "face-to-face confrontation" because of her solicitude for youthful victims of sexual crimes.[11] O'Connor also rejected his textualist reading in *Blakely v. Washington* that the Sixth Amendment right to trial by jury requires that all the facts that have to exist in order to subject a defendant to a legally prescribed punishment must be found by the jury; she considered the "practical consequences"—the additional time and judicial resources needed to comply with this constitutional requirement—"disastrous."[12] Likewise, Kennedy found inconvenient Scalia's textualist reading that due process protects only "long-recognized personal liberties"[13] and is not "the secret repository of all sorts of . . . unenumerated, substantive rights,"[14] and he turned instead to foreign courts and laws to justify declaring unconstitutional the criminalizing of homosexual sodomy in *Lawrence v. Texas*[15] and the juvenile death penalty in *Roper v. Simmons*.[16]

Even Chief Justice Rehnquist has proven to be an unreliable member of the textualist coalition. For Scalia, if the meaning of the text or the traditional understanding of a constitutional text is clear, that ends the matter. The work of the Court is to apply that original meaning, not to gainsay or revise it. The justices are "to rely upon the judgment of the wise men who constructed our system, and of the people who approved it, and of the two centuries of history that have shown it to be sound"[17]—nothing more, nothing less. Not so for Rehnquist, as his majority opinions in *Morrison v. Olson* and *Locke v. Davey* make clear. Thus, Rehnquist held in *Morrison* that even though an independent counsel established under the

Ethics in Government Act did, in fact, exercise some of the president's Take Care powers, the executive branch was nonetheless left, in his view, with "sufficient control . . . to ensure that the President is able to perform his constitutionally assigned duties."[18] The textualist Scalia profoundly disagreed: For him, the Constitution's "division of power" among the branches requires that "all purely executive power must be under the control of the President," not simply those powers "the majority thinks, taking all things into account, . . . ought to be" under the president's control.[19] Likewise, in *Davey*, although Rehnquist acknowledged that Washington State's Promise Scholarship Program clearly imposed a burden on a student who wanted to study devotional theology, he insisted that the burden was "relatively minor" and therefore not in conflict with the Free Exercise Clause.[20] The textualist Scalia strenuously objected to Rehnquist's suggestion that the Court could substitute its judgment for that of those who adopted and ratified the First Amendment and could conclude that the exercise of religion need not be free so long as it is not burdened more than a majority of the Court was willing to tolerate. The First Amendment, Scalia insisted, "guarantees *free* exercise of religion," and, he continued, the $3,000 "financial penalty" the state of Washington imposed on Davey because he wanted to study devotional theology meant that his exercise of religion was "anything *but* free."[21]

Because most of his colleagues chafe at and ultimately reject the constraints imposed by any coherent interpretive approach[22]—including his textualism—Scalia has devoted his energies to persuading the broader legal community. He has confessed that he writes with the verve and panache he does in part to ensure that his opinions are included in constitutional law casebooks, where they will influence the next generation of lawyers and legal scholars.[23]

His strategy has succeeded brilliantly. The leading law school constitutional law casebook is Kathleen Sullivan and Gerald Gunther's *Constitutional Law*.[24] It includes 18 opinions by Scalia, followed by 17 opinions by Justice Stevens, 16 by Justice O'Connor, and 15 by Chief Justice Rehnquist. Another leading law school casebook, William Cohen and David J. Danelski's *Constitutional Law: Civil Liberties and Individual Rights*,[25] includes 15 opinions each by Scalia and O'Connor, followed by 10 opinions each by Stevens and Kennedy. Among the leading political science constitutional law casebooks are the following: Ralph A. Rossum and G. Alan Tarr's *American Constitutional Law*,[26] which includes 29 opinions by Scalia, followed by 27 opinions by Stevens, 22 by Kennedy, and 16 by O'Connor; Alpheus Thomas Mason and Donald Grier Stephenson Jr.'s *American Constitutional Law: Introductory Essays and Selected Cases*,[27] which includes 16 opinions each by Scalia, Rehnquist, and Stevens, followed by 11 by O'Connor; Donald P. Kommers, John Finn, and Gary J. Jacobsohn's *American Constitutional Law*,[28] which includes 22 opinions each by Scalia and Stevens, followed by 17 by Souter and 16 by O'Connor; and Walter F. Murphy, James E. Fleming, Sotirios A. Barber, and Stephen Macedo's *American Constitutional Law*,[29] which includes 15 opinions by Scalia, followed by 14 opinions by Stevens, 13 by O'Connor, and 12 by Rehnquist.

Scalia's textualist jurisprudence and his eminently quotable writing style have also made him the subject of more academic inquiry and debate in the law reviews than any of his colleagues.[30] Table 7.7 reports the results of a Lexis-Nexis search for law review articles that have the name of a current justice of the Supreme Court in their titles; it shows that Scalia's name has appeared in the title of 120 articles since he joined the Court in 1986; William Rehnquist, on the Court since 1971, follows in second place with his name in the title of 57 articles.

Justice Scalia's textualist arguments and opinions—all carefully wrought and powerfully argued—command the attention and engagement of the broader legal community. It is impossible to think of separation of powers, the "negative" Commerce Clause, executive power and the Take Care Clause, the Free Exercise Clause, the political speech rights of candidates and their parties and contributors, the reach of the Fourth Amendment, the meaning of due process, the Takings Clause, the Confrontation Clause, the right to trial by jury, the meaning of the Cruel and Unusual Punishments Clause, state sovereignty immunity, Congress's enforcement powers under § 5 of the Fourteenth Amendment, the abortion controversy, and the debates over the use of legislative history and foreign law without immediately thinking of Scalia's opinions on these matters. He has largely

Table 7.7.	Number of Law Review Articles with Name of a Current Justice of the Supreme Court in Title

Justice*	Number of Articles
Rehnquist	57
Stevens	5
O'Connor	48
Scalia	120
Kennedy	9
Souter	3
Thomas	16
Ginsburg	8
Breyer	2

**The justices are listed with the chief justice first, followed by the most senior associate justice down to the most junior associate justice framed the debate on these and other constitutional provisions and issues through a generally faithful application of his textualist jurisprudence. He has reminded both his colleagues and his readers of what the various provisions of the Constitution meant to those who adopted them, and he has labored diligently to ensure that the Court adheres to that original meaning. He has therefore harshly condemned the Court when it has tolerated actions by "transient majorities" that result in "backsliding," i.e., in the erosion of rights "our society has always accorded in the past." And he has objected with equal outrage when the Court has succumbed to the temptation of expanding constitutional rights to "progressively higher degrees."[31] That power, he insists, has been assigned to the popular branches, not to an unelected committee of nine lawyers.

Conclusions

At bottom, Scalia's original-meaning jurisprudence is devoted to checking judicial discretion. For Scalia, the job of the Court is to preserve constitutional structure and to protect those rights found in the original Constitution and its subsequent amendments—nothing more but also nothing less. Accordingly, it is not the job of the justices to determine, for example, whether Congress's intrusions on executive power violate a system of separation of powers among the three branches that they would devise but rather the system of separation of powers devised by the Framers and actually found in the Constitution. Likewise, it is not their job to eliminate traditional rights or to create new ones but rather to secure those, and only those, included by the Framers and the ratifiers in the Constitution itself. Finally, it is not their job to keep the Constitution up to date—treating it as a "Living Constitution, a 'morphing' document that means, from age to age, what it ought to mean"[32]—but rather to understand that it is a permanent Constitution that means the same from age to age until such time as the people choose to alter it. As Scalia has written, "Changes in the Constitution, when thought necessary, are to be proposed by Congress or conventions and ratified by the States. The Founders gave no such amending power to this Court. Our duty is simply to interpret the Constitution, and in doing so the test of constitutionality is not whether a law is offensive to our conscience ..., but whether it is offensive to the Constitution."[33]

During his long and distinguished career on the Supreme Court, Scalia has remained faithful to the "text and tradition" of the written U.S. Constitution. He has steadfastly rejected the idea of a "Living Constitution" and all other intellectual fads and novel theories of interpretation that have the invariable effect of transferring power from the popular branches to the judges. He has sought to constrain judicial discretion and has fought with all the considerable intellectual tools at his disposal the tendency of judges to substitute their beliefs for society's. In so doing, he has reminded his colleagues of the most important right of the people in a democracy—the right to govern themselves as they see fit and not to be overruled in their governance unless the clear text or traditional understanding of the Constitution they have adopted demands it.

Cases in Which Justice Scalia
Has Cited Dictionaries

Tennessee v. Lane, 541 U.S.509, 559 (2004). N. Webster, *An American Dictionary of the English Language* (1860), and J. Worcester, *Dictionary of the English Language* (1860).

Engine Manufacturers Association v. South Coast Air Quality Management District, 541 U.S. 246, 253 (2004). *Webster's Second New International Dictionary* (1945).

Crawford v. Washington, 541 U.S. 36, 51 (2004). N. Webster, *An American Dictionary of the English Language* (1828).

Dastar Corporation v. Twentieth Century Fox, 539 U.S. 23, 31 (2003). *Webster's New International Dictionary* (2d ed. 1949).

Branch v. Smith, 538 U.S. 254, 264 (2003). *Webster's New International Dictionary* (2d ed. 1949), and *Black's Law Dictionary* 910 (7th ed. 1999).

Republican Party of Minnesota v. White, 536 U.S. 765, 776 (2002). *Webster's New International Dictionary* (2d ed. 1950).

City of Columbus v. Ours Garage & Wrecker Service, 536 U.S. 424, 445 (2002). *Webster's New International Dictionary* (2d ed. 1950).

J.E.M. AgSupply, Inc. v. Pioneer Hi-Bred International, 534 U.S. 124, 146 (2001). *Webster's New International Dictionary* (2d ed. 1950).

Nevada v. Hicks, 533 U.S. 353, 364 (2001). *Black's Law Dictionary* (5th ed. 1979).

Kyllo v. United States, 533 U.S. 27, 33 (2001). N. Webster, *An American Dictionary of the English Language* (1828) (reprint 6th ed. 1989).

Buckhannon Board & Care Home, Inc. v. West Virginia Department of Health and Human Resources, 532 U.S. 598, 615 (2001). *Black's Law Dictionary* (7th ed. 1999).

National Labor Relations Board v. Kentucky River Community Care, Inc., 532 U.S. 706, 712 (2001). *American Heritage Dictionary* (3d ed. 1992).

Semtek International v. Lockheed Martin Corp., 531 U.S. 497, 505 (2001). *Black's Law Dictionary* (7th ed. 1999).

Whitman v. American Trucking Association, 531 U.S. 457, 465 (2001). *Webster's New International Dictionary* (2d ed. 1950).

Artuz v. Bennett, 531 U.S. 4, 8 (2000). *Black's Law Dictionary* (7th ed. 1999).

Hill v. Colorado, 530 U.S. 703, 721 (2000). *Webster's Third New International Dictionary* (1993).

Johnson v. United States, 529 U.S. 694, 704 (2000). *Webster's Third New International Dictionary* (1981).

Reno v. Bossier Parish School Board, 528 U.S. 320, 333 (2000). *Webster's New International Dictionary* (2d ed. 1950), and *American Heritage Dictionary* (3d ed. 1992).

City of Chicago v. Morale, 527 U.S. 41, 93 (1999). *American Heritage Dictionary* (1992).

Holloway v. United States, 526 U.S. 1, 12 (1999). *Black's Law Dictionary* (6th ed. 1990).

Department of Commerce v. United States House of Representatives, 525 U.S. 316, 342 (1999). *Webster's Ninth New Collegiate Dictionary* (1983).

AT&T Corp. v. Iowa Utilities Board, 525 U.S. 366, 394 (1999). *Webster's Ninth New Collegiate Dictionary* (1988).

National Endowment for the Arts v. Finley, 524 U.S. 569, 591 (1998). *American Heritage Dictionary* (3d ed. 1992).

Pennsylvania Department of Corrections v. Yeskey, 524 U.S. 206, 211 (1998). *Webster's New International Dictionary* (2d ed. 1949).

Textron Lycoming Reciprocating Engine Division v. United Automobile, Aerospace & Agricultural Implement Workers, 523 U.S. 653, 656 (1998). *Webster's New International Dictionary* (2d ed. 1950).

Feltner v. Columbia Pictures Television, 523 U.S. 340, 356 (1998). *Webster's New International Dictionary* (2d ed. 1949), and *Black's Law Dictionary* (5th ed. 1979).

Almendarez-Torres v. United States, 523 U.S. 224, 264 (1998). *Webster's New International Dictionary* (2d ed. 1949).

Brogan v. United States, 522 U.S. 398, 400 (1998). *Webster's New International Dictionary* (2d ed. 1950).

Allentown Mack Sales & Service v. National Labor Relations Board, 522 U.S. 359, 823 (1998). *Webster's New International Dictionary* (2d ed. 1949), *The New Shorter Oxford English Dictionary* (1993), and *American Heritage Dictionary* (3d ed. 1992).

City of Boerne v. Flores, 521 U.S. 507, 539 (1997). N. Webster, *American Dictionary of the English Language* (1828), and *Dictionary of American Biography* (1943).

Commissioner of Internal Revenue v. Estate of Hubert, 520 U.S. 93, 118 (1997). *American Heritage Dictionary* (2d ed. 1985).

Auer v. Robbins, 519 U.S. 452, 461 (1997). *American Heritage Dictionary* (3d ed. 1992), and *Webster's New International Dictionary* (2d ed. 1950).

Walters v. Metropolitan Educational Enterprises, 519 U.S. 202, 207 (1997). *The New Shorter Oxford English Dictionary* (1993), *American Heritage Dictionary* (3d ed. 1992), *Webster's New International Dictionary* (2d ed. 1950).

Smiley v. Citibank (South Dakota), N.A., 517 U.S. 735, 745 (1996). J. Bouvier, *A Law Dictionary* (6th ed. 1856), A. Burrill, *A Law Dictionary and Glossary* (2d ed. 1860), *American and English Encyclopedia of Law* (J. Merrill ed. 1890), and J. Wharton, *Law Lexicon or Dictionary of Jurisprudence* (2d. Am. ed. 1860).

Capitol Square Review and Advisory Board v. Pinette, 515 U.S. 753, 764 (1995). *The New Shorter Oxford English Dictionary* (1993); *Webster's New Dictionary* (2d ed. 1950).

Babbitt v. Sweet Home Chapter of Communities for a Great Oregon, 515 U.S. 687, 2422 (1995). *Webster's Third New International Dictionary* (1966).

United States v. Aguilar, 515 U.S. 593, 611 (1995). *Webster's New International Dictionary* (2d ed. 1950), and *The New Shorter Oxford English Dictionary* (1993).

Asgrow Seed Co. v. Winterboer, 513 U.S. 179, 187 (1995). *Oxford Universal Dictionary* (3d ed. 1955), and *Webster's New International Dictionary* (2d ed. 1950).

MCI Telecommunications Corp. v. American Telephone & Telegraph Company, 512 U.S. 218, 225–26 (1994). *Random House Dictionary of the English Language* (2d ed. 1987), *Webster's Third New International Dictionary* (1976), *Oxford English Dictionary* (2d ed. 1989), *Black's Law Dictionary* (6th ed. 1990), *Webster's Ninth New Collegiate Dictionary* (1991), *Webster's Eighth New Collegiate Dictionary* (1973), *Webster's Seventh New Collegiate Dictionary* (1963), and *Webster's New Collegiate Dictionary* (6th ed. 1949).

BFP v. Resolution Trust Corp., 511 U.S. 531, 538 (1994). *Black's Law Dictionary* (6th ed. 1990).

Liteky v. United States, 510 U.S. 540, 552 (1994). *American Heritage Dictionary* (3d ed. 1992).

ABF Freight System v. National Labor Relations Board, 510 U.S. 317, 328 (1994). *American Heritage Dictionary* (3d ed. 1992).

Hartford Fire Insurance Co. v. California,. 509 U.S. 764, 781 (1993). *Webster's New International Dictionary* (2d ed. 1942).

United States v. Dixon, 509 U.S. 688, 705 (1993). *Black's Law Dictionary* (6th ed. 1990), and J. Bouvier, *Law Dictionary* (1883).

Austin v. United States, 509 U.S. 602, 614 (1993). T. Sheridan, *A General Dictionary of the English Language* (1780).

Smith v. United States, 508 U.S. 223, 242 (1993). *Webster's New International Dictionary* (2d ed. 1950).

Deal v. United States, 508 U.S. 129, 131 (1993). *Webster's New International Dictionary* (2d ed. 1950).

Bray v. Alexandria Women's Health Clinic, 506 U.S. 263, 274 (1993). *Webster's Second International Dictionary* (1954).

Wisconsin Department of Revenue v. William Wrigley, Jr., 505 U.S. 214, 223 (1992). *Black's Law Dictionary* (6th ed. 1990); *Webster's Third New International Dictionary* (1981).

Republic of Argentina v. Weltover, Inc., 504 U.S. 607, 614 (1992). *Black's Law Dictionary* (6th ed. 1990).

Morales v. Trans World Airlines, 504 U.S. 374, 383 (1992). *Black's Law Dictionary* (5th ed. 1979).

Dewsnup v. Timm, 502 U.S. 410, 428 (1992). *Black's Law Dictionary* (6th ed. 1990).

Harmelin v. Michigan, 501 U.S. 957, 976 (1991). *Webster's American Dictionary* (1828), and *Webster's Second International Dictionary* (1954).

Freytag v. Commissioner of Internal Revenue, 501 U.S. 868, 920 (1991). N. Webster, *An American Dictionary of the English Language* (1828).

Chisom v. Roemer, 501 U.S. 380, 410 (1991). *Webster's Second New International Dictionary* (1950).

California v. Hodari D., 499 U.S. 621, 624 (1991). N. Webster, *An American Dictionary of the English Language* (1828).

Maryland v. Craig, 497 U.S. 836, 864 (1990). N. Webster, *An American Dictionary of the English Language* (1828).

Grady v. Corbin, 495 U.S. 508, 529 (1990). J. Kersey, *A New English Dictionary* (1702), T. Sheridan, *A General Dictionary of the English Language* (1780), J. Walker, *A Critical Pronouncing Dictionary* (1791), and N. Webster, *An American Dictionary of the English Language* (1828).

National Labor Relations Board v. Curtin Matheson Scientific, Inc., 494 U.S. 775, 814 (1990). *Black's Law Dictionary* (5th ed. 1979).

Crandon v. United States, 494 U.S. 152, 171 (1990). *Webster's Second New International Dictionary* (1957).

Sullivan v. Everhart, 494 U.S. 83, 91 (1990). *Webster's Third New International Dictionary* (1981).

FW/PBS, Inc. v. Dallas, 493 U.S. 215, 260 (1990). *Webster's Third New International Dictionary* (1981).

Chan v. Korean Air Lines, Ltd., 490 U.S. 122, 127 (1989). *Webster's Second International Dictionary* (1950).

Bowen v. Massachusetts, 487 U.S. 879, 914 (1988). *Webster's Third New International Dictionary* (1981), and *Black's Law Dictionary* (5th ed. 1979).

Morrison v. Olson, 487 U.S. 654, 720 (1988). S. Johnson, *Dictionary of the English Language* (6th ed. 1785).

Pierce v. Underwood, 487 U.S. 552, 564 (1988). *Webster's New International Dictionary* (2d ed. 1945).

K Mart Corp. v. Cartier, Inc., 486 U.S. 281, 325 (1988). *Webster's Third New International Dictionary* (1981).

Honig v. Doe, 484 U.S. 305, 333 (1988). *Webster's Third New International Dictionary* (1981).

Lukhard v. Reed, 481 U.S. 368, 374 (1987). *Webster's Third New International Dictionary* (1976).

NOTES

Chapter One. Introduction

1. Jerry Goldman, "Antonin Scalia: Biography," OYEZ Project: U.S. Supreme Court Multimedia, available at http://www.oyez.org/oyez/resource/legal_entity/103/biography, accessed February 17, 2004.

2. Glen Elsasser, "No Contest: Top Court's Top Fighter Is Scalia," *Chicago Tribune*, May 27, 1997, section 1, p. 1.

3. *Chisom v. Roemer*, 501 U.S. 380, 417 (1991).

4. *R.A.V. v. City of St. Paul*, 505 U.S. 377, 396 (1992).

5. *Planned Parenthood of Southeastern Pennsylvania v. Casey*, 505 U.S. 833, 981 (1992).

6. *Roper v. Simmons*, 125 S. Ct. 1183 (2005).

7. Scalia's text-and-tradition jurisprudence is discussed at length in Chapter Two.

8. Antonin Scalia, *A Matter of Interpretation: Federal Courts and the Law* (Princeton, N.J.: Princeton University Press, 1997), p. 38.

9. By the end of the 2004 term of the Court (i.e., the end of June 2005), Scalia had written a total of 613 opinions: they included 191 opinions for the Court, 234 concurring opinions, and 188 dissents.

10. Robert Marquand, "High Court's Colorful Man in Black," *Christian Science Monitor*, March 3, 1998, section 1, p. 1.

11. Personal interview with Justice Antonin Scalia, Washington, D.C., June 11, 2003.

12. Their son, Paul, is an ordained Catholic priest.

13. E. R. Shipp, "Scalia's Midwest Colleagues Cite His Love of Debate, Poker, and Piano," *New York Times*, July 26, 1986, section 1, p. 7.

14. 487 U.S. 654 (1988).

15. 504 U.S. 555 (1992).

16. 521 U.S. 898 (1997).

17. Stuart Taylor, "A Time of Transition for No. 2 Court," *New York Times*, September 8, 1982, section 2, p. 4.

18. Laura A. Kiernan and Fred Barbash, "Appeals Judge Plans to Leave U.S. Court Here," *Washington Post*, April 2, 1982, section 2, p. 1.

19. *Valley Forge Christian College v. Americans United*, 454 U.S. 464, 473, 472 (1982).

20. 698 F.2d 1239 (1983).

21. Ibid., at 1257.

22. *Lujan v. Defenders of Wildlife*, 504 U.S. 555 (1992).

23. 698 F.2d at 1256–57.

24. 733 F.2d 946 (1984).

25. That clause provides that all "bills for raising revenue" shall originate in the House, although the Senate may make amendments as on other bills.

26. 733 F.2d at 954.

27. Ibid., at 957. Once on the Supreme Court, Scalia addressed a similar issue. See his opinion concurring in the judgment in *United States v. Munoz-Flores*, 495 U.S. 385 (1990), discussed in Chapter Three.

28. 733 F.2d at 959. (emphasis in original).

29. 738 F.2d 1375 (1984).

30. Ibid., at 1380.

31. Ibid., at 1378.

32. Ibid., at 1380 (emphasis in original).

33. 793 F.2d 1322 (1986).

34. Ibid., at 1324.

35. Ibid., at 1342.

36. Ibid., at 1344.

37. See *Lujan v. Defenders of Wildlife*, 504 U.S. 555 (1992), and *Franklin v. Massachusetts*, 505 U.S.788 (1992).

38. 793 F.2d at 1344.

39. 5 U.S.C. § 701 (a)(1), (2).

40. 756 F.2d 902 (1985).

41. 38 U.S.C. § 211(a) (1982).

42. 756 F.2d at 910.

43. Ibid., at 919.

44. Ibid., at 916. See also *Thompson v. Clark*, 741 F.2d 401 (1984), in which Scalia wrote a unanimous opinion affirming the district court's dismissal of a developer's challenge to a final rule increasing the application and rental fees charged for certain noncompetitive federal oil and gas leases promulgated by the secretary of the interior. He held that judicial review was precluded by the Regulatory Flexibility Act of 1980, 5 U.S.C. §§ 601–612 (1982).

45. 718 F.2d 1174 (1983). *International Union, United Automobile, Aerospace & Agricultural Implement Workers of America v. Donovan*, 746 F.2d 855 (1984), is another example. In this case, the union had challenged a decision of the secretary of labor not to allocate any of the agency's appropriations to a job-training program, although such a program was included among the permissible uses of the funds. Scalia held that the court of appeals lacked jurisdiction over the secretary of labor's discretionary allocation of a lump-sum budgetary appropriation from Congress.

46. 718 F.2d at 1192.

47. 21 U.S.C. §§ 352, 355.

48. 718 F.2d at 1177.

49. Ibid., 1192.

50. *Chaney v. Heckler*, 724 F.2d 1030 (1984).

51. Ibid., at 1197.

52. Ibid., at 1192.

53. Ibid., at 1200. In *Heckler v. Chaney*, 470 U.S. 821 (1985), the Supreme Court agreed with Scalia, reversed the D.C. Circuit, and held that the FDA's action was an unreviewable exercise of discretion.

54. 777 F.2d 1 (1985).

55. Ibid., at 7 (emphasis in original).

56. Ibid., at 8 (emphasis in original).

57. Richard Nagareda, "The Appellate Jurisprudence of Justice Antonin Scalia," 54 *University of Chicago Law Review* (Spring 1987): 705, 723.

58. *Illinois Commerce Commission v. Interstate Commerce Commission*, 749 F.2d 875, 887 (1984).

59. H.R. Rep. No. 1430, 96th Cong., 2d Sess. 106 (1980).

60. 749 F.2d at 887.

61. Ibid., at 889.

62. Ibid., at 893.

63. 756 F.2d at 914.

64. Ibid., at 926–27.

65. Ibid., at 914.

66. *In Re the Reporters Committee for Freedom of the Press*, 773 F.2d 1325, 1332 (1985).

67. *Ollman v. Evans and Novak*, 750 F.2d 970, 1038 (1984).

68. 703 F.2d 586 (1983).

69. Ibid., at 622.

70. Ibid., at 627.

71. Ibid., at 622.

72. Ibid., at 623. "Where expressive conduct unrelated to speech is at issue, I think it worthwhile to engage in the preliminary step of analysis that separates conduct-prohibiting from expression-prohibiting laws and exempts the former from rigorous First Amendment scrutiny." Ibid., at 626.

73. Ibid., at 622.

74. 750 F.2d at 1036.

75. "The Marxist Professor's Intentions," *Washington Post*, May 4, 1978.

76. Ibid., at 996.

77. Ibid., at 997.

78. Ibid., at 996.

79. Scalia, *A Matter of Interpretation*, p. 44.

80. 750 F.2d at 1038.

81. He reminded his colleagues what the existing test for libel required: Ollman, as a public-figure plaintiff, had to establish by "clear and convincing proof" not only that Evans and Novak's allegation was false but also that they knew it to be so or acted with reckless disregard of its falsity. Ibid., at 1037.

82. Ibid., at 1036. In *Liberty Lobby v. Anderson*, 746 F.2d 1563 (1984), decided just a few weeks earlier, Scalia had applied this existing test for a unanimous panel to reject outright twenty-one of thirty defamation claims made against the columnist Jack Anderson.

83. 750 F.2d at 1038. In n. 2, Scalia answered Bork's criticism that he had failed to appreciate the importance of changing circumstances: "In opposing such unguided 'evolution' I am not in need of the concurrence's reminder that the fourth amendment must be applied to modern electronic surveillance, the commerce clause to trucks and the first amendment to broadcasting. The application of existing principles to new phenomena—either new because they have not existed before or new because they have never been presented to a court before—is what I would call not 'evolution' but merely routine elaboration of the law. What is under discussion here is not application of preexisting principles to new phenomena, but rather *alteration* of preexisting principles in their application to preexisting phenomena on the basis of judicial perception of changed social circumstances." Ibid., at 1039 (emphasis in original).

84. Ibid., at 1038–39.

85. Ibid., at 1039. Bork felt sufficiently stung by Scalia's dissent that he devoted four full pages to his attempt to clarify his *Ollman* concurrence in his *The Tempting of America: The Political Seduction of the Law* (New York: Free Press, 1990), pp. 167–70. He ended with a direct challenge to Scalia's abilities as a judge and, before that, as a law professor: "If one cannot see where . . . the adjustment of doctrine to protect an existing

value ends and the creation of new values begins, then one should not aspire to be a judge or, for the matter of that, a law professor" (p. 170).

86. 773 F.2d 1325 (1985).

87. Ibid., at 1331–32.

88. Ibid., at 1336 (emphasis in original).

89. 793 F.2d 1303 (1986).

90. Ibid., at 1312 (emphasis in original).

91. Ibid., at 1313.

92. Ibid., at 1314.

93. 626 F.Supp. 1374 (1986).

94. See James G. Wilson, "Constraints on Power: The Constitutional Opinions of Judges Scalia, Bork, Posner, Easterbrook, and Winter," 40 *University of Miami Law Review* (1986): 1200. See also Christopher E. Smith, *Justice Antonin Scalia and the Supreme Court's Conservative Moment* (Westport, Conn.: Praeger, 1993), p. 40.

95. 626 F.Supp. at 1400, 1403.

96. See "Antonin Scalia" at http://www.supremecourthistory.org/myweb/justice/scalia.htm, accessed February 17, 2004.

97. 626 F.Supp. at 1390.

98. Ibid., at 1400.

99. Ibid., at 1401.

100. U.S. 211 (1995).

101. 626 F.Supp. at 1403.

102. Ibid., at 1404.

103. 487 U.S. 654, 699 (1988).

104. 488 U.S. 361, 421 (1989).

105. 626 F.Supp. at 1404.

106. See, for example, Stuart Taylor, "The One-Pronged Test for Federal Judges," *New York Times*, April 22, 1984, section 4, p. 5; Fred Barbash, "Election Also Could Determine Future Course of Supreme Court," *Washington Post*, July 15, 1984, p. A3; and Stuart Taylor, "The Reaganization of the Federal Courts," *New York Times*, August 23, 1984, section B, p. 8.

107. See, for example, Al Kamen, "U.S. Court's Liberal Era Ending: Reagan's Nominees Seen Giving Conservatives a Majority," *Washington Post*, January 27, 1985, p. A1; Curtis J. Sitomer, "Reagan's Judicial Legacy

Will Linger Long," *Christian Science Monitor*, May 16, 1985, p. 23; Stuart Taylor, "Some Legal Landmarks Are Facing Reconstruction," *New York Times*, January 22, 1986, section 4, p. 5; Al Kamen, "Time Running Out for Reagan to Reshape Court: High-Bench Nominee Would Face Difficulty in 1988, Even If Republicans Hold Senate," *Washington Post*, January 22, 1986, p. A17.

108. Stephen Wermiel, "Judge Scalia's Central Role in Decision Boosts Prospects for High Court Post," *Wall Street Journal*, February 10, 1986, section 1, p. 12.

109. Chief Justice Burger explained he was leaving the Court to devote all of his time to his other job, as head of the Bicentennial Commission of the United States; the commission was planning to celebrate the 200th anniversary of the Constitution beginning on Burger's 80th birthday, September 17, 1987.

110. Al Kamen, "Burger Quits; Rehnquist Chosen to Lead Court; President Intends to Nominate Appellate Judge Scalia," *Washington Post*, June 18, 1986, p. A1.

111. Edward Walsh, "Confirmation of Justices Predicted by End of Year: Reactions of Key Senators Suggest Rehnquist Nomination May Be the More Controversial," *Washington Post*, June 18, 1986, p. A13; James Reston, "Hear Ye in the Court," *New York Times*, June 18, 1986, section A, p. 35; Irvin Molotsky, "The Supreme Court: Man in the News—Judge with Tenacity and Charm: Antonin Scalia," *New York Times*, June 19, 1986, section A, p. 31; Stuart Taylor, "More Vigor for the Right: Court Would Ease toward Conservatism without Abruptly Changing Direction," *New York Times*, June 18, 1986, section A, p. 1.

112. Stuart Taylor, "Scalia's Views, Stylishly Expressed, Line Up with Reagan's," *New York Times*, June 19, 1986, section D, p. 27. In the same article, Bruce Sanford, a Washington lawyer and libel expert, called Scalia "one of the worst judges in the country on First Amendment and libel issues" but nevertheless added: "He's enormously intelligent.

Ironically he is one of the best writers currently serving on the courts of appeals. What that man does with language in opinions is beautiful. He's humorous, he's savagely subtle, he's absolutely scathing at times, and just in reading it you can feel the emotional commitment that he has to his views in the libel area."

113. The article was quoting then University of Chicago law professor (and now Tenth Circuit Court of Appeals judge) Michael McConnell. Shipp, "Scalia's Midwest Colleagues." The only negative note was sounded by the president of the National Urban League, who declared that the Senate should reject the nominations of both Rehnquist and Scalia because "both have been insensitive to minority rights." Lena Williams, "Head of Urban League Assails Court Nominees," *New York Times*, July 21, 1986, section A, p. 18.

114. See Eugene W. Hickok and Gary L. McDowell, *Law v. Justice: Courts and Politics in American Society* (New York: Free Press, 1993), pp. 137–47, for an excellent discussion of Rehnquist's confirmation as chief justice.

115. "People in the News," Associated Press, August 31, 1986, Sunday AM cycle.

116. *Hearings before the Committee on the Judiciary on the Nomination of Judge Antonin Scalia to Be Associate Justice of the Supreme Court of the United States*, Committee on the Judiciary, United States Senate, 99th Cong., 2d sess., J-99–119 (Washington, D.C.: Government Printing Office, 1987), p. 47. (Hereafter *Hearings on the Nomination of Scalia*.) For other observations from members of the Senate Judiciary Committee on how well Scalia's testimony was going, see the comments of Orrin G. Hatch (p. 53), Patrick J. Leahy (p. 78), Joseph Biden (p. 100), and Strom Thurmond (p. 109).

117. 5 U.S. 137 (1803).

118. *Hearings on the Nomination of Scalia*, pp. 33, 45, 83–84.

119. Ibid., p. 37; see also p. 102.

120. Ibid., pp. 40, 58, 84–87. See also Howard Kurtz, "Judicial Reticence Frustrates Senators," *Washington Post*, September 9, 1986, p. A4.

121. *Hearings on the Nomination of Scalia*, p. 85.

122. Ibid., pp. 86–87.

123. 98 U.S. 145 (1878).

124. *Hearings on the Nomination of Scalia*, p. 44.

125. 163 U.S. 537 (1896).

126. *Hearings on the Nomination of Scalia*, p. 86.

127. Ibid., p. 96.

128. Ibid., p. 108. See also pp. 48–49.

129. Ibid., p. 48.

130. Ibid., p. 49. Once on the Court and after thinking through the consequences of his "original-meaning" jurisprudence, he came to a different conclusion, and in *Harmelin v. Michigan*, he argued that the Cruel and Unusual Punishments Clause outlawed only "particular modes of punishments" that inevitably resulted in cruel and horrible death. 501 U.S. 957, 981 (1991).

131. *Hearings on the Nomination of Scalia*, pp. 48–49.

132. Ibid., p. 89.

133. Ibid., p. 101.

134. Ibid., pp. 66–67.

135. Ibid., p. 105.

136. Ibid., p. 107. See also Scalia's exchange of views on legislative history with Senator Howell Heflin (p. 75), and Senator Charles Mathias (p. 107).

137. Ibid., p. 41. As he said to Senator Dennis DeConcini, "You write it; I will enforce it" (p. 60).

138. Ibid., p. 64.

139. Ibid., p. 81.

140. Ibid., p. 82.

141. Scalia also touched on the issue of federalism in response to a series of questions about the incorporation doctrine posed by Senator Specter. Scalia conceded that the Supreme Court's incorporation through the Fourteenth Amendment of most of the Bill of Rights guarantees to apply to the states was "an accepted part of current law" and that "it would be quite a jolt to the existing system to suddenly discover that those series of protections against State actions do not exist." Ibid., pp. 87–88. Yet he did not categorically rule out voting to overturn this case law. He had earlier drawn a distinction between those Court "mistakes" that are now "so woven in the fabric of the law" that they "are too late to correct" and those that are not (p. 38). He did not explain to Senator Specter which kind of mistake he thought overturning incorporation would be.

142. William Safire, "Free Speech v. Scalia," *New York Times*, April 29, 1985, section A, p. 17.

143. *Hearings on the Nomination of Scalia*, p. 33.

144. Ibid., pp. 51–52.

145. Ibid. See also Senator Hatch's comments (p. 56).

146. Ibid., p. 53.

147. Ibid., pp. 111–12, 141, 168–69, 203.

148. Linda Greenhouse, "Senate, 65 to 33, Votes to Confirm Rehnquist as 16th Chief Justice," *New York Times*, September 18, section A, p. 1.

149. 479 U.S. 27 (1986).

150. Al Kamen, "Court Restricts Fees in Civil Rights Cases; Scalia Writes First Opinion in Tax Ruling," *Washington Post*, November 5, 1986, p. A5.

151. 479 U.S. at 31, 35.

Chapter Two. "Text and Tradition": Scalia's Understanding of the Interpretative Enterprise

1. Scalia searches out the ordinary meaning of the words used when the provision was adopted, frequently consulting dictionaries of the era. In fact, he consults dictionaries more often than any of his colleagues. See Note, "Looking It Up: Dictionaries and Statutory Interpretation," 107 *Harvard Law Review* (1994): 1437, 1439. For a complete list of

cases in which Scalia has cited dictionaries, see the Appendix in this book.

2. See Scalia's concurrence in the judgment in *Green v. Bock Laundry Machine Co:* "The meaning of terms on the statute books ought to be determined, not on the basis of which meaning can be shown to have been understood by a larger handful of the Members of Congress; but rather on the basis of which meaning is (1) most in accord with context and ordinary usage, and thus most likely to have been understood by the *whole* Congress which voted on the words of the statute (not to mention the citizens subject to it), and (2) most compatible with the surrounding body of law into which the provision must be integrated—a compatibility which, by a benign fiction, we assume Congress always has in mind." 490 U.S. 504, 528 (1989) (emphasis in original).

3. For Justice Scalia, separation of powers represents such a critical structural principle. See Antonin Scalia, "The Doctrine of Standing as an Essential Element of the Separation of Powers," 17 *Suffolk University Law Review* (1983): 881, where he stated: "Indeed, with an economy of expression that many would urge as a model for modern judicial opinions, the principle of separation of powers is found only in the structure of the [Constitution,] which successively describes where the legislative, executive, and judicial powers shall reside. One should not think, however, that the principle was less important to the federal framers. Madison said of it, in *Federalist* No. 47, that 'no political truth is certainly of greater intrinsic value, or is stamped with the authority of more enlightened patrons of liberty.' And no less than five of the *Federalist Papers* were devoted to the demonstration that the principle was adequately observed in the proposed Constitution."

4. By the most specific legal tradition, Scalia means "the most specific level at which a relevant tradition protecting, or denying protection to, the asserted right can

be identified." *Michael H. v. Gerald D.*, 491 U.S. 110, 127, n. 6 (1989). See also *Hearings before the Committee on the Judiciary on the Nomination of Judge Antonin Scalia to Be Associate Justice of the Supreme Court of the United States,* Committee on the Judiciary, United States Senate, 99th Cong., 2d sess., J-99–119 (Washington, D.C.: Government Printing Office, 1987), p. 108. (Hereafter *Hearings on the Nomination of Scalia.*) It should be stressed that Justice Scalia uses tradition to interpret only ambiguous constitutional texts; as he said in his dissent in *Rutan v. Republican Party,* 497 U.S. 62, 96, n. 1 (1990), "[N]o tradition can supersede the Constitution."

5. "What I do when I interpret the American Constitution is, I try to understand what it meant, what was understood by the society to mean when it was adopted. And I don't think it changes since then." "Transcript of Discussion between U.S. Supreme Court Justices Antonin Scalia and Stephen Breyer," American University, Washington College of Law, January 13, 2005, p. 12. (Hereafter Scalia/Breyer Transcript.)

6. See, for example, *Stenberg v. Carhart,* 530 U.S. 914 (2000); *Department of Commerce v. Clinton,* 525 U.S. 316, 349 (1999); *Minnesota v. Carter,* 525 U.S. 83, 92 (1998); *Lewis v. Casey,* 518 U.S. 343, 368 (1996); *Witte v. United States,* 515 U.S. 389, 407 (1995); *Plaut v. Spendthrift Farms,* 514 U.S. 211, 217 (1995); *Waters v. Churchill,* 511 U.S. 661, 684 (1994); *Callins v. Collins,* 510 U.S. 1141 (1994); *Herrera v. Collins,* 506 U.S. 390, 427 (1993); *Richmond v. Lewis,* 506 U.S. 40, 54 (1992); *Planned Parenthood of Southeastern Pennsylvania v. Casey,* 505 U.S. 833, 980, 983, 998–1001 (1992); *Morgan v. Illinois,* 504 U.S. 719, 751 (1992); *California v. Acevedo,* 500 U.S. 565, 581 (1991); *Cruzan v. Director, Missouri Department of Health,* 497 U.S. 261, 300 (1990); *Rutan v. Republican Party of Illinois,* 497 U.S. 62, 97 (1990); and *McKoy v. North Carolina,* 494 U.S. 433, 466 (1990).

7. 510 U.S. 1141.

8. 501 U.S. 624, 650 (1991).

9. For a discussion of how textualism restricts judicial discretion, see Leslie Friedman Goldstein, *In Defense of the Text: Democracy and Constitutional Theory* (Savage, Md.: Rowman & Littlefield, 1991), pp. 194–95.

10. See Gregory E. Maggs, "Reconciling Textualism and the *Chevron* Doctrine: In Defense of Justice Scalia," 28 *Connecticut Law Review* (1996): 393, and Bradley C. Karkkainen, "Plain Meaning: Justice Scalia's Jurisprudence of Strict Statutory Construction," 17 *Harvard Journal of Law and Public Policy* (1994): 401.

11. Scalia, "Originalism," p. 857.

12. Scalia's textualism was evident in his dissent in *Troxel v. Granville*, 530 U.S. 57, 91–92 (2000); in this case, the Court struck down a Washington law permitting "[a]ny person" to petition for visitation rights for a child "at any time" and authorizing state superior courts to grant such rights whenever visitation might serve a child's best interest on the ground that the law unconstitutionally infringed on the fundamental right of parents to rear their children. "In my view," Scalia argued, "a right of parents to direct the upbringing of their children is among the . . . 'other rights retained by the people' which the Ninth Amendment says the Constitution's enumeration of rights 'shall not be construed to deny or disparage.'" However, he continued, "the Constitution's refusal to 'deny or disparage' other rights is far removed from affirming any one of them, and even farther removed from authorizing judges to identify what they might be, and to enforce the judges' list against laws duly enacted by the people. Consequently, while I would think it entirely compatible with the commitment to representative democracy set forth in the founding documents to argue, in legislative chambers or in electoral campaigns, that the state has no power to interfere with parents' authority over the rearing of their

children, I do not believe that the power which the Constitution confers upon me as a judge entitles me to deny legal effect to laws that (in my view) infringe upon what is (in my view) that unenumerated right."

13. *Hearings on the Nomination of Scalia*, p. 89.

14. 518 U.S. 668 (1996).

15. 518 U.S. 712 (1996).

16. 518 U.S. at 686.

17. Ibid., at 688.

18. "[U]nder either the procedural component or the so-called 'substantive' component of the Due Process Clause[, i]t is precisely the historical practices that *define* what is 'due.'" *Schad v. Arizona*, 501 U.S. at 650 (emphasis in original).

19. The meanings of those constitutional provisions that are ambiguous are not fixed in time; tradition can evolve, and for Scalia, the appropriate way for such evolution to take place is through the people via their elected state legislatures and Congress. As he said in *Burnham v. Superior Court*, 495 U.S. 604, 627 (1990): "The difference between [me] and Justice Brennan has nothing to do with whether 'further progress [is] to be made' in the 'evolution of our legal system.' It has to do with whether changes are to be adopted as progressive by the American people or decreed as progressive by the Justices of this Court."

20. 518 U.S. at 695.

21. Timothy Raschke Shattuck, "Justice Scalia's Due Process Methodology: Examining Specific Traditions," 65 *Southern California Law Review* (1992): 2743, 2776–78.

22. 518 U.S. 515 (1996).

23. Ibid., at 568. See Scalia/Breyer Transcript, p. 13. Commenting on the phrase "the evolving standards of decency that mark the progress of a maturing society," Scalia declared: "I detest that phrase, because I'm afraid that societies don't always mature. Sometimes they rot. What makes you think that human progress is one upwardly inclined plane [and that] everyday and every

way we get better and better? It seems to me that the purpose of the Bill of Rights was to prevent change, not to encourage it, and to have it written into the Constitution."

24. 497 U.S. at 95–96. Scalia observed that it is "customary" for the critics of the text-and-tradition jurisprudence to invoke the school desegregation decision of *Brown v. Board of Education*, 347 U.S. 483 (1954), "as demonstrating the dangerous consequences" of his approach to constitutional interpretation. But, he insisted, that allegation "is unsupportable." He proceeded to elaborate: "I argue for the role of tradition in giving content only to *ambiguous* constitutional text; no tradition can supersede the Constitution. In my view the Fourteenth Amendment's requirement of 'equal protection of the laws,' combined with the Thirteenth Amendment's abolition of the institution of black slavery, leaves no room for doubt that laws treating people differently because of their race are invalid. Moreover, even if one does not regard the Fourteenth Amendment as crystal clear on this point, a tradition of *unchallenged* validity did not exist with respect to the practice in *Brown*. To the contrary, in the 19th century the principle of 'separate-but-equal' had been vigorously opposed on constitutional grounds, litigated up to this Court, and upheld only over the dissent of one of our historically most respected Justices. See *Plessy v. Ferguson*, 163 U.S. 537, 555–556 (1896) (Harlan, J., dissenting)." 497 U.S. at 95 (emphasis in original).

25. 501 U.S. 957 (1991).

26. Ibid., at 994.

27. Ibid., at 977.

28. Ibid., at 981. See also his dissent in *Atkins v. Virginia*: "The Eighth Amendment is addressed to always-and-everywhere 'cruel' punishments, such as the rack and the thumbscrew. But where the punishment is in itself permissible, 'the Eighth Amendment is not a ratchet, whereby a temporary consensus on leniency for a particular crime fixes a permanent constitutional maximum, disabling the States from giving effect to altered

beliefs and responding to changed social conditions.'" 536 U.S. 304, 349 (2002).

29. 463 U.S. 277 (1983).

30. Scalia's textualism also led him to conclude in *Payne v. Tennessee*, 501 U.S. 808, 834 (1991), that there is "absolutely no basis in constitutional text, in historical practice, or in logic" to justify using the Cruel and Unusual Punishments Clause to ban victim-impact statements in capital punishment cases.

31. 487 U.S. 1012 (1988).

32. Ibid., at 1016. See also his dissent in *Craig v. Maryland*, 497 U.S. 836, 867 (1990).

33. 532 U.S. 451 (2001).

34. Ibid., at 471.

35. 499 U.S. 1, 31 (1991). See also his rejection of substantive due process in *TXO Production Corp. v. Alliance Resources Corp.*, 509 U.S. 443, 471 (1993), in which he declared: "It is particularly difficult to imagine that 'due process' contains the substantive right not to be subjected to excessive punitive damages, since if it contains *that* it would surely also contain the substantive right not to be subjected to excessive fines, which would make the excessive fines clause of the Eighth Amendment superfluous in light of the due process clause of the Fifth Amendment" (emphasis in original). In his later dissents in *BMW v. Gore*, 517 U.S. 559, 598–607 (1996), and especially in *State Farm Insurance v. Campbell*, 538 U.S. 408 (2003), he merely referred to his earlier opinions.

36. 499 U.S. at 31. Scalia's discussion of "historically approved procedures" needs one important qualification: broad contemporary societal consensus can purge a "historically approved practice." As he said in *Haslip*, ibid., at 39: "State legislatures and courts have the power to restrict or abolish the common-law practice of punitive damages, and in recent years have increasingly done so. . . . It is through those means—State by State, and, at the federal level, by Congress—that the legal procedures affecting our citizens

are improved. Perhaps, when the operation of that process has purged a historically approved practice from our national life, the due process clause would permit this Court to announce that it is no longer in accord with the law of the land." For his understanding of what constitutes a "broad societal consensus" sufficient to purge a "historically approved practice," see his dissent in *Atkins v. Virginia*, 536 U.S. at 342–48.

37. 124 S. Ct. 1769, 1775 (2004).

38. 505 U.S. 577, 641 (1992).

39. 512 U.S. 687, 732 (1994).

40. 494 U.S. 872, 878, 885 (1990).

41. 505 U.S. at 1000.

42. *Hearings on the Nomination of Scalia*, p. 108.

43. 124 S. Ct. at 1790.

44. 491 U.S. 397 (1989).

45. Scalia insists that, to his knowledge, he has never joined an opinion in which he has not agreed with both the holding and the reasoning of that opinion. Personal interview with Justice Antonin Scalia, Washington, D.C., June 11, 2003.

46. *Hearings on the Nomination of Scalia*, p. 51.

47. See, for example, "Congressional Report Defending the Alien and Sedition Law, February 21, 1799," in Lance Banning, ed., *Liberty and Order: The First American Party Struggle* (Indianapolis, Ind.: Liberty Fund, 2004), p. 238.

48. *Hearings on the Nomination of Scalia*, pp. 88, 87.

49. 510 U.S. 266, 275 (1994) (emphasis added).

50. 501 U.S. 775, 779 (1991).

51. *Seminole Tribe of Florida v. Florida*, 517 U.S. 44 (1996); *Florida Prepaid Postsecondary Education Expense Bd. v. College Savings Bank*, 527 U.S. 627 (1999); *College Savings Bank v. Florida Prepaid Postsecondary Education Expense Bd.*, 527 U.S. 666 (1999); *Alden v. Maine*, 527 U.S. 706 (1999); *Kimel v. Florida Board of Regents*, 528 U.S. 62 (2000); *Trustees of the University of Alabama*

v. Garrett, 531 U.S. 356 (2001); and *Federal Maritime Commission v. South Carolina State Ports Authority*, 535 U.S. 743 (2002).

52. 517 U.S. at 54.

53. Antonin Scalia, "The Rule of Law as the Law of Rules," 56 *University of Chicago Law Review* (1989): 1175.

54. This explains why he joined Chief Justice Rehnquist's concurring opinion in *Bush v. Gore*, 531 U.S. 98 (2000). The gravamen of Rehnquist's concurrence was that the Florida Supreme Court had established new standards for resolving presidential election contests and had thereby violated Article II, § 1, cl. 2 of the U.S. Constitution, which provides that "each State shall appoint, in such Manner as the Legislature thereof may direct," electors for president and vice president. Ibid., at 112.

55. 530 U.S. 57 (2000).

56. Ibid., at 91.

57. Ibid., at 92–93.

58. 517 U.S. 620, 651 (1996).

59. Ibid., at 636. He elaborated on this theme in his dissent in *Lawrence v. Texas*, in which the Court invalidated a Texas statute forbidding anal sex with a member of the same sex: "One of the most revealing statements in today's opinion is the Court's grim warning that the criminalization of homosexual conduct is 'an invitation to subject homosexual persons to discrimination both in the public and in the private spheres.' It is clear from this that the Court has taken sides in the culture war, departing from its role of assuring, as neutral observer, that the democratic rules of engagement are observed. Many Americans do not want persons who openly engage in homosexual conduct as partners in their business, as scoutmasters for their children, as teachers in their children's schools, or as boarders in their home. They view this as protecting themselves and their families from a lifestyle that they believe to be immoral and destructive. The Court views it as 'discrimination' which it is the function of our judgments to deter. So

imbued is the Court with the law profession's anti-anti-homosexual culture, that it is seemingly unaware that the attitudes of that culture are not obviously 'mainstream'; that in most States what the Court calls 'discrimination' against those who engage in homosexual acts is perfectly legal; that proposals to ban such 'discrimination' under Title VII have repeatedly been rejected by Congress; that in some cases such 'discrimination' is *mandated* by federal statute (mandating discharge from the armed forces of any service member who engages in or intends to engage in homosexual acts); and that in some cases such 'discrimination' is a constitutional right, see *Boy Scouts of America v. Dale* (2000)." 539 U.S. 558, 602–3 (2003) (emphasis in original). This, he charged, constituted the "invention of a brand-new 'constitutional right' by a Court that is impatient of democratic change." Whether statutes that criminalize homosexual conduct should be repealed was, he said, a judgment "to be made by the people, and not imposed by a governing caste that knows best." Ibid., at 603–4.

60. 497 U.S. 261, 293 (1990).

61. Antonin Scalia, *A Matter of Interpretation: Federal Courts and the Law* (Princeton, N.J.: Princeton University Press, 1997), p. 7.

62. Ibid., p. 9.

63. Ibid., p. 22.

64. 518 U.S. at 711.

65. 518 U.S. at 567. See also his criticisms of the "Living Constitution" approach in *A Matter of Interpretation*, pp. 41–42: "The argument most frequently made in favor of The Living Constitution is a pragmatic one: Such an evolutionary approach is necessary in order to provide the 'flexibility' that a changing society requires; the Constitution would be snapped if it had not been permitted to bend and grow. This might be a persuasive argument if most of the 'growing' that the proponents of this approach have brought upon us in the past, and are determined to bring upon us in the future, were

the *elimination* of restrictions upon democratic government. But just the opposite is true. Historically, and particularly in the past thirty-five years, the 'evolving' Constitution has imposed a vast array of new constraints—new inflexibilities—upon administrative, judicial, and legislative action. . . . [T]he reality of the matter is that, generally speaking, devotees of The Living Constitution do not seek to facilitate change but to prevent it" (emphasis in original).

66. See Larry P. Arnn and Ken Masugi, "The Smoke of a Burning White Flag: Law without a Regime, Form without Purpose," *Perspectives on Political Science* 28 (Winter 1999): 16.

67. Antonin Scalia, "Of Democracy, Morality, and the Majority," lecture presented as part of the series "Left, Right, and the Common Good," Gregorian University, May 2, 1996, in *Origins, CNS Documentary Service* 26, no. 6, pp. 81–90.

68. Scalia, *A Matter of Interpretation*, p. 134. See also *Troxel v. Granville*, 530 U.S. at 91, where Scalia wrote: "In my view, a right of parents to direct the upbringing of their children is among the 'unalienable Rights' with which the Declaration of Independence proclaims 'all Men . . . are endowed by their Creator.' . . . The Declaration of Independence, however, is not a legal prescription conferring powers upon the courts."

Scalia has invoked the Declaration of Independence in ten of his opinions, including *Troxel*. In the other nine instances, however, he has done so merely to support a point he is making. See, for example, his dissent in *Neder v. United States*, 527 U.S. 1, 30–31 (1999), in which he argued that a criminal defendant has the right to have the jury determine his guilt of the crime charged and that this includes his commission of every element of the crime charged: "One of the indictments of the Declaration of Independence against King George III was that he had 'subjected us to a Jurisdiction foreign to our Constitution, and unacknowledged by our Laws' in approving legislation 'for depriving us, in many Cases, of the Benefits of Trial by Jury.' "

By contrast, Justice Clarence Thomas, with whom Scalia votes 86.3 percent of the time (see Chapter Seven), does take the Declaration of Independence seriously, believes that its principles infuse the Constitution, and grounds his opinions explicitly in them. See Thomas's concurrence in *Adarand Constructors v. Pena*, 515 U.S. 200, 240 (1994), holding that the strict scrutiny standard applies to all government classifications based on race: "As far as the Constitution is concerned, it is irrelevant whether a government's racial classifications are drawn by those who wish to oppress a race or by those who have a sincere desire to help those thought to be disadvantaged. There can be no doubt that the paternalism that appears to lie at the heart of this program is at war with the principle of inherent equality that underlies and infuses our Constitution. See Declaration of Independence ('We hold these truths to be self-evident, that all men are created equal, that they are endowed by their Creator with certain unalienable Rights, that among these are Life, Liberty, and the pursuit of Happiness.')."

69. Merrill D. Peterson, ed., *Thomas Jefferson: Writings* (New York: Library of America, 1984), pp. 492–93.

70. Harry V. Jaffa, *Storm over the Constitution* (Lanham, Md.: Lexington Books, 1999), p. 117.

71. Scalia, *A Matter of Interpretation*, p. 134.

72. Ibid., p. 135 (emphasis in original).

73. See, for example, *Doe v. Chao*, 124 S. Ct. 1204 (2004), in which the Court announced that "Souter, J., delivered the opinion of the Court, in which Rehnquist, C. J., and O'Connor, Kennedy, and Thomas, JJ., joined, and in which Scalia, J., joined except as to the penultimate paragraph of Part III and footnote 8." The penultimate paragraph begins: "This inference from the terms of the Commission's mandate is under-

scored by drafting history showing that Congress cut out the very language in the bill that would have authorized any presumed damages." Ibid., at 1209–10. Footnote 8 contains the sentence: "Congress's use of the entitlement phrase actually contained in the statute, however, is explained by drafting history." Ibid., at 1210. Scalia's refusal to join opinions that rely on legislative history is driven by his commitment never to join an opinion in which he does not agree with both the outcome and the reasoning. Personal interview with Justice Antonin Scalia, Washington, D.C., June 11, 2003.

74. William N. Eskridge, "The New Textualism," 37 *UCLA Law Review* (April 1990): 621.

75. Ibid., p. 624.

76. See, e.g., *Kelly v. Robinson*, 479 U.S. 36 (1986); *Offshore Logistics, Inc. v. Tallentire*, 477 U.S. 207 (1986); *Midlantic National Bank v. New Jersey Department of Environmental Protection*, 474 U.S. 494 (1986); *Bob Jones University v. United States*, 461 U.S. 574 (1983); *Dames & Moore v. Regan*, 453 U.S. 654 (1981); *United Steelworkers v. Weber*, 443 U.S. 193 (1979); *United States v. Board of Commissioners*, 435 U.S. 110 (1978); *Simpson v. United States*, 435 U.S. 6 (1978); *Train v. Colorado Public Interest Research Group*, 426 U.S. 1 (1976); and *Thermtron Products, Inc. v. Hermansdorfer*, 423 U.S. 336 (1976).

77. 143 U.S. 457, 459 (1892). In *A Matter of Interpretation*, p. 18, Scalia described *Church of the Holy Trinity* as "the prototypical case involving the triumph of supposed 'legislative intention' (a handy cover for judicial intent) over the text of the law." He continued: "*Church of the Holy Trinity* is cited to us whenever counsel wants us to ignore the narrow, deadening text of the statute, and pay attention to the life-giving legislative intent. It is nothing but an invitation to judicial lawmaking" (p. 21).

78. 443 U.S. at 201–4.

79. 777 F.2d 1, 6 (D.C. Cir. 1985).

80. Ibid., at 3, n. 9.

81. Ibid., at 7–8. In a footnote, he enjoyed providing the following illustration from 128 *Congressional Record* S8659 (daily ed. July 19, 1982):

Several years ago, the following illuminating exchange occurred between members of the Senate, in the course of floor debate on a tax bill:

Mr. ARMSTRONG. . . . My question, which may take [the chairman of the Committee on Finance] by surprise, is this: Is it the intention of the chairman that the Internal Revenue Service and the Tax Court and other courts take guidance as to the intention of Congress from the committee report which accompanies this bill?

Mr. DOLE. I would certainly hope so. . . .

Mr. ARMSTRONG. Mr. President, will the Senator tell me whether or not he wrote the committee report?

Mr. DOLE. Did I write the committee report?

Mr. ARMSTRONG. Yes.

Mr. DOLE. No; the Senator from Kansas did not write the committee report.

Mr. ARMSTRONG. Did any Senator write the committee report?

Mr. DOLE. I have to check.

Mr. ARMSTRONG. Does the Senator know of any Senator who wrote the committee report?

Mr. DOLE. I might be able to identify one, but I would have to search. I was here all during the time it was written, I might say, and worked carefully with the staff as they worked. . . .

Mr. ARMSTRONG. Mr. President, has the Senator from Kansas, the chairman of the Finance Committee, read the committee report in its entirety?

Mr. DOLE. I am working on it. It is not a bestseller, but I am working on it.

Mr. ARMSTRONG. Mr. President, did members of the Finance Committee vote on the committee report?

Mr. DOLE. No.

Mr. ARMSTRONG. Mr. President, the reason I raise the issue is not perhaps apparent on the surface, and let me just state it: . . . The report itself is not considered by the Committee on Finance. It was not subject to amendment by the Committee on Finance. It is not subject to amendment now by the Senate. . . . If there were matter within this report which was disagreed to by the Senator from Colorado or even by a majority of all Senators, there would be no way for us to change the report. I could not offer an amendment tonight to amend the committee report. . . . For any jurist, administrator, bureaucrat, tax practitioner, or others who might chance upon the written record of this proceeding, let me just make the point that this is not the law, it was not voted on, it is not subject to amendment, and we should discipline ourselves to the task of expressing congressional intent in the statute. Ibid., at 7, n. 1.

Scalia quoted this passage again in *A Matter of Interpretation*, pp. 32–34.

82. Comment, "The Appellate Jurisprudence of Justice Antonin Scalia," 54 *University of Chicago Law Review* (1987): 707, 723.

83. 756 F.2d 902 (D.C. Cir. 1985).

84. Ibid., at 926–27.

85. Ibid., at 914. Once on the Supreme Court, he termed it "post-legislation legislative history" and described it as an "oxymoron." *United States v. Carlton*, 512 U.S. 26, 40 (1994).

86. 756 F.2d at 914. Once on the Supreme Court, in an opinion concurring in part in *Sullivan v. Finkelstein*, 496 U.S. 617, 631–32 (1990), Justice Scalia elaborated on his objections to "subsequent legislative history": " 'Subsequent legislative history' — which presumably means the post-enactment history of a statute's consideration and enactment — is a contradiction in terms. The phrase is used to smuggle into judicial consideration legislators' expressions not of what a bill currently under considera-

tion means (which, the theory goes, reflects what their colleagues understood they were voting for), but of what a law previously enacted means." He continued: "It seems to be a rule for the use of subsequent legislative history that the legislators or committees of legislators whose post-enactment views are consulted must belong to the institution that passed the statute. Never, for example, have I seen floor statements of Canadian MPs cited concerning the meaning of a United States statute; only statements by Members of Congress qualify. No more connection than that, however, is required. It is assuredly not the rule that the legislators or committee members in question must have considered, or at least voted upon, the particular statute in question—or even that they have been members of the particular Congress that enacted it. The subsequent legislative history [employed in] today's [decision], for example, tells us (according to the Court's analysis) what committees of the 99th and 95th Congresses thought the 76th Congress intended." Continuing, he stated: "In my opinion, the views of a legislator concerning a statute already enacted are entitled to no more weight than the views of a judge concerning a statute not yet passed. . . . Arguments based on subsequent legislative history, like arguments based on antecedent futurity, should not be taken seriously."

87. *Hearings on the Nomination of Scalia*, p. 106.

88. 480 U.S. 421, 452–53 (1987).

89. *Thompson v. Thompson*, 484 U.S. 174, 191 (1988). However, even Scalia himself has occasionally succumbed to the allure of legislative history. See his reliance on Senate reports in his majority opinion for the Supreme Court in *United States v. Fausto*, 484 U.S. 439, 443, 449 (1988), and his extensive use of the legislative history surrounding the passage of Louisiana's Balanced Treatment Act (requiring the state's public schools to give a "balanced treatment" to "creation science" and "evolution science") in

Edwards v. Aguillard, 482 U.S. 578, 619–26 (1987).

90. 484 U.S. at 191–92. See Scalia's recent reaffirmation of this position in his concurrence in the judgment in *Intel v. Advanced Micro Devices*, 124 S. Ct. 2466, 2484–85 (2004): "As today's opinion shows, the Court's disposition is required by the text of the statute. None of the limitations urged by petitioner finds support in the categorical language of 28 U.S.C. § 1782(a). That being so, it is not only (as I think) improper but also quite unnecessary to seek repeated support in the words of a Senate Committee Report—which, as far as we know, not even the full committee, much less the full Senate, much much less the House, and much much much less the President who signed the bill, agreed with. Since, moreover, I have not read the entire so-called legislative history, and have no need or desire to do so, so far as I know the statements of the Senate Report may be contradicted elsewhere. Accordingly, because the statute—the only sure expression of the will of Congress—says what the Court says it says, I join in the judgment."

91. 125 S. Ct. 460, 474 (2005).

92. 487 U.S. 326, 345 (1988).

93. *A Matter of Interpretation*, p. 36. See also *Conroy v. Aniskoff*, 507 U.S. 511, 519 (1993).

94. 490 U.S. 545, 556 (1989).

95. As one critic of Scalia's rejection of legislative history complained, individual members of Congress "can no longer express their intentions effectively in any way other than incorporating them in the legislation itself." Note, "Justice Scalia's Use of Sources in Statutory and Constitutional Interpretation: How Congress Always Loses," 1990 *Duke Law Journal* (1990): 160, 188.

96. 749 F.2d 875, 893 (D.C. Cir. 1984). This court of appeals opinion provides further evidence of Scalia's keen appreciation for the workings of the legislative process.

97. 503 U.S. 291, 309 (1992).

98. Scalia's rejection of the use of legislative history extends as well to Congress's deliberations concerning the adoption of constitutional amendments. See, for example, *City of Boerne v. Flores*, 521 U.S. 507, 510 (1997), in which Scalia joined all of Justice Kennedy's majority opinion in this case invalidating the Religious Freedom Restoration Act of 1993 except for Part III-A-1, which addressed the debates in the Thirty-ninth Congress concerning the adoption of the Fourteenth Amendment.

99. 501 U.S. 597 (1991).

100. Ibid., at 621. In his concurring opinion in *Thunder Basin Coal Co. v. Reich*, 510 U.S. 200, 219 (1994), Scalia declared that he found "unnecessary" the majority's discussion of the legislative history of the statute under consideration. He wrote: "It serves to maintain the illusion that legislative history is an important factor in this Court's deciding of cases, as opposed to an omnipresent makeweight for decisions arrived at on other grounds."

101. 530 U.S. 363 (2000).

102. Ibid., at 390–91 (emphasis in original). Scalia had made many of these same points before in his powerful concurrence in *Conroy v. Aniskoff*, in which he concurred in the judgment: "The Court begins its analysis with the observation: 'The statutory command . . . is unambiguous, unequivocal, and unlimited.' In my view, discussion of that point is where the remainder of the analysis should have ended. Instead, however, the Court [Justice Stevens] feels compelled to demonstrate that its holding is consonant with legislative history, including some dating back to 1917—*a full quarter century* before the provision at issue was enacted. That is not merely a waste of research time and ink; it is a false and disruptive lesson in the law. It says to the bar that even an 'unambiguous (and) unequivocal' statute can never be dispositive; that, presumably under penalty of malpractice liability, the oracles of legislative history, far into the dimmy past, must always be consulted. This undermines the clarity of law,

and condemns litigants (who, unlike us, must pay for it out of their own pockets) to subsidizing historical research by lawyers. The greatest defect of legislative history is its illegitimacy. We are governed by laws, not by the intentions of legislators." Ibid., at 518–19 (emphasis in original).

103. 501 U.S. 380 (1991).

104. 125 S. Ct. at 474.

105. 501 U.S. at 406. See Ralph A. Rossum, "Applying the Voting Rights Act to Judicial Elections: The Supreme Court's Misconstruction of Section 2 and Misconception of the Judicial Role," in Anthony A. Peacock, ed., *Affirmative Action and Representation: Shaw v. Reno and the Future of Voting Rights* (Durham, N.C.: Carolina Academic Press, 1997), pp. 317–41.

106. 504 U.S. 505, 521 (1992).

107. Ibid., at 516, n. 8. Souter was quoting Frankfurter's dissent in *United States v. Monia*, 317 U.S. 424, 432 (1943).

108. Patricia M. Wald, "Some Observations on the Use of Legislative History in the 1981 Supreme Court Term," 68 *Iowa Law Review* (1983): 195: "[A]lthough the Court still refers to the 'plain meaning' rule, the rule has effectively been laid to rest. No occasion for statutory construction now exists when the Court will *not* look at the legislative history" (emphasis in original).

109. Gregory E. Maggs, "The Secret Decline of Legislative History: Has Someone Heard a Voice Crying in the Wilderness?" in Roger Clegg and Leonard A. Leo, eds., *The Public Interest Law Review 1994* (Washington, D.C.: National Legal Center for the Public Interest, 1994), p. 72. See also Eskridge, "The New Textualism," pp. 625, 657–63.

110. "Congress Keeps Eye on Justices as Court Watches Hill's Words," *Congressional Quarterly Weekly Report* 49 (1991): 2863.

111. See, for example, Scalia, "Originalism."

112. Eskridge made this criticism of Scalia in "The New Textualism," pp. 625, 683.

113. 513 U.S. 150, 167 (1995).

114. Scalia, "The Rule of Law as the Law of Rules," p. 1184.

115. See *Hearings on the Nomination of Scalia*, pp. 48, 108.

116. Although, as he pointed out in *A Matter of Interpretation*, p. 38, "the Great Divide with regard to constitutional interpretation is not that between Framers' intent and objective meaning, but rather that between original meaning (whether derived from Framers' intent or not) and current meaning . . . [or] what is called The Living Constitution."

117. Ibid.

118. 533 U.S. 27 (2001).

119. Ibid., at 34.

120. Ibid (emphasis in original). See also Scalia's concurring opinion in *Minnesota v. Dickerson*, 508 U.S. 366, 379 (1993): "I take it to be a fundamental principle of constitutional adjudication that the terms in the Constitution must be given the meaning ascribed to them at the time of their ratification. Thus, when the Fourth Amendment provides that 'the right of the people to be secure in their persons, houses, papers, and effects, against unreasonable searches and seizures, shall not be violated,' it 'is to be construed in the light of what was deemed an unreasonable search and seizure when it was adopted.' The purpose of the provision, in other words, is to preserve the degree of respect for the privacy of persons and the inviolability of their property that existed when the provision was adopted—even if a later, less virtuous age should become accustomed to considering all sorts of intrusion 'reasonable.'" Although he did not employ the language he used in *United States v. Virginia*, 518 U.S. at 568, in these cases, they exemplify Scalia's efforts "to prevent backsliding from the degree of restriction the Constitution imposed upon democratic government."

121. Scalia, "Originalism," p. 852.

122. Ibid., p. 862. See his argument in *A Matter of Interpretation*, pp. 44–45: "Perhaps the most glaring defect of Living Constitutionalism, next to its incompatibility with the whole antievolutionary purpose of a constitution, is that there is no agreement, and no chance of agreement, upon what is to be the guiding principles of the evolution."

123. Scalia, "Originalism," pp. 862–63.

124. 487 U.S. 1012 (1988).

125. Scalia, "Originalism," p. 856.

126. Ibid., pp. 856–57. Scalia also identified a second "serious objection to originalism: In its undiluted form, at least, it is medicine that seems too strong to swallow." Ibid., p. 861. He confessed that "in a crunch I may prove a faint-hearted originalist. I cannot imagine myself, any more than any other federal judge, upholding a statute that imposes the punishment of flogging. But then I cannot imagine such a case arising either." Ibid., p. 864. See also his testimony during his Senate confirmation hearing, *Hearings on the Nomination of Scalia*, p. 49. In truth, however, Scalia has proven to be anything but a "faint-hearted originalist," as his opinion in *Harmelin v. Michigan* attests.

127. Scalia, "Originalism," p. 864.

128. Ibid., p. 862.

129. Ibid. See also Antonin Scalia, "Assorted Canards of Contemporary Legal Analysis," 40 *Case Western Reserve Law Review* (1990): 581. In that article, he argued: "To keep government up-to-date with modern notions of what good government ought to be, we do not need a constitution but only a ballot-box and a legislature." Ibid., p. 595. He also stated, "[C]hanges in the Constitution, when thought necessary, are to be proposed by Congress or conventions and ratified by the States. The Founders gave no such amending power to this Court. Our duty is simply to interpret the Constitution, and in doing so the test of constitutionality is not whether a law is offensive to our conscience or to the 'good old common law,' but whether it is offensive to the Constitution." Ibid., p. 596.

130. 17 U.S. 316, 431 (1819).

131. *Panhandle Oil Co. v. Mississippi ex rel. Knox*, 277 U.S. 218, 223 (1928).

132. Scalia, "Assorted Canards of Contemporary Legal Analysis," p. 590.

133. 493 U.S. 165, 181 (1989).

134. Shattuck, "Justice Scalia's Due Process Methodology," p. 2782.

135. 356 U.S. 86, 100–101 (1958).

136. Ibid., at 102.

137. Although see the Court majority opinions invalidating the death penalty in cases involving the rape of an adult woman, *Coker v. Georgia*, 433 U.S. 584 (1977), and in felony murder cases where the defendant did not kill, attempt to kill, or intend to kill, *Enmund v. Florida*, 458 U.S. 782 (1982). Footnotes in both these cases reference practices in other countries.

138. 487 U.S. 815, 830, n. 31 (1988).

139. 536 U.S. 304, 316 (2002).

140. 539 U.S. 558, 576 (2003).

141. 125 S. Ct. 1183, 1198 (2005).

142. Ibid., at 1200, 1198.

143. "In considering this question, then, we must never forget, that it is a constitution we are expounding." 17 U.S. 316, 407 (1819).

144. 487 U.S. at 869.

145. 536 U.S. at 348.

146. 539 U.S. at 598 (emphasis in original).

147. 125 S. Ct. at 1225. Six weeks earlier, Scalia had engaged in a highly unusual debate with Justice Stephen Breyer at the Washington College of Law at American University over the constitutional relevance of foreign court decisions. He repeated more systematically and acerbically in his *Simmons* dissent many of the same points he had made more extemporaneously and humorously there. See Scalia/Breyer Transcript, pp. 7–41.

148. 125 S. Ct. at 1199.

149. Ibid., at 1226 (emphasis in original).

150. Ibid., at 1226–27.

151. Ibid., at 1227. Scalia acknowledged that "we share a common history with the United Kingdom, and that we often consult English sources." But, as he insisted, the Court does so only because it is "asked to discern the meaning of a constitutional text written against the backdrop of eighteenth century English law and legal thought." Ibid., at 1228. As he said in his discussion with Justice Breyer at American University: "[F]oreign law is irrelevant with one exception: Old English law, because phrases like 'due process,' the 'right of confrontation,' and things of that sort were all taken from English law. So, the reality is I use foreign law more than anybody on the Court. But it's all old English law." Scalia/Breyer Transcript, p. 12.

152. 125 S. Ct. at 1223. Scalia used the same language in *A Matter of Interpretation*, p. 36, and in *Conroy v. Aniskoff*, 507 U.S. at 519.

153. 125 S. Ct. at 1228 (emphasis in original).

154. Scalia, *A Matter of Interpretation*, p. 23. But see Eskridge, "The New Textualism," p. 691. Eskridge favors what he calls an "anti-formalist" theory of "dynamic statutory interpretation" that asks not "what the legislation means abstractly" nor what it means "even on the basis of legislative history" but rather "what it ought to mean in terms of the needs and goals of our present society." See Eskridge, "Dynamic Statutory Interpretation," 135 *University of Pennsylvania Law Review* (July 1987): 1479, 1480. Yet he says of Scalia's textualism that it "has already been a valuable intellectual contribution to theoretical literature on statutory interpretation," "appeals to the sophisticated legal analyst," "is a fascinating theory," and is "more sophisticated than the traditional approach." Eskridge, "The New Textualism," pp. 666, 667, and 690.

155. Scalia, *A Matter of Interpretation*, p. 23.

Chapter Three. Constitutional Structure and Separation of Powers

1. Quoted in Christopher E. Smith, *Justice Antonin Scalia and the Supreme Court's Conservative Moment* (Westport, Conn.: Praeger, 1993), p. 39.

2. U.S. 654, 699 (1988).

3. Ibid., at 712.

4. *Hearings before the Committee on the Judiciary on the Nomination of Judge Antonin Scalia to Be Associate Justice of the Supreme Court of the United States,* Committee on the Judiciary, United States Senate, 99th Cong., 2d sess., J-99–119 (Washington, D.C.: Government Printing Office, 1987), p. 32. (Hereafter *Hearings on the Nomination of Scalia.*)

5. Ibid., p. 108.

6. Antonin Scalia, "The Doctrine of Standing as an Essential Element of the Separation of Powers," 17 *Suffolk University Law Review* (1983): 881. See also Scalia's dissent in *Morrison v. Olson,* 487 U.S. 654, 697–98 (1988): "The principle of separation of powers is expressed in our Constitution in the first section of each of the first three Articles. Article I, § 1, provides that '[a]ll legislative Powers herein granted shall be vested in a Congress of the United States, which shall consist of a Senate and House of Representatives.' Article III, § 1, provides that '[t]he judicial Power of the United States shall be vested in one supreme Court, and in such inferior Courts as the Congress may from time to time ordain and establish.' And the provision at issue here, Article II, § 1, provides that '[t]he executive Power shall be vested in a President of the United States of America.' "

7. *Hearings on the Nomination of Scalia,* p. 32.

8. Helen E. Veit, Kenneth R. Bowling, and Charlene Bangs Bickford, eds., *Creating the Bill of Rights: The Documentary Record from the First Congress* (Baltimore, Md.: Johns Hopkins University Press, 1991), p. 78. For a detailed analysis of Madison's argument that the Bill of Rights does not create or secure rights but only declares those rights that are secured by constitutional structure, see Ralph A. Rossum, "*The Federalist's* Understanding of the Constitution as a Bill of Rights," in Charles R. Kesler, ed., *Saving the Revolution: The Federalist Papers and the American Founding* (New York: Free Press, 1987), pp. 219–33.

9. Alexander Hamilton, James Madison, and John Jay, *The Federalist,* edited by Jacob E. Cooke (New York: World, 1961), No. 51, p. 351.

10. U.S. 529, 549 (1991). Scalia's interest in preserving separation of powers has been described as greater than his interest in preserving federalism. M. David Gelfand and Keith Werhan, "Federalism and Separation of Powers on a 'Conservative' Court: Currents and Cross-Currents from Justices O'Connor and Scalia," 64 *Tulane Law Review* (1990): 1443. Gelfand and Werhan wrote: "Justice Scalia has been especially vocal and aggressive in advocating a formalist approach to separation of powers, while showing much less concern for the protection of federalism values." See, however, Chapter Four.

11. U.S. 654 (1988).

12. Justice Anthony Kennedy did not participate in this case.

13. U.S. at 691.

14. Ibid., at 695.

15. Ibid., at 692.

16. Ibid., at 695.

17. Ibid., at 694.

18. Ibid., at 719.

19. Ibid., at 699.

20. Ibid., at 733.

21. Ibid., at 704.

22. Ibid. Scalia's reliance on *Federalist* No. 49 was misplaced. In that essay, Madison was not describing the structure of separation of powers established in the Constitution but rather responding to Thomas Jefferson's argument in *Notes on the State of Virginia* that the remedy for encroachments "by any one of the departments" is "recurrence to the people" (p. 329).

23. 487 U.S. at 703.

24. Ibid., at 732. In 1986, while serving on the Court of Appeals for the District of Columbia Circuit, Scalia sat on a special three-judge district court panel that held that the Gramm-Rudman-Hollings budget balancing statute (formally known as the

Balanced Budget and Emergency Deficit
Control Act of 1985) unconstitutionally
infringed on executive power because it gave
to the comptroller of the General Accounting Office (removable only at the initiative of
Congress) the ultimate authority in determining what budget cuts would have to be
made. *Synar v. United States*, 676 F.Supp.
1374 (D.D.C.) (1986). As discussed in Chapter One, Scalia was widely rumored to be the
author of the per curiam opinion. See James
G. Wilson, "Constraints on Power: The Constitutional Opinions of Judges Scalia, Bork,
Posner, Easterbrook, and Winter," 40 *University of Miami Law Review* (1986): 1200. See
also Smith, *Justice Antonin Scalia and the
Supreme Court's Conservative Moment*,
p. 40. The Supreme Court subsequently
affirmed the circuit opinion in *Bowsher v.
Synar*, 478 U.S. 714 (1986).

25. 487 U.S. at 705. See Scalia's similar
formulation of the judicial power in *Freytag
v. Commissioner of Internal Revenue*, 501
U.S. 868, 908 (1991): "Article III begins '*The*
judicial Power of the United States' — not
'*Some of* the judicial Power of the United
States,' or even '*Most of* the judicial Power of
the United States' — 'shall be vested in one
supreme Court, and in such inferior Courts
as the Congress may from time to time
ordain and establish' " (emphasis in original).
In *Freytag*, the Court confronted the question whether a statute authorizing the chief
judge of the Tax Court to appoint special
trial judges and to assign them to "any other
proceeding which the chief judge may designate" violated the Appointments Clause of
Article II, § 2, cl. 2, which states: "[T]he
Congress may by Law vest the Appointment
of such inferior Officers, as they think
proper, in the President alone, in the Courts
of Law, or in the Heads of Departments." Justice Blackmun held for the Court that a special trial judge is an "inferior Officer" within
the meaning of the clause and that, absent
presidential appointment, for his appointment to be valid, he must be appointed by a

court of law or the head of a department. Up
to that point in the argument, Justice Scalia
agreed. But Blackmun then went on to conclude that the Tax Court was a "Court of
Law." On this, Scalia vociferously disagreed,
finding the appointment valid because the
Tax Court is a "Department" and the chief
judge is its head. Scalia's textualism was on
full display as he argued that the Tax Court
could not be a court of law: "A careful reading of the Constitution and attention to the
apparent purpose of the Appointments clause
make it clear that the Tax Court cannot be
one of those 'Courts of Law' referred to
there. The Clause does not refer generally to
'Bodies exercising judicial Functions,' or
even to 'Courts' generally, or even to 'Courts
of Law' generally. It refers to 'the Courts of
Law.' Certainly this does not mean any
'Court of Law' (the Supreme Court of Rhode
Island would not do). The definite article
'the' obviously narrows the class of eligible
'Courts of Law' to those Courts of Law envisioned by the Constitution. Those are Article
III courts, and the Tax Court is not one of
them." 501 U.S. at 902.

26. 487 U.S. at 705.

27. Ibid., at 706.

28. Ibid., at 696.

29. Ibid., at 709. Scalia wondered how
willing the Court would be to have a portion
of its judicial power given to another branch.
He stated, "[T]o bring the point closer to
home, consider a statute giving to non–
Article III judges just a tiny bit of purely judicial power in a relatively insignificant field,
with substantial control, though not total
control, in the courts. . . . Is there any doubt
that we would not pause to inquire whether
the matter was '*so central* to the functioning
of the Judicial Branch' as really to require
complete control, or whether we retained
'*sufficient* control over the matters to be
decided that we are able to perform our constitutionally assigned duties'? We would say
that our 'constitutionally assigned duties'
include *complete* control over all exercises of

the judicial power." Ibid., at 710 (emphasis in original).

30. Ibid., at 711–12.

31. Ibid., at 734.

32. Ibid., at 710.

33. Ibid., at 711.

34. Ibid., at 731 (emphasis in original).

35. Ibid., at 710. Scalia had previously made this argument in his concurrence in the judgment in *Young v. United States ex rel. Vuitton et Fils S.A.*, 481 U.S. 824 (1987), which will be discussed.

36. 487 U.S. at 727.

37. Ibid., at 730.

38. Ibid., at 732.

39. Ibid., at 708.

40. Ibid., at 713.

41. Ibid.

42. For these same reasons, Starr himself argued against the reauthorization of the independent counsel statute when it was set to expire on June 30, 1999. Neil A. Lewis, "Starr to Ask Congress to End Law That Gave Him His Job," *Washington Post*, April 14, 1999, p. A1.

43. Ibid., at 702.

44. Ibid., at 701.

45. Ibid., at 703.

46. Ibid., at 734.

47. Ibid., at 697.

48. 521 U.S. 898 (1997).

49. "[K]nowingly violat[ing]" the act subjected CLEOs to a potential fine or a term of imprisonment "for no more than one year, or both." 18 U.S.C. § 924(a)(5).

50. 521 U.S. at 935.

51. 505 U.S. 144 (1992).

52. Ibid., at 178.

53. Ibid., at 168–69.

54. Ibid., at 177.

55. Ibid., at 156–57.

56. Ibid., at 157.

57. 521 U.S. at 905.

58. Ibid.

59. Ibid., at 949.

60. See Ralph A. Rossum, *Federalism, the Supreme Court, and the Seventeenth Amend-*

ment: The Irony of Constitutional Democracy (Lanham, Md.: Lexington Books, 2001).

61. 521 U.S. at 922.

62. Ibid., at 925.

63. 488 U.S. 361 (1989).

64. Ibid., at 412.

65. Ibid., at 385.

66. Ibid., at 372.

67. Ibid., at 384. Justice Blackmun was quoting *Bowsher v. Synar*, 478 U.S. 714, 736 (1986).

68. Ibid., at 381.

69. Ibid., at 427.

70. Ibid., at 413.

71. Ibid., at 421.

72. Ibid., at 426.

73. Ibid., at 427.

74. Ibid., at 371.

75. Ibid., at 379.

76. Although Scalia agreed with the Court majority that "the doctrine of unconstitutional delegation of legislative authority" had not been violated "because of the lack of intelligible, congressionally prescribed standards to guide the Commission," he fundamentally disagreed with its conclusion that the doctrine had therefore not been violated. Congress, he insisted, cannot delegate its powers to the commission, regardless of the specificity and precision of its standards, because "the power to make law cannot be exercised by anyone other than Congress." Ibid., at 416–17.

77. Ibid., at 421. See Antonin Scalia, "A Note on the Benzene Case," *Regulation* 20 (July-August 1980): 28, in which he called for renewed judicial enforcement of the unconstitutional delegation doctrine. "Recently, however, the notion seems to have taken root that if a constitutional prohibition is not enforceable through the courts it does not exist. Where that mind set obtains, the congressional barrier to unconstitutional action disappears unless reinforced by judicial affirmation. So even those who do not relish the prospect of regular judicial enforcement of the unconstitutional delegation doctrine might well support the

Court's making an example of one—just one—of the many enactments that appear to violate the principle. The educational effect on Congress might well be substantial."

78. 488 U.S. at 422. Elsewhere in *Mistretta*, Scalia declared, "Unlike executive power, judicial and legislative powers have never been thought delegable." Ibid., at 425. See also Scalia's dissent in *Peretz v. United States*, 501 U.S. 923, 956 (1991): "[T]he Constitution guarantees not merely that no Branch will be forced by one of the *other* Branches to let someone else exercise its assigned powers—but that none of the Branches will *itself* alienate its assigned powers. Otherwise, the doctrine of unconstitutional delegation of legislative powers (which delegation cannot plausibly be compelled by one of the other Branches) is a dead letter." (emphasis in original).

79. U.S. at 415. See Scalia, "A Note on the Benzene Case," pp. 27–28: "[T]he second problem . . . [with the unconstitutional delegation doctrine is] the difficulty of enunciating how much delegation is too much. The relevant factors are simply too multifarious: How significant is the power in question (for example, fixing customs duties versus fixing prices and wages for the entire economy)? How technical are the judgments left for executive determination (for example, establishing construction criteria for nuclear reactors versus establishing standards for 'fair' advertising)? What degree of social consensus exists with respect to those nontechnical judgments committed to the executive (for example, defining 'unfair or deceptive trade practices' versus defining acceptable levels of air pollution)? And—most imponderable of all—how great is the need for immediate action (for example, the executive-determined price controls authorized in World War II versus those authorized in 1970, during the Vietnam conflict)?"

80. U.S. at 417. Elsewhere in *Mistretta*, Scalia rejected entirely the use of the term *excessive delegation*. For him, no degree of

delegation is permissible because, "strictly speaking, there is *no* acceptable delegation of legislative power." Ibid., at 419 (emphasis in original). He elaborated on this idea at greater length in his concurring opinion in *Loving v. United States*, 517 U.S. 748, 776–77 (1996): "While it has become the practice in our opinions to refer to 'unconstitutional delegations of legislative authority' versus 'lawful delegations of legislative authority,' in fact the latter category does not exist. Legislative power is nondelegable. Congress can no more 'delegate' some of its Article I power to the Executive than it could 'delegate' some to one of its committees. What Congress does is to *assign responsibilities* to the Executive; and when the Executive undertakes those assigned responsibilities it acts, not as the 'delegate' of Congress, but as the agent of the People. At some point the responsibilities assigned can become so extensive and so unconstrained that Congress has in effect delegated its legislative power; but until that point of excess is reached there exists, not a 'lawful' delegation, but no delegation at all" (emphasis in original). See also Scalia's dissent in *Clinton v. New York*, 524 U.S. 417, 465 (1998), and his opinion for the Court in *Whitman v. American Trucking Association*, 531 U.S. 457, 472 (2001).

81. U.S. at 421.

82. See *The Federalist* No. 51, pp. 347–48: "To what expedient then shall we finally resort for maintaining in practice the necessary partition of power among the several departments, as laid down in the Constitution? The only answer that can be given is . . . by so contriving the interior structure of the government, as that its several constituent parts may, by their mutual relations, be the means of keeping each other in their proper places."

83. U.S. at 421. As he declared: "Until our decision last Term in *Morrison v. Olson*, 487 U.S. 654 (1988), it could have been said that Congress could delegate lawmaking authority only at the expense of increasing the power of

either the President or the courts. Most often, as a practical matter, it would be the President, since the judicial process is unable to conduct the investigations and make the political assessments essential for most policy-making. Thus, the need for delegation would have to be important enough to induce Congress to aggrandize its primary competitor for political power, and the recipient of the policymaking authority, while not Congress itself, would at least be politically accountable."

84. Ibid., at 422.

85. In *Blakely v. Washington*, 124 S. Ct. 2531 (2004), Scalia wrote an opinion for the Court that cast grave doubt on the constitutionality of the sentencing guidelines of the U.S. Sentencing Commission. Scalia held for a five-member majority that when a state judge sentenced the defendant to three years more than the fifty-three-month statutory maximum of the standard range for his offense under Washington's sentencing guidelines because he found that the defendant had acted with deliberate cruelty, he violated the defendant's Sixth Amendment right to trial by jury. "When a judge inflicts punishment that the jury's verdict alone does not allow, the jury has not found all the facts 'which the law makes essential to the punishment,' and the judge exceeds his proper authority. . . . Because the State's sentencing procedure did not comply with the Sixth Amendment, petitioner's sentence is invalid." Ibid., at 2537. Scalia relied on the Sixth Amendment and not, as in *Mistretta*, on the principle of separation of powers. In fact, he never mentioned *Mistretta* in his opinion, but Justice O'Connor, in her dissent, did. See ibid., at 2548 and 2549. She worried that *Mistretta* was on the verge of being undone: "If the Washington scheme does not comport with the Constitution, it is hard to imagine a guidelines scheme that would." Ibid., at 2550. Her worries were confirmed in *United States v. Booker*, 125 S. Ct. 738 (2005), when Justice Stevens held for a five-member majority that the Sixth Amend-

ment as construed in *Blakely* did, in fact, apply to the federal sentencing guidelines. (See Chapter Six for an extended discussion of *Booker*.)

The parallels to *Printz* are not perfect but are worth brief commentary nonetheless. In *Printz*, Scalia sugarcoated his separation-of-powers argument in *Morrison* with a federalism argument and converted his solitary dissent into the opinion of the Court, and in *Blakely*, he sugarcoated his separation-of-powers argument against the U.S. Sentencing Commission in *Mistretta* with a Sixth Amendment argument and converted his solitary dissent into majority opinions in *Blakely* and *Booker*, thereby achieving what he had previously failed to accomplish.

86. U.S. 211 (1995).

87. Justice Stephen Breyer concurred in the judgment. Justice John Paul Stevens dissented, and Justice Ruth Bader Ginsburg joined his dissent.

88. U.S. 350 (1991).

89. Memorandum Opinion and Order, Civil Action, No 87–438 (E.D. Ky, April 13, 1992).

90. F.3d 1487 (1993).

91. U.S. at 218.

92. Ibid., at 240. Justice Breyer refused to join so categorical a statement: "[I]t is far less clear, and unnecessary for the purposes of this case to decide, that separation of powers is violated *whenever* an 'individual final judgment is legislatively rescinded' . . . I do not subscribe to the Court's more absolute statement." Ibid., at 243 (emphasis in original).

93. Ibid., at 249.

94. Ibid., at 254.

95. Ibid., at 264.

96. Ibid., at 265.

97. Ibid., at 247, n. 1.

98. Ibid., at 247.

99. Ibid., at 264.

100. Ibid., at 265.

101. Ibid., at 266.

102. Ibid., at 267. Justice Stevens quoted Justice Robert Jackson's concurring opinion

in *Youngstown Sheet & Tube Co. v. Sawyer,* 343 U.S. 579, 635 (1952): "The actual art of governing under our Constitution does not and cannot conform to judicial definitions of the power of any of its branches based on isolated clauses or even single Articles torn from context. While the Constitution diffuses power the better to secure liberty, it also contemplates that practice will integrate the dispersed powers into a workable government. It enjoins upon its branches separateness but interdependence, autonomy but reciprocity." This passage by Jackson represents the view to which Scalia takes great exception.

103. U.S. at 267.

104. Ibid., at 219.

105. Ibid.

106. Ibid., at 221.

107. Ibid., at 222. See *The Federalist* No. 81, p. 545.

108. U.S. at 225.

109. Ibid., at 228. See Scalia's statement in *Morrison,* 487 U.S. at 699: "That is what this suit is about. Power. The allocation of power among Congress, the President, and the courts in such fashion as to preserve the equilibrium the Constitution sought to establish—so that 'a gradual concentration of the several powers in the same department,' *Federalist* No. 51, can effectively be resisted. Frequently an issue of this sort will come before the Court clad, so to speak, in sheep's clothing: the potential of the asserted principle to effect important change in the equilibrium of power is not immediately evident, and must be discerned by a careful and perceptive analysis. But this wolf comes as a wolf."

110. U.S. at 228.

111. Ibid., at 239.

112. Antonin Scalia, "The Legislative Veto: A False Remedy for System Overload," *Regulation* (November-December 1979): 19–26. As an assistant attorney general in the Ford administration, Scalia had testified before Congress in opposition to the legislative veto, a practice by which an executive agency is given authority by Congress to make policy with the stipulation that one or both houses of Congress can subsequently overturn the executive action. See Barbara Craig, *Chadha: The Story of an Epic Constitutional Struggle* (New York: Oxford University Press, 1988), p. 53.

113. Scalia, "The Legislative Veto," p. 19.

114. Ibid., p. 25. For Scalia, *Chevron U.S.A., Inc. v. Natural Resources Defense Council,* 467 U.S. 837 (1984), and its principle that the courts will accept an agency's reasonable interpretation of the ambiguous terms of a statute that the agency administers raised no separation-of-powers issue. Scalia attributed "an ambiguity in a statute committed to agency implementation" to the fact that "Congress had no particular intent on the subject, but meant to leave its resolution to the agency." Antonin Scalia, "Judicial Deference to Administrative Interpretations of the Law," 1989 *Duke Law Journal* (June 1989): 511, 516. See also his opinion for the Court in *Sullivan v. Everhart,* 494 U.S. 83 (1990), and his dissent in *Pauley v. Bethenergy Mines, Inc.,* 501 U.S. 680, 706 (1991).

115. Scalia, "The Legislative Veto," p. 26. For an elaboration of these views, see Jessica Korn, *The Power of Separation: American Constitutionalism and the Myth of the Legislative Veto* (Princeton, N.J.: Princeton University Press, 1996).

116. U.S. 919 (1983).

117. Scalia wrote the amicus curiae brief opposing the constitutionality of the legislative veto that was filed by the American Bar Association in *Chadha.* See Craig, *Chadha: The Story of an Epic Constitutional Struggle,* p. 186.

118. U.S. at 240.

119. U.S. 787 (1987). See Neal Devins and Steven J. Mulroy, "Judicial Vigilantism: Inherent Judicial Authority to Appoint Contempt Prosecutors in *Young v. United States ex rel. Vuitton et Fils S.A.,*" 76 *Kentucky Law Review* (1988): 861.

120. See also Scalia's concurring opinion in *United States v. Providence Journal*, 485 U.S. 693, 708 (1988).

121. U.S. at 815.

122. Ibid., at 816.

123. Ibid., at 817, n. 2.

124. Ibid., at 797.

125. Ibid., at 817–18.

126. Ibid., at 818. See *The Federalist* No. 78, pp. 522–23 (emphasis added by Justice Scalia).

127. U.S. at 822.

128. Ibid., at 824.

129. U.S. at 824.

130. U.S. 385 (1990).

131. Ibid., at 410.

132. F.2d 654 (1988).

133. U.S. at 396–400. The Court was unanimous in Justice Marshall's judgment that § 3013 did not violate the Constitution; however, both Scalia and Stevens filed separate opinions concurring only in the judgment. Stevens argued that since the Constitution is silent as to the consequences of an Origination Clause violation, any bill passed by both houses and signed by the president should still become law. Ibid., at 401–2.

134. Ibid., at 409.

135. Ibid., at 409–10.

136. Ibid., at 410. Scalia's expressed concern that the Court was manifesting a "lack of respect due a coordinate Branch" mirrored the federal government's contention that *Munoz-Flores* raised a nonjusticiable political question; "the most persuasive factor suggesting non-justiciability," as those factors were identified in *Baker v. Carr*, 369 U.S. 186 (1962), was "the concern that courts not express 'lack of . . . respect' for the House of Representatives." The Court majority denied that the case raised a political question, and interestingly, Scalia, who never mentioned the political question doctrine, left it uncertain whether he was tacitly applying it. Even his final paragraph preserved the uncertainty: "This disposition does not place forever beyond our reach the only issue in this

area that seems to me appropriate for judicial rather than congressional resolution: what sort of bills constitute 'Bills for raising Revenue,' Art. I, § 7, cl. 1. Whenever Congress wishes to preserve the possibility of a judicial determination on this point, all it need do is originate the bill that contains the arguably revenue-raising measure in the Senate, indicating such origination on the enrolled bill, as by the caption 'S.J. Res.' This Court may thereby have the last word on what constitutes a bill for raising revenue, and Congress the last word on where a particular bill has originated—which seems to me as it should be." Ibid., at 410.

137. U.S. 727, 731 (1972).

138. U.S. 447 (1923).

139. Antonin Scalia, "The Doctrine of Standing as an Essential Element in the Separation of Powers," 17 *Suffolk University Law Review* (Winter 1983): 882. See *Baker v. Carr*, 369 U.S. 186, in which the Warren Court described the doctrine of standing as necessary not because of the constitutional limitation of the federal courts' jurisdiction to cases and controversies but because "a personal stake in the outcome of the controversy . . . assure[s] that concrete adverseness which sharpens the presentation of issues upon which the Court so largely depends for illumination of difficult constitutional questions." This passage was quoted by the Court in *Flast v. Cohen*, 392 U.S. 83 (1968), prompting Justice Scalia to observe, in "The Doctrine of Standing as an Essential Element," pp. 891–92: "Standing, in other words, is only meant to assure that the courts can do their work well, and not to assure that they keep out of affairs better left to the other branches. I must note at the outset . . . that if the purpose of standing is 'to assure that concrete adverseness which sharpens the presentation of issues,' the doctrine is remarkably ill designed to that end. Often the very best adversaries are national organizations such as the NAACP [National Association for the Advancement of Colored People] or the

American Civil Liberties Union that have a keen interest in the abstract question at issue in the case, but no 'concrete injury in fact' whatever. Yet the doctrine of standing clearly excludes them, unless they can attach themselves to some particular individual who happens to have some personal interest (however minor) at stake."

140. U.S. 83 (1968).

141. U.S. 669 (1973).

142. U.S. at 102.

143. Scalia, "The Doctrine of Standing as an Essential Element," p. 881. See also Scalia's Court of Appeals dissent in *Center for Auto Safety v. National Highway Traffic Safety Administration*, 793 F.2d 1322, 1341–45 (D.C. Cir. 1986).

144. Ibid., p. 895.

145. Ibid., p. 894 (emphasis in original).

146. U.S. 555 (1992).

147. Ibid., at 560.

148. Ibid.

149. Ibid., at 564.

150. Ibid., 565–66. Defenders of Wildlife also proposed an "ecosystem nexus" whereby any person who uses any part of a "contiguous ecosystem" adversely affected by a funded activity has standing, even if the activity occurs on a different continent. Not even the Court of Appeals for the Eighth Circuit, which found that the plaintiffs had standing on the basis of their other claims, accepted this argument, holding that the ecosystem nexus is limited in application to challenged activity "in the vicinity."

151. Ibid., at 571.

152. Ibid., at 568.

153. Ibid., at 571.

154. 16 U.S.C. § 1540(g).

155. 504 U.S. 573.

156. Ibid., at 574.

157. Ibid., at 576.

158. Ibid., at 577. See Scalia's opinion for the Court in *Lewis v. Casey*, 518 U.S. 343, 357 (1996), in which he elaborated on the need for the Court to enforce strictly the actual-injury requirement as a means of

keeping the Court from exceeding its proper role: "The actual-injury requirement would hardly serve the purpose . . . of preventing courts from undertaking tasks assigned to the political branches . . . if once a plaintiff demonstrated harm from one particular inadequacy in government administration, the court were authorized to remedy *all* inadequacies in that administration. The remedy must of course be limited to the inadequacy that produced the injury in fact that the plaintiff has established" (emphasis in original). See also Gene R. Nichols Jr., "Injury and the Disintegration of Article III," 74 *California Law Review* (1986): 1915, 1942: "A judiciary that reviews every claim of government illegality may truly threaten separation of powers." However, see Nichols, "Justice Scalia, Standing, and Public Law Litigation," 42 *Duke Law Journal* (1993): 1141.

159. U.S.788 (1992). *Lujan* was decided on June 12, 1992, *Franklin* on June 26. Scalia has not invariably lost in subsequent cases when he has employed his three-element standing test of *Lujan*. See *Steel Company, AKA Chicago Steel and Pickling Company v. Citizens for a Better Environment*, 523 U.S. 83 (1998), in which he held for a five-member majority that plaintiffs lacked standing to vindicate "the 'undifferentiated public interest' in faithful execution" of the law. "[A]lthough a suitor may derive great comfort and joy from the fact that the United States Treasury is not cheated, that a wrongdoer gets his just desserts, or that the nation's laws are faithfully enforced," he argued, "that psychic satisfaction is not an acceptable Article III remedy because it does not redress a cognizable Article III injury. Relief that does not remedy the injury suffered cannot bootstrap a plaintiff into federal court; that is the very essence of the redressability requirement." Ibid., at 107.

160. F.Supp. 230 (D. Mass.) (1992).

161. U.S. at 803–6.

162. Technically, Scalia concurred in part and concurred in the judgment; however, his

concurrence in the Court's opinion was limited to its discussion of the Administrative Procedure Act, which is not germane to this discussion.

163. 505 U.S. at 824.

164. Ibid., at 824–25.

165. Ibid., at 826.

166. In *Department of Commerce v. Montana*, 503 U.S. 442 (1992), the Court did reach the merits of the president's use of what is called the method of equal proportions in calculating the number of representatives each state receives. Scalia relied on *Hagans v. Lavine*, 415 U.S. 528, 533, n. 5 (1974), to avoid his need to reach a "contrary conclusion" in *Franklin*: "When questions of jurisdiction have been passed on in prior decisions, *sub silentio*, this Court has never considered itself bound when a subsequent case finally brings the jurisdictional issue before us." 505 U.S. at 829, n. 4.

167. 505 U.S. at 827. Scalia, of course, acknowledged that presidential actions are reviewable: "Review of the legality of Presidential action can ordinarily be obtained in a suit seeking to enjoin the officers who attempt to enforce the President's directive." Ibid., at 828.

168. Ibid., at 829.

169. 110 Stat. 1200, 2 U.S.C. § 691 *et seq.* (Supp. II, 1994).

170. 956 F.Supp. 25 (1997).

171. *Raines v. Byrd*, 521 U.S. 811, 830 (1997).

172. 524 U.S. 417 (1998).

173. Ibid., at 463.

174. Ibid., at 457.

175. Ibid., at 459. See Scalia's objections to "hypothetical jurisdiction" in *Steel Company v. Citizens for a Better Environment*, 523 U.S. at 101–2: "Hypothetical jurisdiction produces nothing more than a hypothetical judgment—which comes to the same thing as an advisory opinion, disapproved by this Court from the beginning. Much more than legal niceties are at stake here. The statutory and (especially) constitutional elements of jurisdiction are an essential ingredient of separation and equilibration of powers, restraining the courts from acting at certain times, and even restraining them from acting permanently regarding certain subjects. For a court to pronounce upon the meaning or the constitutionality of a state or federal law when it has no jurisdiction to do so is, by very definition, for a court to act *ultra vires*."

176. 524 U.S. at 459 (emphasis in original).

177. Ibid., at 432.

178. Ibid., at 460.

179. Ibid., at 463.

180. Ibid.

181. Ibid., at 469.

182. Ibid., at 463–64 (emphasis in original).

183. Ibid., at 464–65 (emphasis in original).

184. Ibid., at 466. Scalia provided several "examples of appropriations committed to the discretion of the President" that he said "abound in our history": "From 1789–1791, the First Congress made lump-sum appropriations for the entire Government—'sums not exceeding' specified amounts for broad purposes. From a very early date Congress also made permissive individual appropriations, leaving the decision whether to spend the money to the President's unfettered discretion. In 1803, it appropriated $50,000 for the President to build 'not exceeding fifteen gun boats, to be armed, manned and fitted out, and employed for such purposes as in his opinion the public service may require.' President Jefferson reported that 'the sum of fifty thousand dollars appropriated by Congress for providing gun boats remains unexpended. The favorable and peaceable turn of affairs on the Mississippi rendered an immediate execution of that law unnecessary.' During the Civil War, an Act appropriated over $76 million to be divided among various items 'as the exigencies of the service may require.' During the Great Depression, Congress appropriated $950 million 'for such projects and/or purposes and under such rules and regulations as the President in his discretion may prescribe,' and $4 billion for

general classes of projects, the money to be
spent 'in the discretion and under the direction of the President.' The constitutionality
of such appropriations has never seriously
been questioned." Ibid., at 467.

185. Ibid., at 469.

186. 124 S. Ct. 2711 (2004). The Court held
that Padilla's petition, filed in a federal district
court in New York, should have been filed in
a federal district court in South Carolina.

187. 124 S. Ct. 2686 (2004).

188. 124 S. Ct. 2633 (2004).

189. 124 S. Ct. at 2711.

190. Ibid., at 2693.

191. Ibid., at 2701.

192. Ibid., at 2707. In *Sosa v. Alvarez-
Machain*, 124 S. Ct. 2739, 2776 (2004),
Scalia referred to *Rasul* as an example of
what he called the Court's "Never Say Never
Jurisprudence," in which "[t]his Court seems
incapable of admitting that some matters—
any matters—are none of its business"
(emphasis in original).

193. 124 S. Ct. at 2701 (emphasis in
original).

194. Ibid., at 2706.

195. Ibid., at 2707.

196. Ibid., at 2711.

197. Ibid.

198. Scalia's dissent in *Hamdi*, 124 S. Ct. at
2660–61, was a pure expression of his text-
and-tradition jurisprudence: "Where the
Government accuses a citizen of waging war
against it, our constitutional tradition has
been to prosecute him in federal court for
treason or some other crime. Where the exigencies of war prevent that, the Constitution's Suspension Clause, Art. I, § 9, cl. 2,
allows Congress to relax the usual protections temporarily. Absent suspension, however, the Executive's assertion of military
exigency has not been thought sufficient to
permit detention without charge. No one
contends that the congressional Authorization for Use of Military Force, on which the
Government relies to justify its actions here,
is an implementation of the Suspension

Clause. Accordingly, I would reverse the
decision below."

199. Ibid., at 2642.

200. Ibid., at 2640.

201. Ibid., at 2648.

202. Ibid., at 2671.

203. Ibid., at 2672.

204. Ibid.

205. Ibid., at 2673.

206. Ibid.

207. Alexis de Tocqueville, *Democracy in
America*, ed. Phillips Bradley (New York:
Random House, 1945), 2:344.

208. U.S at 549.

209. *Steel Company v. Citizens for a Better
Environment*, 523 U.S. at 102.

210. U.S. at 732.

211. U.S. at 824. Scalia was quoting from
The Federalist No. 78, which in turn was
quoting Montesquieu's *Spirit of the Laws*.

212. *Hamdi v. Rumsfeld*, 124 S. Ct. at 2661.

213. Ibid., at 2673–74. Scalia continued: "If
civil rights are to be curtailed during
wartime, it must be done openly and democratically, as the Constitution requires, rather
than by silent erosion through an opinion of
this Court."

214. 514 U.S. at 245.

Chapter Four. Constitutional Structure and Federalism

1. *Hearings before the Committee on the
Judiciary on the Nomination of Judge
Antonin Scalia to Be Associate Justice of the
Supreme Court of the United States*, Com-
mittee on the Judiciary, United States Sen-
ate, 99th Cong., 2d sess., J–99–119
(Washington, D.C.: Government Printing
Office, 1987), p. 32. (Hereafter *Hearings on
the Nomination of Scalia*.)

2. Alexander Hamilton, James Madison,
and John Jay, *The Federalist*, edited by Jacob
E. Cooke (New York: World Publishing,
1961), No. 51, p. 351.

3. In matters affecting separation of powers, Scalia seeks no more than to "preserve"

from the actions of the other branches (and especially the Congress) the basic constitutional structure the Framers put in place. *James B. Beam Distilling Company v. Georgia*, 501 U.S. 529, 549 (1991). In matters affecting federalism, not only does he seek to "preserve" that original constitutional structure — even when it has been subsequently altered by the Fourteenth and Seventeenth Amendments — but he also is frequently willing to vote to invalidate the results produced by that constitutional structure. See Scalia's opinion concurring in part and concurring in the judgment in *South Carolina v. Baker*, 485 U.S. 505, 528 (1988), rejecting the view that "'national political process' is the States' only constitutional protection, and that nothing except the demonstration of 'some extraordinary defects' in the operation of that process can justify judicial review" and indicating only that constitutional "structure does not prohibit what the Federal Government has done here."

4. 17 U.S. 316, 405 (1819).

5. See Ralph A. Rossum and G. Alan Tarr, *American Constitutional Law*, vol. 1, *The Structure of Government*, 6th ed. (Belmont, Calif.: Wadsworth, 2003), pp. 236–65, for a sustained discussion of these issues.

6. 22 U.S. 1 (1824).

7. 14 U.S. 304 (1816).

8. 19 U.S. 264 (1821).

9. M. David Gelfand and Keith Werhan, "Federalism and Separation of Powers on a 'Conservative' Court: Currents and Cross-Currents from Justices O'Connor and Scalia," 64 *Tulane Law Review* (1990): 1443. "Justice Scalia has been especially vocal and aggressive in advocating a formalist approach to separation of powers, while showing much less concern for the protection of federalism values."

10. *Hearings on the Nomination of Scalia*, p. 81.

11. Scalia recognizes, as Madison argued in *Federalist* No. 46, p. 317, that the people might "in [the] future become more partial

to the federal than to the State governments, . . . and in that case, the people ought not surely to be precluded from giving most of their confidence where they may discover it to be most due."

12. Antonin Scalia, "The Legislative Veto: A False Remedy for System Overload," *Regulation* (November-December 1979): 20. See also Antonin Scalia, "On the Merits of the Frying Pan," *Regulation* (January-February 1985): 13: "The most important, enduring, and stable portions of the Constitution represent such a deep social consensus that one suspects that if they were entirely eliminated, very little would change. And the converse is also true. A guarantee may appear in the words of the Constitution, but when society ceases to possess an abiding belief in it, it has no living effect. Consider the fate of the principle expressed in the Tenth Amendment that the federal government is a government of limited powers."

13. 501 U.S. 775, 779 (1991).

14. *American Trucking Association v. Smith*, 496 U.S. 167, 202 (1990). The negative Commerce Clause is more typically known as the "dormant Commerce Clause." The dormant Commerce Clause, however, has come to mean different things at different times to different people. For example, what Scalia terms contemporary "'negative' Commerce Clause jurisprudence" clearly differs from the theory of the "dormant" Commerce Clause as it was initially enunciated by Justice William Johnson in his concurring opinion in *Gibbons v. Ogden*, 22 U.S. 1, 222 (1824). Johnson wrote that the grant of the commerce power to Congress in Article I, § 8, even though unexercised by Congress, necessarily prevented the states from regulating commerce and required the Court to invalidate all state regulations that touched on commerce.

15. *Dennis v. Higgins*, 498 U.S. 439, 448 (1991).

16. *Westinghouse Electric Corp. v. Tully*, 466 U.S. 388, 402–3 (1984) (emphasis added).

17. See *Camps Newfound/Owatonna v. Harrison*, 520 U.S. 564, 603 (1997), however, in which Scalia charges the Court with abandoning even the need to consider the state's justification for the discriminatory burden: "The most remarkable thing about today's judgment is that it is rendered without an inquiry into whether the purposes of the tax exemption *justify* its favoritism. Once having concluded that the statute is facially discriminatory, the Court rests" (emphasis in original).

18. *Pharmaceutical Research and Manufacturers Association of America v. Walsh*, 538 U.S. 644, 674 (2003). See also *Tyler Pipe Industries v. Washington State Department of Revenue*, 483 U.S. 232, 254 (1987); *American Trucking Association v. Smith*, 496 U.S. at 202; *State of Wyoming v. State of Oklahoma*, 502 U.S. 437, 469 (1992); and *Oklahoma Tax Commission v. Jefferson Lines*, 514 U.S. 175, 200 (1995).

19. 496 U.S. at 202.

20. Ibid., at 202, 203.

21. 486 U.S. 888, 906 (1988). See also *Quill Corporation v. North Dakota*, 504 U.S. 298, 320 (1992).

22. 53 U.S. 299, 319 (1852).

23. 82 U.S. 232 (1873).

24. Ibid., at 275.

25. Ibid., at 282.

26. But see Felix Frankfurter, *The Commerce Clause under Marshall, Taney, and White* (Chapel Hill: University of North Carolina Press, 1937), p. 19: "The doctrine that state authority must be subject to such limitations as the Court finds it necessary to apply for the protection of the national community . . . [is] an audacious doctrine, which, one may be sure, would have been publicly avowed in support of the adoption of the Constitution." See also David P. Currie, *The Constitution in the Supreme Court: The First Hundred Years, 1789–1888* (Chicago: University of Chicago Press, 1985), p. 234, who describes the Court's negative Commerce Clause jurisprudence as

"arbitrary, conclusory, and irreconcilable with the constitutional text."

27. 483 U.S. 232, 260 (1987).

28. Ibid., at 258.

29. Ibid., at 259. As Scalia remarked in *Itel Containers International Corp. v. Huddleston*, 507 U.S. 60, 80–81 (1993), "The National Government can always explicitly pre-empt the offending state law."

30. 483 U.S. at 259.

31. 22 U.S. 1, 209 (1824).

32. 483 U.S. at 261.

33. See 82 U.S. at 279. See *Itel Containers International Corp. v. Huddleston*, 507 U.S. at 80, in which Scalia rejects Justice Strong's argument concerning the states' power to regulate foreign commerce: "I have not hitherto had occasion to consider an asserted application of the negative Commerce Clause to commerce 'with foreign Nations'—as opposed to commerce 'among the several States'—but the basic point that the Commerce Clause is a power conferred upon Congress (and not a power denied to the States) obviously applies to all portions of the Clause."

34. 483 U.S. at 261.

35. Ibid., at 263–64 (emphasis in original).

36. Ibid., at 264.

37. 317 U.S. 111 (1942).

38. 402 U.S. 146 (1971).

39. 483 U.S. at 261.

40. Ibid., at 261–62.

41. 496 U.S. at 203.

42. 483 U.S. at 262. He quoted from Justice Blackmun's unanimous opinion for the Court in *Alaska Airlines v. Brock*, 480 U.S. 678, 686 (1987): "Congress's silence is just that—silence."

43. 496 U.S. at 202–3.

44. 483 U.S. at 262–63.

45. *State of Wyoming v. State of Oklahoma*, 502 U.S. at 469.

46. 483 U.S. at 265.

47. *Baldwin v. Montana Fish and Game Commission*, 436 U.S. 371, 382 (1978).

48. See Chapter Two.

49. 6 Fed. Cas. 546 (1825).

50. 436 U.S. at 387.

51. 483 U.S. at 265.

52. There are a few exceptions: Chief Justice Rehnquist joined Scalia's opinions in *Tyler Pipe, American Trucking Association v. Scheiner*, 483 U.S. 266 (1987), and *State of Wyoming v. State of Oklahoma*, 502 U.S. 437 (1992); Justice Kennedy joined Scalia's opinion in *Quill Corporation v. North Dakota*, 504 U.S. 298 (1992); and Justice Thomas joined Scalia's opinion in *State of Wyoming v. State of Oklahoma* and *Quill*.

53. *Itel Containers International Corporation v. Huddleston*, 507 U.S. at 78.

54. Ibid., at 78–79. He has repeated this announcement in *West Lynn Creamery v. Healy*, 512 U.S. 186, 210 (1994); *Barclays Bank v. Franchise Tax Board*, 512 U.S. 298, 332 (1992); *General Motors Corporation v. Tracy*, 519 U.S. 278, 312 (1997); and *American Trucking Associations v. Michigan Public Service Commission*, 125 S. Ct. 2419 (2005).

55. 507 U.S. at 78–79. See Scalia's concurring or dissenting opinions in which he debates with his colleagues whether a particular state regulation or tax is "facially discriminatory" in *American Trucking Association v. Scheiner*, 483 U.S. 266, 305 (1987); *New Energy Company of Indiana v. Limbach*, 486 U.S. 269, 280 (1988); *Amerada Hess v. Division of Taxation, New Jersey Department of the Treasury*, 490 U.S. 66, 80 (1989); *Healy v. Beer Institute*, 491 U.S. 324, 344 (1989); and *Trinova Corporation v. Michigan Department of Treasury*, 498 U.S. 358, 387 (1991).

56. 507 U.S. at 78–79.

57. 520 U.S. 564 (1997).

58. Ibid., at 595.

59. Ibid., at 608.

60. Ibid., at 605.

61. Ibid., at 601–2.

62. Ibid., at 602 (emphasis in original). For Scalia, "the theory underlying the exemption is that it is a *quid pro quo* for uncompensated expenditures that lessen the State's burden of providing assistance to its residents."

63. Ibid., at 608.

64. See Rossum and Tarr, *American Constitutional Law*, pp. 366–67, for a useful overview of preemption.

65. 480 U.S. 572 (1987).

66. 536 U.S. 424 (2002).

67. One of these statutes prohibited a health insurer from discriminating against any provider who was willing to meet the conditions established by the insurer for participation in the insurer's health benefit plan, and the other required a health benefit plan that included chiropractic benefits to permit any licensed chiropractor who agreed to abide by the plan's conditions to serve as a participating primary chiropractor.

68. 538 U.S. 329 (2003).

69. 501 U.S. 597 (1991).

70. 504 U.S. 374 (1992).

71. Ibid., at 383. See his dissent in *Cipollone v. Liggett Group, Inc.*, 505 U.S. 504, 545 (1992): "The ultimate question in each case, as we have framed the inquiry, is one of Congress's intent, as revealed by the text, structure, purposes, and subject matter of the statutes involved."

72. 480 U.S. at 608.

73. Ibid., at 610.

74. Ibid., at 613.

75. Ibid., at 614. See also Scalia's opinion for the Court in *Engine Manufacturers Association v. South Coast Air Quality Management District*, 124 S. Ct. 1756 (2004).

76. 536 U.S. at 444 (emphasis in original).

77. Ibid., at 445 (emphasis in original).

78. Ibid., at 446.

79. Ibid., at 445.

80. Ibid., at 447.

81. Ibid., at 448.

82. Ibid., at 449.

83. 538 U.S. at 333.

84. Ibid., at 337–38 (emphasis in original).

85. 501 U.S. at 616.

86. Although, given the fact that the Court majority relied heavily on the use of legislative history to reach the same judgment that Scalia reached simply on the basis of the

text, he felt the need to say more—much more—about the Court's "weird endeavor." Ibid., at 622.

87. For another example of this same kind of analysis by Scalia, see his opinion for a seven-member majority in *American Telephone and Telegraph Co. v. Central Office Telephone*, 524 U.S. 214 (1998).

88. 504 U.S. at 383. The phrase *relating to* also appeared in ERISA's language, and in *Kentucky Association of Health Plans*, 538 U.S. 329, Scalia for the Court majority did not read it to hold that Kentucky's AWP statutes were preempted. The difference, of course, is that, unlike the Airline Deregulation Act, ERISA contained potentially competing provisions—§ 1144(a) preempting state laws as they "relate to any employee benefit plan" and § 1144(b) excepting from preemption all state laws "which regulate insurance."

89. 504 U.S. at 385. Scalia makes a similar argument concerning the phrase *relating to* in his concurrence in *Egelhoff v. Egelhoff*, 532 U.S. 141, 153 (2001).

90. 504 U.S. at 385–86.

91. 485 U.S. 495, 503 (1988).

92. He is also eager to employ the threshold question of federal court jurisdiction to avoid reaching a decision on preemption, and this, too, works to the advantage of the states. See *DeBuono v. NYSA-ILA Medical and Clinical Services Fund*, 520 U.S. 806, 820–21 (1997): "Because I am uncertain of the federal courts' jurisdiction over this case, I would set the jurisdictional issue for briefing and argument, and would resolve that issue before reaching the merits of respondents' ERISA pre-emption claim. Accordingly, I respectfully dissent from today's opinion."

93. 485 U.S. at 501, 503. See his majority opinion in *Morales*, 504 U.S. at 386.

94. 501 U.S. at 499.

95. 485 U.S. at 501.

96. 501 U.S. at 622.

97. Ibid., at 617.

98. Ibid., at 620–21 (emphasis in original).

99. Ibid., at 621.

100. Under the rule of *Chevron* deference, Scalia is willing to defer to an administrative agency's determination that a federal statute preempts state regulations. See *Mississippi Power & Light Co. v. Mississippi ex rel. Moore*, 487 U.S. 354, 380 (1988): "What the case comes down to, then, is whether FERC's [Federal Energy Regulation Commission's] asserted jurisdiction to examine the prudence of a particular utility's joining a pooling arrangement with affiliated companies is supported by the provisions of the Federal Power Act. If so, there is no regulatory gap for the States to fill, and they are pre-empted from examining that question of prudence in calculating the rates chargeable to retail customers. In considering the Federal Power Act question we will defer, of course, to FERC's construction if it does not violate plain meaning and is a reasonable interpretation of silence or ambiguity. See, e.g., . . . *Chevron U.S.A. Inc. v. Natural Resources Defense Council, Inc.*, 467 U.S. 837, 842–44 (1984)."

101. Occasionally, the statutory cat may be sporting an "anti-preemptive grin"—or would that be a grimace? On those occasions, Scalia will give it an equally full anti-preemptive effect—to the advantage of the states. See *California Federal Savings & Loan Association v. Guerra*, 479 U.S. 272, 296 (1987).

102. 505 U.S. at 545.

103. Ibid., at 544.

104. Ibid., at 548.

105. 511 U.S. 531, 546 (1994).

106. 505 U.S. 144 (1992).

107. Ibid., at 178.

108. Ibid., at 177.

109. Ibid.

110. Ibid., at 159.

111. Ibid., at 156–57.

112. 521 U.S. 898 (1997).

113. Ibid., at 935.

114. Ibid., at 925.

115. Ibid., at 905.

116. 487 U.S. 654 (1988).

117. Antonin Scalia, "Originalism: The Lesser Evil," 57 *University of Cincinnati Law Review* (1989): 849, 851.

118. 521 U.S. at 922.

119. 521 U.S. at 922–23.

120. 538 U.S. 254 (2003).

121. Ibid., at 301.

122. Ibid., at 280.

123. Ibid., at 302.

124. Ibid., at 280.

125. 2 U.S. 419 (1793).

126. See Ralph A. Rossum, "Congress, the Constitution, and the Appellate Jurisdiction of the Supreme Court: The Letter and Spirit of the Exceptions Clause," 24 *William and Mary Law Review* (1983): 385–428. See also Rossum, *Congressional Control of the Judiciary: The Article III Option* (Washington, D.C.: Center for Judicial Studies, 1988).

127. Jurisdiction "between a State, or the Citizens thereof, and foreign States, Citizens or Subjects," provided as well in Article III, § 2, is also known as "state citizen diversity" jurisdiction.

128. The words are from Justice John Blair in his opinion in *Chisholm v. Georgia*, 2 U.S. at 450.

129. *The Federalist* No. 81, pp. 548–49 (emphasis in original): "It is inherent in the nature of sovereignty not to be amenable to the suit of an individual *without its consent.* This is the general sense, and the general practice of mankind; and the exemption, as one of the attributes of sovereignty, is now enjoyed by the government of every State in the Union. Unless, therefore, there is a surrender of this immunity in the plan of the convention, it will remain with the States, and the danger intimated must be merely ideal. The circumstances which are necessary to produce an alienation of State sovereignty were discussed in considering the article of taxation, and need not be repeated here. A recurrence to the principles there established will satisfy us, that there is no

color to pretend that the State governments would, by the adoption of that plan, be divested of the privilege of paying their own debts in their own way, free from every constraint but that which flows from the obligations of good faith. The contracts between a nation and individuals are only binding on the conscience of the sovereign, and have no pretensions to a compulsive force. They confer no right of action, independent of the sovereign will. To what purpose would it be to authorize suits against States for the debts they owe? How could recoveries be enforced? It is evident, it could not be done without waging war against the contracting State; and to ascribe to the federal courts, by mere implication, and in destruction of a pre-existing right of the State governments, a power which would involve such a consequence, would be altogether forced and unwarrantable."

Of course, Hamilton also assumed (and in this instance, clearly incorrectly) that the president would not be able to remove any officer without the advice and consent of the Senate. See *Federalist* No. 77, p. 515: "It has been mentioned as one of the advantages to be expected from the co-operation of the Senate, in the business of appointments, that it would contribute to the stability of the administration. The consent of that body would be necessary to displace as well as to appoint. A change of the Chief Magistrate, therefore, would not occasion so violent or so general a revolution in the officers of the government as might be expected, if he were the sole disposer of offices. Where a man in any station had given satisfactory evidence of his fitness for it, a new President would be restrained from attempting a change in favor of a person more agreeable to him, by the apprehension that a discountenance of the Senate might frustrate the attempt, and bring some degree of discredit upon himself. Those who can best estimate the value of a steady administration, will be most disposed to prize a provision which connects the official existence of public men with the approbation or disapprobation of that body which, from the greater permanency of its own composition, will in all probability be less subject to inconstancy than any other member of the government."

130. 2 U.S. at 471–72.

131. 1 Statutes at Large 73 (1789).

132. This statement is in need of one qualification: § 13 actually confers on the Supreme Court "original but not exclusive jurisdiction" in all controversies "between a state and its citizens."

133. Wythe Holt reported that "[m]ost observers agreed with Congressman Benjamin Goodhue that 'no material alterations' had been made in 'the Judicial bill . . . as it came from the Senate.'" Holt, "'To Establish Justice': Politics, the Judiciary Act of 1789, and the Invention of the Federal Courts," 1989 *Duke Law Journal* (1989): 1421, 1516, n. 348. See also Wilfred J. Ritz, *Rewriting the History of the Judiciary Act of 1789: Exposing Myths, Challenging Premises, and Using New Evidence*, ed. Wythe Holt and L. H. LaRue (Norman: University of Oklahoma Press, 1990), p. 18. See Julius Goebel Jr., *The Oliver Wendell Holmes Devise History of the Supreme Court of the United States*, vol. 1, *Antecedents and Beginnings to 1801* (New York: Macmillan, 1971), pp. 504–7, for a discussion of four "novel" but not material alterations made by the House.

134. See Ralph A. Rossum, *Federalism, the Supreme Court, and the Seventeenth Amendment: The Irony of Constitutional Democracy* (Lanham, Md.: Lexington Books, 2001), pp. 93–123.

135. Henry J. Bourguignon, "The Federal Key to the Judiciary Act of 1789," 46 *South Carolina Law Review* (1995): 647, 700. In his "'To Establish Justice,'" p. 1513, Holt went even further: "The judiciary bill's passage through Congress significantly blunted the momentum of the drive to amend the Constitution."

136. Consider, for example, that the Senate followed state boundaries in establishing districts for the new federal courts. It imposed state procedures and state common law on the federal courts hearing cases in the states. It severely restricted the jurisdiction of the newly created district and circuit courts, and it allowed the state courts to retain a great deal of the jurisdiction many had thought to be rendered exclusively federal by the Constitution. It imposed a $500 jurisdictional minimum on the circuit courts, thereby preventing "the poorer and midling class of citizen" from being taken into federal court and "excluding a huge number of the British debt claims." It limited alienage jurisdiction so that cases brought by British creditors that were already pending in state courts could not be transferred to federal courts. It imposed a $2,000 jurisdictional minimum on the Supreme Court, saving many litigants from having to travel to the seat of the federal government for appeals. Finally, the Senate provided state courts maximum concurrent jurisdiction with the federal courts, and it granted them exclusive jurisdiction over most cases arising under federal law, treaties, and the Constitution. See Rossum, *Federalism, the Supreme Court, and the Seventeenth Amendment*, pp. 138–39. As Bourguignon noted, the omission of general federal questions jurisdiction from the judicial powers granted to the federal courts was no "oversight." Although the district courts were "little more than admiralty courts" and, therefore, unlikely candidates to receive general federal question jurisdiction, the circuit courts "would seem to have been the ideal courts to receive this important area of jurisdiction, but they did not." He attributed this "enormous concession of federal judicial power to the often distrusted state courts" to the Senate's desire to protect the interests of the states as states. Bourguignon, "The Federal Key to the Judiciary Act of 1789," p. 694.

137. 2 U.S. 419.

138. It was the practice at the time for each justice to write a separate opinion in each case. Since there was no majority opinion of the Court, it is necessary to provide language from those who concluded that neither the Constitution nor the Judiciary Act of 1789 acknowledged the principle of state sovereign immunity. See, therefore, the language of Justice John Blair, 2 U.S. at 451: "It seems to me, that if this Court should refuse to hold jurisdiction of a case where a State is Defendant, it would renounce part of the authority conferred, and, consequently, part of the duty imposed on it by the Constitution; because it would be a refusal to take cognizance of a case where a State is a party."

See also the language of Justice James Wilson, ibid., at 466: "Could the strictest legal language; could even that language, which is peculiarly appropriated to an art, deemed, by a great master, to be one of the most honorable, laudable, and profitable things in our law; could this strict and appropriated language, describe, with more precise accuracy, the cause now depending before the tribunal? Causes, and not parties to causes, are weighed by justice, in her equal scales: On the former solely, her attention is fixed: To the latter, she is, as she is painted, blind."

Finally, see also the language of Chief Justice Jay, ibid., at 479: "The extension of the judiciary power of the United States to such controversies, appears to me to be wise, because it is honest, and because it is useful. It is honest, because it provides for doing justice without respect of persons, and by securing individual citizens as well as States, in their respective rights, performs the promise which every free Government makes to every free citizen, of equal justice and protection. It is useful, because it is honest, because it leaves not even the most obscure and friendless citizen without means of obtaining justice from a neighbouring State; because it obviates occasions of quarrels between States

on account of the claims of their respective citizens; because it recognizes and strongly rests on this great moral truth, that justice is the same whether due from one man or a million, or from a million to one man; because it teaches and greatly appreciates the value of our free republican national Government, which places all our citizens on an equal footing, and enables each and every of them to obtain justice without any danger of being overborne by the weight and number of their opponents; and, because it brings into action, and enforces this great and glorious principle, that the people are the sovereign of this country, and consequently that fellow citizens and joint sovereigns cannot be degraded by appearing with each other in their own Courts to have their controversies determined. The people have reason to prize and rejoice in such valuable privileges; and they ought not to forget, that nothing but the free course of Constitutional law and Government can ensure the continuance and enjoyment of them."

139. Justice James Iredell was the lone dissenter, but his dissent focused solely on the construction of the Judiciary Act of 1789, not on the meaning of Article III, § 2. In his view, states sued under the federal courts' state-citizen diversity jurisdiction retained common-law sovereign immunity "as it existed in England (unaltered by any statute) at the time of the first settlement of the country." Ibid., at 435. That immunity, however, could be qualified or abrogated by a "special act of Legislation [that] controuls it, to be in force in each State." He readily conceded that states could be held liable to "the authority of the United States" if such liability were clearly expressed in "laws passed under the Constitution and in conformity to it." Ibid., at 436. However, since he found in the Judiciary Act of 1789 no language clearly abrogating the states' common-law immunity, he therefore concluded that Georgia should not be liable to suit.

140. *Gazette of the United States and Philadelphia Daily Advertiser*, February 20, 1793, p. 303.

141. 517 U.S. at 111.

142. 19 U.S. 264, 383 (1821).

143. Ibid., at 407. See also Marshall's language in *Osborn v. Bank of the United States*, 22 U.S. 738, 847 (1824), in which the Court held that the Eleventh Amendment was no bar to an action against a state that sought the return of an unconstitutional tax. Marshall omitted any reference to federal-question jurisdiction and declared only that "the eleventh amendment of the constitution has exempted a State from the suits of the citizens of other States, or aliens."

144. 491 U.S. 1 (1989).

145. Ibid., at 31–32.

146. 134 U.S. 1 (1890).

147. See Scalia's opinion concurring in the judgment in *Welch v. Texas Department of Highways and Public Transportation*, 483 U.S. 468, 496 (1987), in which he found the question of "the correctness of *Hans* as an original matter" to be "complex" enough that he was "unwilling to address" it in a case that "focused on other matters."

148. 134 U.S. at 15.

149. Ibid., at 11.

150. 491 U.S. at 32. (Interestingly, Scalia did not consider the key premise on which *Chisholm* was based to be fidelity to the actual text of Article III, § 2.)

151. Ibid., at 37.

152. Scalia, "Originalism," pp. 856–57.

153. 292 U.S. 313, 322–23 (1934).

154. Scalia, "Originalism," p. 857.

155. 491 U.S. at 33.

156. *Federalist* No. 10, 63–64.

157. Ibid., No. 51, 353.

158. Ibid., p. 349.

159. See, for example, his very effective use of this argument in his concurrence in the judgment of the Court in *City of Richmond v. Croson*, 488 U.S. 469, 523 (1989).

160. 491 U.S. at 34.

161. Ibid. He pointed out that forty-nine Congresses since *Hans* had legislated under the assurance that private damages actions created by federal law do not extend against the states, and he stressed that "[i]t is impossible to say how many extant statutes would have included an explicit preclusion of suits against States if it had not been thought that such suits were automatically barred." Ibid., at 35. "Indeed," he continued, "it is not even possible to say that, without *Hans*, all constitutional amendments would have taken the form they did." Further, he stated: "The Seventeenth Amendment, eliminating the election of senators by state legislatures, was ratified in 1913, 23 years after *Hans*. If it had been known at that time that the Federal Government could confer upon private individuals federal causes of action reaching state treasuries; and if the state legislatures had had the experience of urging the Senators they chose to protect them against the proposed creation of such liability; it is not inconceivable, especially at a time when voluntary state waiver of sovereign immunity was rare, that the Amendment (which had to be ratified by three-quarters of the same state legislatures) would have contained a proviso protecting against such incursions upon state sovereignty."

Scalia's discussion of the Seventeenth Amendment is especially interesting. It was based on speculation, not on the historical research that his textualist approach would demand of him. Had he researched the history of the adoption and ratification of the Seventeenth Amendment, he would have found the consequences that direct election of the Senate would have on federalism (much less state sovereign immunity) went completely unexplored, and the people, in their desire to make the Constitution more democratic, inattentively abandoned what the Framers regarded as the crucial constitutional means for protecting the federal-state balance and the interests of the states as states. See Rossum, *Federalism, the Supreme Court, and the Seventeenth Amendment,* pp. 219–20.

162. 501 U.S. 775 (1991).

163. Ibid., at 779.

164. This majority included Scalia plus Chief Justice Rehnquist and Justices Kennedy, O'Connor, and Thomas.

165. This statement must be qualified to a certain extent: The same five-member majority acknowledged in each of these cases that Congress does have the power to abrogate state sovereign immunity under the enforcement sections of the post–Civil War amendments. Later amendments trump the original Constitution and earlier amendments, and on the basis of that logic, Chief Justice Rehnquist held in the very first of these cases, *Seminole Tribe of Florida v. Florida,* 517 U.S. 44, 65–66 (1996), that § 5 of the Fourteenth Amendment—passed, of course, after the Eleventh Amendment—was able to trump its state protections: "[T]he Fourteenth Amendment, adopted well after the adoption of the Eleventh Amendment and the ratification of the Constitution, operates to alter the preexisting balance between the state and federal power achieved by Article III and the Eleventh Amendment."

166. Ibid., at 54.

167. Ibid., at 69–70.

168. 527 U.S. 627 (1999).

169. 527 U.S. 666 (1999).

170. Ibid., at 669.

171. In *College Savings Bank,* the Court considered the constitutionality of the Trademark Remedy Clarification Act (TRCA), which subjected states to suits brought under the Trademark Act of 1946 for false and misleading advertising. College Savings Bank, a New Jersey institution that offered an annuity contract for financing future college tuition expenses, sued Florida Prepaid Postsecondary Education Expense Board, a state-created entity that provided a similar tuition prepayment contract available to Florida res-

idents, alleging that Florida Prepaid was guilty of misrepresenting its own program. In his opinion for the Court, Justice Scalia first denied that Congress had power under § 5 of the Fourteenth Amendment to pass the TRCA to remedy and prevent state deprivations of property without due process. There simply is no property right, he insisted, to be free from a "competitor's false advertising about its own product." Ibid., at 672. There was, therefore, no constitutional violation for Congress to remedy and, hence, under *City of Boerne v. Flores,* 521 U.S. 507 (1997) (a case that will be discussed in the next section of this chapter), no power under § 5 for Congress to abrogate state sovereign immunity. There was nothing new in that portion of Scalia's opinion; in journeyman fashion, he was dutifully applying a formula already worked out in much greater detail by Chief Justice Rehnquist in *College Savings Bank v. Florida Prepaid Postsecondary Education Expense Board* and by Justice Kennedy in *Alden v. Maine,* 527 U.S. 706 (1999). Scalia then turned, however, to the question whether Florida had voluntarily waived its immunity by its activities in interstate commerce. College Savings had relied on the Court's 1964 decision in *Parden v. Terminal Railroad Co.,* 377 U.S. 184 (1964), to argue that Florida Prepaid had "'impliedly' or 'constructively' waived its immunity," 527 U.S. at 676, since Congress had provided unambiguously in the TRCA that states would be subject to private suit if they engaged in certain federally regulated conduct and Florida Prepaid had thereafter voluntarily elected to engage in that conduct. In by far the most interesting portion of his opinion, Scalia announced that *Parden* was no longer good law. Declaring it to be "expressly overruled," ibid., at 676, 680, he argued that it could not be squared with the Court's "cases requiring that a state's express waiver be unequivocal." As Scalia pointed out, "There is a fundamental difference between a State's expressing unequivocally that it waives its immunity, and Congress's expressing unequivocally its intention that if the State takes certain action it shall be deemed to have waived that immunity." Ibid., at 681. Nor, he continued, could it be squared with the principle that a state's waiver must be voluntary; he insisted that "the voluntariness of waiver" is destroyed "when what is attached to the refusal to waive is the exclusion of the State from otherwise lawful activity" such as, in the instant case, engaging in interstate marketing. Ibid., at 687. This argument is not so much a defense of federalism as a display of the textualist Scalia demanding that words of the statute mean what they say, if ironically in the midst of an opinion in which he ignores what the words of the Constitution themselves say.

172. 527 U.S. 706, 729 (1999).

173. 528 U.S. 62, 73 (2000).

174. 531 U.S. 356 (2001). The two *Florida Prepaid* cases, *Kimmel* and *Garrett*, were also based on the Court's interpretation in *City of Boerne v. Flores*, 521 U.S. 507, of § 5 of the Fourteenth Amendment. See the next section of this chapter.

175. 535 U.S. 743, 753 (2002).

176. 521 U.S. 507.

177. Ibid., at 536. The Court also claimed that *City of Boerne* violated separation of powers, in that it asserted Congress was attempting to contradict the Court's previous interpretation of the Free Exercise Clause in *Employment Division, Department of Human Resources of Oregon v. Smith*, which will be discussed later. However, as David Cole argued in "The Value of Seeing Things Differently: *Boerne v. Flores* and the Congressional Enforcement of the Bill of Rights," in Dennis J. Hutchinson, David A. Strauss, and Geoffrey R. Stone, eds., *1997 Supreme Court Review* (Chicago: University of Chicago Press, 1998), 31–77, 41: "The [Court's] separation of powers argument . . . is easily rebutted. The argument's premise is

that, in enacting RFRA, Congress sought to 'alter the Fourteenth Amendment's meaning.' But it did no such thing. RFRA provided a statutory right, not a constitutional right. It did not change the Constitution, but only the United States Code. It cannot possibly be inconsistent with the separation of powers for Congress to protect, by statute, rights not protected by the Constitution. Innumerable federal statutes—directed at private and government conduct alike—do precisely that." The real question in *City of Boerne*, therefore, was not whether Congress was free to disagree with the Court concerning how much protection should be afforded to religious liberty but whether Congress had the power to impose such an expanded understanding on the states—that is to say, the real question is a question of federalism.

178. 494 U.S. 872 (1990).

179. Ibid., at 879.

180. 374 U.S. 398 (1963).

181. Public Law No. 103–141, 107 Stat. 1488 (1993).

182. 406 U.S. 205 (1972).

183. Its impact on the administration of prisons was especially perverse. See, for example, Lino A. Graglia, "*Church of Lukumi Babalu Aye*: Of Animal Sacrifice and Religious Persecution," 85 *Georgetown Law Journal* (November 1996): 1, 60–69. See also Christopher L. Eisgruber and Lawrence G. Sager, "Congressional Power and Religious Liberty after *City of Boerne v. Flores*," in Dennis J. Hutchinson, David A. Strauss, and Geoffrey R. Stone, eds., *1997 Supreme Court Review* (Chicago: University of Chicago Press, 1998), 79–139.

184. 310 U.S. 296 (1940).

185. 521 U.S. at 525, 532.

186. Ibid., 520. See Michael W. McConnell, "The Supreme Court, 1996 Term: Comment—Institutions and Interpretation: A Critique of *Boerne v. Flores*," 111 *Harvard Law Review* (November 1997): 153, 165, 170.

187. 521 U.S. at 530–31.

188. Ibid., at 532.

189. 100 U.S. 339 (1880).

190. Matt Pawa, "When the Supreme Court Restricts Constitutional Rights, Can Congress Save Us?: An Examination of Section 5 of the Fourteenth Amendment," 141 *University of Pennsylvania Law Review* (January 1993): 1029, 1057. The "shield" aspect of the Fourteenth Amendment was upheld in *Strauder v. West Virginia*, 100 U.S. 303 (1879).

191. 100 U.S. at 345–46.

192. Ibid., at 347.

193. Ibid., at 346.

194. 384 U.S. 641 (1966). *Katzenbach v. Morgan* upheld the constitutionality of § 4(e) of the Voting Rights Act of 1965, which provided that no state could bar any person from voting solely on grounds of English literacy if that person could demonstrate that he had been educated in an American-flag school "in which the predominant classroom language was other than English." In a seven-to-two opinion written by Justice William Brennan, the Supreme Court declared that "[a] construction of § 5 that would require a judicial determination that the enforcement of the state law precluded by Congress violated the Amendment, as a condition of sustaining the congressional enactment, would depreciate both congressional resourcefulness and congressional responsibility for implementing the Amendment. It would confine the legislative power in this context to the insignificant role of abrogating only those state laws that the judicial branch was prepared to adjudge unconstitutional, or of merely informing the judgment of the judiciary by particularizing the 'majestic generalities' of § 1 of the Amendment." Ibid., at 648–49. It concluded by explaining that "by including § 5, the draftsmen sought to grant to Congress, by a specific provision applicable to the Fourteenth Amendment, the same broad powers expressed in the Necessary and Proper Clause." Ibid., at 650.

195. 392 U.S. 409 (1968). In *Jones v. Alfred H. Mayer Company*, the Supreme Court held that Congress had the power to regulate purely private property transactions in which racial discrimination was present. In his opinion for a seven-member majority, Justice Potter Stewart exhumed the Civil Rights Act of 1866 and held that it "bars all racial discrimination, private as well as public, in the sale or rental of property, and that the statute, thus construed, is a valid exercise of the power of Congress to enforce the Thirteenth Amendment." Ibid., at 413.

196. 400 U.S. 112 (1970). In *Oregon v. Mitchell*, among other conclusions, the Court unanimously held that Congress had power under § 2 of the Fifteenth Amendment to include language in the Voting Rights Act of 1970 that suspended the use of literacy tests throughout the United States for both federal elections and state and local elections, even though it continued to adhere to its belief, expressed in *Lassiter v. Northampton Election Board*, 360 U.S. 45 (1959), that the use by the states of literacy tests did not violate the Fifteenth Amendment.

197. 427 U.S. 445 (1976). Unlike the other cases in this series, *Fitzpatrick v. Bitzer* involved a form of discrimination other than race or rights other than voting. *Fitzpatrick* was a gender-discrimination, class-action suit against the state of Connecticut brought on behalf of all of its current and retired male employees claiming discrimination in its state retirement benefit plan in violation of the 1972 amendments of Title VII of the Civil Rights Act of 1964. These amendments extended Title VII's coverage to the states and were enacted by a Congress that explicitly cited § 5 of the Fourteenth Amendment for its authority to do so. Speaking for a seven-member majority, then-Justice Rehnquist held that, under § 5 of the Fourteenth Amendment, Congress was authorized to make states liable for damages and attorneys' fees for unlawful employment discrimination. He declared: "[W]e think that the

Eleventh Amendment, and the principles of state sovereign immunity which it embodies, are necessarily limited by the enforcement provisions of § 5 of the Fourteenth Amendment. In that section Congress is expressly granted authority to enforce 'by appropriate legislation' the substantive provisions of the Fourteenth Amendment, which themselves embody significant limitations on state authority. When Congress acts pursuant to § 5, not only is it exercising legislative authority that is plenary within the terms of the constitutional grant, it is exercising that authority under one section of a constitutional Amendment whose other sections by their own terms embody limitations on state authority." Ibid., at 456. *Fitzpatrick* was decided prior to *Craig v. Boren*, 429 U.S. 190 (1976), in which the Court for the first time held that gender was a protected class in equal protection cases, and so *Fitzpatrick* is yet another case in which the Court held that Congress could use its enforcement powers under the post–Civil War amendments to bar conduct that the Court, based on its own interpretation of the relevant provision, could not have prohibited on its own.

198. 446 U.S. 156 (1980). In *City of Rome v. United States*, the Supreme Court held that Congress, under § 2 of the Fifteenth Amendment, could prohibit electoral schemes with discriminatory effects, even though, on the same day in *City of Mobile v. Bolden*, 446 U.S. 156 (1980), it held that such schemes do not of themselves violate the Fifteenth Amendment. Justice Thurgood Marshall wrote for a six-member majority when he declared that "under § 2 of the Fifteenth Amendment Congress may prohibit practices that in and of themselves do not violate § 1 of the Amendment, so long as the prohibitions attacking racial discrimination in voting are 'appropriate,' as that term is defined in *McCulloch v. Maryland* and *Ex Parte Virginia*." 446 U.S. at 177.

199. See Erwin Chemerinsky, "Reflections on *City of Boerne v. Flores*: The Religious Freedom Restoration Act Is a Constitutional Expansion of Rights," 39 *William and Mary Law Review* (February 1998): 601, 610. See also Frank B. Cross, "Institutions and Enforcement of the Bill of Rights," 85 *Cornell Law Review* (September 2000): 1529.

200. 529 U.S. 598 (2000).

201. It also held that Congress lacked power to enact VAWA under the Commerce Clause in Article I, § 8 of the Constitution, which Congress had also explicitly identified as the source of its authority. In his majority opinion, Chief Justice Rehnquist expressed concern that if the Court were to uphold Congress's authority under the Commerce Clause to enact VAWA, the result would be "to completely obliterate the Constitution's distinction between national and local authority." Ibid., at 615.

202. Ibid., at 621.

203. Ibid., at 627.

204. In *College Savings Bank v. Florida Prepaid Postsecondary Education Expense Board*, 527 U.S. 666 (1999), he wrote the majority opinion.

205. The Court found that Congress had exceeded its § 5 powers (in that its abrogation of state sovereign immunity was an excessive remedy not congruent and proportional to the injury caused by the states that Congress was seeking to prevent) in *Florida Prepaid Postsecondary Education Expense Board v. College Savings Bank*, in which Chief Justice Rehnquist concluded that there was no widespread state violation of the Patent Remedy Act of 1992 sufficient for Congress to enforce the Fourteenth Amendment's Due Process Clause by allowing states to be sued for patent violations; in *College Savings Bank v. Florida Prepaid Postsecondary Education Expense Board*, when Scalia declared that there was no property right under the Due Process Clause to be free from false advertising by a state for Congress to enforce and therefore no constitutional authorization for Congress to abrogate state sovereign immunity in the Trademark

Remedy Clarification Act; in *Kimel v. Florida Board of Regents*, when Justice O'Connor found insufficient evidence of age discrimination by the states for Congress to enforce the Fourteenth Amendment's Equal Protection Clause by subjecting states to suits filed by state employees for age discrimination in the Age Discrimination in Employment Act of 1967; and in *Trustees of the University of Alabama v. Garrett*, when Chief Justice Rehnquist followed O'Connor's argument in *Kimel* and held that there was insufficient evidence of states discriminating against disabled state employees for Congress to enforce the Equal Protection Clause by allowing suits in federal court by state employees seeking to recover money damages by reason of a state's failure to comply with the Title I of the Americans with Disabilities Act of 1990.

206. 538 U.S. 721 (2003).

207. 541 U.S. 509 (2004).

208. 538 U.S. at 736–37.

209. Ibid., at 741–42 (emphasis in original).

210. Ibid., at 742.

211. 541 U.S. at 526–27.

212. Ibid., at 531.

213. Ibid., at 532.

214. Ibid., at 533.

215. Ibid., at 555.

216. Ibid., at 556.

217. Ibid., at 557–58.

218. Ibid., at 558. At this juncture, Scalia quoted from his majority opinion in *Plaut v. Spendthrift Farm* that "low walls and vague distinctions will not be judicially defensible in the heat of interbranch conflict." 514 U.S. at 239.

219. 541 U.S. at 558–59 (emphasis in original). Scalia was not content to say only what the word *enforce* does not authorize; he offered a powerful example of what it does: "The Ku Klux Klan Act of April 20, 1871, 17 Stat. 13, entitled '*An Act to enforce the Provisions of the Fourteenth Amendment to the Constitution of the United States, and for other Purposes.*' § 1 of that Act, later codified as Rev. Stat. § 1979, 42 U.S.C. § 1983, authorized a cause of action against 'any person who, under color of any law, statute, ordinance, regulation, custom, or usage of any State, shall subject, or cause to be subjected, any person within the jurisdiction of the United States to the deprivation of any rights, privileges, or immunities secured by the Constitution of the United States.'" Ibid., at 559–60.

220. Ibid., at 560 (emphasis in original). "Giving § 5 more expansive scope with regard to measures directed against racial discrimination by the States accords to practices that are distinctively violative of the principal purpose of the Fourteenth Amendment a priority of attention that this Court envisioned from the beginning, and that has repeatedly been reflected in our opinions." Ibid., at 561.

221. Ibid., at 562–63.

222. Ibid., at 564. Citing *Hibbs*, he declared that he "would not, however, abandon the requirement that Congress may impose prophylactic § 5 legislation only upon those particular States in which there has been an identified history of relevant constitutional violations."

223. Ibid., at 565 (emphasis in original).

224. Scalia argued that "one does not 'enforce' the right of access to the courts at issue in this case by requiring that disabled persons be provided access to *all* of the 'services, programs, or activities' furnished or conducted by the State." Ibid., at 558. That argument, however, seems backward. The case in which to argue that Congress lacks the power to require the states to provide disabled persons with all such "services, programs, and activities" would be one in which the state is being sued for denying access to a service, program, or activity that has no connection to due process or equal protection.

225. *Senate Reports*, 103rd Cong., 1st sess., no. 111, p. 14 (emphasis added).

226. 491 U.S. at 42.

227. 501 U.S. at 788.

228. 541 U.S. at 518.

229. "In textual interpretation, context is everything, and the context of the Constitution tells us not to expect nit-picking detail, and to give words and phrases an expansive rather than narrow interpretation—though not an interpretation that the language will not bear." Antonin Scalia, *A Matter of Interpretation: Federal Courts and the Law* (Princeton, N.J.: Princeton University Press, 1997), p. 37.

230. As David Cole pointed out, § 5 simply does not say that Congress has power only to "provide remedies for constitutional violations identified by the courts"; rather, it says in much more expansive terms that Congress has the power to enforce, by "appropriate" means, the provisions of § 1. Cole continued: "Had the Framers [of the Fourteenth Amendment] sought to restrict Congress's power to remedial measures, they could have done so expressly." Cole, "The Value of Seeing Things Differently," p. 49.

231. Scalia, *A Matter of Interpretation*, p. 37.

232. 521 U.S. at 922.

Chapter Five. Scalia's Textualism Applied to Substantive Rights

1. *Hearings before the Committee on the Judiciary on the Nomination of Judge Antonin Scalia to Be Associate Justice of the Supreme Court of the United States*, Committee on the Judiciary, United States Senate, 99th Cong., 2d sess., J-99–119 (Washington, D.C.: Government Printing Office, 1987), p. 32. (Hereafter *Hearings on the Nomination of Scalia*.)

2. Alexander Hamilton, James Madison, and John Jay, *The Federalist*, edited by Jacob E. Cooke (New York: World Publishing, 1961), No. 51, p. 351.

3. *Hearings on the Nomination of Scalia*, p. 32.

4. Ibid.

5. *United States v. Virginia*, 518 U.S. 515, 568 (1996).

6. *Rutan v. Republican Party of Illinois*, 497 U.S. 62, 95 (1990).

7. *United States v. Virginia*, 518 U.S. at 568.

8. 495 U.S. 604, 627 (1990).

9. *Texas Monthly v. Bullock*, 489 U.S. 1, 42 (1989). This is obviously not the place to launch into an extended discussion of what Scalia has termed the *irrationality* of the Court's contemporary Religion Clause jurisprudence. Those interested in this subject should see ibid., at 45. See also chapter 6 in Ralph A. Rossum and G. Alan Tarr, *American Constitutional Law*, vol. 2, *The Bill of Rights and Subsequent Amendment*, 6th ed. (Belmont, Calif.: Wadsworth, 2003).

10. The language is from Scalia's judgment for the Court in *Capitol Square v. Pinette*, 515 U.S. 753, 768 (1995).

11. The Court made applicable to the states the Free Exercise Clause in *Cantwell v. Connecticut*, 310 U.S. 296 (1940), and the Establishment Clause in *Everson v. Board of Education*, 330 U.S. 1 (1947).

12. *Kiryas Joel v. Grumet*, 512 U.S. 687, 751 (1994).

13. For an excellent discussion of the full implications of a no privileges, no penalties approach to the Religion Clauses, see Vincent Phillip Muñoz, "Establishing Free Exercise," *First Things*, No. 138 (December 2003): 14–20. See also his "James Madison's Principle of Religious Liberty," *American Political Science Review* 97, no. 1 (February 2003): 17–32.

14. In *McCreary County v. ACLU of Kentucky*, 125 S. Ct. 2722 (2005), Scalia denied that governmental acknowledgment of a "single Creator" gave official status to monotheistic religions: "If religion in the public forum had to be entirely nondenominational, there could be no religion in the public forum at all. One cannot say the word 'God,' or 'the Almighty,' one cannot offer public supplication or thanksgiving, without contradicting the beliefs of some people that there are many gods, or that God or the gods

pay no attention to human affairs. With respect to public acknowledgment of religious belief, it is entirely clear from our Nation's historical practices that the Establishment Clause permits this disregard of polytheists and believers in unconcerned deities, just as it permits the disregard of devout atheists."

15. 512 U.S. at 748.

16. 505 U.S. 577, 641 (1992).

17. Because his colleagues have refused to read the Establishment Clause as narrowly as Scalia, he has been forced to defend tax exemptions for religions in general from Court majorities who see such exemptions as constituting an establishment of religion. See his dissent in *Texas Monthly v. Bullock*, 489 U.S. at 43: "[W]e have set our face against the subsidizing of religion—and in other contexts we have suggested that tax exemptions and subsidies are equivalent. We have not treated them as equivalent, however, in the Establishment Clause context, and with good reason. 'In the case of direct subsidy, the state forcibly diverts the income of both believers and nonbelievers to churches. In the case of an exemption, the state merely refrains from diverting to its own uses income independently generated by the churches through voluntary contributions.' In *Walz* [*v. Tax Commission of New York City*, 397 U.S. 664 (1990)], we pointed out that the *primary* effect of a tax exemption was not to sponsor religious activity but to 'restric[t] the fiscal relationship between church and state' and to 'complement and reinforce the desired separation insulating each from the other.' 397 U.S. at 676." Of course, given his view that nondiscriminatory aid to religion is perfectly constitutional, there is no reason to believe that he would not be willing to defend actual subsidies with the same conviction. See the Free Press Clause case of *Arkansas Writers' Project v. Ragland*, 481 U.S. 221, 236 (1987), where he made exactly that argument.

18. In the 2005 Ten Commandments case of *McCreary County v. ACLU of Kentucky*,

125 S. Ct. 2722, Scalia considered the "principle that government cannot favor religion over irreligion" to be "demonstrably false." For elaborations on this point, see Michael J. Malbin, *Religion and Politics: The Intentions of the Authors of the First Amendment* (Washington, D.C.: AEI Press, 1978), and Walter F. Berns, *The First Amendment and the Future of American Democracy* (New York: Basic Books, 1976).

19. 508 U.S. 384, 401 (1993).

20. See George Anastaplo, *The Amendments to the Constitution: A Commentary* (Baltimore, Md.: Johns Hopkins University Press, 1995), p. 57.

21. In fact, in *McCreary*, 125 S. Ct. 2722, Scalia actually criticized the view that "if one is serious about following the original understanding of the Establishment Clause, he must repudiate its incorporation into the Fourteenth Amendment, and hold that it does not apply against the States. This is more smoke." An indication that Scalia has not thought through the full implications of either the original understanding of the Establishment Clause or the incorporation doctrine is that he went on to say: "The notion that incorporation empties the incorporated provisions of their original meaning has no support in either reason or precedent."

22. The closest he has come to delivering the opinion of the Court in an Establishment Clause case is his judgment for the Court in *Capitol Square v. Pinette*, in which the Court held that Ohio's denial of an application by the Ku Klux Klan to display an unattended cross on the statehouse square was unjustified on the grounds that the permit would constitute an establishment of religion. Scalia was able to convince six other justices that private religious speech is protected under the Free Speech Clause of the First Amendment and that, although compliance with the Establishment Clause is a sufficiently compelling state interest to justify content-based restrictions on speech, Ohio's denial of the Klan's application to

display the cross on the statehouse square was not justified on that basis. He was able, however, to convince only three other justices as to his reasons: (1) governmental favoritism did not exist in the case at hand because Capitol Square was a genuinely public forum, was known to be a public forum, and had been widely used as a public forum for many years; (2) the state could not, on the claim of misperception of official endorsement, ban all private religious speech from the square or discriminate by requiring religious speech alone to disclaim public sponsorship; and (3) religious expression could not violate the Establishment Clause when that expression was purely private and occurred in a traditional or designated public forum that was publicly announced and open to all on equal terms. See 515 U.S. at 762–70. These arguments are far removed from his view expressed in *Kiryas Joel* that the Establishment Clause merely "prohibits the favoring of one religion over others." 512 U.S. at 748. Yet even these were regarded by a majority of the Court as too narrow a construction of what constitutes an establishment of religion.

23. 403 U.S. 602, 612–13 (1971).

24. *Kiryas Joel,* 512 U.S. at 748.

25. *Edwards v. Aguillard,* 482 U.S. 578, 613 (1987).

26. 508 U.S. 520, 558 (1993).

27. 482 U.S. at 610 (emphasis in original). See also Scalia's dissent in *Kiryas Joel,* 512 U.S. at 737: "I turn, next, to Justice Souter's second justification for finding an establishment of religion: his facile conclusion that the New York Legislature's creation of the Kiryas Joel school district was religiously motivated. But in the Land of the Free, democratically adopted laws are not so easily impeached by unelected judges."

28. 482 U.S. at 615. See also Scalia's criticisms of the Court's concern for legislative motivation in *Church of Lukumi Bababu Aye v. City of Hialeah,* 508 U.S. at 558–59.

29. *Lamb's Chapel,* 508 U.S. 384, 399 (1993). As Scalia noted in the Ten Command-

ments case of *McCreary,* 125 S. Ct. 2722, "As bad as the *Lemon* test is, it is worse for the fact that, since its inception, its seemingly simple mandates have been manipulated to fit whatever result the Court aimed to achieve."

30. 482 U.S. at 636.

31. 508 U.S. at 398–99.

32. 465 U.S. 668, 688 (1984).

33. Ibid., at 691.

34. Ibid., at 692.

35. For other cases employing the endorsement test, see *County of Allegheny v. American Civil Liberties Union, Greater Pittsburgh Chapter,* 492 U.S. 573 (1989); *Lamb's Chapel,* 508 U.S. 384 (1993); *Kiryas Joel,* 512 U.S. 687 (1994); and *Zelman v. Simmons-Harris,* 536 U.S. 639 (2002).

36. 508 U.S. at 400 (emphasis in original).

37. 515 U.S. at 772.

38. Ibid., at 764 (emphasis in original).

39. Ibid., at 767 (emphasis in original). See also his concurring opinion in *Good News Club v. Milford Central School,* 533 U.S. 98, 121 (2001).

40. 515 U.S. at 767 (emphasis in original).

41. Ibid., at 774.

42. 505 U.S. 577 (1992). Justices Stevens, Blackmun, O'Connor, and Souter also understood the prayer as constituting an unconstitutional official endorsement of religion.

43. 505 U.S. at 588, 593.

44. Ibid., at 633.

45. Ibid., at 633–35. Scalia rehearsed many of these same examples in his dissent in *McCreary,* 125 S. Ct. 2722.

46. 505 U.S. at 635.

47. Ibid., at 644. See also ibid., at 632: "Today's opinion shows more forcefully than volumes of argumentation why our Nation's protection, that fortress which is our Constitution, cannot possibly rest upon the changeable philosophical predilections of the Justices of this Court, but must have deep foundations in the historic practices of our people."

48. Ibid., at 641 (emphasis in original).

49. Ibid., at 642. See Scalia's concurring opinion in *Good News Club,* 533 U.S. at 121.

50. 505 U.S. at 632. Scalia clearly saw how the coercion test put at risk the phrase *under God* in the Pledge of Allegiance and thereby anticipated the legal controversy present in *Elk Grove Unified School District v. Newdow*, 524 U.S. 1 (2004), when he declared: "The opinion manifests that the Court itself has not given careful consideration to its test of psychological coercion. For if it had, how could it observe, with no hint of concern or disapproval, that students stood for the Pledge of Allegiance, which immediately preceded Rabbi Gutterman's invocation? Since the Pledge of Allegiance has been revised . . . to include the phrase 'under God,' recital of the Pledge would appear to raise the same Establishment Clause issue as the invocation and benediction. If students were psychologically coerced to remain standing during the invocation, they must also have been psychologically coerced, moments before, to stand for (and thereby, in the Court's view, take part in or appear to take part in) the Pledge. Must the Pledge therefore be barred from the public schools (both from graduation ceremonies and from the classroom)? Logically, that ought to be the next project for the Court's bulldozer." See 505 U.S. at 638–39.

Interestingly, however, when this issue reached the high court in *Newdow*, Scalia recused himself and took no part in the consideration or decision of the case. At a Religious Freedom Day event on January 12, 2003, in Fredericksburg, Virginia, he had spoken critically of the Ninth Circuit Court of Appeals decision that the pledge's reference to God turned daily recitations by public school children into an unconstitutional, state-sponsored religious ritual. He cited its decision as an example of what he considered mistaken attempts to "exclude God from the public forums and from political life"; see Charles Lane, "High Court to Consider Pledge in Schools; Scalia Recuses Himself from California Case," *Washington Post*, October 15, 2003, p. A01.Ultimately, a five-

member majority of the Court ducked the central constitutional question by concluding that Michael Newdow, noncustodial parent of the child on whose behalf he brought the suit, lacked standing to do so because Sandra Banning, the child's mother, had exclusive legal custody and because, as her daughter's sole legal custodian, she felt it was not in the child's best interest to be a party to Newdow's suit.

51. 505 U.S. at 636. Contrast Kennedy's use of psychology to ban religion from the public square with Scalia's understanding of the political utility of fostering religious observance: "The Founders of our Republic knew the fearsome potential of sectarian religious belief to generate civil dissension and civil strife. And they also knew that nothing, absolutely nothing, is so inclined to foster among religious believers of various faiths a toleration—no, an affection—for one another than voluntarily joining in prayer together, to the God whom they all worship and seek. Needless to say, no one should be compelled to do that, but it is a shame to deprive our public culture of the opportunity, and indeed the encouragement, for people to do it voluntarily. The Baptist or Catholic who heard and joined in the simple and inspiring prayers of Rabbi Gutterman on this official and patriotic occasion was inoculated from religious bigotry and prejudice in a manner that cannot be replicated. To deprive our society of that important unifying mechanism, in order to spare the nonbeliever what seems to me the minimal inconvenience of standing or even sitting in respectful nonparticipation, is as senseless in policy as it is unsupported in law." Ibid., at 646.

52. 494 U.S. 872 (1990).

53. Ibid., 877 (emphasis in original).

54. Ibid., at 878. Scalia added: "Our decisions reveal that [this] reading is the correct one. We have never held that an individual's religious beliefs excuse him from compliance with an otherwise valid law prohibiting

conduct that the State is free to regulate." In support of his claim, he cited *Reynolds v. United States*, 98 U.S. 145 (1879), where, he noted, "we rejected the claim that criminal laws against polygamy could not be constitutionally applied to those whose religion commanded the practice. 'Laws,' we said, 'are made for the government of actions, and while they cannot interfere with mere religious belief and opinions, they may with practices. . . . Can a man excuse his practices to the contrary because of his religious belief? To permit this would be to make the professed doctrines of religious belief superior to the law of the land, and in effect to permit every citizen to become a law unto himself.'" 494 U.S. at 878–79.

55. Ibid. Scalia did acknowledge one exception: "The only decisions in which we have held that the First Amendment bars application of a neutral, generally applicable law to religiously motivated action have involved not the Free Exercise Clause alone, but the Free Exercise Clause in conjunction with other constitutional protections, such as freedom of speech and of the press." Ibid., at 881.

56. 374 U.S. 398 (1963).

57. 494 U.S. at 884.

58. Ibid., at 891.

59. Ibid., at 885, 892.

60. Ibid., at 890.

61. Ibid., at 877.

62. 512 U.S. at 747.

63. Eighteenth Amendment (emphasis added).

64. 494 U.S. at 890.

65. 521 U.S. 507 (1997).

66. Ibid., at 546.

67. Ibid., at 544.

68. *Smith*, 494 U.S. at 890.

69. *U.S. v. Virginia*, 518 U.S. at 568.

70. *Smith*, 494 U.S. at 890.

71. Scalia seems to rule out any means for doing so short of a constitutional amendment, but he has never argued that the only way society can enhance the level of the rights of the people the government must

respect is by this difficult supermajoritarian process.

72. 540 U.S. 712 (2004).

73. Ibid., at 715.

74. 508 U.S. 520 (1993).

75. Ibid., at 546, 533.

76. 540 U.S. at 721.

77. Ibid., at 725.

78. 330 U.S. 1, 16 (1947).

79. 540 U.S. at 727. See also his concurrence in the judgment in *Lukumi*, in which he stressed that if a law "singles out a religious practice for special burdens," it is "invalid" even if the "legislature consists entirely of the purehearted." 508 U.S. at 559.

80. Rehnquist's words are found at 540 U.S. at 525.

81. Ibid., at 731 (emphasis in original).

82. Ibid., at 729. He also suggested another solution: "The State could also simply abandon the scholarship program altogether. If that seems a dear price to pay for freedom of conscience, it is only because the State has defined that freedom so broadly that it would be offended by a program with such an incidental, indirect religious effect." Ibid.

83. Ibid.

84. Ibid., at 730 (emphasis in original).

85. Ibid., at 733.

86. Ibid., at 734.

87. Ibid., at 730.

88. Ibid., at 734.

89. *McIntyre v. Ohio Elections Commission*, 514 U.S. 334, 378 (1995). Since tradition "cannot alter the core meaning of a constitutional guarantee," he argued in *McIntyre* that even flag burning is protected by the First Amendment: "Prohibition of expression of contempt for the flag, whether by contemptuous words or by burning the flag . . . [comes] within that 'bedrock principle.'" Ibid., at 377–78.

90. The words are from Scalia's combined dissenting opinion in *Board of County Commissioners, Wabaunsee County, Kansas v. Umbehr*, and *O'Hare Truck Service Inc. v. City of Northlake*, 518, U.S. 668, 700 (1996).

See also his opinion concurring in part and dissenting in part in *McConnell v. Federal Election Commission*, 540 U.S. 93, 786 (2003): "[T]he heart of what the First Amendment is meant to protect . . . [is] the right to criticize the government."

91. *Barnes v. Glen Theatre, Inc.*, 501 U.S. 560, 576 (1991). Justice Scalia concurred in the judgment.

92. 494 U.S. 872 (1990).

93. *Barnes*, 501 U.S. at 576, 579.

94. Ibid., at 577 (emphasis in original).

95. Because he limits the Free Speech and Press Clauses to "oral and written speech" traditionally covered by their protection and to conduct that can clearly be identified as having been undertaken for no other reason than to communicate an idea, he has refused to extend the First Amendment's full protections to commercial speech, which, he argues, does not involve the communication of an idea but merely "proposes a commercial transaction." See his opinion for the Court in *Board of Trustees of the State University of New York v. Fox*, 492 U.S. 469, 482 (1989). In his concurrence in the judgment in *44 Liquormart v. Rhode Island*, 517 U.S. 484, 517 (1996), he declared that he will accord commercial speech only the amount of protection that state legislatures accorded it "at the time the First Amendment was adopted, since almost all of the States had free speech constitutional guarantees of their own, whose meaning was not likely to have been different from the federal constitutional provision derived from them. Perhaps more relevant still are the state legislative practices at the time the Fourteenth Amendment was adopted, since it is most improbable that that adoption was meant to overturn any existing national consensus regarding free speech. Indeed, it is rare that any nationwide practice would develop contrary to a proper understanding of the First Amendment itself." For other opinions in which he makes clear that he is grounding his First Amendment jurisprudence not only in the text but also

in the traditional understanding of that text, see also *Rutan*, 497 U.S. 62, 103 (1990); *Barnes*, 501 U.S. at 573; *Burson v. Freeman*, 504 U.S. 191, 216 (1992); and *McIntyre*, 514 U.S. at 375.

96. *Republican Party of Minnesota v. White*, 536 U.S. 765, 774–75 (2002). Although Scalia uses the language of strict scrutiny because that has become standard practice for the Court, he clearly remains wedded to Justice Holmes's "clear and present danger" test. See his dissent in *Austin v. Michigan State Chamber of Commerce*, 494 U.S. 652, 689 (1990), and his majority opinion in *California Democratic Party v. Jones*, 530 U.S. 567, 578 (2000).

97. *Republican Party of Minnesota v. White*, 536 U.S. at 782. This view explains in part his opinion expressed in *McConnell v. FEC* that "this is a sad day for the freedom of speech." 540 U.S. at 720.

98. The rule did allow judicial candidates to make statements that were critical of past judicial decisions but only if they also declared that they embraced stare decisis and, if elected, would not seek to overturn what they considered erroneous decisions. 536 U.S. at 772.

99. Ibid., at 781 (emphasis in original).

100. Ibid., at 784.

101. Ibid., at 783.

102. Ibid., at 780.

103. See Scalia's dissent in *McConnell v. FEC*, 540 U.S. at 720.

104. *California Democratic Party v. Jones*, 530 U.S. 567.

105. 530 U.S. at 581–82 (emphasis in original). In this context, Scalia also referred to the parties' First Amendment "right of association," although it is clear that his principal concern in his opinion was the message that the state was compelling the parties to make or not make.

106. Ibid., at 586.

107. Ibid., at 585 (emphasis in original).

108. 540 U.S. at 720.

109. Ibid., at 721.

110. Ibid., at 722.

111. He quoted *Buckley v. Valeo*, 424 U.S. 1, 16 (1976): " 'This Court has never suggested that the dependence of a communication on the expenditure of money operates itself to introduce a nonspeech element or to reduce the exacting scrutiny required by the First Amendment.' " 540 U.S. at 722.

112. 540 U.S. at 722 (emphasis in original).

113. Ibid.

114. Ibid., at 723. As Scalia noted: "History and jurisprudence bear this out. The best early examples derive from the British efforts to tax the press after the lapse of licensing statutes by which the press was first regulated. The Stamp Act of 1712 imposed levies on all newspapers, including an additional tax for each advertisement. It was a response to unfavorable war coverage, 'obvious[ly] . . . designed to check the publication of those newspapers and pamphlets which depended for their sale on their cheapness and sensationalism.' It succeeded in killing off approximately half the newspapers in England in its first year. In 1765, Parliament applied a similar Act to the Colonies. The colonial Act likewise placed exactions on sales and advertising revenue, the latter at 2s. per advertisement, which was 'by any standard . . . excessive, since the publisher himself received only from 3 to 5s. and still less for repeated insertions.' " Ibid., at 722–23.

115. Ibid., at 724 (emphasis in original). As this passage makes abundantly clear, although Scalia agreed with that portion of the per curiam opinion in *Buckley v. Valeo* that invalidated the expenditure limitations of the Federal Election Campaign Act of 1971, he profoundly disagreed with that portion of the opinion affirming the act's contribution limitations. See ibid., at 720. See also his comments on that portion of the per curiam opinion in *Buckley* invalidating expenditure limitations in *Austin*, 494 U.S. at 683.

116. 540 U.S. at 724. To support this statement, Scalia referred to the Declaration of Independence (for only the ninth time in any of his opinions) and its conclusion that "for the support of this Declaration, . . . we mutually pledge to each other our Lives, *our Fortunes* and our sacred Honor." Ibid. (emphasis in original).

117. Ibid., at 725.

118. Ibid.

119. 435 U.S. 765, 776–77 (1978), quoted in *McConnell*, 540 U.S. at 725. Scalia could have quoted James Madison in *Federalist* No. 40 to the same effect: "The prudence inquiry in all cases, ought surely to be not so much *from whom* the advice comes, as whether the advice be *good*." *The Federalist*, No. 40, p. 267 (emphasis in original).

120. 494 U.S. 652 (1990).

121. Ibid., at 693–94.

122. 540 U.S. at 725–26.

123. Ibid., at 726 (emphasis in original).

124. Ibid.

125. Ibid., at 728.

126. 494 U.S. at 679.

127. 540 U.S. at 726 (emphasis in original). Scalia also noted that a report prepared for Congress concluded that the total amount, in hard and soft money, spent on the 2000 federal elections was between $2.4 and $2.5 billion and that other studies determined that all campaign spending in the United States, including for state elections, ballot initiatives, and judicial elections, amounted to $3.9 billion for 2000. This prompted him to remark: "Even taking this last, larger figure as the benchmark, it means that Americans spent about half as much electing all their Nation's officials, state and federal, as they spent on movie tickets ($7.8 billion); about a fifth as much as they spent on cosmetics and perfume ($18.8 billion); and about a sixth as much as they spent on pork (the nongovernmental sort) ($22.8 billion). If our democracy is drowning from this much spending, it cannot swim." Ibid., at 728.

128. Ibid., at 726 (emphasis in original). In *Austin*, Scalia noted what logically should follow from the Court's willingness to uphold

restrictions on speech if it "has the mere *potential* for producing social harm": "The principle the Court abandons today—that the mere potential for harm does not justify a restriction upon speech—had its origin in the 'clear and present danger' test devised by Justice Holmes in 1919 and championed by him and Justice Brandeis over the next decade in a series of famous opinions opposing the affirmance of convictions for subversive speech. The Court finally adopted their view in 1937. Today's reversal of field will require adjustment of a fairly large number of significant First Amendment holdings. Presumably the State may now convict individuals for selling books found to have a potentially harmful influence on minors, ban indecent telephone communications that have the potential for reaching minors, restrain the press from publishing information that has the potential for jeopardizing a criminal defendant's right to a fair trial or the potential for damaging the reputation of the subject of an investigation, compel publication of the membership lists of organizations that have a potential for illegal activity, and compel an applicant for bar membership to reveal her political beliefs and affiliations to eliminate the potential for subversive activity." 494 U.S. at 689 (emphasis in original). Scalia repeated this concern in *McConnell* when he argued that the Court, in the name of "fairness," had abandoned "most of its First Amendment weaponry," leaving it "even less equipped to resist" future efforts by Congress to restrict speech. 540 U.S. at 729.

129. Ibid., at 726 (emphasis in original).

130. Ibid., at 727.

131. Scalia, of course, recognizes that free speech is subject to the restrictions of content-neutral time, manner, and place regulations. See his unanimous opinion for the Court in *Thomas v. Chicago Park District*, 534 U.S. 316 (1002). He also has written opinions proclaiming that the Free Speech and Press Clauses allow a grand jury witness to make public "what he knew before he

entered the grand jury room," "even while the grand jury is sitting," *Butterworth v. Smith*, 494 U.S. 624, 636 (1990); protect "the solicitation of money by charities" as fully as they protect "the dissemination of ideas," *Riley v. National Federation of the Blind of North Carolina*, 487 U.S. 781, 803 (1988); bar laws allowing for civil judgments against newspapers that publish the names of victims of sexual offenses, *Florida Star v. B.J.F.*, 491 U.S. 524, 542 (1989); and protect nonunion members from paying union fees "for any expenses except those incurred for the conduct of activities in which the union owes a duty of fair representation to the nonmembers being charged," *Lehnert v. Ferris Faculty Association*, 500 U.S. 507, 558 (1991).

132. *Hill v. Colorado*, 530 U.S. 703, 750 (2000).

133. Ibid., at 742. See also Scalia's dissents in *Madsen v. Women's Health Center, Inc.*, 512 U.S. 753, 785 (1994), and *Schenck v. Pro-choice Network of Western New York*, 519 U.S. 357, 386 (1997). See also his concurrence in the Court's decision to deny a petition for a writ of certiorari in *Lawson v. Murray*, 525 U.S. 955 (1998): "I believe that what New Jersey has approved here makes a mockery of First Amendment law."

134. 530 U.S. at 741. Scalia has consistently opposed the Court's abortion jurisprudence. For present purposes, his view, discussed at greater length in Chapter Six, is well captured in the following passage from his dissent in *Planned Parenthood v. Casey*, 505 U.S. 833 (1992): "My views on this matter are unchanged from those I set forth in my separate opinions in *Webster v. Reproductive Health Services*, 492 U.S. 490, 532 (1989), and *Ohio v. Akron Center for Reproductive Health*, 497 U.S. 502, 520 (1990). The States may, if they wish, permit abortion on demand, but the Constitution does not *require* them to do so. The permissibility of abortion, and the limitations upon it, are to be resolved like most important questions in

our democracy: by citizens trying to persuade one another and then voting. . . . [T]he issue in these cases [is] whether [the power of a woman to abort her unborn child] is a liberty protected by the Constitution of the United States. I am sure it is not. I reach that conclusion . . . because of two simple facts: (1) the Constitution says absolutely nothing about it, and (2) the longstanding traditions of American society have permitted it to be legally proscribed." Ibid., at 980 (emphasis in original).

135. 530 U.S. 703.

136. Ibid., at 723.

137. Ibid., at 742 (emphasis in original).

138. Ibid., at 744 (emphasis in original).

139. 530 U.S. at 748–49.

140. 277 U.S. 438, 478 (1928).

141. 530 U.S. at 716–17.

142. Ibid., at 753.

143. Ibid., at 751 (emphasis in original). See also his dissent in *Schenck*, 519 U.S. at 386. Later in his opinion in *Hill*, Scalia explained the importance of "the right of the speaker in the public forum to be free from government interference of the sort Colorado has imposed here": "The possibility of limiting abortion by legislative means—even abortion of a live-and-kicking child that is almost entirely out of the womb—has been rendered impossible by our decisions from *Roe v. Wade* to *Stenberg v. Carhart*. For those who share an abiding moral or religious conviction (or, for that matter, simply a biological appreciation) that abortion is the taking of a human life, there is no option but to persuade women, one by one, not to make that choice. And as a general matter, the most effective place, if not the only place, where that persuasion can occur, is outside the entrances to abortion facilities. By upholding these restrictions on speech in this place the Court ratifies the State's attempt to make even that task an impossible one." 530 U.S. at 763.

144. Ibid., at 748–49.

145. *R.A.V. v. City of St. Paul*, 505 U.S. 377, 383 (1992).

146. Ibid., at 386.

147. Ibid., at 381.

148. Ibid., at 382–83.

149. Ibid., at 384 (emphasis in original).

150. Ibid., at 386.

151. Ibid., at 391.

152. Ibid., at 392.

153. Ibid., at 396. As Scalia remarked, "The point of the First Amendment is that majority preferences must be expressed in some fashion other than silencing speech on the basis of its content."

154. Ibid., at 396. In *Virginia v. Black*, 538 U.S. 343, 369 (2003), Scalia joined the Court majority in holding that a state, consistent with the First Amendment, may ban cross burning carried out with the intent to intimidate. Unlike the city ordinance at issue in *R.A.V.*, the Virginia statute did not single out for opprobrium only that speech directed toward "one of the specified disfavored topics." The statute banned cross burning whether undertaken to intimidate because of the victim's race, gender, or religion or undertaken because of the victim's political affiliation, union membership, or homosexuality. Justice O'Connor argued for the Court majority on this point, and Scalia agreed, that "a ban on cross burning carried out with the intent to intimidate is fully consistent with our holding in *R.A.V.* and is proscribable under the First Amendment, for just as a State may regulate only that obscenity which is the most obscene due to its prurient content, so, too, a State may choose to prohibit only those forms of intimidation that are most likely to inspire fear of bodily harm." See 538 U.S. at 363.

155. Scalia's combined dissent in *Umbehr* and *O'Hare Truck Service Inc.*, 518 U.S. at 699.

156. 497 U.S. 62 (1990).

157. 427 U.S. 347 (1976).

158. 445 U.S. 507 (1980).

159. 497 U.S. at 110. He observed the irony of federal courts' enforcing a ban on patronage hiring: "If there is any category of jobs

for whose performance party affiliation is not an appropriate requirement, it is the job of being a judge, where partisanship is not only unneeded but positively undesirable. It is, however, rare that a federal administration of one party will appoint a judge from another party. And it has always been rare. Thus, the new principle that the Court today announces will be enforced by a corps of judges (the Members of this Court included) who overwhelmingly owe their office to its violation. Something must be wrong here, and I suggest it is the Court." Ibid., at 92–93.

160. 518 U.S. 668 (1996).

161. 518 U.S. at 712 (1996).

162. Ibid., at 710 (emphasis in original).

163. Ibid., at 687.

164. 497 U.S. at 94.

165. See, for example, *Public Workers v. Mitchell*, 330 U.S. 75 (1947); *Civil Service Commission v. Letter Carriers*, 413 U.S. 548 (1973); and *Broadrick v. Oklahoma*, 413 U.S. 601, 616–17 (1973).

166. 497 U.S. at 95.

167. Ibid., at 99.

168. 518 U.S. at 700.

169. Ibid., at 688.

170. 497 U.S. at 102 (emphasis in original). Tradition also explains why Scalia concurred in the judgment in *Burson*, 504 U.S. 191 (1992), when the Court rejected a First Amendment challenge to a Tennessee statute that prohibited solicitation of votes and display or distribution of campaign literature within 100 feet of the entrance to a polling place: "[T]he environs of a polling place, on election day, are simply not a 'traditional public forum'—which means that they are subject to speech restrictions that are reasonable and viewpoint neutral." Ibid., at 215. "The widespread and longstanding traditions of our people" also explains why he dissented from the Court's decision in *McIntyre* striking down, on First Amendment grounds, an Ohio statute banning distribution of anonymous campaign literature: "A governmental

practice that has become general throughout the United States, and particularly one that has the validation of long, accepted usage, bears a strong presumption of constitutionality." 514 U.S. at 375.

171. 497 U.S. at 104–08. In his combined dissent in *Umbehr* and *O'Hare Truck Services*, Scalia continued on the theme of social integration, this time in the context of government contracting: "The ability to discourage eccentric views through the mild means that have historically been employed, and that the Court has now set its face against, may well be important to social cohesion. To take an uncomfortable example from real life: An organization (I shall call it the White Aryan Supremacist Party, though that was not the organization involved in the actual incident I have in mind) is undoubtedly entitled, under the Constitution, to maintain and propagate racist and antisemitic views. But when the Department of Housing and Urban Development lets out contracts to private security forces to maintain law and order in units of public housing, must it really treat this bidder the same as all others? Or may it determine that the views of this organization are not political views that it wishes to 'subsidize' with public funds, nor political views that it wishes to hold up as an exemplar of the law to the residents of public housing?" 518 U.S. at 700.

172. 497 U.S. at 110.

173. 524 U.S. 569 (1998).

174. Ibid., at 590.

175. Ibid., at 523.

176. Ibid., at 595.

177. Ibid., at 595–96 (emphasis in original).

178. As Scalia noted, Karen Finley, the plaintiff, had sought NEA funding for her "controversial show, 'We Keep Our Victims Ready,'" in which she "visually recounts a sexual assault by stripping to the waist and smearing chocolate on her breasts and by using profanity to describe the assault." Ibid., at 596.

179. As an example, see Scalia's opinion for the Court in *Johanns v. Livestock Marketing*

Association, 125 S. Ct. 2055 (2005), in which he held that the federal policy of promoting and marketing beef and beef products by imposing an assessment, or "checkoff," on all sales and importation of cattle by members of the Livestock Marketing Association did not unconstitutionally compel respondents to subsidize speech to which they objected. The beef checkoff funded the government's own speech, he argued, and therefore was not susceptible to a First Amendment compelled-subsidy challenge. "'Compelled support of government'—even those programs of government one does not approve—is of course perfectly constitutional, as every taxpayer must attest. And some government programs involve, or entirely consist of, advocating a position. 'The government, as a general rule, may support valid programs and policies by taxes or other exactions binding on protesting parties. Within this broader principle it seems inevitable that funds raised by the government will be spent for speech and other expression to advocate and defend its own policies.' We have generally assumed . . . that compelled funding of government speech does not alone raise First Amendment concerns." Ibid., at 2062.

180. Ibid., at 598. See also his dissent in *Legal Services Corporation v. Velazquez,* in which the Court held unconstitutional, on First Amendment grounds, a congressional restriction on the Legal Services Corporation (LSC) from funding any organization that represented clients in efforts to amend or otherwise challenge existing welfare laws. "The LSC Act is a federal subsidy program, not a federal regulatory program, and there is a basic difference between the two. Regulations directly restrict speech; subsidies do not." 531 U.S. 533, 552 (2001).

181. For Scalia, the classic example of conduct that is undertaken for no other reason than to communicate an idea is flag burning: "'If there is a bedrock principle underlying the First Amendment, it is that the govern-

ment may not prohibit the expression of an idea simply because society finds the idea itself offensive or disagreeable.' Prohibition of expression of contempt for the flag, whether by contemptuous words or by burning the flag, come within this 'bedrock principle.'" *McIntyre,* 514 U.S. at 378.

182. *Barnes v. Glen Theatre,* 501 U.S. at 572. See his similar arguments in his concurrences in the judgment in *City of Erie v. PAP's,* 529 U.S. 277, 310 (2000), and in *Watchtower Bible and Tract Society of New York v. Village of Stratton,* 536 U.S. 150, 223 (2002).

183. 501 U.S. at 576 (emphasis in original).

184. Ibid., at 577 (emphasis in original). As mentioned earlier, he declared that "[w]e have explicitly adopted such a regime in another First Amendment context: that of free exercise. In *Employment Division, Department of Human Resources of Oregon v. Smith* (1990), we held that general laws not specifically targeted at religious practices did not require heightened First Amendment scrutiny even though they diminished some people's ability to practice their religion." *Barnes,* 501 U.S. at 579.

185. Ibid., at 580. Scalia has defended prohibitions of certain conduct simply on the basis of morality: "Our society prohibits, and all human societies have prohibited, certain activities not because they harm others but because they are considered, in the traditional phrase, 'contra bonos mores,' i.e., immoral. In American society, such prohibitions have included, for example, sadomasochism, cockfighting, bestiality, suicide, drug use, prostitution, and sodomy. While there may be great diversity of view on whether various of these prohibitions should exist (though I have found few ready to abandon, in principle, all of them), there is no doubt that, absent specific constitutional protection for the conduct involved, the Constitution does not prohibit them simply because they regulate 'morality.'" Ibid., at 575. See also his dissent in *Lawrence v. Texas,* 539 U.S. 558, 599 (2003).

186. In *R.A.V. v. City of St. Paul*, 505 U.S. at 382–83, Scalia declared that the First Amendment permits restrictions on obscenity because it is "'of such slight social value as a step to truth that any benefit that may be derived from [it] is clearly outweighed by the social interest in order and morality.'"

187. *FW/PBS, Inc. v. Dallas*, 493 U.S. 215, 253 (1990). He has also called it "the business of obscenity," *United States v. Playboy Entertainment Group*, 529 U.S. 803, 831 (2000), and "pornographic commerce," *United States v. X-Citement Video, Inc.*, 513 U.S. 64, 85 (1994).

188. *Playboy Entertainment Group, Inc.*, 529 U.S. at 831.

189. 493 U.S. at 251–64. His concurrence in the judgment in *City of Littleton v. Z. J. Gifts*, 124 S. Ct. 2219, 2226 (2004), and his dissent in *Ashcroft v. American Civil Liberties Union*, 124 S. Ct. 2783, 2797 (2004), are little more than citations to his *FW/PBS* dissent.

190. 493 U.S. at 259.

191. Ibid., at 256.

192. Ibid., at 253.

193. Ibid., at 260.

194. 383 U.S. 463, 470 (1966).

195. 529 U.S. at 835.

196. Ibid., at 832.

197. Ibid., at 831.

198. 98 U.S. 403, 406 (1879).

199. 32 U.S. 243 (1833).

200. 166 U.S. 226 (1887).

201. Ibid., at 236–37.

202. 260 U.S. 393, 415 (1922).

203. 438 U.S. 104, 124 (1978).

204. Ibid., at 136.

205. 458 U.S. 419 (1982). In that case, the Supreme Court held that a New York statute requiring landlords to allow television cable companies to install cable facilities in their apartment buildings constituted a taking, even though the facilities occupied no more than 1.5 cubic feet of the landlords' property.

206. 447 U.S. 255, 260 (1980).

207. Ibid.

208. 483 U.S. 825 (1987).

209. 485 U.S. 1, 21 (1988).

210. 505 U.S. 1003 (1992).

211. Ibid., at 1057–58.

212. Ibid., at 1028, n. 15. Such a reading is "consistent with the historical compact recorded in the Takings Clause that has become part of our constitutional culture." Ibid.

213. *Pennell*, 485 U.S. at 22.

214. 483 U.S. at 841–42.

215. Ibid., at 837 (emphasis added).

216. 485 U.S. at 21.

217. Ibid., at 22.

218. Ibid., at 23. This is necessary to prevent what he called, in *Brown v. Legal Foundation of Washington*, 538 U.S. 216, 252 (2003), a "Robin Hood Taking."

219. Since *Bolling v. Sharpe*, 347 U.S. 497 (1954), the Court has formally recognized an equal protection component in the Fifth Amendment's Due Process Clause and has held the federal government to the same standards as the states. In Chief Justice Earl Warren's words in *Bolling*, "The Fifth Amendment, which is applicable in the District of Columbia, does not contain an equal protection clause as does the Fourteenth Amendment which applies only to the states. But the concepts of equal protection and due process, both stemming from our American ideal of fairness, are not mutually exclusive. The 'equal protection of the laws' is a more explicit safeguard of prohibited unfairness than 'due process of law,' and, therefore, we do not imply that the two are always interchangeable phrases. But, as this Court has recognized, discrimination may be so unjustifiable as to be violative of due process." Ibid., at 499.

220. 83 U.S. 36, 81 (1873).

221. 347 U.S. 483 (1954).

222. 497 U.S. at 95, n. 1 (1990) (emphasis in original).

223. In *Croson*, 488 U.S. 469, 521 (1989), Scalia had declared that "only a social emergency rising to the level of imminent danger to life and limb—for example, a prison race

riot, requiring temporary segregation of inmates—can justify an exception to the principle embodied in the Fourteenth Amendment that '[o]ur Constitution is color-blind, and neither knows nor tolerates classes among citizens,' *Plessy v. Ferguson*, 163 U.S. 537, 559 (1896) (Harlan, J., dissenting)."

224. Harlan argued in *Plessy* that "[t]he Thirteenth Amendment does not permit the withholding or the deprivation of any right necessarily inhering in freedom. It not only struck down the institution of slavery as previously existing in the United States, but it prevents the imposition of any burdens or disabilities that constitute badges of slavery or servitude. It decreed universal civil freedom in this country. . . . But that amendment having been found inadequate to the protection of the rights of those who had been in slavery, it was followed by the Fourteenth Amendment. . . . These two amendments, if enforced according to their true intent and meaning, will protect all the civil rights that pertain to freedom and citizenship." 163 U.S. at 555.

225. 109 U.S. 3, 20 (1883).

226. 392 U.S. 409, 424 (1968).

227. Although see *Croson*, 488 U.S. at 528: "The relevant proposition is not that it was blacks, or Jews, or Irish who were discriminated against, but that it was individual men and women, 'created equal,' who were discriminated against."

228. 515 U.S. 200, 240 (1995). Thomas declared in his concurrence in the judgment in that case that "[t]here can be no doubt that the paternalism that appears to lie at the heart of this program is at war with the principle of inherent equality that underlies and infuses our Constitution. See Declaration of Independence ('We hold these truths to be self-evident, that all men are created equal, that they are endowed by their Creator with certain unalienable Rights, that among these are Life, Liberty, and the pursuit of Happiness')."

229. *Rutan*, 497 U.S. at 95, n. 1. He is therefore able to avoid the intellectual complications confronted by those other originalists who argue that the drafters of the Fourteenth Amendment did not intend to prohibit segregated schools. See, for example, Raoul Berger, *Government by Judiciary: The Transformation of the Fourteenth Amendment* (Cambridge, Mass.: Harvard University Press, 1977), pp. 177–83; Robert H. Bork, *The Tempting of America: The Political Seduction of the Law* (New York: Free Press, 1990), pp. 74–84; and Lino A. Graglia, " 'Interpreting' the Constitution: Posner on Bork," 44 *Stanford Law Review* (May 1922): 1019, 1037–43.

230. 488 U.S. at 520.

231. 515 U.S. at 239.

232. Ibid. (emphasis in original). Scalia had previously made the same point in *Croson*, 488 U.S. at 520–21: "The difficulty of overcoming the effects of past discrimination is as nothing compared with the difficulty of eradicating from our society the source of those effects, which is the tendency—fatal to a Nation such as ours—to classify and judge men and women on the basis of their country of origin or the color of their skin. A solution to the first problem that aggravates the second is no solution at all." See also his dissenting language in *Johnson v. Santa Clara County*, 480 U.S. 616, 668 (1987).

233. 488 U.S. at 524. See also ibid., at 528: "Racial preferences appear to 'even the score' (in some small degree) only if one embraces the proposition that our society is appropriately viewed as divided into races, making it right that an injustice rendered in the past to a black man should be compensated for by discriminating against a white. Nothing is worth that embrace." See also Antonin Scalia, "The Disease's Cure: 'In Order to Get Beyond Racism, We Must First Take Account of Race,' " 1979 *Washington University Law Quarterly* (1979): 146–57.

234. Ibid., at 524 (emphasis in original). Although Scalia did not address the question whether the state can provide back pay for these employees, his comments in his con-

curring opinion in *Freeman v. Pitts*, 503 U.S. 467, 506 (1992), make it clear that he believes the state both can and must: "[W]e must continue to prohibit, without qualification, all racial discrimination in the operation of public schools, and to afford remedies that eliminate not only the discrimination but its identified consequences."

This need "to eliminate their own maintenance of a system of unlawful racial classification," *Croson*, 488 U.S. at 524, also explains Scalia's defense of "our school desegregation cases, in which we have made plain that States and localities sometimes have an obligation to adopt race conscious remedies." *Freeman*, 503 U.S. at 506. However, the longer these race-conscious remedies remain in place, the less Scalia is willing to defend them. As he remarked in *Freeman*: "At some time, we must acknowledge that it has become absurd to assume, without any further proof, that violations of the Constitution dating from the days when Lyndon Johnson was President, or earlier, continue to have an appreciable effect upon the current operation of schools. We are close to that time. . . . [W]e . . . must soon revert to the ordinary principles of our law, of our democratic heritage, and of our educational tradition." Ibid. What are those "ordinary principles of our law" in such a case? Scalia alluded to them in *Freeman*, and two months later in his dissenting opinion in *United States v. Fordice*, 505 U.S. 717, 757 (1992), he laid them out expressly: for public schools, no less than for public universities, "the standard for dismantling a dual system [as announced by the Court in *Bazemore v. Friday*, 478 U.S. 385, 395–96 (1986),] ought to control here: discontinuation of discriminatory practices and adoption of a neutral admissions policy."

235. 488 U.S. at 526.

236. Ibid., at 528.

237. 539 U.S. 306, 347–48 (emphasis in original). As Scalia declared, "The Constitution proscribes government discrimination on the basis of race, and state-provided education is no exception." Ibid., at 349.

238. *Rutan*, 497 U.S. at 95.

239. 511 U.S. 127, 159 (1994). See also his dissents in *Edmonson v. Leesville Concrete Co.*, 500 U.S. 614, 644–45 (1991), and *Georgia v. McCollum*, 505 U.S. 42, 69 (1992).

240. *United States v. Virginia*, 518 U.S. at 570.

241. Ibid., at 568.

242. Ibid., at 569. See his dissent *in Romer v. Evans*, 517 U.S. 620, 641 (1996). The Constitution, he insisted, does not "change to suit current fashions."

243. 518 U.S. at 568 (emphasis in original).

244. As he declared in *United States v. Virginia*, 518 U.S. at 567: "Since it is entirely clear that the Constitution of the United States—the old one—takes no sides in this educational debate, I dissent."

245. Ibid., at 569.

246. In *Romer v. Evans*, he noted: "The only denial of equal treatment it contends homosexuals have suffered is this: They may not obtain *preferential* treatment without amending the state constitution. That is to say, the principle underlying the Court's opinion is that one who is accorded equal treatment under the laws, but cannot as readily as others obtain *preferential* treatment under the laws, has been denied equal protection of the laws. If merely stating this alleged 'equal protection' violation does not suffice to refute it, our constitutional jurisprudence has achieved terminal silliness." 517 U.S. 638–39 (emphasis in original).

247. Ibid., at 636.

248. Ibid., at 653.

249. *Lawrence v. Texas*, 539 U.S. 558, 601 (2003). He stated, "Even if the Texas law *does* deny equal protection to 'homosexuals as a class,' that denial *still* does not need to be justified by anything more than a rational basis, which our cases show is satisfied by the enforcement of traditional notions of sexual morality" (emphasis in original).

250. Ibid., at 599.

251. Ibid., at 603–4.

252. *Romer*, 517 U.S. at 648 (emphasis in original).

253. Ibid., at 652.

254. *Lawrence*, 539 U.S. at 604–5 (emphasis in original). Scalia's prediction came to pass only a few months later, albeit at the state level. In *Goodridge v. Department of Public Health*, 440 Mass. 309; 798 N.E.2d 941 (2003), the Supreme Judicial Court of Massachusetts repeatedly cited *Lawrence* in its majority opinion declaring that the Massachusetts Constitution forbids the Commonwealth from denying the protections, benefits, and obligations conferred by civil marriage to two individuals of the same sex who wish to marry.

255. Ibid., at 604.

256. *United States v. Virginia*, 518 U.S. at 567.

257. Ibid., at 600.

258. *Michael H. v. Gerald D.*, 491 U.S. 110, 122 (1989).

259. *United States v. Virginia*, 518 U.S. at 568.

260. 539 U.S. at 599.

261. *United States v. Virginia*, 518 U.S. at 570.

262. Ibid., at 579.

263. 539 U.S. at 590, 603.

264. 501 U.S. 597, 621 (1991).

265. *United States v. Virginia*, 518 U.S. at 570.

266. "Transcript of Discussion between U.S. Supreme Court Justices Antonin Scalia and Stephen Breyer," American University, Washington College of Law, January 13, 2005, p. 33.

267. *McNeil v. Wisconsin*, 501 U.S. 171, 182 (1991).

Chapter Six. Scalia's Textualism Applied to Procedural Rights

1. 518 U.S. 515, 568 (1996).

2. See Ralph A. Rossum and G. Alan Tarr, *American Constitutional Law*, vol. 2, *The Bill of Rights and Subsequent Amendment*, 6th ed. (Belmont, Calif.: Wadsworth, 2003), pp. 48–65.

3. *United States v. Carlton*, 512 U.S. 26, 40 (1994). Scalia concurred in the judgment.

4. 495 U.S. 604, 623 (1990).

5. The language is from Scalia's dissent in *Shafer v. South Carolina*, 532 U.S. 36, 55 (2001). See also his opinion for the Court in *Sullivan v. Louisiana*, 508 U.S. 275, 278 (1993).

6. 499 U.S. 1, 28 (1991).

7. Ibid., at 31 (emphasis in original). See also Scalia's opinions for the Court in *Griffin v. United States*, 502 U.S. 46, 51 (1991), and *United States v. Gaudin*, 515 U.S. 506, 518 (1995); his concurrence in *Cruzan v. Director, Missouri Department of Health*, 497 U.S. 261, 294 (1990); and his concurrence in the judgment in *Schad v. Arizona*, 501 U.S. 624, 650 (1991).

8. See, for example, his judgment for the Court in *Montana v. Egelhoff*, 518 U.S. 37, 48 (1996): "The burden remains upon the respondent to show that the 'new common-law' rule [in this case, that intoxication must be considered by the jury as a matter of criminal intent] was so deeply rooted at the time of the Fourteenth Amendment . . . as to be a fundamental principle which that Amendment enshrined." See also his opinion for the Court in *Sun Oil v. Wortman*, 486 U.S. 717, 730 (1988): "Here again neither the tradition in place when the constitutional provision was adopted, nor subsequent practice supports the contention."

9. *Pacific Mutual Life Insurance Co. v. Haslip*, 499 U.S. at 31. See Scalia's opinion for the Court in *Reno v. Flores*, 507 U.S. 292, 303 (1993). The question before the justices was whether regulations of the Immigration and Naturalization Service that allowed the release of alien juveniles detained pending deportation hearings only to their parents or other close relatives denied these juveniles due process of law. The Ninth Circuit Court of Appeals said yes, but the Supreme Court

said no, and Scalia explained why: "We are unaware, however, that any court—aside from the courts below—has ever held that a child has a constitutional right not to be placed in a decent and humane custodial institution if there is available a responsible person unwilling to become the child's legal guardian but willing to undertake temporary legal custody. The mere novelty of such a claim is reason enough to doubt that 'substantive due process' sustains it; the alleged right certainly cannot be considered 'so rooted in the traditions and conscience of our people as to be ranked as fundamental.'"

10. In his judgment for the Court in *Michael H. v. Gerald D.*, 491 U.S. 110, 127, n. 6 (1989), Scalia also limits the Due Process Clauses to "the most specific level at which a relevant tradition protecting, or denying protection to, the asserted right can be identified." The issue in this case was whether California's law, under which a child born to a married woman living with her husband is presumed to be the child of the marriage, infringed on the due process rights of a man who wished to establish his paternity of a child born to the wife of another man. General traditions regarding parenthood provided, Scalia noted, "imprecise guidance" and allowed Justice Brennan to "dictate rather than discern the society's views." Ibid. The "most specific tradition available," ibid., however, protected "the marital family," ibid., at 124, and "unqualifiedly denie[d] protection" to "the rights of the natural father of a child adulterously conceived." Ibid., at 127, n. 6. On that basis, Scalia affirmed the constitutionality of California's law as consistent with the traditional "aversion of declaring children illegitimate" and the traditional "interest in promoting the 'peace and tranquility of states and families,' a goal that is obviously impaired by facilitating suits against husband and wife asserting that their children are illegitimate." Ibid., at 125.

11. *Haslip*, 499 U.S. at 38.

12. Ibid., at 32. Moreover, he is willing to concede that if most state legislatures come to protect statutorily a right that has not been traditionally protected by the Due Process Clauses, this right becomes part of a new tradition and is subject to judicial protection. As he acknowledged in his judgment for the Court in *Egelhoff*, 518 U.S. at 51, if a right comes to receive "sufficiently uniform and permanent allegiance" from the states, it then "qualifies" as "fundamental" and "displaces the lengthy common law tradition." His standard, however, for what constitutes "the uniform and continuing acceptance we would expect for a rule that enjoys 'fundamental principle' status" is high. In *Egelhoff*, he observed that "fully one-fifth of the states either never adopted the 'new common-law' rule at issue here or have recently abandoned it." Ibid., at 48. See also Scalia's dissent in *Simmons v. South Carolina*, 512 U.S. 154, 180 (1994): "[T]he parties and their *amici* point to only 10 States that arguably employ the procedure which, according to today's opinions, the Constitution requires. This picture of national practice falls far short of demonstrating a principle so widely shared that it is part of even a current and temporary American consensus."

13. See Scalia's dissent in *Lawrence v. Texas*, 539 U.S. 558, 603–4 (2003): "But it is the premise of our system that those judgments are to be made by the people, and not imposed by a governing caste that knows best."

14. *Weiss v. United States*, 510 U.S. 163, 197 (1994).

15. *Rutan v. Republican Party*, 497 U.S. 62, 95 (1990).

16. 532 U.S. 451 (2001).

17. Ibid., at 471.

18. Ibid., at 466.

19. Ibid., at 467–68.

20. Ibid., at 468.

21. Ibid., at 471.

22. Ibid., at 460.

23. Ibid., at 478 (emphasis in original).

24. Ibid. Contrast that language with Scalia's reflections in *Herrera v. Collins*, 506 U.S. 390, 427–28 (1993): "We granted certiorari on the question whether it violates due process or constitutes cruel and unusual punishment for a State to execute a person who, having been convicted of murder after a full and fair trial, later alleges that newly discovered evidence shows him to be 'actually innocent.' I would have preferred to decide that question, particularly since, as the Court's discussion shows, it is perfectly clear what the answer is: There is no basis in text, tradition, or even in contemporary practice (if that were enough) for finding in the Constitution a right to demand judicial consideration of newly discovered evidence of innocence brought forward after conviction. In saying that such a right exists, the dissenters apply nothing but their personal opinions to invalidate the rules of more than two-thirds of the States, and a Federal Rule of Criminal Procedure for which this Court itself is responsible. If the system that has been in place for 200 years (and remains widely approved) 'shocks' the dissenters' consciences, perhaps they should doubt the calibration of their consciences, or, better still, the usefulness of 'conscience shocking' as a legal test. I nonetheless join . . . the Court's opinion because there is no legal error in deciding a case by assuming, *arguendo*, that an asserted constitutional right exists, and because I can understand, or at least am accustomed to, the reluctance of the present Court to admit publicly that Our Perfect Constitution lets stand any injustice, much less the execution of an innocent man who has received, though to no avail, all the process that our society has traditionally deemed adequate. With any luck, we shall avoid ever having to face this embarrassing question again, since it is improbable that evidence of innocence as convincing as today's opinion requires would fail to produce an executive pardon."

25. The language is from Scalia's concurring opinion in *Albright v. Oliver*, 510 U.S. 266, 275 (1994).

26. 32 U.S. 243 (1833).

27. Ibid., at 250.

28. See Charles Fairman, "Does the Fourteenth Amendment Incorporate the Bill of Rights? The Original Understanding," 2 *Stanford Law Review* (1949): 5–138, and Raoul Berger, *The Fourteenth Amendment and the Bill of Rights* (Norman: University of Oklahoma Press, 1989).

29. 510 U.S. at 275. See also his statement in his concurring opinion in *TXO Production Corp. v. Alliance Resources Corp.*, 509 U.S. 443, 470 (1993): "I am willing to accept the proposition that the Due Process Clause of the Fourteenth Amendment, despite its textual limitation to procedure, incorporates certain substantive guarantees specified in the Bill of Rights."

30. 499 U.S. at 35.

31. *Rutan*, 497 U.S. at 95.

32. 509 U.S. at 470. See Scalia's concurring opinion in *City Of Cuyahoga Falls v. Buckeye Community Hope Foundation*, 538 U.S. 188, 200 (2003): "The judicially created substantive component of the Due Process Clause protects, we have said, certain 'fundamental liberty interests' from deprivation by the government. . . . Freedom from delay in receiving a building permit is not among these 'fundamental liberty interests.'" See also his opinion for the Court in *Castle Rock v. Gonzales*, 125 S. Ct. 2796 (2005), in which he declared that individuals do not, "for purposes of the Due Process Clause, have a property interest in police enforcement" of a restraining order. "[T]he benefit that a third party may receive from having someone else arrested for a crime generally does not trigger protections under the Due Process Clause, neither in its procedural nor in its 'substantive' manifestations."

33. Scalia concurred in part in the judgment. 538 U.S. 760, 781 (2003). See also his

statement in his concurring opinion in *Albright:* "The Bill of Rights sets forth, in the Fifth and Sixth Amendments, procedural guarantees relating to the period before and during trial, including a guarantee (the Grand Jury Clause) regarding the manner of indictment. Those requirements are not to be supplemented through the devise of 'substantive due process.'" 510 U.S. at 276.

34. See *Haslip,* 499 U.S. at 24–25; *TXO Production Corp.,* 509 U.S. at 470; *BMW of North America v. Gore,* 517 U.S. 559, 599 (1996); *Cooper Industries v. Leatherman Tool Group,* 532 U.S. 424, 443 (2001); and *State Farm Mutual Automobile Insurance Co. v. Campbell,* 538 U.S. 408, 429 (2003).

35. *BMW v. Gore,* 517 U.S. at 599 (emphasis in original). See Scalia's concurring opinion in *Honda Motor Co. v. Oberg,* 512 U.S. 415, 436 (1994), in which he agreed with the Court majority that due process requires judicial review of the size of punitive-damage awards. But see his inexplicable comment in *Martinez v. Court of Appeal of California,* 528 U.S. 152, 165 (2000): "[T]here is no constitutional right to appeal."

36. *Haslip,* 499 U.S. at 24–25.

37. *TXO Production Corp.,* 509 U.S. at 471 (emphasis in original).

38. 410 U.S. 113 (1973). See Scalia's concurrence in the judgment in *Webster v. Reproductive Health Services,* 492 U.S. 490, 532 (1989); his concurring opinion in *Ohio v. Akron Center for Reproductive Health,* 497 U.S. 502, 520 (1990); his opinion concurring in part and dissenting in part in *Planned Parenthood of Southeastern Pennsylvania v. Casey,* 505 U.S. 833, 979 (1992); and his dissenting opinion in *Stenberg v. Carhart,* 530 U.S. 914, 956 (2000).

39. 497 U.S. at 520. "On the question of abortion, as an originalist, I would look at the text of the Constitution, which says nothing about the subject either way. I look at the text; it says nothing about it. And I look at 200 years of history; nobody ever thought it

said anything about it. That's the end of the question for me." "Transcript of Discussion between U.S. Supreme Court Justices Antonin Scalia and Stephen Breyer," American University, Washington College of Law, January 13, 2005, p. 30. (Hereafter Scalia/Breyer Transcript.)

40. 505 U.S. at 980.

41. 497 U.S. 417, 479–80 (1990).

42. 505 U.S. at 980. See Scalia's statement in his article "God's Justice and Ours," *First Things* 123 (May 2002): 17–21, 18: "[M]y difficulty with *Roe v. Wade* is a legal rather than a moral one: I do not believe (and, for two hundred years, no one believed) that the Constitution contains a right to abortion. And if a state were to permit abortion on demand, I would—and could in good conscience—vote against an attempt to invalidate that law for the same reason that I vote against the invalidation of laws that forbid abortion on demand: because the Constitution gives the federal government (and hence me) no power over the matter." This article was adapted from remarks Scalia gave at a conference sponsored by the Pew Forum on Religion and Public Life at the University of Chicago Divinity School.

43. 505 U.S. at 979.

44. 497 U.S. at 520–21.

45. 530 U.S. 57 (2000).

46. Ibid., at 91–92 (emphasis in original). He also declared that "I would think it entirely compatible with the commitment to representative democracy set forth in the founding documents to argue, in legislative chambers or in electoral campaigns, that the state has *no power* to interfere with parents' authority over the rearing of their children." Ibid., at 92 (emphasis in original).

47. Ibid., at 93.

48. 497 U.S. 261 (1990).

49. Ibid., at 293.

50. Ibid., at 294.

51. Ibid. Some societies have adopted the view, Scalia noted, that "it is none of the

state's business if a person wants to commit suicide." And he asserted that it is a view "our states are free to adopt if they wish." But, he insisted, "it is not a view imposed by our constitutional traditions, in which the power of the state to prohibit suicide is unquestionable." Ibid., at 300.

52. Ibid., at 300–301.
53. 539 U.S. 558 (2003).
54. Ibid., at 597.
55. Ibid., at 592.
56. Ibid., at 578.
57. Ibid., at 577.
58. Scalia, "God's Justice and Ours," p. 17.
59. Ibid., at 578–79.
60. Ibid., at 599. Scalia had previously elaborated on this point at greater length in his concurrence in the judgment in *Barnes v. Glen Theatre, Inc.*, 501 U.S. 560, 575 (1991): "Our society prohibits, and all human societies have prohibited, certain activities not because they harm others but because they are considered, in the traditional phrase, '*contra bonos mores,*' *i.e.,* immoral. In American society, such prohibitions have included, for example, sadomasochism, cockfighting, bestiality, suicide, drug use, prostitution, and sodomy. While there may be great diversity of view on whether various of these prohibitions should exist (though I have found few ready to abandon, in principle, all of them), there is no doubt that, absent specific constitutional protection for the conduct involved, the Constitution does not prohibit them simply because they regulate 'morality.'"

61. Ibid., at 599 (emphasis in original).
62. Ibid., at 603–4.
63. Ibid., at 604–5.
64. The passage is from Scalia's concurring opinion in *Minnesota v. Dickerson*, 508 U.S. 366, 379 (1993). For similar language, see also his concurring opinion in *Minnesota v. Carter*, 525 U.S. 83, 92 (1998); his concurrence in the judgment in *Cheek v. United States*, 498 U.S. 192, 209 (1991); and his dissenting opinion in *Alabama v. Shelton*, 535 U.S. 654, 681 (2002).

65. *Carter*, 525 U.S. at 98.
66. *Dickerson*, 508 U.S. at 380.
67. 518 U.S. 1, 19 (1996).
68. *Dickerson*, 508 U.S. at 380. For Scalia, the question is occasionally whether there has even been a search or seizure. In *Ferguson v. City of Charleston*, 532 U.S. 67 (2001), he dissented when the Court held that a state hospital's performance of urine tests to obtain evidence of cocaine use by maternity patients for law-enforcement purposes was, absent patient consent, an unreasonable search in violation of the Fourth Amendment. He argued, first, that "the hospital's reporting of positive drug-test results to police . . . is obviously not a search" and, second, that "[i]t is rudimentary Fourth Amendment law that a search which has been consented to is not unreasonable" and that "[t]here is no contention in the present case that the urine samples were extracted forcibly." Ibid., at 92–93. He continued: "Because the defendant had voluntarily provided access to the evidence, there was no reasonable expectation of privacy to invade. Abuse of trust is surely a sneaky and ungentlemanly thing, and perhaps there should be . . . laws against such conduct by the government. That, however, is immaterial for Fourth Amendment purposes, for '*however strongly* a defendant may trust an apparent colleague, his expectations in this respect are not protected by the Fourth Amendment.'" Ibid., at 94 (emphasis in original).

And in *California v. Hodari D.*, 499 U.S. 621 (1991), he wrote the majority opinion, holding that a juvenile defendant had not been "seized" within the meaning of the Fourth Amendment when he had been ordered by the police to stop but only when he had been tackled by the police after his unsuccessful effort to run away. As the juvenile ran away, he disposed of a rock of cocaine that the police recovered and used as evidence against him. He argued that the evidence should have been suppressed as unreasonably obtained without probable cause after his arrest; the police argued that it had been abandoned prior to his arrest and was therefore admissible. Scalia wrote a textualist opinion for the seven-member majority: "The language of the Fourth Amendment, of course, cannot sustain respondent's contention. The word 'seizure' readily bears the meaning of a laying on of hands or application of physical force to restrain movement, even when it is ultimately unsuccessful. ('She seized the purse-snatcher, but he broke out of her grasp.') It does not remotely apply, however, to the prospect of a policeman yelling 'Stop, in the name of the law!' " at a fleeing suspect who continues to flee. That, Scalia insisted, "is no seizure." An arrest, he continued, "requires *either* physical force (as described above) *or*, where that is absent, *submission* to the assertion of authority." Ibid., at 626 (emphasis in original).

69. 500 U.S. 44, 60 (1991).

70. Ibid., at 52–53.

71. Ibid., at 60 (emphasis in original).

72. Ibid., at 61.

73. Ibid., at 66 (emphasis in original).

74. Ibid., at 69. "I would treat the time limit as a presumption; when the 24 hours are exceeded the burden shifts to the police to adduce unforeseeable circumstances justifying the additional delay." Ibid., at 70.

75. Ibid., at 71 (emphasis in original).

76. 533 U.S. 27 (2001).

77. Ibid., at 34.

78. Ibid., at 35–36.

79. Ibid., at 34. As he declared, "Where, as here, the Government uses a device that is not in general public use, to explore details of the home that would previously have been unknowable without physical intrusion, the surveillance is a 'search' and is presumptively unreasonable without a warrant." Ibid., at 40.

80. *Vernonia School District v. Acton*, 515 U.S. 646, 652 (1995). See Scalia's majority opinion in *Arizona v. Hicks*, 480 U.S. 321

(1987), in which Scalia found unreasonable the following search. A bullet, fired through the floor of Hicks's apartment, struck and injured a man in the apartment below. Police officers were called to the scene and entered Hicks's apartment, searching for the shooter, other shooting victims, and weapons. They found and seized three weapons; one of the officers also noticed, in plain view, expensive Bang and Olufsen stereo equipment, which seemed out of place in an otherwise squalid apartment. Suspecting that the equipment was stolen, the officer recorded the equipment's serial numbers, moving some of the equipment to do so. Upon reporting the serial numbers to police headquarters, the officer was advised that some of the equipment had been taken in an armed robbery, and he seized that equipment immediately. In an opinion for the Court holding that this search was unreasonable, Scalia declared that moving these stereo pieces was an action unrelated to the objectives of the authorized intrusion into Hicks's apartment and produced a new invasion of Hicks's privacy unjustified by the exigent circumstances that validated the entry. Even though the equipment was in plain view, Scalia declared that probable cause, and not the lesser test of "reasonable suspicion," was required to move it, even if only a few inches. He responded to the charge that his decision insulated "the criminality of the few" by declaring that it protected "the privacy of us all," and he declared that his disagreement with the dissenters in this case pertained "to where the proper balance should be struck." In unsurprising language, he declared, "We choose to adhere to the textual and traditional standard of probable cause." 480 U.S. at 329.

81. *Acton*, 515 U.S. at 652.

82. The language is from Scalia's dissenting opinion in *National Treasury Employees Union v. Von Raab*, 489 U.S. 656, 681 (1989). Sometimes, he contended, the circumstances are so compelling that there is

no need to address "social necessity." See *Brower v. County of Inyo*, 489 U.S. 593 (1989), in which Scalia found "unreasonable" the seizure described in his opinion for the Court as follows: "On the night of October 23, 1984, William James Caldwell (Brower) was killed when the stolen car that he had been driving at high speeds for approximately 20 miles in an effort to elude pursuing police crashed into a police roadblock. His heirs, petitioners here, . . . allege that 'under color of statutes, regulations, customs and usages,' the police (1) caused an 18-wheel tractor-trailer to be placed across both lanes of a two-lane highway in the path of Brower's flight, (2) 'effectively concealed' this roadblock by placing it behind a curve and leaving it unilluminated, and (3) positioned a police car, with its headlights on, between Brower's oncoming vehicle and the truck, so that Brower would be 'blinded' on his approach. Petitioners further alleged that Brower's fatal collision with the truck was 'a proximate result' of this official conduct." Ibid., at 594.

83. *Schenck v. United States*, 249 U.S. 47, 52 (1919).

84. *Patterson v. Shumate*, 504 U.S. 753, 767 (1992).

85. 489 U.S. at 680.

86. Ibid., at 683 (emphasis in original).

87. Ibid., at 681.

88. Ibid., at 687.

89. See *Griffin v. Wisconsin*, 483 U.S. 868, 876–77 (1987), in which Scalia wrote for the Court majority that a warrantless search of a probationer's home by state probation officers was reasonable with the meaning of the Fourth Amendment because it was conducted pursuant to a Wisconsin regulation that was itself a reasonable response to the "special needs" of a probation system.

90. 515 U.S. at 654.

91. Ibid., at 657.

92. Ibid., at 663.

93. Ibid., at 665.

94. *Murray v. United States*, 487 U.S. 533 (1988). In his opinion for the Court, Scalia wrote: "The Government argues that . . . evidence initially discovered during, or as a consequence of, an unlawful search, but later obtained independently from activities untainted by the initial illegality [is reasonably obtained]. We think the Government's view has better support in both precedent and policy." Ibid., at 537.

95. *Illinois v. Rodriguez*, 497 U.S. 177 (1990). In his opinion for the Court, Scalia declared: "The Constitution is no more violated when officers enter without a warrant because they reasonably (though erroneously) believe that the person who has consented to their entry is a resident of the premises, than it is violated when they enter without a warrant because they reasonably (though erroneously) believe they are in pursuit of a violent felon who is about to escape." Ibid., at 186.

96. See, for example, *California v. Acevedo*, 500 U.S. 565, 585 (1991); *Whren v. United States*, 517 U.S. 806, 810 (1996); *Wyoming v. Houghton*, 526 U.S. 295, 305 (1999); and *Thornton v. United States*, 541 U.S. 615 (2004).

97. 495 U.S. 508 (1990).

98. Ibid., at 526.

99. Ibid., at 542.

100. 509 U.S. 688 (1993).

101. Ibid., at 704.

102. See his concurrence in the judgment in *Witte v. United States*, 515 U.S. 389, 407 (1995), and his concurring opinion in *Hudson v. United States*, 522 U.S. 93, 106 (1997). See also his majority opinion in *Sattazahn v. Pennsylvania*, 537 U.S. 101, 112–13 (2003), in which he explained why the state's action constituted a single prosecution: "Petitioner was convicted in the guilt phase of his first trial of the lesser offense of first-degree murder. During the sentencing phase, the jury deliberated without reaching a decision on death or life, and without making any find-

ings regarding aggravating or mitigating circumstances. After 3½ hours the judge dismissed the jury as hung and entered a life
sentence in accordance with Pennsylvania
law. . . . [N]either judge nor jury 'acquitted'
petitioner of the greater offense of 'first-
degree murder plus aggravating circum-
stance(s).' Thus, when petitioner appealed
and succeeded in invalidating his conviction
of the lesser offense, there was no double-
jeopardy bar to Pennsylvania's retrying petitioner on both the lesser and the greater
offense; his 'jeopardy' never terminated with
respect to either."

103. 511 U.S. 767 (1994).

104. Ibid., at 798.

105. *Department of Revenue of Montana v.
Kurth Ranch*, 511 U.S. at 798–808.

106. *Witte*, 515 U.S. at 406–7.

107. *Hudson*, 522 U.S. at 496–97. Scalia
offered an important clarification of his view
that the Double Jeopardy Clause does not
prohibit successive punishments in his dissent in *Jones v. Thomas*, 491 U.S. 376 (1989):
"If, for example, a judge imposed only a 15-
year sentence under a statute that permitted
15 years to life, he could . . . [not] have second thoughts after the defendant has served
that time, and add on another 10 years. I am
sure that cannot be done, because the Double Jeopardy Clause is a statute of repose for
sentences as well as for proceedings. Done is
done." Ibid., at 392. He concluded his dissent observing that "[t]he Double Jeopardy
Clause is and has always been, not a provision designed to assure reason and justice
in the particular case, but the embodiment
of technical, prophylactic rules that require
the Government to turn square corners.
Whenever it is applied to release a criminal
deserving of punishment it frustrates justice
in the particular case, but for the greater purpose of assuring repose in the totality of
criminal prosecutions and sentences." Ibid.,
at 396.

108. 384 U.S. 436 (1966).

109. The passage is from Scalia's dissent in
Dickerson v. United States, 530 U.S. 428,
461, 465 (2000).

110. Ibid., at 450.

111. 498 U.S. 146, 167 (1990) (emphasis in
original).

112. *Dickerson*, 530 U.S. at 461.

113. 501 U.S. 171 (1991).

114. Ibid., at 175.

115. Ibid., at 176–77.

116. Ibid., at 177–78 (emphasis in original).
Even though the Court concluded that he
had suffered no constitutional violation, the
accused asked it to declare "as a matter of
sound policy" that invocation of the Sixth
Amendment right includes an invocation of
the Fifth Amendment right. Scalia declined
to do so, saying, "It would not wisely be exercised." "Since the ready ability to obtain
uncoerced confessions is not an evil but an
unmitigated good, society would be the loser.
Admissions of guilt resulting from valid
Miranda waivers are more than merely
'desirable'; they are essential to society's compelling interest in finding, convicting, and
punishing those who violate the law." Ibid.,
at 181.

117. 512 U.S. 452, 464 (1994).

118. Ibid., at 465.

119. Ibid., at 464.

120. Ibid., at 431.

121. Ibid., at 445–46 (emphasis in original).

122. As Scalia declared, "We have already
pointed out that the Constitution does not
require any specific code of procedures for
protecting the privilege against self-incrimination during custodial interrogation. Congress and the States are free to develop their
own safeguards for the privilege." 384 U.S.
436, 491 (1966).

123. 422 U.S. 806, 818 (1975).

124. 541 U.S. 36, 54 (2004).

125. Ibid., at 43.

126. Ibid. In *Lilly v. Virginia*, 527 U.S. 116,
143 (1999), Scalia had anticipated his opinion in *Crawford* and described a somewhat

similar use of tape-recorded statements at trial without providing the defendant with a prior opportunity for cross-examination as "a paradigmatic Confrontation Clause violation."

127. 541 U.S. at 60.

128. Ibid., at 61. He also asserted: "Dispensing with confrontation because testimony is obviously reliable is akin to dispensing with a jury trial because a defendant is obviously guilty. This is not what the Sixth Amendment prescribes." Ibid., at 62.

129. 487 U.S. 1012, 1016 (1988).

130. Ibid., at 1020.

131. 497 U.S. 836 (1990).

132. Ibid., at 867.

133. 527 U.S. 1, 30 (1999) (emphasis added).

134. Ibid., at 32.

135. 124 S. Ct. 2531, 2539 (2004).

136. *Neder*, 527 U.S. at 30 (emphasis in original). See also his concurrence in the judgment in *Yates v. Evatt*, 500 U.S. 391, 414 (1991); his opinion for the Court in *Sullivan*, 508 U.S. at 280 (1993); and his opinion for the Court in *Gaudin*, 515 U.S. at 511 (1995).

137. 527 U.S. at 32.

138. Ibid.

139. 530 U.S. 466, 498 (2000).

140. *Blakely v. Washington*, 124 S. Ct. at 2543.

141. 530 U.S. at 499 (emphasis in original).

142. 536 U.S. 584, 612 (2002) (emphasis in original).

143. 124 S. Ct. at 2537.

144. 524 U.S. 721, 740 (1998).

145. See, for example, O'Connor's apprehensions at 124 S. Ct. at 2548.

146. Ibid., at 2539, n. 9.

147. Ibid., at 2540.

148. Ibid., at 2543.

149. Ibid., at 2542.

150. 125 S. Ct. 738 (2005).

151. Ibid., at 746–56. Justice Stevens wrote the opinion for this five-member majority, which also included Justices Ginsburg, Scalia, Souter, and Thomas.

152. Ibid., at 756–71. Justice Stevens wrote the opinion for this five-member majority, which also included Chief Justice Rehnquist and Justices Ginsburg, Kennedy, and O'Connor.

153. Ibid., at 772.

154. Ibid., at 790.

155. 124 S. Ct. 2519 (2004).

156. 489 U.S. 288 (1989).

157. 527 U.S. at 30. Scalia's defense of his argument in *Schriro* was not up to the task: "The question here is not, however, whether the Framers believed that juries are more accurate factfinders than judges (perhaps — they certainly thought juries were more independent). Nor is the question whether juries actually *are* more accurate factfinders than judges (again, perhaps so). Rather, the question is whether judicial factfinding so '*seriously* diminishes' accuracy that there is an 'impermissibly large risk' of punishing conduct the law does not reach. The evidence is simply too equivocal to support that conclusion." 124 S. Ct. at 2424 (emphasis in original).

158. *Schriro* is not the only case in which Scalia has affirmed without question *Teague*'s refusal to give full retroactive effect to the Court's criminal procedural decisions. See *Lambrix v. Singletary*, 520 U.S. 518 (1997).

159. 381 U.S. 618 (1965).

160. 381 U.S. at 628.

161. William Blackstone, *Commentaries on the Laws of England*, 3rd ed. (Dublin: John Exshaw, Henry Saunders, Boulter Grierson, and James Williams, 1769), p. 69.

162. Ibid.

163. Ibid., p. 70 (emphasis in original).

164. Herman Schwartz, 33 *University of Chicago Law Review* (1966): 719, 753. See also Ralph A. Rossum, "New Rights and Old Wrongs: The Supreme Court and the Problem of Retroactivity," 23 *Emory Law Journal* (1974): 381, 386–88.

165. 366 U.S. 213, 225 (1961).

166. 401 U.S. 667, 677 (1971).

167. 509 U.S. 602, 623 (1993).

168. The passage is from Scalia's judgment for the Court in *Harmelin v. Michigan*, 501 U.S. 957, 976 (1991).

169. Ibid., at 981.

170. Ibid., at 976.

171. The passage is from Scalia's dissenting opinion in *Thompson v. Oklahoma*, 487 U.S. 815, 873 (1988).

172. *Ewing v. California*, 538 U.S. 11, 31 (2003) (emphasis in original). See Scalia's opinion for the Court in *Wilson v. Seiter*, 501 U.S. 294, 303 (1991), in which he wrote that the standard to employ in cases where prisoners claim that "inadequate conditions of confinement" (e.g., inadequate food, warmth, medical care, etc.) constitute cruel and unusual punishment is "deliberate indifference" on the part of prison officials.

173. 501 U.S. 957 (1991).

174. Ibid., at 994. Scalia frequently refers to "text and tradition" when addressing Eighth Amendment issues. See, for example, *McKoy v. North Carolina*, 494 U.S. 433, 467 (1990); *Richmond v. Lewis*, 506 U.S. 40, 54 (1992); and *Atkins v. Virginia*, 536 U.S. 304, 337 (2002).

175. 501 U.S. at 977.

176. Ibid., at 977. Scalia also observed that "[b]oth the New Hampshire Constitution, adopted 8 years before ratification of the Eighth Amendment, and the Ohio Constitution, adopted 12 years after, contain, in separate provisions, a prohibition of 'cruel and unusual punishments' ('cruel or unusual,' in New Hampshire's case) *and* a requirement that 'all penalties ought to be proportioned to the nature of the offence.'" Ibid., at 977–78 (emphasis in original).

177. Ibid., at 979 (emphasis in original).

178. Ibid., at 980.

179. Ibid., at 980–81.

180. Ibid., at 985–86 (emphasis in original).

181. 463 U.S. 277 (1983).

182. Ibid., at 965.

183. 538 U.S. 11, 31 (2003).

184. *Harmelin*, 501 U.S. at 976.

185. *Simmons v. South Carolina*, 512 U.S. 154, 185 (1994). See also Scalia's use of the phrase "death-is-different jurisprudence" in *Shafer v. South Carolina*, 532 U.S. 36, 55 (2001), and *Wiggins v. Smith*, 539 U.S. 510, 557 (2003).

186. 501 U.S. at 980. See also his essay "God's Justice and Ours," p. 17. The death penalty "was clearly permitted when the Eighth Amendment was adopted (not merely for murder, by the way, but for all felonies — including, for example, horse-thieving, as anyone can verify by watching a western movie). And so it is clearly permitted today."

187. 433 U.S. 584 (1977).

188. 458 U.S. 782 (1982).

189. *Harmelin v. Michigan*, 501 U.S. at 993.

190. 492 U.S. 361, 379 (1989) (emphasis in original). The passage in *Enmund* is found at 458 U.S. at 797.

191. 492 U.S. at 379 (emphasis in original).

192. 536 U.S. 304, 348 (2002) (emphasis in original). The passage the Court majority quoted from *Coker* is found at 433 U.S. at 597.

193. *Atkins*, 536 U.S. at 348.

194. 125 S. Ct. 1183 (2005).

195. Ibid., at 337.

196. 487 U.S. at 859–78.

197. Ibid., at 864.

198. Ibid., at 864–65. The quoted passage is from Chief Justice Earl Warren's plurality opinion in *Trop v. Dulles*, 356 U.S. 86, 101 (1958).

199. 487 U.S. at 865. "It will," he declared, "rarely if ever be the case that the Members of this Court will have a better sense of the evolution in views of the American people than do their elected representatives."

200. Ibid., at 872, 868.

201. Ibid., at 873.

202. 492 U.S. 361 (1989).

203. Ibid., at 368, 370.

204. Ibid., at 378 (emphasis in original).

205. 125 S. Ct. at 1218.

206. Ibid.

207. Ibid. (emphasis in original). Scalia's rejection of Kennedy's reliance on foreign law in *Simmons* has already been addressed in Chapter Two.

208. 492 U.S. 302 (1989). Scalia dissented in part from the Court's conclusion that Texas unconstitutionally limited the jury's discretion to consider the mitigating evidence of the accused's mental retardation and background of child abuse. Ibid., at 350–60.

209. 536 U.S. at 342 (emphasis in original).

210. Ibid., at 346.

211. Ibid.

212. Ibid., at 337–38.

213. Ibid., at 353.

214. *Harmelin v. Michigan*, 501 U.S. at 976.

215. 482 U.S. 496, 459–60 (1987).

216. Ibid.

217. 490 U.S. 805, 825 (1989).

218. 501 U.S. 808 (1991).

219. Ibid., at 833.

220. *Walton v. Arizona*, 497 U.S. 639, 670 (1990).

221. For the same reason, Scalia also denies that the Eighth Amendment is violated when a trial court refuses to ask potential jurors during voir dire in capital cases whether they would automatically impose the death penalty if the defendant is convicted. As he declared in his dissent in *Morgan v. Illinois*, 504 U.S. 719, 751–52 (1992): "Sixteen years ago, this Court decreed—by a sheer act of will, with no pretense of foundation in constitutional text or American tradition—that the People (as in We, the People) cannot decree the death penalty, absolutely and categorically, for any criminal act, even (presumably) genocide; the jury must always be given the option of extending mercy. Today, obscured within the fog of confusion that is our annually improvised Eighth Amendment, 'death is different' jurisprudence, the Court strikes a further blow against the People in its campaign against the death penalty. Not only must mercy be allowed, but now

only the merciful may be permitted to sit in judgment. Those who agree with the author of Exodus, or with Immanuel Kant, must be banished from American juries—not because the People have so decreed, but because such jurors do not share the strong penological preferences of this Court. In my view, that not only is not required by the Constitution of the United States; it grossly offends it."

222. 497 U.S. at 671.

223. 428 U.S. 280 (1976).

224. 408 U.S. 238 (1972).

225. 497 U.S. at 670.

226. Ibid., at 671. See Scalia's concurring opinion in *Tuilaepa v. California*, 512 U.S. 967, 980 (1994): "It is my view that once a State has adopted a methodology to narrow the eligibility for the death penalty, thereby ensuring that its imposition is not 'freakish,' the distinctive procedural requirements of the Eighth Amendment have been exhausted."

227. See his dissenting opinion in *Richmond*, 506 U.S. at 54.

228. Ibid. See also Scalia's opinion concurring in part and dissenting in part in *Sochor v. Florida*, 504 U.S. 527, 554 (1992), and his concurring opinion in *Buchanan v. Angelone*, 522 U.S. 269, 279 (1998).

229. *Tennard v. Dretke*, 124 S. Ct. 2562, 2575 (2004).

230. Ibid. (emphasis in original). Fourteen years earlier in his concurrence in the judgment in *Walton*, Scalia had already written: "Today a petitioner before this Court says that a state sentencing court (1) had unconstitutionally *broad* discretion to sentence him to death instead of imprisonment, *and* (2) had unconstitutionally *narrow* discretion to sentence him to imprisonment instead of death. An observer unacquainted with our death penalty jurisprudence (and in the habit of thinking logically) would probably say these positions cannot both be right. The ultimate choice in capital sentencing, he would point out, is a unitary one—the choice between death and imprisonment.

One cannot have discretion whether to select the one yet lack discretion whether to select the other. Our imaginary observer would then be surprised to discover that, under this Court's Eighth Amendment jurisprudence . . ., petitioner would have a strong chance of winning on *both* of these antagonistic claims, simultaneously—as evidenced by the facts that four Members of this Court think he should win on both, and that an *en banc* panel of a Federal Court of Appeals so held in an essentially identical case. But that just shows that our jurisprudence and logic have long since parted ways." 497 U.S. at 656 (emphasis in original). See also his concurring opinion in *Johnson v. Texas*, 509 U.S. 350, 374 (1993).

231. 495 U.S. 604, 627 (1990).

Chapter Seven. The Impact of Scalia's Textualism on His Colleagues

1. The completion of the 2003–2004 term of the Court marked the first time in history that nine justices had served together for a full decade. During that decade, the Court handed down a total of 175 five-to-four decisions; the voting bloc that prevailed most frequently (in 82 of these cases) was composed of Chief Justice Rehnquist and Justices O'Connor, Scalia, Kennedy, and Thomas. It was followed by a bloc composed of Justices Stevens, O'Connor, Souter, Ginsburg, and Breyer that prevailed in 28 cases. "Nine Justices, Ten Years: A Statistical Retrospective," 118 *Harvard Law Review* (November 2004): 510, 521.

2. During the 1991–1992 term of the Court, Scalia found himself on the opposite side of Justices Kennedy and O'Connor in several key cases. He filed or joined vigorous dissents in *Hudson v. McMillian*, 503 U.S. 1 (1992), in which Justice O'Connor held for the Court that the use of excessive physical force against an inmate may constitute cruel and unusual punishment, even in the absence of significant injury; *Lee v. Weisman*,

505 U.S. 577 (1992), in which Justice Kennedy held for the Court that prayers at public school graduation ceremonies indirectly coerce religious observance and therefore violate the First Amendment; *Doggett v. United States*, 505 U.S. 647 (1992), in which Justice Souter held for a five-member majority that the petitioner, who had not been brought to trial until eight and a half years after his indictment, had been denied his Sixth Amendment right to a speedy trial, despite the facts that the petitioner did not even know he had been indicted and that the government believed he was in prison in Panama; and *Planned Parenthood of Southeastern Pennsylvania v. Casey*, 505 U.S. 833 (1992), in which Justices O'Connor, Kennedy, and Souter jointly signed an opinion acknowledging that *Roe v. Wade*, 410 U.S. 113 (1973), had been wrongly decided but refusing to overturn it because to do so would result "in profound and unnecessary damage to the Court's legitimacy, and to the Nation's commitment to the rule of law." During that term, Scalia ended up joining the same opinions with O'Connor only 68.9 percent of the time and with Kennedy only 72.4 percent. And the sharp dissents Scalia filed that term, especially in *Planned Parenthood*, had lingering effects: during the 1992–1993 term of the Court, Scalia joined in the same opinions with O'Connor only 53.5 percent of the time and with Kennedy only 62.3 percent—representing the lowest levels of agreement for any of the terms Scalia has served on the Court with these two justices.

3. Scalia dissented and Thomas joined the majority opinion in the following cases: *Richmond v. Lewis*, 506 U.S. 40 (1992); *American National Red Cross v. S. G. and A. E.*, 505 U.S. 247 (1992); *Smith v. United States*, 508 U.S. 223 (1993); *McIntyre v. Ohio Elections Commission*, 514 U.S. 334 (1995); *Ornelas v. United States*, 517 U.S. 690 (1996); *Jaffee v. Redmond*, 518 U.S. 1 (1996); *Commissioner of Internal Revenue v.*

Hubert, 520 U.S. 93 (1997); Almendarez-Torres v. United States, 523 U.S. 224 (1998); Bryan v. United States, 524 U.S. 184 (1998); Monge v. California, 524 U.S. 721 (1998); Johnson v. United States, 529 U.S. 694 (2000); United States v. Playboy Entertainment Group, Inc., 529 U.S. 803 (2000); United States v. Mead Corp., 533 U.S. 218 (2001); Miller v. Barnhart, 535 U.S. 789 (2002); and City of Columbus v. Ours Garage, 536 U.S. 424 (2002).

Thomas dissented and Scalia joined the majority opinion in the following cases: Dawson v. Delaware, 503 U.S. 159 (1992); Rowland v. California Men's Colony, 506 U.S. 194 (1993); Musick, Peeler, and Garrett v. Employers Insurance of Wausau, 508 U.S. 286 (1993); John Hancock Mutual Life Insurance v. Harris Trust and Savings Bank, 510 U.S. 86 (1993); Northwest Airlines v. County of Kent, Michigan, 510 U.S. 355 (1994); Powell v. Nevada, 511 U.S. 79 (1994); Security Services v. Kmart, 511 U.S. 431 (1994); Thomas Jefferson University v. Shalala, 512 U.S. 504 (1994); Mastrobuono v. Shearson Lehman Hutton, Inc., 514 U.S. 52 (1995); Garlotte v. Fordice, 515 U.S. 39 (1995); Thompson v. Keohane, 516 U.S. 99 (1996); Commissioner of Internal Revenue v. Lundy, 516 U.S. 235 (1996); Henderson v. United States, 517 U.S. 654 (1996); Doctor's Associates v. Casarotto, 517 U.S. 681 (1996); Lopez v. Monterey County, 525 U.S. 266 (1999); Cedar Rapids Community School District v. Garret F., 526 U.S. 66 (1999); Saenz v. Roe, 526 U.S. 489 (1999); Harris v. United States, 536 U.S. 545 (2002); Miller-El v. Cockrell, 537 U.S. 322 (2003); Archer v. Warner, 538 U.S. 314 (2003); Green Tree Financial Corp v. Bazzle, 539 U.S. 444 (2003); and Pennsylvania State Police v. Suders, 124 S. Ct. 2342 (2004).

4. In United States v. Williams, 504 U.S. 36 (1992), Scalia wrote the majority opinion and Thomas joined the dissent. In Sims v. Apfel, 530 U.S. 103 (2000), Thomas wrote the judgment of the Court and Scalia joined the dissent.

5. In AT&T Corp. v. Iowa Utilities Board, 525 U.S. 336 (1999), United States v. McDermott, 507 U.S. 447 (1993), and Clark v. Martinez, 125 S. Ct. 716 (2005), Scalia wrote the majority opinion and Thomas wrote the dissent. In United States v. Rodriguez-Moreno, 526 U.S. 275 (1999), Olympic Airways v. Husain, 124 S. Ct. 1221 (2004), and National Cable & Telecommunications Association v. Brand X Internet Services, 125 S. Ct. 2688 (2005), Thomas wrote the majority opinion and Scalia wrote the dissent.

6. 526 U.S. at 281. Scalia's dissent was a textualist classic: "If to state this case is not to decide it, the law has departed further from the meaning of language than is appropriate for a government that is supposed to rule (and to be restrained) through the written word." Ibid., at 285.

7. See, for example, Christopher Smith, Justice Antonin Scalia and the Supreme Court's Conservative Moment (Westport, Conn.: Praeger, 1993), p. 20, who rather gleefully reports on Scalia's failure as a "coalition-builder" to achieve a "judicial counterrevolution." See also David A. Schultz and Christopher Smith, The Jurisprudential Vision of Justice Antonin Scalia (Lanham, Md.: Rowman & Littlefield, 1996), p. 210.

8. Callins v. Collins, 510 U.S. 1141 (1994).

9. 505 U.S. 833, 851 (1992).

10. Pacific Mutual Life Insurance Co. v. Haslip, 499 U.S. 1, 28, 31 (1991) (emphasis in original).

11. 487 U.S. 1012, 1022–23 (1988).

12. 124 S. Ct. 2531, 2544 (2004).

13. Rutan v. Republican Party, 497 U.S. 62, 95 (1990).

14. TXO Production Corp. v. Alliance Resources Corp., 509 U.S. 443, 470 (1993).

15. 539 U.S. 558, 576 (2003).

16. 125 S. Ct. 1183 (2005).

17. Morrison v. Olson, 487 U.S. 654, 734 (1988).

18. Ibid., at 696.

19. Ibid., at 733.

20. 540 U.S. 712, 725 (2004).

21. Ibid., at 731 (emphasis in original).

22. For confirmation of this claim, see the essays on the individual justices of the Rehnquist Court in Earl M. Maltz, ed., *Rehnquist Justice: Understanding the Court Dynamic* (Lawrence: University Press of Kansas, 2003). Key words in the titles of these essays are revelatory: *Accommodationism*—O'Connor; *Respectable Conservatism*—Kennedy; *Realism, Pragmatism*—Stevens; *Liberal Constitutionalism*—Souter; *Limits of Formal Equality*—Ginsburg; and *Synthetic Progressivism*—Breyer. These are not words that suggest the presence of an overarching interpretative principle in the thinking of these justices.

23. Personal interview with Justice Antonin Scalia, Washington, D.C., June 11, 2003.

24. Kathleen M. Sullivan and Gerald Gunther, *Constitutional Law*, 15th ed. (New York: Foundation Press, 2004).

25. William Cohen and David J. Danelski, *Constitutional Law: Civil Liberties and Individual Rights*, 5th ed. (New York: Foundation Press, 2002).

26. Ralph A. Rossum and G. Alan Tarr, *American Constitutional Law*, vol. 1, *The Structure of Government*, and vol. 2, *The Bill of Rights and Subsequent Amendments*, 6th ed. (Belmont, Calif.: Wadsworth, 2003).

27. Alpheus Thomas Mason and Donald Grier Stephenson Jr., *American Constitutional Law: Introductory Essays and Selected Cases*, 14th ed. (Upper Saddle River, N.J.: Pearson–Prentice Hall, 2005).

28. Donald P. Kommers, John Finn, and Gary J. Jacobsohn, *American Constitutional Law*, vol. 1, *Governmental Powers and Democracy*, and vol. 2, *Liberty, Community, and the Bill of Rights*, 2d ed. (Lanham, Md.: Rowman & Littlefield, 2004).

29. Walter F. Murphy, James E. Fleming, Sotirios A. Barber, and Stephen Macedo, *American Constitutional Law*, 3d ed. (New York: Foundation Press, 2003).

30. I wish to acknowledge Kevin A. Ring, ed., *Scalia Dissents: Writings of the Supreme Court's Wittiest, Most Outspoken Justice* (Washington, D.C.: Regnery, 2004), p. 19, for prompting the analysis that follows.

31. *United States v. Virginia*, 518 U.S. 515, 568 (1996).

32. Antonin Scalia, *A Matter of Interpretation: Federal Courts and the Law* (Princeton, N.J.: Princeton University Press, 1997), p. 47.

33. Antonin Scalia, "Assorted Canards of Contemporary Legal Analysis," 40 *Case Western Reserve Law Review* (1990): 581, 596.

INDEX